John Young

Sermons on Various Important Subjects

Vol. 2

John Young

Sermons on Various Important Subjects
Vol. 2

ISBN/EAN: 9783337087531

Printed in Europe, USA, Canada, Australia, Japan

Cover: Foto ©Lupo / pixelio.de

More available books at **www.hansebooks.com**

CONTENTS.

SERMON I.
A sinless Redeemer made sin for us. — Page 1

2 Cor. v. 21. *For he hath made him to be sin for us, who knew no sin; that we might be made the righteousness of God in him.*

SERMON II.
Guilty sinners made the righteousness of God in Christ. 30

From the same text.

SERMON III.
God's Covenant with the New Testament church considered. Part I. - - 91

Heb. viii. 12. *I will be to them a God, and they shall be to me a people.*

SERMON IV.
God's Covenant with the New Testament church considered. Part II. - - 135

From the same text.

SERMON V.
The first promise illustrated. Part I. 181

Gen. iii. 15. *I will put enmity between thee and the woman, and between thy seed and her seed.*

SERMON VI.
The first promise illustrated. Part II. 214

Gen. iii. 15. *He shall bruise thy head, and thou shalt bruise his heel.*

SERMON VII.
The Invocation; or, The Church's prayer for the influences of the Holy Ghost, to qualify her for communion with Christ. - - 249

Song iv. 16. *Awake, O north wind, and come, thou south; blow upon my garden, that the spices thereof may flow out.*

SERMON VIII.
The Invitation; or, A prayer of the church for the presence of Christ, and for his gracious acceptance of the fruits of his Spirit in her. - - 276

Song iv. 16. *Let my Beloved come into his garden, and eat his pleasant fruits.*

SERMON IX.

The Invitation accepted and returned; or, Christ's gracious presence vouchsafed to the church, in answer to her prayer.   -   -   Page 296

Song v. 1. *I am come into my garden, my sister, my spouse: I have gathered my myrrh with my spice; I have eaten my honey-comb with my honey; I have drunk my wine with my milk: eat, O friends, drink, yea drink abundantly, O beloved.*

SERMON X.

Israel's power with God; or, The blessing of God upon his people, a happy consequence of his gracious interviews with them.   -   -   336

Gen. xxxii. 29. *And he blessed him there.*

SERMON XI.

The Returning Prodigal's attire; or, The robe of imputed righteousness actually put upon every penitent sinner. 365

Luke xv. 22. *Bring forth the best robe, and put it on him.*

SERMON XII.

The returning Prodigal's hand adorned.   -   392

Luke xv. 22. *And put a ring on his hand.*

SERMON XIII.

The Returning Prodigal's feet shod; or, The penitent sinner furnished with the preparation of the gospel of peace.
403

Luke xv. 22. *And put shoes on his feet.*

SERMON XIV.

The Returning Prodigal's Entertainment; or, The penitent sinner abundantly satisfied with the fatness of God's house.   -   -   435

Luke xv. 23. *And bring hither the fatted calf, and kill it; and let us eat and be merry.*

SERMON I.

A sinless Redeemer made Sin for us.

2 Cor. v. 21.

HE HATH MADE HIM TO BE SIN FOR US, WHO KNEW NO SIN; THAT WE MIGHT BE MADE THE RIGHTEOUSNESS OF GOD IN HIM.

AS every one of us has, one way or other, a deep concern in that great event, which we propose, this day, symbolically to commemorate; and as there can be no proper commemoration of it, without an eye had to the end and design of it; so it cannot be unsuitable exercise, in the entry of the day's work, to take a view of the character in which Christ died, and of the design which he pursued in dying. Both these are set before us in the words of this text.

The Apostle Paul, having been informed of various abuses that prevailed in the church at Corinth, wrote his first epistle to that church, from Ephesus, about the year of our Lord 57, with a view to rectify those abuses. And being informed by Titus what effect it had upon them, he wrote them this second epistle from Philippi, a city in Macedonia, about a year after the other. His defign was, to fet in a clearer light fome things in the former, which they had not fufficiently underftood; to encourage fome among them, who were too much caft down by the other; and fharply to reprove fuch as continued to defpife both him and his writings.

In the beginning of this chapter, the Apoftle continues that difcourfe which he had begun in the preceding; about the manner of being fupported under the trials of this life, by the happy profpect of a better life in another world. This was it that enabled Paul himfelf, and his brethren, the firft preachers of Chriftianity, to *glory in* all their *tribulations*. And this makes every true Chriftian, when grace is in exercife, to *rejoice with joy unfpeakable*, even while he is *in heavinefs through manifold temptations*.

From the 11th verfe downward, he makes a kind of apology for his fevere manner of writing in his firft epiftle; as flowing from a zeal, which was animated by various confiderations. It was animated by a fenfe of that folemn appearance which he, as well as all other men, was, in a little, to make before the judgment-feat of Chrift, and the impartial account that he muft there give of his ftewardfhip; by the irrefiftible influence of the love of Chrift, which conftrained him to faithfulnefs and diligence in his work; and by the vaft importance of the work in which he was employed, as an ambaffador of Jefus Chrift. Thefe are motives that ought to bear out all minifters of the gofpel, in a faithful difcharge of the duties of their office; whatever cenfures they may incur, and whatever hardfhips they may fuffer on that account,

account, whether from profeffed friends or open enemies.

Having mentioned it as the main bufinefs of his office, as an ambaffador for Chrift, to publifh, in his name, the doctrine of reconciliation to God through him; and to deal with finners, that they might be reconciled accordingly; he takes occafion to profecute the great end of his miniftry, in a fervent addrefs to his Corinthians, ver. 20. to the following purpofe:

'Since *God hath committed to us*, who are Apoftles
' of Chrift, and preachers of his gofpel, *the miniftry*
' *of reconciliation;* we are, by that means, clothed
' with the honourable character of *Ambaffadors for*
' *Chrift;* and appointed to ufe our influence, in dependence upon his affiftance, for having peace made
' up between God and finners. In profecution of
' that important truft, which God hath committed
' unto me, I take this opportunity to befeech and
' intreat you, in the moft preffing and importunate
' manner, to lay afide your natural enmity againft
' God, and be thoroughly reconciled unto him. And
' I certify you, that if what I fay is neglected or defpifed, it will be at your peril: For, as earthly princes expect the fame deference to be paid to what
' their ambaffadors fpeak in their name, that would
' be due to themfelves, if they fpake the fame things
' in perfon; fo God expects and requires, that you
' confider our words as his own; and yield the fame
' attention and obedience to what we fay in his name,
' as you would to God himfelf, if he were praying
' and befeeching you by a voice from heaven, as he
' now does by my mouth, to be reconciled unto him.'

What Paul said to the Corinthians, the Spirit of God as really says to us. And ministers of the gospel, being Paul's successors in office, have the same warrant as he had, to address their hearers in this manner. In the entry, therefore, of the work of this solemn day, and in the great name of God, whose ambassador I am honoured to be, however unworthy of that dignity, I earnestly call, beseech, and obtest every person in this numerous assembly, to be *reconciled unto God*. God has no objections against a present and perfect reconciliation with you. And surely it cannot be your interest to reject the offers of peace, and refuse to be reconciled to him. The call that is addressed to you is the call of God; and, if it is rejected, it is God, and not man, to whom you must be accountable.

God is, indeed, an enemy to every person who continues in a natural estate; as every such person is an enemy to him. And it would be vain to call you to be reconciled to him, if his wrath were not appeased, and he ready and willing to be reconciled unto you. But God has laid a sure foundation for the restoration of peace between him and you, and given the surest proof of his willingness to be reconciled, in that he has exposed his own eternal Son to the punishment which your sin deserved; and that with this express view, that such sinners as you are might enjoy all the blessed fruits of his righteousness.

To set this important truth before us, as the strongest argument for our being reconciled unto God; and as a satisfying answer to all our objections against a present compliance with his gracious invitation to that purpose; is the scope of what we have in ver. 21.

The sense of which may be summed up in the following paraphrase:

'In order that the way might be paved, for the reconciliation of sinners unto God; it pleased God the Father, to make his own eternal Son an offering for our sin, though he was altogether without sin in himself: that we, through him, might be accounted perfectly righteous in the sight of God.'

THE text evidently consists of two parts: It informs us,

I. What our Lord Jesus Christ submitted to become for us, according to his Father's appointment.

II. What we may expect to be made through him; or, what was God's end and design in that appointment.

A FEW words concerning the first of these is all that we can expect to overtake at present. We have it in the first clause of the verse; *He hath made him* to be *sin for us, who knew no sin.* In which words, more particularly, we may take notice of the following things.

I. What Christ was, and still is, in his true and original character; he *knew no sin.*

II. What he became, in consequence of his undertaking for us; he was *made to be sin.*

III. How this wonderful event was brought about; it was by virtue of a divine appointment and constitution: *He*, that is God the Father, *hath made him to be sin.*

IV. On whose account, or for whose behoof this appointment was made and executed; it was *for us.*

We

We shall speak a little concerning each of these, and conclude with some improvement.

I. WHAT Christ was, in his original character, we have in these words, *who knew no sin*. No person, surely, that knows to whom the words refer, will imagine that they are to be understood so literally, as to mean that Christ knew not what sin was, or could not discern sin from duty. Nay, he knows all things. He is the great Author of all law. He cannot but know the exact meaning of every article of the law which he made. And he is intimately acquainted with all the creatures, and all their actions. Thus he has a more perfect knowledge than any mere creature can have, what is sin, and what is not. How else should he be the final judge of the quick and the dead, at his second coming? Such is his infinite knowledge, in this respect, that no person can be guilty of sin, even in his most secret thought, but he is privy to it. And many things he knows to be sinful, which men are disposed to consider in an opposite light.

But the expression must be understood of an experimental knowledge of sin. He had no experience of what it was to commit sin. " He did no evil, neither " was guile found in his mouth *." In this sense the word is frequently used in Scripture. We shall mention but one instance. " False witnesses," says David, " did rise up; they laid to my charge things that I " knew not †;" that is, things of which I was not, in the smallest degree, guilty. In this sense it was that our Lord knew no sin; never having been chargeable, in his own person, with the least transgression of

the

the law of God. In his divine nature he could not commit sin; being essentially above all law; and being absolutely free from any possibility of doing amiss. Sin being opposite to all his adorable perfections, he cannot be the author or the actor of sin, without doing violence to his own infinite and unchangeable nature. Even in human nature, he did no sin. He was not, like other men, "shapen in iniquity, and " conceived" by his *mother* in sin. That which was *born* of the Virgin Mary, being sanctified by the supernatural influence of the Holy Ghost, was an *holy thing* *. And he was as free from actual, as he was from original sin; for, during the whole course of his humbled life, he was *holy, harmless, undefiled, and separated from sinners* †.

That he should be thus free from all sin was absolutely necessary; otherwise he could have never been *made sin for us*. He who was our Surety to divine justice, behoved to perform a spotless obedience to the law, in all its precepts, in our name and stead. The least defect in his obedience would have rendered the whole unacceptable to God, and therefore unprofitable to us. The law, to which he was subject, extended to the nature, as well as to the actions of life; and, had there been the least depravity in his nature, he had been a transgressor of that law. Hence the holiness of his human nature is the ground-work of that righteousness, which he wrought out for us. It behoved him also to become a sacrifice for our sin. And every sacrifice must be pure and unblemished. Under the law, no typical sacrifice could be accepted that was not without blemish. Hereby it was plainly signified,

* Luke i. 35. † Heb. vii. 26.

nified, that the great facrifice, by which a real atonement was to be made, muft be abfolutely free from all moral pollution or defect.

Yet the confideration of his being without fin, in his own perfon, rendered his being *made fin for us* fo much the more wonderful. It could not have been furprifing, to find a perfon who had been really chargeable with fin, fuftained a finner in law, and fuffering the punifhment that was due for fin. But to fee one who was abfolutely without fin in himfelf, who was known to be fo by God, and even proved to be fo before men, feized and apprehended, not only by a band of murderers, but even by the hand of an infinitely holy and juft God; to fee him " led as a " lamb to the flaughter," nailed to an accurfed tree by the hands of wicked men; ftricken to death by the fword of divine juftice, and forfaken of God under all his fufferings: This furpaffes, incomparably furpaffes, all that is wonderful among men.

II. WHAT Chrift became, in confequence of his undertaking for us, we are informed in thefe words, *he bath made him to be fin.* Concerning the meaning of this expreffion, interpreters are not wholly agreed. Moft of them confider the word *fin,* as put, by a figure, for a facrifice or offering for fin. It is certain that the word is fometimes ufed in that fenfe in Scripture. So it is, for inftance, in that paffage, where the Spirit of God complains of the priefts thus, " They eat up the fin of my people; and they fet " their heart on their iniquity *." By the law of Mofes every fin-offering was to be eaten by the priefts,

* Hof. iv. 8.

priests, except that part of it which was to be burnt in the fire *. The priests in Hosea's time considering this, took pleasure in the sins of the people; because, by that means, their tables were plentifully supplied. Because " they *did* eat up the sin-*offerings* " of *the* people; *therefore* they set their heart upon " their iniquity." We have no objection against understanding the word in this sense here, provided the nature and use of a sin-offering be properly attended unto.

Under the law, when any person had sinned, and brought a sin-offering unto the Lord; it was required that the beast, which was to be offered, should be brought to the door of the tabernacle of the congregation. There the sinner was to lay his hand upon the head of it, and to confess his sin over it; hereby to signify the transferring of his guilt to it, and the substitution of it in his place. In consequence of this the beast was to be slain; to signify the execution of the judgment of God upon the beast, which would otherwise have been due to him that offered it. Thus, by God's appointment, the sin-offering was dealt with as the sinner himself deserved to have been. The guilt of the sin was typically transferred from the sinner, to the sacrifice; and the punishment due for the sin was laid upon the beast which was offered, that the sinner himself might go free.

What was done typically and symbolically to the beast that was made a sin-offering, was really and truly done to Christ, when he was *made sin for us*. Our sins were imputed to him. The guilt of them was transferred from us to him. He was esteemed, declared,

* See Lev. xiv. 13.

declared, and dealt with as a sinner in the eye of God's law. And, in consequence of this, he suffered all the punishment that was due to us for all our sins. Though he had no sin of his own, justice considered him as a sinner; and inflicted upon him all that punishment which would have been due, if, in his own person, he had committed all those sins that ever were or will be committed by all those whom he represented, and for whom he was *made sin*. Have you not good reason, believer, when you " look upon him " whom *you have thus* pierced, *to* mourn for him ?" You are welcome to make use of his atonement, and to claim all the benefits that result from his being made a sin-offering for you : And you have reason to praise God because that is the case. But it is your indispensible duty, at the same time, to mourn, and mourn deeply, for those sins that made such an atonement necessary.

III. How it was that he who was himself without sin was made a sacrifice for sin, we may gather from the first words of the verse. *He hath made him to be sin*. It was God the Father, who, by a free and voluntary constitution, made him so. In the making of the covenant of grace, from all eternity, God the Father, as therein representing the Deity, proposed and stipulated that Christ should be *made sin for us*. This proposal being cheerfully assented to by Christ; a decree was past, in the council of peace, appointing and ordaining that it should be so. Accordingly, " when the fulness of the *appointed* time was come, " *Christ* made his soul an offering for sin." And God the Father not only accepted this offering, but he
actually

actually made him to be an offering; by inflicting
upon him, with his own hand, that punishment which
was due to us. He came into the world, and continued in it all the time of his humbled life, under the
legal imputation of our guilt: And God exacted of
him the full payment of our criminal debt. It is said,
that when God accepted a sacrifice of old, he testified
that acceptance by sending fire from heaven to burn
it. We are sure this was sometimes the case. Perhaps
it was so always, unless while the sacred fire was kept
burning in the tabernacle, and afterwards in the temple. This was a lively type of what took place in
relation to Christ. In token of his being fully pleased
with this glorious sacrifice, and in consequence of
that divine appointment by which it was provided,
God himself struck the blow by which the sacrifice
was cut off; he consumed it by fire from heaven.
With his own hand he inflicted upon Christ the punishment that was due for all those *sins*, which he
" bare in his own body on the tree." You cannot
have room to doubt of God's being perfectly pleased
with this wonderful Sacrifice for sin, while there is
such work in the church as that about which we are
now met. While you commemorate the death of Christ,
you may therein see the fire of God coming down
from heaven, and consuming the great Sacrifice. And
it is your duty, on such an occasion, to follow the
example of the people of Israel, in Solomon's time:
Who, " when they saw the fire come down, and the
" glory of God upon the house, bowed themselves
" with their faces upon the pavement; and worship-
" ped and praised the Lord, saying, For he is good,
" for his mercy endureth for ever *."

But,

But, though Christ was thus made sin by an appointment of God the Father, it was not without his own free and voluntary consent. As soon as the proposal was made, when the " council of peace *was* " between them both," he cheerfully assented to it. " Lo! I come," said he, " (it is written of *him* in the " volume of God's book) : I delight to do thy will, " O my God; and thy law is within my heart." When the appointed time came, he did not repent of his undertaking. " He was not rebellious, nor " turned away back : but, gave his *blessed* back to " the smiters ; and his cheeks to them that plucked " off the hair : he hid not his face from shame " and spitting." So far from it, that he was even *straitened, till* his bloody *baptism was accomplished.* As Isaac freely suffered himself to be bound, and laid upon the altar, in the *land of Moriah*, while his godly father lifted the knife to slay him; so our Lord Jesus Christ, the first-born child of the promise, willingly suffered himself, not only to be bound, and laid upon the altar; but actually to be slain, and consumed by the fire of God's wrath, as a sacrifice for our sin. Indeed, such a thing could never have taken place, if Christ had not been as willing as his Father. Being God equal with the other persons of the Trinity, none had power to compel him. But, on the other hand, it was equally impossible that he should refuse his consent to his Father's proposal. What was the Father's will, could not fail to be his also : for he and his *Father are one*.

What a strange and astonishing event is this? The eternal Son of God, the Father's equal and his darling, made a victim for sin ! The sword of divine justice sheathed in the heart of him who used to wield it !

it! The supreme object of the Father's love become the supreme object of his tremendous wrath! Is not this he, concerning whom the voice from heaven was heard to say, and to repeat it, " This is my beloved " Son, in whom I am well pleased?" Does God, then, cease to be well pleased with him now? Does his eternal Father delight in him no more? Or " what " meaneth the heat of this great *anger?*" Nay, Christian: It was not any defect of love to him, but an excess of love to you, that produced all this. God so " loved the world, that he gave his only begotten Son" to the death; " that whosoever believeth in him " should not perish, but have everlasting life." Without this there could have been no egress for the love of God to you; nor was there any other method of averting his wrath from you. And, rather than suffer you to lie for ever under the stroke which your sin deserved, God would level that stroke at the heart of his only begotten Son; that you, and such as you, might escape.

But, is the love of God to sinners stronger than his love to Christ? Or, is the rage of his justice beyond the yearning of his bowels towards his beloved Son? By no means. Even while the vials of his wrath were poured into the soul of Christ, he still continued to be the supreme object of his love. Abraham never loved his Isaac more than when he stretched out his hand to slay him; and never did God love *his* Son more than when he slew him indeed. Yea, his love to Christ, as the Head of the body mystical, as well as his love to the members, moved the Father, thus to " make his soul an offering for sin." The mediatory glory of Christ is the genuine fruit of his sufferings,

ings. The splendor of his crown rose from the ignominy of his cross. And God brought him to the cross, that he might bring him to the crown. He *brought* him " to the dust of death," that he might exalt him to the " right hand of the throne of the Majesty in " the heavens. He made him," for a very short time, " to be sin for" the church; that he might make him *to be head*, and that through all eternity, " over all things to the church."

IV. On whose account, or for whose behoof this wonderful appointment was made, we see in the last words of this clause of the verse. It was *for us*. The apostle includes himself, and all the believing Corinthians, and all believers in Christ, from the beginning to the end of the world. It was not only *for us*, as being intended for our good and benefit. It was also *for us*, as being in our room and stead. He was made a sacrifice to *put away sin* from us; in such a manner that " his own self bare our sins, in his own body on " the tree." He substituted himself in our place. He was considered, by the law of God, in the same light as we should have been. Our sin was reckoned to his account. And that same punishment was inflicted upon him, which was originally due to us.

It is no wonder, that some men speak of sacrifices for sin, as apparently inconsistent with reason; when they make a sacrifice to be something widely different from what God ever intended it to be: and something that no reason whatsoever is able to comprehend. What can they mean by a sacrifice to *put away sin*, when they do not allow it to make any proper satisfaction for sin? Who, in the Jewish church,

or

or even in the heathen world, ever offered a sacrifice, with a view to put away sin; unless in a way of having his guilt, and so his punishment, transferred from himself to the victim? Or in what other manner is a sacrifice capable to take away sin? If Christ had meant to take away sin from us, without making satisfaction for it; what need was there for his subjecting himself to the curse, and to the Father's wrath at all? Or how can it consist with the justice of God, to inflict such miseries upon his own eternal Son, if there was not a proper imputation of our guilt to him? It is true, the Scripture says that he "put away sin by "the sacrifice of himself:" and who goes about to deny it? But it says also, that God "laid on him the " iniquities of us all; *that* his own self bare our sins; " and *that he* was made sin for us." And surely the Scriptures do not contradict themselves. It is easy to understand his putting away sin from us, in a way of bearing it *in his own body*. But how he should bear our sins, without a formal imputation of them to him; or how he should be made a sin-offering for us, and yet make no proper satisfaction for our sin, is perfectly unintelligible. It is worse—It is highly injurious to the wisdom, the goodness, the justice, and all the other perfections of God.

If it should be asked, more particularly, for whom, or in whose stead Christ was thus *made sin?* We cannot now stay to discuss the question at large, so as to obviate all the cavils of adversaries on this head. What may satisfy the conscience of every exercised person, we shall endeavour to comprize in the following propositions.

1. God, in appointing Christ to be a sacrifice for
sin,

sin, and Christ himself, in undertaking to that purpose, had their eye, from all eternity, upon a certain select number of mankind, who were and still are known to God only. For these only was this sacrifice strictly and properly intended. And for them only it shall be finally and ultimately effectual. As Christ *prayed not*, so he died not " for the world ; but " for them whom *God* had given *him* out of the " world." These are *the sheep, for* whom he *laid down* his *life* *.

2. The sacrifice that Christ offered was, in itself, sufficient to make atonement for the sins of all mankind, had it been so intended. While he bare all that was due to the elect for their sins, he bare as much as was due to all the seed of Adam. Indeed, his sacrifice could not have been sufficient for any, if it had not been sufficient for all. An atonement of infinite value was necessary for every individual. And more could not be necessary for all the world. This intrinsic sufficiency of Christ's sacrifice was, doubtless, attended to, in the divine appointment concerning it. God purposely made provision of such a sacrifice as was not only sufficient effectually to take away the sins of all the elect; but also sufficient to be laid before all mankind, in the dispensation of the gospel. If this is all that some have understood by an *ordinate sufficiency* of the death of Christ for all men ; the sense might be admitted, though the expression would be dangerous

3 The sacrifice of Christ, thus all-sufficient in itself. is, by God's appointment, offered to all that hear the gospel. All mankind are invited to make use of
it,

---

* John x. 15. compare chap. xvii.

it, in their dealings with God for pardon and acceptance, as freely and as fully as if they knew that God had defigned it for them from all eternity. In the gofpel-offer, no mention is made of election or reprobation. No difference is made between one finner and another. Without any diftinction, the call is addreffed, and a gracious welcome proclaimed, to all the children of Adam, " Unto you, O men, I call," fays divine Wifdom; " and my voice is to the fons of " man *."

4. As it is impoffible for any creature to know who are elect, or who are reprobate, till the event declare it; fo neither election nor reprobation can have any cafual influence in bringing any perfon to Chrift, or in keeping any from him. They ought to have no influence upon us, in making ufe of the facrifice of Chrift; and they will have no *judicial* influence with God, in admitting us to enjoy the benefit of that facrifice, or keeping us from it. God will, doubtlefs, execute his own eternal decree, in bringing all the elect to falvation; and likewife in the final condemnation of all others. Yea every man will execute God's purpofe; either in making ufe of Chrift's facrifice, or in rejecting it. But in no part of God's judicial procedure towards us does he pay any regard to his own decree, or to the intention of Chrift's death, as the ground of his decifions; but folely to our receiving or rejecting of Chrift. It is not faid, he that is elected, but " he that believeth and is baptized fhall be faved." Neither are we told that he who was not elected; but that " he who believeth not fhall be damned." The firft, indeed, would have been true; but

* Prov. viii. 4.

the laſt only is capable to have any influence upon us, as a motive of our conduct. And it only will be attended to by God, in his judicial dealings with us. Therefore,

5. It is the immediate duty of every ſinner that hears the goſpel, preſently to accept the gracious offer that God makes him of Chriſt, as a proper ſacrifice for his ſin: and that without ever thinking whether he be elect or reprobate; any more than a drowning man would think whether it was decreed from all eternity, that he ſhould periſh in the water or be ſaved out of it, before he would catch at a rope that were thrown in for his relief. For ſuch a man to lie ſtill in the water, till he could reſolve ſuch a queſtion, would evidently be the greateſt folly. Every perſon would ſee it to be ſo. Yet it was as really decreed from eternity, whether the man's life ſhould be ſaved, by means of the rope, or not; as whether any ſoul ſhall be ſaved by Chriſt, or be finally condemned. Yea, the man, by neglecting, on ſuch a fooliſh account, the means of his preſervation, would certainly contribute to the execution of God's purpoſe, in the deſtruction of his life. But if he ſhould immediately graſp at the rope, without aſking queſtions, as every rational man would do; then his life would be ſaved; and he would be ſure that God, from all eternity, fore-ordained it to be ſo. In like manner, it is our preſent and indiſpenſible duty to lay hold, by faith, upon the ſacrifice of Chriſt, as God holds it forth to us in the goſpel; to hold it up to God, as the only ground of our reconciliation and ſalvation; and firmly to truſt the promiſe of God, that, on this footing, he " will be merciful to our unrighteouſ-
" neſſes:

" ouſneſſes; and will remember our ſins no more." When any perſon is determined to take this courſe, it ſhall aſſuredly be to him according to his faith. And this he ſhall have as a ſure evidence, that God had an eye to him in particular, when he appointed Chriſt to be a ſacrifice for ſin: or, in other words, that he was elected from eternity. Having thus, in the manner that the Holy Ghoſt preſcribes, made our calling ſure; our election will come to be ſure of courſe. Having ſecured an intereſt in the ſacrifice of Chriſt, we may be firmly aſſured that he was intentionally *made ſin for us.*

And who were we, or what was our houſe, that the Son of God ſubmitted to become *ſin for us?* Were we friends to God? Nay; but enmity itſelf againſt him. Were we perſons, from whoſe ſalvation God could derive any advantage; or whoſe ruin would prove any loſs to him? Nay; to every one of us it might juſtly have been ſaid, as Elihu ſaid to Job, "If thou ſinneſt," and dieſt for ever in thy ſin, " what " doſt thou againſt him? Or if thy tranſgreſſions be " multiplied, what doſt thou unto him? If thou be " righteous, what giveſt thou him? Or what receiveth " he of thine hand *?" Were we perſons of ſuch value in ourſelves, or of any ſuch rank among the creatures, as to entitle us to all, or any part of this? By no means. Juſtly might David ſay; juſtly may we all ſay after him, " What is man that thou art mind-" ful of him? or the Son of man that thou viſiteſt " him?" In our beſt eſtate we were but vanity. In our fallen eſtate we are leſs than nothing and vanity: the vileſt, the moſt deſpicable, the worſt things in all

* Job xxxv. 6, 7.

all the visible world; and yet God " hath made him " to be sin for us, who knew no sin!"

We have heard of Abraham giving his son, his only son to God; and surely God was worthy of such an offering. Yet this is the only instance that ever the world produced, of such love among men, even to him who deserves it above all others. We have heard of wicked idolaters giving their children to Moloch, in the vain hope of keeping their own souls from misery: and " what will *not* a man give in ex- " change for his soul?" We know, the king of the children of Ammon offered his first-born son upon the wall; with a view to procure deliverance from an imminent danger, that threatened himself, his country, and all the rest of his kindred. But can any of these, or any thing else that ever took place among men, deserve a comparison with what is mentioned in the text? God gave his eternal, his only begotten, his well-beloved Son; he gave him to the death, and made him a sin-offering; not for his best friends, not for his own safety or advantage; not for his dutiful subjects, or for those who were allied to him; but for his most inveterate enemies, who were utterly worthless in themselves, and utterly unprofitable to him. Herein, indeed, is the love of God magnified, and the riches of his condescending mercy, that while we were yet sinners, and we can never be called by a worse name, " he made him to be sin for us, who " knew no sin."

We shall conclude for the time, with the following inferences for the improvement of the subject.

1. From what you have heard, you may learn, what

what is the difmal condition of all mankind by nature. We ftand in abfolute need of a fin-offering: otherwife there had been no reafon why Chrift fhould have been *made fin for us*. The elect of God are not in better circumftances than the reft of mankind in this refpect. They " were, by nature, children of wrath, " even as others *." Yes; every perfon in this affembly, and every other perfon upon earth, came into the world a finner. As fuch you were fubject to the curfe of God's broken law. A fentence of eternal condemnation had paffed againft you; and the wrath of God *abode upon* you. You were in imminent danger of the full execution of your fentence, and fo of becoming eternal victims to the devouring juftice of God. Nor was there any way for you to obtain deliverance, unlefs by means of the glorious fin-offering mentioned in the text. If any perfon among you has efcaped that condemnation, under which you naturally lay, and is reftored to the favour of God; let it never be forgotten, that you owe that happinefs, and all that you expect in confequence of it, to his free and unmerited love and goodnefs, who *made* Chrift *to be fin for* you.

2. You may here fee, how rigoroufly ftrict and fevere the juftice of God is. He " fpared not his own " Son," when our fin was imputed to him; but " de-" livered him up," without relenting, to that fearful ftroke, which, had it fallen upon all the rational world, would have reduced the whole to a ftate of inconceivable and endlefs mifery. Who are they, after all this, that dare affirm, that if God had pleafed, he might have forgiven our fin, and reftored us

* Eph. ii. 3.

to his favour, without any satisfaction to justice? Surely, if God could have pardoned sin without a satisfaction, he would not have exacted a satisfaction from his own eternal Son. If the whole punishment of sin, or any part of it, could have been remitted at all, it would have been remitted to Christ. And now, sinner, " if these things were done in the green tree, " what shall be done in the dry?" If Christ himself could not be discharged, till he had paid the last farthing of that criminal debt, which his voluntary undertaking had made his; how shall you be released, without a full payment of that debt, which is originally your own? Your sins, being an infinite evil, can never be expiated but by an infinite satisfaction. And is it possible that ever you should make payment of such a debt? " Can you drink of that cup which " *Christ* drank; or be baptized with the baptism that " he was baptized with?" Yes; you certainly shall, if divine mercy prevent it not. But the cup which he drank up at once, you shall never be able to exhaust: and therefore you must eternally drink of it, and be drunken. Nor can inexorable justice admit of your exemption from this dreadful doom; unless you are determined to lay hold, by faith, of this sacrifice, and to improve it as the foundation of all your hopes of deliverance.

3. You may see the absolute vanity and unprofitableness of all methods of creature-invention, for appeasing the wrath of God, which is kindled against sinners. God *has made* Christ *to be sin for us;* and he has neither appointed nor approved any other sacrifice. In that mournful breach, that sin made between God and us, God was the party offended and injured.

injured. He might juftly have refufed to admit of any fatisfaction, and infifted upon the inflicting of punifhment upon every finner in perfon. And furely, if a fatisfaction was to be admitted, it belonged to him only to determine what the fatisfaction fhould be. Under the law, no typical facrifices could be accepted, but fuch as God had appointed. Even under the New Teftament, no acts of worfhip can be pleafing to him, but fuch as wear the ftamp of his own authority. All will-worfhip is fuperftition and idolatry. And, furely, no fin-offering, properly fo called, might be accepted with God, which himfelf had not provided. Even the facrifice of Chrift might have been rejected, if God himfelf had not made him to be fin for us.

But if it had been lawful for the finner to have propofed a method of appeafing divine juftice, it would not have been poffible. All the wifdom of men and angels could never have devifed, either that method which God has provided, or any other. No facrifice could have been accepted that was not of infinite value. No other facrifice of infinite value, but that of Chrift, has ever been thought of, nor ever will. And this, which infinite wifdom has found out, was as far beyond creature-conception as any thing elfe can be. Who but God himfelf could ever have conceived it poffible, that the fecond perfon of the bleffed Trinity fhould " make his foul an offering for " fin?" If it could have been thought of, who durft have mentioned it? The very thought had been blafphemous in the higheft degree, if God had not been the author of it.

If any other method were poffible, it would be altogether

gether superfluous. This answers all the ends of God's glory, and all our spiritual necessities, in the most perfect manner. And, seeing this is the only method that God approves, every other must be rejected with disdain. It was because " sacrifice and " offering *God* would not ;" because, " in burnt-sa-" crifice, and sacrifice for sin, *he* had no pleasure," that Christ said, " Lo! I come ; I delight to do thy will ". O my God." Beware of attempting to " come be-" fore *God* with burnt-offerings ;" to bring your own righteousness in your hand, as the price of your restoration to his favour, or to make peace with him upon any other terms than those which the gospel reveals. If you truly wish to have his wrath appeased, and to be reconciled unto him, be concerned speedily to betake yourself to him whom God *hath made to be sin for us.*

4. You see how low the Son of God was pleased to stoop for our sakes. Not only did he take upon him our nature, and suffer all the miseries of an abased and afflicted life: not only did he condescend to encounter all our spiritual enemies, and to subject himself to the law of God in our room : not only was he brought to the dust of death, and continued three days and three nights in the heart of the earth : He even submitted to become a sinner, that we might be made righteous through him ! A sinner he could not be—in himself considered. In this respect, you have heard, *he knew no sin;* no sin was ever inherent in him. But he was made a sinner in our name, in the same sense in which we are made righteous through him. Our sin being imputed to him, he was reckoned a sinner in the eye of the law ; and, as such, he
was

was punished to the death. Indeed, when we are made righteous in law, through the imputation of his righteousness,—a principle of inherent righteousness is likewise implanted in us by his holy Spirit; whereas, he continued still *holy* and *harmless* in himself, absolutely free from all inherent sin, even when he became a sinner by imputation. But, in respect of guilt, he became a sinner, as really as we are made the righteousness of God in him. To become man for us was much; to become a dead man was still more: but that he should be made sin for us, or become a sinner in our stead, was a step of condescension surpassing all others. Men and angels will admire it eternally, without ever being able to admire it enough.

5. Here you may obtain the clearest discovery of the love of God to mankind; that love which *passeth all understanding*. Turn aside, then, gospel-hearer: turn aside, intended communicant, and see this great sight. Behold how he loved you! Behold the love of the Father, manifested in appointing his own eternal Son to be a sin-offering for you; in imputing your sin to him; and inflicting upon him that punishment which was due to you on account of it. Such was God's love to you, Christian, and such his resolution to make you happy; that, rather than suffer you to be miserable for ever, he made his Son miserable in your stead! Rather than you should be eternally shut out from his presence, he withdrew his comfortable presence from him, who had been, from unbeginning ages, his bosom-delight! Rather would he pour out his wrath upon his Christ, till law and justice should be satisfied; than have you subjected, through eternity, to that wrath, without ever being able to satisfy it.

Behold,

Behold, in the fame glafs, the no lefs amazing love of the Son of God, who fubmitted thus to be *made fin for* you. He loved you to fuch a degree, that he not only died for you, while you were yet enemies; tho' this had been more than ever took place among men: He even fubmitted to his Father's wrath, and to the hidings of his face, which were worfe than ten thoufand deaths, for you. But who can tell the ftrength and vehemence of his love! It was not only *ftrong as death;* the ftrength of it was equal to *the power of* God's *wrath.* Even the *floods* of Almighty vengeance could not *drown it.* Through thefe he voluntarily fwimmed, that he might fnatch you from that tremendous ocean, in which you were ready to fink eternally, and bring you home, a fpotlefs bride to himfelf, into thofe chambers where you fhall abide forever. Continue to look, with wonder and admiration, at this love; till you find your heart kindled with the flame, in fuch a manner as that *the love of Chrift* may *conftrain* you, not only to go forward to his table, over the belly of much unworthinefs, and of many doubts and fears about your condition; but likewife to encounter reproaches, and perfecutions, and dangers, and devils, and death for his fake, whenever he fhall call you to it.

6. From hence you may learn your duty, on fuch an occafion as this. Let me, therefore, take an opportunity to exhort every perfon before me, always to maintain a lively fenfe of your indifpenfible need of Chrift, as a fin-offering for you; and of the abfolute impoffibility of regaining the favour of God in another way. Keep ever in view the exact fuitablenefs of this facrifice; both to reftore the honour of
God's

God's law and juſtice, and to ſupply all the neceſſities of your ſouls. And ſee that you accept of this atonement, as offered to you in the goſpel. Offer it up by faith unto God, as the ground of all your pleadings with him : And truſt him for the pardon of ſin, and for a complete ſalvation, on that footing. You " have *all* ſinned againſt heaven, and in" God's ſight. None of you can make the ſmalleſt reparation to God on that account. The arm of divine vengeance is lifted up againſt you in your natural eſtate ; and neither you nor any creature can do any thing to divert the ſtroke. But, behold ! the eternal Son of God, equal in glory, bleſſedneſs, and perfection, to the Father, hath interpoſed to avert it. He averts it, not by oppoſing force to force, though he " hath an " arm like God, and can thunder with a voice like " him;" but by ſubjecting himſelf to it in your room: and ſuffering that unrelenting fury to vent itſelf upon him, which would otherwiſe have fallen upon you. And now, on account of what Chriſt has done, a free pardon of all ſin, a full indemnity for all your crimes, is exhibited, by God's authority, to every one of you. Thus ſaith the Lord to every one in this aſſembly, communicant and ſpectator, ſaint and ſinner, man and woman, old and young ; he ſays it to every one alike; every one has an equal warrant to apply it to himſelf, and to look for the preſent accompliſhment of it ; " I, even I, am he that blotteth out thy tranſ- " greſſions for mine own ſake, and will not remember " thy ſins *."

You that have received tokens of admiſſion to the Lord's table, ſee that you forget not in what character

* Iſa. xliii. 25.

racter and capacity it was, that Chrift accomplifhed that deceafe which you are about to commemorate. He died as a fin-offering for you. Forget not the promife, by which God has fecured you a free pardon on Chrift's account. And while you confider both what God hath promifed, and what a broad foundation is laid for the accomplifhment of the promife, by the facrifice of Chrift; beware of fuffering any fin that ever you committed, or any corruption that you feel prevailing againft you, or any thing elfe whatfoever, to deter you from ufing all that holy boldnefs and freedom with the King, at his table, that he gracioufly allows and requires. But come forward with cheerfulnefs and joy; and caft in your mite, fmall and inconfiderable as it may be, to keep up the remembrance of that death which made a full atonement for your fin; of that love which bound the facrifice as " with *invincible* cords, to the horns of the " altar;" and of all that power and wifdom, juftice and faithfulnefs, grace and love, which were manifefted in that glorious conftitution, by which God " made him to be fin for us, who knew no fin."

I muft not conclude without a word to you, who ftill continue in your natural eftate, and have *the wrath of God abiding* upon you. Such there undoubtedly are in this affembly, though we cannot point them out. O finner, confider the miferable fituation in which you are. The flaming fword of divine juftice is brandifhed over your guilty head; and is ready, every moment, to ftrike the blow that fhall render your condition eternally defperate. Neither is there any other remedy, but this which God has provided. If, therefore, you love your immortal fou', foul, and would not have it loft for ever; if you fear the wrath of Almighty God, and wifh to efcape from it; if you have any defire to be happy, in this world, or in the world to come: we earneftly call and befeech you, in the great name of the Lord our God; yea, we charge you, as you fhall anfwer to Chrift himfelf at his fecond coming; that you perfift not a moment longer in rejecting *fo great a falvation*. God is fo far pleafed with the facrifice of Chrift, that he has no further claim upon you; if you are but willing to owe your pardon and falvation to the merit of this facrifice. He is as willing to make you righteous; yea, to " make *you* the righteoufnefs of God in " *Chrift* ;" as ever he was to " make him to be fin " for us, who knew no fin." He fays to the greateft finner among you, what he faid, long ago, to the people of Ifrael, by the mouth of the prophet Ifaiah, " Come and let us reafon together: though your fins " be as fcarlet, they fhall be as white as fnow; though " they be red like crimfon, they fhall be as wool *."

* Ifaiah i. 18.

SERMON II.

Guilty Sinners made the Righteousness of God in Christ.

2 COR. V. 21.

HE HATH MADE HIM TO BE SIN FOR US, WHO KNEW NO SIN; THAT WE MIGHT BE MADE THE RIGHTEOUSNESS OF GOD IN HIM.

WHATEVER God requires of us is not only our reasonable service, it is likewise our interest to perform it; and we have reason to do it with pleasure and satisfaction. This is not the case more remarkably with regard to any other duty, than it is with respect to the work about which we are now met. It is natural for a person to think, with pleasure, of those whom he loves, though at a distance from him. It is equally natural to remember with pleasure any event, from which one has reaped, or expects to reap, any considerable advantage. A loving wife thinks with pleasure on her absent husband: and she commemorates, with delight, the day when she was united to him; or the day when he first made proposals propofals of love to her. And why fhould not the fpoufe of Chrift take pleafure in remembering her abfent Lord, and in commemorating that remarkable day, in which the foundation of her union to him was laid, in the fhedding of his precious blood? Surely the criminal, who had obtained a free pardon from his prince, after having been condemned to fuffer death, would count it no hardfhip to commemorate the day when his pardon was fealed. And why fhould we think with indifference about that wonderful deceafe, by which our glorious furety procured our freedom from condemnation and wrath? Or why fhould we give ourfelves up to difcouragement, when about to commemorate that event in the facrament of the fupper? Surely the dying command of Chrift will not be grievous to any, who duly attends to the end and defign of his death; as it is expreft in the words of this text. He died in confequence of his being *made fin for us*. He died *that we*, who were the moft atrocious finners, *might be made the righteoufnefs of God in him*.

It will, doubtlefs, be remembered by fome, that we read thefe words, on the laft occafion of this nature that we had in this place. And, after fome fhort account of the Apoftle's fcope in the context, we endeavoured to give you the fenfe of this verfe in the following paraphrafe.

'In order that the way might be paved, for the
' reconciliation of finners unto God; it pleafed God
' the Father, to make his own eternal Son an offer-
' ing for our fin; that we, through him, might be
' accounted perfectly righteous in the fight of God.'

We

We told you that the text plainly fets before us two things,

I. What our Lord Jefus Chrift fubmitted to be for our fakes, according to his Father's appointment; as we have it in the firft part of the verfe. *He hath made him to be fin for us, who knew no fin.*

II. What was God's end and defign, in this folemn tranfaction; as in the laft claufe. It was *that we might be made the righteoufnefs of God in him.*

We fpake at large concerning the firft of thefe: and now propofe, through divine affiftance, to offer you fome thoughts concerning the fecond.

In the laft part of the verfe, as in the firft, there are four particulars deferving confideration.

I. What God intends that we fhould be, in confequence of Chrift's being *made fin for us:* He defigns that we fhould be *righteoufnefs.*

II. What kind of righteoufnefs it is, with which he propofes to endow us; *the righteoufnefs of God.*

III. How we obtain an intereft in this divine righteoufnefs; intimated in the word *made.*

IV. In what right we are to enjoy it. It is only *in him;* that is, in Chrift.

After fome fhort explication of each of thefe, we fhall conclude with fome improvement of the fubject.

I. It is propofed to fpeak of what God intended us to be, in confequence of Chrift's being *made fin for us.* He became what he was not, that we might be the oppofite of what we were. He who knew no fin was made fin, that we, who knew nothing but fin, might become righteous; yea, righteoufnefs in the abftract.

Righteoufnefs

Righteousness, as well as sin, is something relative. As sin consists in the want of conformity to the law of God; so righteousness, the opposite of sin, consists in conformity to that unerring rule. That law which was first written upon Adam's heart, and afterwards summed up in those *ten words*, which were delivered by the voice of God, from mount Sinai; being a transcript of the holy nature of God, and agreeable to all his moral perfections; is the supreme rule, and original standard, of all moral rectitude and perfection among men. Every action that is conformable to this law, is a work of righteousness; and every thing contrary to it is an act of sin. And, as that law extends to those habits and dispositions that belong to the constitution of the nature, as well as to outward actions; it is the standard by which we should judge ourselves, and by which we must be judged in the sight of God. The man, therefore, whose nature and actions are conformable to that law, is righteous; whereas he who is deficient in this conformity, in whole or in part, in his nature, or in any of his actions, must be deemed a sinner.

Now, it is manifest, that a person may live conformably to any law, or yet contrary to it, without being tried in a court of justice, so as to be pronounced either righteous or wicked. Among men, it is but a small number of those who are subject to the law, that ever have been tried before any judge. Indeed no person, in ordinary cases, is so, till he is suspected of some crime. And of those who are tried, some who have lived according to law may be pronounced guilty; while others are declared righteous, who have really acted contrary to law. Hence arises a plain distinction,

diſtinction, betwixt a *real* and a *legal* righteouſneſs. That man is *really* juſt and righteous, whoſe life is conformable to the law; and he who has committed any tranſgreſſion of the law, is *really* guilty and a ſinner. On the other hand, he is *legally* righteous, who has been judged and declared to be ſo in a court of juſtice; whether he has indeed lived according to law or not. And he is *legally* guilty, who is judicially pronounced and declared to be ſo; even though his life has been agreeable to law and equity. And, becauſe all human judges are liable to err, and capable of being impoſed upon by falſe evidence; it frequently happens, that the ſame perſon is *really* guilty and *legally* righteous: while another, who is righteous *in fact*, may be *legally* guilty; having been declared to be ſuch in a court of juſtice.

With God it is not as with men, in this reſpect. All the ſubjects of his government are not only bound by his laws; they are alſo tried in a court of juſtice,— even in the ſupreme court of heaven. A ſentence of that court has actually paſt, and ſtands on record, concerning every man and every woman. Some, being ſuſtained righteous in law, are adjudged to life and happineſs: while others, and theſe by far the greateſt part, are found guilty in judgment; they are declared to be ſinners, and, as ſuch, are " condem-" ned already, *and* the wrath of God abideth on " them." God himſelf, being the omniſcient witneſs of all actions; yea, having an intimate knowledge of all hearts, is incapable of erring in judgment, or of being impoſed upon by any means. His judgment, therefore, " is always according to truth."

If we were to judge of God's procedure, in this reſpect,

fpect, by the rules of human reafon; we would readily apprehend, that the juft *Judge of all the earth* would pronounce all thofe to be guilty, and deal with them as guilty perfons,—who are really guilty in themfelves; and that none fhould be pronounced righteous, or fuftained fuch in law, but them whofe natures and actions had been found, upon trial, to be perfectly agreeable to that law which is the rule of judgment. Indeed it would have been fo, if the covenant of works had ftood ; or if men had only been judged by the law of nature. And it will eventually be fo, with regard to all thofe who continue under the covenant of works, and all who fhall finally be judged by the law of nature only. But, by the covenant of grace, a new method of procedure is introduced; a method far above the reach of unenlightened reafon. By this method, perfons who are really guilty, and finners in themfelves, are fuftained, pronounced, and declared righteous in the eye of the law. They are dealt with as righteous perfons, and entitled to all the privileges that are connected with that character; in the fame manner as they would have been, if they had never finned : yea, in a manner far more ample and glorious than, in that cafe, they ever could have been. Yet all this is done in a full confiftency with all the rules of juftice; and with all the adorable perfections of that holy and juft God, who is the fupreme *Judge of all the earth.*

It is true, indeed, that no perfon is thus made legally righteous, who is not made really and perfonally righteous at the fame time. Every perfon who is pronounced righteous in law, is likewife endued with a principle of inherent righteoufnefs, and enters upon a courfe of obedience to that law which is the fupreme rule of righteoufnefs. But, contrary to all the dictates of human reafon, and to all the courfe of human procedure, in the adminiftration of juftice; our perfonal inherent righteoufnefs is fo far from being the ground of that fentence, by which we become legally righteous, that it is only a fruit and confequence of that fentence. All our actions, before we are declared righteous in law, are fo egregioufly finful, that any one of them would have been fufficient to condemn us. And, in the paffing of our fentence, no refpect is had to any works of righteoufnefs that we are to perform afterwards. Our juftification, our being affoilzied and declared righteous, proceeds upon a very different, an infinitely more fure and noble footing.

This wonderful fentence is folely owing to Chrift's having been *made fin for us*. It is founded upon that righteoufnefs which he wrought out for us. All they, for whom Chrift was made fin, are, in due time, brought, in the manner that fhall be explained in a little, if the Lord will, to enjoy an actual intereft in what Chrift did and fuffered, when our fin lay upon him. On that footing, they are abfolved from the curfe of the law; that dreadful fentence by which they ftood condemned before. A new fentence is paffed in their favours, by which they are fuftained and declared righteous in the eye of God's law, and entitled to all that happinefs which they might have expected to enjoy if the covenant of works had ftood, and much more. In the fame inftant the Holy Ghoft takes up his refidence in the foul, and begins to make it really and inherently righteous. And, under his influence,

they

they grow in conformity, both of nature and actions, to the law of God; till their inherent righteousness also is made perfect, and they are completely freed from all the remainders of their natural corruption. Both these may be included in the text,—our legal and our real or personal righteousness; as both are the fruits of Christ's being *made sin for us.* But it is undoubtedly the first that is primarily and directly intended.

Thus it is, that we become righteous through Christ; yea, *righteousness* itself, as the text expresses it, by an usual figure; the *abstract* being put for the *concrete*, as grammarians speak: and this figure may be here used to intimate the two following things.

1. The perfection and excellency of that righteousness, with which we are endued. We are made righteous in the eye of God's law, in the very highest degree, so that it is impossible for us to be more so than we are. This is the usual import of the figure. Thus, the *carnal mind* is said to be, not only an enemy, but *enmity* itself *against God* * ; as if the whole substance of the soul were exhausted by that one quality. Carnal men are enemies to God in the very highest degree. They could not be more so, if they had no other quality belonging to them; but their whole nature and constitution were made up of nothing else but this enmity. So, when we are here said to be made *righteousness,* the meaning is, that we are made righteous in such a degree as admits of no addition. We could not be more righteous if our whole nature and constitution were made up of this one attribute, and there were nothing about us but righteousness.

2. The

* Rom. viii. 7.

2. The similarity of the manner in which we are made righteous through Christ, to the manner in which he became guilty for us. His righteousness is transferred to us, in the same manner in which our sin was transferred upon him. He is said to have been made not only sinful, but sin; and, therefore, we are said to be made righteousness. The same form of speech is used in both parts of the verse; because both the wonderful changes mentioned in it were brought about in the same manner. Our character was originally the opposite of Christ's: He knew no sin; and we had no experimental knowledge of any thing but sin. But he was put into our place in law; and we are put into his. He was pronounced a sinner, and dealt with accordingly. And we are judicially declared to be righteous; and as such we are dealt with. Christ bare all the punishment that was due to us for all the sins that were imputed to him; and we enjoy all the blessings and benefits that were due to the merits of Christ, when he *fulfilled all righteousness*. He was made sin by the imputation of our sins to him, though he continued to be without sin in himself. And we, even while we continue sinners, are made righteousness; by having his righteousness imputed to us, and reckoned to our account.

II. WHAT kind of righteousness it is, with which the people of God are endued, in consequence of Christ's being made sin for them, was the next thing observed in the words. It is *the righteousness of God*.

This strange expression some take to signify no more, than that this righteousness with which we are endued is most noble and excellent. By an usual Hebraism

Hebraism, that which is moſt excellent in its kind is aſcribed to God, or called his, in Scripture. Thus, the cedars are called *the trees of God* *; becauſe they are the moſt noble and ſtately of all trees.—In this ſenſe, indeed, our righteouſneſs may, with the greateſt propriety, be called the righteouſneſs of God. No other righteouſneſs is comparable with it; unleſs the eſſential righteouſneſs of the divine nature. The righteouſneſs of Adam, in his eſtate of original integrity, could not be compared with it. Though perfect while it continued, it was ſo ſhort lived, that " man in ho- " nour lodged not a night †." The perſonal righteouſneſs of the ſaints deſerves not to be mentioned along with it. While they are in this world, it is but *as filthy rags;* it is both imperfect and defiled. And though it ſhall be perfect in another world, none of them will ever be diſpoſed to compare it with this. Even the righteouſneſs of confirmed angels is not like it. Their righteouſneſs can be profitable to none but themſelves, as it barely correſponds to the demands that the law of their Creator has upon them. Nay, all the righteouſneſs that can be found among mere creatures muſt be infinitely inferior to it. All creatures muſt be finite and dependent. Their righteouſneſs can never be wholly their own; as they muſt depend upon the great Firſt Cauſe, in this, as in every other reſpect. It muſt be finite, in itſelf and in its value, as proceeding from a finite nature. But this righteouſneſs, being wrought out by an infinite perſon, is itſelf infinite in value and in duration. It not only anſwers all the demands of the law; it even exceeds them. By it the law is " magnified and made honour-

---

* Pſal. civ. 16. † So the word might be read, Pſal. xlix. 12.

"honourable *. The law had demands upon every mere man, for all that obedience that a finite nature could perform. But that the great Author of the law should subject himself to it, and yield an obedience, infinite as the person who yielded it, this surpassed all that ever the law could demand; and hereby was an honour conferred upon it, beyond any thing that could have taken place if it had never been dishonoured by sin. Thus the righteousness which is conferred upon us is infinitely more noble than any other; and, on that account, may, with propriety, be called *the righteousness of God.*

But I apprehend it is so denominated chiefly on another account; because it is a righteousness in which God has a principal interest and concern. And, indeed, in whatever light we view it, it is, in the strictest sense, God's righteousness. If we view it in the original spring of it; it was God alone that contrived it. None but he had any right to make Christ a sacrifice for us; and none but he had sufficient wisdom to find out so strange and wonderful an invention. View it in the actual fulfilment of it; and it was God who wrought it out. Our glorious Surety, though made a partaker of flesh and blood, like his brethren, was from all eternity, and to all eternity is, the supreme and self-existent God, equal in every respect with the Father and the Holy Ghost. Consider it in respect of its end and tendency: it was a righteousness designed for God; to promote his glory as the righteous Judge of all the earth, and to restore the honour of his broken law. To God, therefore, it was offered by Christ; as the full payment of all that debt

for

---

* Isaiah xlii. 21.

for which he became furety. To God it is offered by the Chriſtian, in the day of believing, as the ſole ground of his pardon and acceptance. And God has accepted it, from the hand of the Surety firſt, and then from the ſinner himſelf. Of this he has given aſſurance, in that he hath raiſed Chriſt from the dead; and in that he bleſſes every Chriſtian, " with all ſpiritual " bleſſings, in heavenly places, in Chriſt Jeſus." In a word, take a view of this righteouſneſs in its actual communication to us, and it is the gift of God. It is God who exhibits it to us in the goſpel. And it is he alone by whom it is actually conferred upon us, and made ours. By him it is that we are *made the righteouſneſs of God in* Chriſt. This naturally leads us to enquire,

III. How it is that we obtain an intereſt in this incomparable and truly divine righteouſneſs. This is expreſt, in the text, by our being *made righteouſneſs*.

It was hinted above, that we are *made* the righteouſneſs of God in Chriſt, in the very ſame manner in which he was *made* ſin for us. Now, in Chriſt's being made ſin for us, four things may, and ought to be attended to.

The propoſal made to Chriſt from all eternity; wherein the Father declared it as his will, that he ſhould be made ſin for us.

The Son's conſent to that propoſal; whereby he undertook to ſatisfy juſtice in our name.

The actual imputation of our ſin to him, in the fulneſs of time, when God laid on him the iniquities of us all. And,

His being dealt with as a ſinner, in conſequence of all

all this; and fubjected to the punifhment that our fin deferved.

Correfponding to thefe, there are four things, that may be confidered as fo many fteps, by which we are brought forward to be the righteoufnefs of God in Chrift.

1. Correfponding to the propofal which the Father made to Chrift from all eternity; there is the gracious propofal that God makes to us, in the difpenfation of the gofpel, of making us righteous through Chrift. The righteoufnefs of Chrift, having firft been accepted at his hand, by God the Father, as the full accomplifhment of his undertaking, is, by God's authority, freely offered, exhibited, and *brought near* to every hearer of the gofpel; and every perfon is warranted, invited, and intreated, to receive and ufe it; as the fole ground of his acceptance with God, of the pardon of his fin, and of his title to eternal life and happinefs. We, then, have the honour to be " ambaffa-
" dors for Chrift: as though God did befeech you by
" us; we pray you in Chrift's ftead," to accept this precious righteoufnefs, as the ground of your reconciliation unto God. You need not bring any thing in your hand, with which to purchafe it; it is offered " without money and without price." You have no occafion to wait for any previous qualifications or endowments to recommend you; it is brought near even to them " that are ftout-hearted and far from righ-
" teoufnefs." The very offer of this righteoufnefs to you neceffarily fuppofes you to be unrighteous and guilty in yourfelf. You could have no need of this, if you had a fufficient righteoufnefs of your own, or any thing that could effectually recommend you to
God.

God. Come, then, juſt as you are. And, if you are a deſcendent of Adam, and have a rational ſoul, in union to that body which we ſee; you are as welcome as God can make you, to this precious, this ineſtimable, this *unſpeakable gift*.

2. There is the act of juſtifying faith; whereby the ſinner, in the day of his effectual calling, lays hold of this righteouſneſs, as it is thus offered to him in the goſpel. This may be viewed as correſponding to Chriſt's acceptance of the Father's propoſal, whereby he undertook to become *ſin for us*. The poor ſinner, finding himſelf purſued by the fiery law, with curſes and denunciations of vengeance; ſeeing the ſword of divine juſtice ready to ſtrike him to the loweſt hell; having tried all methods to appeaſe the juſtice of God, to ſatisfy the demands of the law, and to allay the terrors of his guilty conſcience; and having found all methods of his own deviſing in vain: his ears are opened by the Holy Spirit of Chriſt; he hears the voice of God in the goſpel, to which he was altogether inattentive before ; and now, for the firſt time, he conſiders that offer of Chriſt and his righteouſneſs, which the goſpel contains, as made to him in particular, and as made by God himſelf. His will, being, at the ſame inſtant, ſubdued by a day of almighty power, conſents, with cheerfulneſs, to the gracious propoſal; and he ſays, " Surely in the Lord have I righteouſ- " neſs *." Thus he actually receives what God offered to him before, and makes it his own. He holds it up to God, as a full and ſatisfactory anſwer to all the cravings of his law, and a ſufficient atonement to his incenſed juſtice. He pleads for the pardon of his

ſin,

* Iſaiah xlv. 24.

fin, the acceptance of his perfon, and an intereſt in all the benefits of God's covenant, folely on that footing; and fays, *Behold, O God, my ſhield; and look upon the* righteouſneſs *of thine anointed.*

3. There is the actual communication of this righteouſneſs to us, correſponding to the laying of our fins upon Chriſt. This includes two things.

(1.) The actual imparting of it unto us, upon our receiving it by faith, in the manner juſt now deſcribed. You can eaſily perceive, that when any perfon has fomething valuable offered and held out to him by another; he can never get poſſeſſion of it, unleſs there is an act of giving on the part of him that offered it, as well as an act of receiving on his part. So it is here. When the finner, by the aſſiſtance of divine grace, puts forth his hand to receive this righteouſneſs, God actually makes good his offer. He gives him the real and perſonal poſſeſſion of it, and it becomes his indeed. The *beſt robe* is *put upon him;* and he is accordingly qualified to partake in the marriage-feaſt that God has made for his Son; to lift up his face with confidence in the preſence of God, and before that throne of which " juſtice and judgment are " made the dwelling-place."

(2.) The judicial imputation of this righteouſneſs to us, fuſtaining it as ours in law, to all intents and purpofes, as really and effectually as if it had been wrought out by our own hands. *Imputation* properly ſignifies the putting of any thing to a perfon's account; and it is uſually underſtood in a forenfic fenfe. The imputation of Chriſt's righteouſneſs to us is that *judicial ſentence,* or *judgment of the court of heaven, whereby it is declared to be ours in law.* Now, as
the

the judgment of God is always *according to truth;* it is manifest that this righteousness cannot be sustained as ours till it be received by us, and put upon us in the manner above explained. But a moment does not pass, after we have received it by faith, or after it is put upon us by God, till it is likewise sustained for us in law, and we pronounced righteous by him who is the supreme and sovereign Judge of all the earth. Yes, believer: however guilty you are in yourself, and however much your conscience may be burdened with a sense of your guilt, God accounts you righteous in as high a degree as if you had never committed a sin. Yea, in the eye of his law, you are incomparably more righteous, than, in that case, you could have been; for you are considered as *made the righteousness of God in* Christ. In consequence of all this,

4. There is God's dealing with us as righteous persons; and bestowing upon us all the fruits of that righteousness which is judicially put to our account: corresponding to Christ's being dealt with as a sinner, in consequence of the imputation of our sin to him. In making " his soul an offering for sin," God had no respect to the unspotted holiness and righteousness of his personal character; but punished him in the same unrelenting manner, as he would have done if he had been the greatest of all sinners; because he stood before God as our Surety, and all the guilt of our sins was found upon him. In like manner, Christian, from the moment that you are clothed upon with the righteousness of your Redeemer, God pays no regard at all, in judgment, to the sinfulness and vileness of your real character: but, in all his judicial dealings

with

with you, he conducts himself in the same manner as he would have done if you had never been guilty of any sin; yea, in the same manner as if you, in your own person, had performed every article of that which Christ performed in your name. Having freely *forgiven* your *iniquities*, he remembers not, he never " will remember your sins *any* more *." The reason of this is assigned in the text. Christ having been *made sin for* you, you are *made the righteousness*, not of a mere man, but of a divine person, for such Christ was. You are even *made the righteousness of God in him*

Wonderful change! amazing dignity! a vile, sinful, cursed, condemned worm *made the righteousness of God!* Is every true believer then made so absolutely righteous? Is he considered, by law and justice, in the same light as Christ is? Or, is it possible that the righteousness of an infinite person can be imparted to a sinful creature; and that creature made such in law as Jesus Christ is, with regard to perfection of righteousness? Rejoice, Christian, in your privilege. But beware of suffering a licentious imagination to lead you into blasphemy and absurdity. Christ has not done for you what the devil said the forbidden fruit would do, made you equal with God. The words of the text, when understood in their proper sense, contain a precious and consolatory truth; abundantly consistent with all the distance that must ever subsist between the Creator and the creature. But, if stretched, they may seem to give countenance to the blasphemous absurdities of some ranting sectaries, who spake of being *Godded with God*, and *Christed with Christ:*

* Jer. xxxi. 34.

Christ: as if Christians were incorporated with the essence of God, or made partakers of his incommunicable perfections. Nay, the thing is simply impossible. And the very thought is injurious, in the highest degree, to the infinite and inaccessible majesty of God. You are *made the righteousness of God;* not by a participation of the essential righteousness of God's nature; nor by having the righteousness of God, in any respect, inherent in you. Nay; at the same that you are thus righteous in the eye of the law, your inherent righteousness continues to be as filthy rags. But you are made so, in the manner already described; by being interested in that righteousness, which was wrought out by a person who is God; and by having that perfect, infinite, and truly divine righteousness judicially put to your account. No change is hereby made in your real and personal character. You still continue that sinful, unrighteous, and filthy creature that you feel yourself to be. But you are considered, and dealt with, by the law and justice of God, as a person interested in an infinite righteousness. You are intitled to all the happiness that a divine righteousness can procure, and are as free from any possibility of condemnation as *the righteousness of God* can make you. You are interested in a better inheritance than a finite obedience could ever have procured; and so are entitled to hope for a higher degree of glory and blessedness, through eternity, than any of mankind could have enjoyed if sin had never entered. You have and hold this inheritance, by the very same right by which it is held by Christ your Head. And you have the same security that he has, against ever falling under the wrath or curse of God a

second

second time. The infinitude of his righteousness, or its being *the righteousness of God*, gives you a title to the one, and a security against the other, as unchangeable as the divine nature itself. But this arises from nothing inherent in you: it is wholly owing to Christ your Surety. You are *made the righteousness of God* only *in him*.

IV. To consider the meaning of these last words of the text, or to enquire in whose right believers are *made the righteousness of God*, is all that remains of the doctrinal part of our subject. We are made thus righteous *in him*. The expression imports two things.

1. That no persons can be thus *made the righteousness of God* till they are really *in Christ*, and enjoy a vital union to his person. There is a twofold union that subsists between Christ and the believer; a *legal* and a *vital* union. The legal union is our being sustained in law as one with him; and so entitled to be dealt with according to his merits. This is much the same with what, in the text, is called a being *made the righteousness of God*." The vital union consists in our being partakers of the same spirit with him; and being endued with that faith by which we hold him as our Head. Our real union commences in regeneration, and our legal union in justification. Hence it is manifest, that, though there is no difference in point of time, yet, in the order of nature, regeneration must be prior to justification. Till we be really united to Christ, we cannot be judicially declared to be one with him; otherwise the judgment of God would not be according to truth, nor could we be said to be made the righteousness of God *in him*.

2. That

2. That when any person is thus *made the righteousness of God*, being accounted righteous in the eye of God's law; it is only in Christ's right, and on his account. As Christ could not be accounted a sinner, or dealt with as such, unless on our account; so neither can we be accounted righteous, nor entitled to any part of the reward due to a righteous person, unless on his account. In our justification God has no more respect to any righteousness of our own, than he had to any sin inherent in Christ, when he subjected him to his wrath and curse. We are justified on account of his righteousness imputed to us, in the same manner as he was condemned for our sin imputed to him; and for the same good and sufficient reason. He *knew no sin*, and we knew no righteousness. He could not be punished for his own sin; because he was " holy, harmless, undefiled, and separa-" ted from sinners." And we cannot be justified on account of our own righteousness; because it is but *filthy rags*.

- It is true, that, in consequence of Christ's being made sin for us, a principle of inherent personal righteousness is implanted in us, as has been said already. And it is equally true, that this inherent righteousness begins to be wrought in us in regeneration; which is prior, as we have just now seen, to the legal imputation of Christ's righteousness to us in justification. We are not made the righteousness of God in Christ, without having an image of God's righteousness and holiness stamped upon us. But it is equally true, and a truth that can never be too much attended to, that this our personal righteousness comes not at all into consideration before God, when he judicially declares us to be righteous perfons. Indeed, it is utterly impoffible that it fhould. Nothing that is about us when we are juftified, nor any thing that we can attain to in any after period, can fo far anfwer the demands of the law as to procure acceptance for itfelf; or to be pronounced, in ftrict juftice, a righteous action: much lefs can it procure acceptance *for us;* or be any part of the ground upon which we are pronounced righteous perfons. The truth is, we never could be juftified, unlefs every thing wrought in us, and done by us, were wholly out of the queftion. As all our fins, whether committed in a natural, or in a gracious ftate, are wholly overlooked, on the one hand; fo are all our righteoufneffes on the other: whether that which we vainly pretend to in our unregenerate ftate, or that which we really attain to, under the influence of divine grace, in our eftate of union to Chrift. Imputed righteoufnefs is only attended to, in God's judicial procedure towards us. We are *made the righteoufnefs of God*, only *in* Chrift.

WE are now to conclude with fome improvement of the fubject. We fhall fatisfy ourfelves, at prefent, with the following inferences: referving any further application, till it can be overtaken, if the Lord will, in the progrefs of the work of this day.

1. From what has been faid, we may fee what is the true fpring of all that legality which does fo much harm in the Church, and in the hearts of profeffed Chriftians. It is nothing elfe than mens attempting to meafure the great things of God by the ftandard of human reafon. We know that, among men, there is no way of being acquitted in a court of law, or being pronounced

pronounced righteous by a juft judge, upon ftanding a legal trial before him; unlefs the perfon is really innocent, or elfe the proof of his guilt fails. We are difpofed to think that God is fuch an one as ourfelves; and therefore we have no profpect of acquitment in his prefence, unlefs upon the footing of our own perfonal righteoufnefs or innocence. The method of juftification by the imputed righteoufnefs of another, is not fit to be practifed among men. It lies beyond the reach of human wifdom; fo far, that it appears to be *foolifhnefs* in the carnal eye. Therefore it is, that carnal men reject it in their dealings with God. Never will a finner be reconciled to it, till he find the bottom beaten out of all his own fchemes; his refuges of lies fwept way, his own wifdom befooled, and all hopes of fatisfying the demands of God's law by his own doings utterly cut off: never—till he be determined, by divine grace, to deny himfelf; and have his eyes fupernaturally opened, to fee the infinite wifdom of God, appearing in the myftery of redemption through the blood of Chrift. Hence every natural man is a legalift; and every Chriftian has a remainder of legality about him, proportioned to the prevalence of the unrenewed part.

Whence is it that fo many of thofe who profefs to be *mafters* in our *Ifrael*, fubftitute a fyftem of legality or Arminianifm in the place of the gofpel of Chrift? Men are early taught to fet up human reafon, as the touchftone even of revelation itfelf. A doctrine fo flattering to human pride is readily drunk in. And, being greedily received, is afterwards retailed even from the pulpit. The doctrine of imputed righteoufnefs they confequently reject, as one of thofe which reafon explodes. All other doctrines which exceed their fhallow comprehenfion fhare the fame fate; and one argument ferves to confute them all—' They are 'contrary to reafon, and God is the Author of reafon; 'he cannot therefore be the Author of fuch doctrines, 'becaufe he cannot contradict himfelf.' Some other fenfe muft be fought for thofe paffages of Scripture where thefe doctrines are taught; and invention is put to the rack, to get the word of God perverted from its genuine and obvious meaning. Would it not be more honeft, and equally native, to reafon as others do, from the fame principle, that the Scriptures cannot be the word of God at all; becaufe they contain doctrines that feem inconfiftent with human reafon? Truly, whenever reafon is fet up as the judge of revelation, *Deifm* is the native confequence.

But knoweft thou not, O vain man, that God's " ways are not as *our* ways, nor *his* thoughts as *our* " thoughts?" Haft thou no experience of the imperfection of *human* reafon, and of its liablenefs to err, even in natural things? Are the *deep things of God* more within the reach of this boafted reafon, than the things of this corporeal world? Or are *thefe* the only things about which *thy* reafon cannot err? God is, indeed, the Author of *right* reafon; and cannot be the Author of any thing that is really contrary to it. But art thou fure that *thine* is that very reafon, of which God is the Author? Or art thou fuch a complete mafter of *right* reafon, as to know infallibly what is agreeable, and what is contrary to it? A much better method of arguing would be this; God has exprefsly told me, in his word, that " there is no falva-
" tion in any other *name but* the name of Jefus; *that*
" by

" by the works of the law no flesh living shall be juf-
" tified;" and that, " as by one man's disobedience
" many were made sinners, so by the obedience of
" one shall many be made righteous:" And, seeing
these are the very words of God, I must believe them
to be agreeable to right reason, though to my shal-
low apprehension it would seem to be otherwise.
Much better suspect my own reason, which I know
to be erring and imperfect, than bring any imputation upon the veracity of the unchangeable God, or
any of his other perfections. This we are sure of, that
you must learn to argue in this manner, and to have
your practice influenced by such reasonings, in relation to this and many other doctrines in the Christian
system, if ever you enjoy real and saving advantage
by divine revelation. And we are equally sure, that,
whatever be the views of carnal men, this doctrine of
imputed righteousness, in particular, will ever be precious in the eyes of every genuine Christian. The
doctrine of salvation through the merits of a crucified
Redeemer may be, as it ever has been, " to the
" Jews a stumbling block, and to the Greeks foolish-
" ness; but still it *will be* the wisdom of God and the
" power of God unto salvation, to every one that be-
" lieveth *."

2. We may see, that neither faith nor repentance,
nor sincere obedience, nor all these together, nor any
thing else that is wrought in us, or done by us, can
be the proper condition of that covenant which God
makes with believers through Jesus Christ. Indeed,
there is a covenant entered into between God and
every believer; as really as between God the Father

and

* 1 Cor. i. 23.

and his eternal Son. But, in this covenant, no mention is made of any condition to be performed by us, as the ground of our title to the promifes of it. Nothing is required of us, but freely to receive what God as freely gives; and to give ourfelves and our fervices to him, not as the ground of our title to what he beftows upon us, but as a teftimony of our gratitude on account of it. The reafon of this is manifeft. The covenant that is made with us is the fame that was made with Chrift from eternity. The whole condition of this covenant was to be fulfilled by Chrift, and he has fulfilled it accordingly. What he did, in fulfilling the condition of it, is gracioufly imputed to us, when we are brought within the bond of the covevenant; and on that footing we are not only abfolved from guilt and from punifhment, but likewife adjudged to the poffeffion of all the bleffings of the covenant. Our faith, our repentance, our evangelical obedience, inftead of being the condition of the covenant, are all contained in the promife of it; and are all gracioufly beftowed upon us, as the fruits of Chrift's purchafe. Thefe are not the righteoufnefs on the footing of which we are juftified; but they are all beftowed upon us through Chrift, as fo many branches of that happinefs to which we are adjudged, when we are made the righteoufnefs of God in him.

3. We may hence be informed, in what fenfe it is that God fees no fin in his people. Balaam was conftrained, under the unwelcome influence of the Spirit of God, to fay, " He hath not beheld iniquity in " Jacob, nor perverfenefs in Ifrael." If our tranflators have given a proper verfion of this paffage, it furely means, that, in fome fenfe or other, God fees no

fin

sin in his people. No person, who has any competent acquaintance with himself, will pretend to be without sin in this world. And it cannot be apprehended, without blasphemy, that there can be sin any where, to which an omniscient God is not privy. Nay, Christian, your mournful experience testifies that there is still much sin about you. And the many chastisements that you suffer may assure you that God sees it; for by these he takes *vengeance* on your *inventions*. But he sees no sin in you, or about you, as he is the supreme Judge of all the earth. He takes no judicial notice, or cognizance of it. It is all covered, from the eye of vindictive justice, by the garment of your Surety's righteousness, with which you are clothed. And it is impossible that any judicial knowledge should ever be taken of it in the court of heaven. In all God's legal procedure towards you, he must deal with you as if you had never sinned; for himself has graciously made you *the righteousness of God in* Christ.

4. Though our sin was imputed to Christ, in the same manner as his righteousness is imputed to us; yet there is a very great difference, in regard to the duration of the effects of these two transactions. Christ was *made sin for us*, only for a short time: we continue to be the righteousness of God in him, not only while time remains, but even through all eternity. Christ was reputed a sinner, and dealt with as such, only during the continuance of his humbled state: and as soon as, by his death, he had " finished " transgression and made an end of sin," he was freed from all the dismal effects of the imputation of our sin to him. But we shall continue for ever to be

dealt

dealt with as righteous perfons; and when death fhall have put an end to all the remainders of fin in us, then only fhall we begin to enjoy, in perfection, all the happy fruits of his imputed righteoufnefs. The reafon of this is manifeft. No fentence of the court of heaven can be abolifhed, or ceafe to have effect, till it be executed to the full. When our fins were imputed to Chrift, a fentence paft in that court, appointing him to fuffer all the punifhment that was due to them. Being an infinite perfon, he bare a punifhment by which the whole contents of his fentence were exhaufted, and that in a fhort time. When we are *made the righteoufnefs of God in him*, a fentence in like manner paffes, appointing us to enjoy the full reward of Chrift's obedience unto death. And the full reward of an infinite righteoufnefs muft needs be infinite. But we, being finite creatures, are as incapable to exhauft an infinite inheritance, in any limited fpace of duration, as we are to fuffer an infinite punifhment. Our fentence, therefore, can never have its full effect, unlefs we continue, through all eternity, in poffeffion of the fruits of this divine righteoufnefs.

5. We may fee a ready method for intended communicants to be properly dreffed out for the banquet of wine, to which the great King is inviting them. If you, who propofe to join in the great work of this day, have not been greatly deficient in your duty, you have been endeavouring previoufly to examine yourfelves. And the great enquiry, with you, has been, whether or not you have on that wedding-garment, in which alone you can fit with acceptance at the King's table? And, perhaps, it is ftill matter of doubt;

doubt, whether you have it or not. But here is a ready method to have all such doubts resolved. You have heard in what manner we obtain an interest in the righteousness of Christ; and this righteousness is the very garment which you want. This righteousness God presently offers to you, as well as to every other hearer of the gospel. We are expressly commanded by him to " bring forth this *robe*, and put it " on you." And, whether ever you had it before or not, it is your indispensible duty *now* to put it on, by the renewed actings of faith. In this way, no sin of which you are conscious, nor any sin that may have escaped your memory, shall stand in the way of your enjoying the most intimate communion with God at his table. Yea, in this way, you may have all your doubts, relative to your state, resolved: you may have *the Spirit* of God *bearing witness with* your *spirits, that* you *are the children of God:* and may come to the Lord's table, in full assurance of your being the genuine friends of Christ. Reflecting upon the present exercise of your faith, you may have that as an infallible mark of your present interest in Christ, and of your present right to partake in this solemn ordinance. " Put ye on the Lord Jesus Christ," therefore: put on the *wedding-garment* of his righteousness. And so go forward " to the altar of God, and " to God *your* exceeding joy; that *you* may publish " with the voice of thanksgiving, and tell of all his " wondrous works:" but chiefly of this most wonderful of all his works, that *he hath made him to be sin for us who knew no sin; that we might be made the righteousness of God in him.*

6. Here is a door of hope set open before the greatest

est and most atrocious of all sinners. It is " a faithful " saying, and worthy of all acceptation, that Jesus " Christ came to save sinners," even *the chief* of them. He came to save them by being *made sin for* them; *that* they *might be made the righteousness of God in him.* To every sinner in this assembly, even to him that has been guilty of the greatest sins, and to him that has continued in sin the longest, is Jesus Christ offered, as *made of God unto you righteousness.* God is now giving you an opportunity to chuse, whether you will be dealt with, both now and hereafter, according to what you deserve, or according to the merits of Christ. If you choose the last, you shall inherit all that Christ has purchased, and is now in possession of: but if you finally choose the former, you must dwell, for ever, among "snares, fire and brim- " stone, and an horrible tempest;" which justly belongs " to sinners as the portion of their cup." And perhaps this may be the last time that ever you will have it in your power to make the choice. Let your present choice, therefore, be such as you would wish to stand for eternity; and beware of trifling in a matter of such vast importance.

Perhaps you are still dreaming of salvation by your own righteousness. But have you never any suspicions that it may fail you? If there is but a possibility that it may fail, it must be your wisdom to renounce it, and take up your standing on the righteousness of Christ; for this can never fail you. Surely you can never dream that your righteousness is equal, in any respect, to the righteousness of God. And is it not the greatest folly to trust your eternal happiness to a righteousness that is finite and imperfect,

fect, when you have one that is infinite and absolutely perfect in your offer? If you will be saved by the works of the law, you must fulfil all its demands. If you fail in the least article, you are exposed to the curse; nor will any punctuality in your after-services make atonement for the least offence. "Cursed is "every one that continued not in all things which are "written in the book of the law, to do them." Be not deceived. It is as impossible for you to be saved by your own righteousness, as it is for any person to perish who embraces and puts on the righteousness of Christ. As soon may you see a real Christian in hell, as see one who lived and died a legalist in heaven. Neither is it possible that you can retain your own righteousness, and yet have an interest in Christ's. This spotless robe needs no patching—It admits of none. Either you must receive Christ, and renounce your own righteousness; or, by retaining it, you renounce him.

Neither have you any reason to be afraid, that the greatness of your sin will be a bar in the way of your being saved by Christ's righteousness. Surely your sin can never bear a comparison with the infinite holiness of Christ's person. Yet God made him to be sin; and why should he hesitate to make you righteous? Your sin can never deserve the wrath and curse of God more richly than the righteousness of Christ deserves eternal life. Even to the *stout-hearted*, and them *that are far from righteousness*, is the righteousness of God brought near in this gospel. And the greater your sin is, the more glory will redound to the merits of Christ, and to the grace of God through him, by your salvation. Be concerned, therefore,

while

while it is called to-day, to lay hold on Chrift's righteoufnefs, by an appropriating faith ; and improve it as the fole ground of all your expectations from a God of grace, either in time or through eternity. For, by God's authority, we declare unto you, that " he " that believeth not in *Chrift* is condemned already ; " *and* the wrath of God abideth on him." But, on the other hand, *there is no condemnation*, through eternity there never will be any, *to them who are in Chrift Jefus*. How fhould there? " It is God that " juftifieth, who is he that condemneth ? It is Chrift " that died; yea, rather that is rifen again : who is " even at the right hand of God; who alfo maketh " interceffion for us."

The

The Difcourfe in fencing the Tables: containing an Ufe of Trial, drawn from the Subject of the foregoing Difcourfe.

NO perfon can partake acceptably in the folemn ordinance, which is about to be difpenfed among us, unlefs in the way of carefully examining himfelf; that he may caft out all *the old leaven* which he finds about himfelf, and be in a condition to keep this New-Teftament paffover " with the unleavened " bread of fincerity and truth." The fubject, from which we have been fpeaking, affords you various marks by which you may try yourfelves. We fhall endeavour to fet a few of them before you. And we charge every perfon, who has a-token of admiffion to the Lord's table, to apply them to his own confcience as we go along. Nor is there any perfon prefent who has no concern in what we are about to fay. It muft be the intereft of every man to know himfelf, and of every woman. And if the glafs is faithfully held up, every perfon may fee his own face in it, on the one fide or on the other.

The great queftion, then, with every one in this company fhould be, Whether you have been *made the righteoufnefs of God in* Chrift, in the manner that has been

been spoken of, or not? If you have, and come forward in the exercise of the sacramental graces, Christ makes you welcome to a feast upon his body that was broken, and his blood which was shed, when God *made him to be sin for* you. But if it is otherwise with you; in coming to this holy table, you will become accessory to the sin of those who murdered him: you will be *guilty of the body and blood of the Lord*. Would you desire to avoid this sin; and know whether you have on the wedding-garment, in which alone you can be welcome to participate in this feast, or not? Then ask your consciences, as in the sight of God, the following questions.

1. What knowledge have you of Christ, and of the method of justification through his imputed righteousness? You have heard, that this whole device is foolishness to the natural man; and if it continues to be so in your eye, you cannot be welcome at his holy table. But if your eyes have been opened to see this method of salvation to be worthy of all the perfections of God, exactly suitable to all your necessities, and free from all those defects that you have found about every other method that ever you tried or thought of; and if you are presently disposed to say of it, as David in his dying day, It " is all my " salvation, and all my desire;" then your knowledge of it is saving; and you may be welcome at this table. I only say you *may* be welcome; I dare not say you *shall*. For, though your knowledge be saving in its nature, you cannot be a worthy communicant; unless, for the degree of it, it be such as may qualify you to discern the Lord's body through the outward elements. Not only those hypocrites whose, knowledge

ledge is all carnal and speculative; but also those Christians, whose knowledge of the nature, ends, and uses of this ordnance, is incompetent, are debarred from the holy table of the Lord.

2. Have you ever been determined to accept the offer that God makes to you in the gospel, of Christ and his righteousness; and to improve that righteousness, as the sole ground of your pardon and acceptance in the sight of God? You have heard, that this is one thing necessarily included in the manner of our being made the righteousness of God in Christ. Have you therefore, when pinched with a sense of sin, and of your dangerous condition while exposed to the wrath and curse of God, been enabled to hear the voice of God in the Gospel, as addressed to you? Have you been satisfied that the offer of Christ and salvation through him was made to you in particular, as really as ever it was to any other of Adam's lost family? And was you determined, in a day of almighty power, to accept the gracious proposal; and to say, in raptures of love and joy, " in the Lord have I righteous- " ness?" Was you disposed to renounce all dependence upon your own righteousness, whatever was your attachment to it before; and to cast it away as *filthy rags?* Are you of the same disposition still? and is it your present desire and aim, to lay hold on Christ anew; as *made of God unto* you, not only *wisdom and righteousness,* but also *sanctification and redemption?* In a word, do you propose to go forward to the Lord's table in the faith of being accepted in that service, and strengthened for it, only in Christ, your beloved? Then we are warranted to invite, and we hereby do kindly invite you to a seat at this holy table.

ble. But if you are a stranger to this faith; if you have never seen your indispensible need of this divine righteousness; if you are disposed to accept of Christ, only as he is *made righteousness*, but not as *made sanctification;* if you put all the calls and offers of the gospel from yourself; or if you content yourself with having embraced them some time heretofore, and are not concerned to renew the actings of faith upon Christ and his righteousness *now:* we declare you unfit, for the present, to partake in this solemn feast. For, not only all habitual unbelievers, but all faithless and unbelieving Christians; that is, all who are not in the present exercise of faith, are debarred from this holy table of the Lord.

3. What views have you of that evil and bitter thing, which brought the eternal Son of God to suffer his Father's wrath, when *he made him to be sin for us?* Has God *poured upon* you, according to his promise, *the spirit of grace and of supplications;* enabling you to *look upon* him *whom you have pierced, and to mourn for him?* Do you not only fear sin and abstain from it, on account of its dangerous consequences to yourself; but also hate and abhor it for its lothsome and abominable nature, for the dishonour it does to God, and for the wounds that it gave to Christ? Do you turn from it with a sincere abhorrence; and even lothe and abhor yourself on account of it? Do you turn from it unto God, with full purpose of, and endeavour after new obedience? Are you presently in the exercise of repentance? And is it your resolution, through grace, to eat the New-Testament passover, this day, with these bitter herbs? Then we invite you to partake in this feast, as a genuine

nuine friend of Chrift. But if you ftill continue to love fin, though you fear the punifhment of it; if you refolve to continue in fome fins, while you refolve to forfake others; if you would choofe to continue in fin, provided you might with impunity; if you have never been grieved for the injury that fin has done to Chrift, nor affected with fhame and felf-lothing on account of it: then there is fad reafon to conclude, that you are ftill in the gall of bitternefs, and in the bond of iniquity; and while this is the cafe, you muft be debarred from this holy table of the Lord.

4. What think you of Chrift, whom God *hath made to be fin for us?* Have you got fuch a view of his glory, his excellency and beauty, as convinces you that he is *altogether lovely?* And do you love him above all creatures whatfoever? Is your love to himfelf productive of love to his law, to his ordinances, and to his people? Do you ftudy to give proper evidence of your love to him, by keeping his commandments? And is it this love that powerfully conftrains you to fet about keeping his dying command to-day, over the belly of many doubts and fears, and difcouragements? In a word, are you prefently humbled in the fight of God for the weaknefs of your love; and earneftly longing for an increafe of this grace, that your love to him may correfpond, as far as your finite nature will admit of, to his incomparable love to you? Then he warrants us to invite you to his holy table; *there will* he *give* you his *loves.* But, on the other hand, if you are no lover of the Lord Jefus Chrift, nor ever faw him " fairer than the children of men ;" if you love not his laws, but count his fervice a burden; if you love not his ordinances, but are *detained,* like

Doeg, *before the Lord;* if you imagine that you love him, or ever loved him enough; if you have never been fenfible of your natural enmity againft him, nor difpofed to mourn on account of it, but apprehend that you have loved him all your days: then you are ftill under that dreadful *anathema,* which an infpired apoftle pronounces againft all them who " love not " the Lord Jefus Chrift;" and, while that is the cafe, you can have nothing to do with this love-feaft, this pledge of his dying love.

5. Are you made really and inherently righteous, as well as righteous by imputation? You have heard, that when a perfon is *made the righteoufnefs of God in* Chrift, then the Spirit of Chrift takes up his refidence in his foul, and begins to imprint upon him an image of the righteoufnefs of God: which he will make perfect in due time. Are you, then, a partaker of that Spirit? Is it your daily endeavour to " walk, " not after the flefh, but after the Spirit;" keeping always in your eye the law of Chrift as your rule, the example of Chrift as your pattern, and the glory of God in Chrift as your ultimate end, in all that you do? Are you careful to obey every precept of the divine law, and that on every occafion? Do you confider it as the law of Chrift, and obey from refpect to his royal authority, as well as to the authority of God his Father? Do you obey in the ftrength of borrowed grace, and count yourfelf ftill an unprofitable fervant after all that you can do? Then you are *made the righteoufnefs of God in* Chrift; and your *garments are of wrought gold;* for you prove yourfelf to be the king's daughter, by being *all glorious within.* We, therefore, invite you to this holy table. But if
you

you indulge yourself habitually in any sin; if you satisfy yourself with obedience to the letter of the law, and do not consider its spirituality, nor its *exceeding breadth;* if you obey from a principle of slavish fear only, or in the vain hope of procuring for yourself a title to eternal life; if you pretend to obey by your own power, and *go not in the strength of the Lord God;* if you are not humbled for the legal and slavish principle that too often influences your obedience, for the many imperfections that attend it, and for the many sins that are intermixed with it;—then you are a stranger to the righteousness of Christ; for you have no principle of inherent righteousness in you; and you have no warrant to touch the sacred symbols of his body and blood with such unclean hands.

It is necessary that we be a little more particular here. You ought to examine your obedience by the several precepts of the law of God; and to consider what respect you have to each of them, in their order.

- Is it your sincere desire, to *love the Lord* your *God, with all* your *heart, with all* your *soul, with all* your *strength, and with all* your *mind?* Have you chosen Christ's God for your God and Father; for your portion and everlasting inheritance? Are you concerned to worship, love, fear, obey, and honour him, as God; to believe and rejoice in him as your God; to take up the rest of your soul in him, to look for eternal happiness only in the enjoyment of him; and presently to cast away all your idols, of every kind, " to " the moles and to the bats?" Have you a due respect for all the ordinances of his worship? And is it, through grace, your study to keep them pure and entire?

entire? Do you confider it as your duty to contend earneftly for the purity of that doctrine and worfhip, and for the prefervation and exercife of that government and difcipline, which Chrift hath inftituted in his church? Do you make confcience of attending the difpenfation of the word, and partaking in the facraments, as occafion requires; of performing fecret duty, and performing or attending family worfhip, morning and evening? And, in whatfoever act of outward worfhip you are engaged, are you concerned that the exercife of your heart correfpond to your outward appearance? Are you careful, at all times, and in all refpects, to make a holy and reverend ufe of all that whereby God makes himfelf known; avoiding all profane or irreverend mentioning of his names, titles, attributes, ordinances, words, or works? Are you peculiarly careful to avoid all falfe, needlefs, profane, or fuperftitious fwearing; and all ufe of lots, in gaming or in trivial matters? Do you make confcience of vowing to the Lord your God, and paying your vows daily in the prefence of his people? And are you concerned to fanctify the Sabbath to the Lord: calling it a " delight, the holy of the " Lord, honourable;" and to honour him on that day, " not doing your own ways, nor finding your " own pleafure, nor fpeaking your own words?" Then you are made the righteoufnefs of God in Chrift; for you love and honour the God of righteoufnefs: and we invite you to his holy table.

But if you are under the power of habitual enmity againft God; if you continue to purfue happinefs among the creatures; if you allow that place in your heart and affections to any other, that is due to God only;

only; or allow yourself in applying to creatures, good or bad, for what God alone has to give; if you believe not God, nor trust in his salvation; if you indulge yourself in the neglect of any divine ordinance; if you satisfy yourself with a formal, careless, drowsy, or hypocritical attendance upon them; if you allow yourself, or countenance others, in adding to them, or taking from them; if you dare profane the name of God, by swearing, or imprecations, in ordinary conversation; by swearing false, unnecessary, or contradictory oaths, whether imposed by public authority, or required by any private society or corporation: if you are an avowed enemy to the duty of vowing and swearing to the Lord of Hosts, either publicly or personally; or are not careful to *perform to the Lord* your *oaths*, and other engagements; if you are a habitual breaker of the Sabbath, indulging yourself in profaning that holy day, by idleness, by carnal conversation, by worldly employments or recreations:— if any of those sins lie on your conscience, not repented of; or if you are not presently disposed to mourn before God for every breach of any of the precepts of the first table, that your heart is privy to; then you have not yet " attained to the law of righteous-" ness:" and therefore we debar you from this holy table of the Lord.

In vain will you pretend to perform the duties of the first table, if you live in the neglect of those of the second. " If a man love not his brother whom " he hath seen, how shall he love God whom he hath " not seen?" Is it, therefore, your concern to *love* your *neighbour* as *yourself;* and to give evidence of it, by doing good, according to your ability and opportunity,

portunity, to all men, especially to them that are of the household of faith? More particularly, Are you conscientious in the performance of relative duties, according to that station in which adorable Providence has placed you; as husbands or wives, parents or children, masters or servants, ministers or people; as superiors, inferiors, or equals; in church, state, or family; taking the word of God for your rule, and performing your duties to one another, *as unto the Lord?* Are you careful to use all lawful endeavours to preserve your own life and the life of others; avoiding all immoderate use of meat, drink, physic, labour, or any thing that may tend to shorten your own life, or to hurt its well-being; and using every lawful mean to preserve your bodily health or restore it; guarding against all striking, quarrelling, and every thing that may tend to the taking away of your neighbour's life, or rendering it uncomfortable; and striving, by the exercise of meekness, gentleness, compassion, charity and forbearance, to contribute all in your power to make your neighbour's life easy and agreeable? Have you, like Job, *made a covenant with* your *eyes;* watching over them and your other senses, shunning all occasions and appearances of uncleanness, and all provocations thereunto; hating the garments spotted with the flesh, and counting yourself defiled, even by unclean imaginations? Are you conscientious in rendering to every man his own; and ready, according to your ability, to use every endeavour for promoting your neighbour's wealth and outward estate; being diligent, at the same time, in a lawful calling, and otherways careful to *provide* for yourself, and " for those of *your* own house, things
" honest

" honeſt in the ſight of all men?" Do you wiſh and endeavour always to ſpeak the truth to your neighbour, eſpecially in matters of judgment and juſtice; " to be valiant for the truth upon the earth;" to rejoice in your neighbour's good name as in your own; and, in every reſpect, to follow the things that are true, honeſt, lovely, and of good report? And, in one word, Do you rejoice in all the good that your neighbour poſſeſſes, as if it were your own; and ſubmit, or ſtrive to ſubmit, without repining, to all the evils that are in your lot; *committing* yourſelf, in all things, " to him that judgeth righteouſly?" Then you bear the image of him who " did no evil, neither was guile " found in his mouth." This is a ſure evidence that you have been *made the righteouſneſs of God in him;* and you are welcome to his holy table.

But if you hate your brother in your heart, and habitually ſhew that hatred in your practice, by the neglect of relative duties, or by the commiſſion of the oppoſite ſins; particularly, if you are an undutiful huſband, a diſobedient wife, a cruel or too indulgent parent, a prodigal or rebellious child, a rigid maſter, or a mere eye-ſervant; if you are a haughty ſuperior, an uſurping inferior, or an equal void of brotherly love: if you ſhew your hatred of your brother, by giving way to ſinful anger, wrath, ſtrife, ſedition, or deſire of revenge; by oppreſſion, quarrelling, ſtriking, wounding, or whatever elſe tends to render his life ſhort or unhappy: if you indulge yourſelf in outward acts of uncleanneſs, in unclean imaginations, in filthy or obſcene diſcourſe; in wanton looks, immodeſt apparel, the uſe of laſcivious ſongs, books, pictures, dancings, ſtage-plays, or any thing elſe unbecoming the

character

character of a *chaste virgin* unto *Christ:* if you are habitually guilty of theft, fraud, oppression, extortion, or injustice of any kind, whereby you may hurt the outward estate of your neighbour; or yet indulge yourself in idleness, luxury, drunkenness, wasteful gaming, vexatious law-suits, or any thing else tending to hurt your own: If you are a liar, a slanderer, a backbiter, a tale-bearer, a false witness, or perjured person; if you are an open enemy to any of the truths of God; if you receive not the truth in the love thereof, or if you hold the truth in unrighteousness: If you allow yourself in discontentment, envy, repining at the disposals of Providence, or " covetousness which " is idolatry."—In one word, If your conscience tells you, that, in any part of your past life, you have been guilty of any of these sins, and have never truly repented of them; if you think you have repented sufficiently already, and are not desirous presently to be humbled for them; or if you think you have always been so innocent, in all these respects, as to need no repentance on any such account;—then you are a stranger to inherent, and therefore to imputed righteousness; and we should do an injury to you, as well as be unfaithful to our great Master, if we did not, as we now do, debar you, while in your present condition, from this holy table of the Lord.

Now, if any of you that have received tokens find yourselves characterized among them who are unfit for a seat at the sacramental table, we charge you, as you shall answer to Christ himself, at his coming, that you venture not to partake in this holy ordinance, without first betaking yourselves, by faith, to him

whom

whom God has *made to be fin for us; that* you may *be made the righteoufnefs of God in him.* We call every intended communicant, to renew the actings of faith, repentance, love to God, to Chrift, and to one another, and true evangelical obedience. In that way, let them who find themfelves invited, come forward with cheerfulnefs; to get their graces confirmed and ftrengthened, their intereft in Chrift and his righteoufnefs fealed, fome comfortable fruits of this righteoufnefs communicated; and both Chrift himfelf and his Father manifefted to them, as they never manifeft themfelves to the world.

, *The*

The Discourse at serving the first Table: Containing an Use of Consolation.

COMMUNICANTS,

THE approach that is made to God in this ordinance is very near and very solemn. The advantage of an acceptable participation in it is unspeakable; but the danger of eating and drinking unworthily is proportionably great. If you are accepted guests at this table, you shall have reason, through eternity, to praise God for the seat you occupy; but if you are not, there is danger that you shall eternally bewail what you are now employed about. God " will be sanctified in all that draw near " unto *him;* and before all the people will *he* be glo- " rified." If he is not glorified by you in an active manner, by an acceptable performance of your duty, you have reason to fear lest he sanctify himself upon you, by consuming, with the fire of his jealousy, those who presume to offer strange fire upon his altar. How is it, then, that you hope to be accepted, or on what footing do you expect to " stand before this holy " LORD God?" If you have any dependance upon your own doings, your attainments, or any grace that you have received; if your hopes are founded upon

any

any thing that ever was done by you, or any thing that ever was wrought in you; we can affure you, that you ftand upon a wrong bottom. And after all the length you are come, we charge you that you provoke not the jealoufy of the Mafter of the feaft; by partaking of his provifion that has been prepared at fuch a vaft expence, in a way of hugging his rivals in your bofom. Either, therefore, give up with your own righteoufnefs prefently, and betake yourfelf to the divine righteoufnefs of him whom God *made to be fin for us;* or rife from his table, and be gone.

But methinks I hear fome poor foul *bemoaning himfelf thus:* 'Alas! I dare not fay that I have no
' dependence upon any thing of my own; but God
' is my witnefs that I defire to have none. I feel
' about myfelf a ftrange prevalence of legality; but
' it is matter of fincere grief to me: and I mean to
' offer my petition at the banquet of wine, for the de-
' ftruction of it. Though heretofore I have counted
' my own works and attainments gain; henceforth it
' is my fincere defire to *count* them *lofs. Yea, doubt-*
' *lefs,* I wifh to *count all things but lofs for the excel-*
' *lency of Chrift Jefus my Lord; and to count them*
' *but dung that I may win him, and be found in him;*
' *not having mine own righteoufnefs which is of the*
' *law, but that which is through the faith of Chrift;*
' *the righteoufnefs which is of God by faith.'* If this is your language, communicate; if you are but aiming to lifp out fuch language within yourfelf, however fenfible you are of the prevalence of an oppofite difpofition; it is a fure evidence that you have been made *the righteoufnefs of God in* Chrift: and we are warranted to difpenfe unto you the fymbols of his body

dy which was broken, and of his blood which was shed, when God *made him to be sin for us :* For,

Our Lord Jesus, the same night in which he was betrayed, took bread, &c.

' *Do this in remembrance of* my having been made
' *sin for* you. And do it in the grateful remembrance
' of that grace, by which you are *made the righteouf-*
' *ness of God in* me. Do it in remembrance of that
' love which I bore to you, when I *made my soul an*
' *offering for* your *sin;* and of that tender care which
' I had of you, when I prepared you such a feast :
' even while I was struggling with the weight of your
' guilt, which I had taken upon my shoulders ; and
' with the weight of that wrath, which my own eter-
' nal Father poured into my soul on that account.'
Yes, believing communicant; he knew that the traitor had struck his infamous bargain with the chief priests and elders, and sought an opportunity to betray him. He knew that it was but a few moments till his bitter agony would begin. Already was he sensible, that the prince of this world was a-coming. He came against him, armed with all his infernal rage ; which was not now restrained by any exertions of the power of God, as it is when he makes his assaults upon you. He saw the bloody sword of divine justice already drawn ; and the arm of omnipotence lifted up, to fetch the terrible stroke, that was to bring him to the dust of death ; a stroke that would have driven the whole creation headlong into the lowest hell! Yet even in this situation he did not forget you. In this dreadful crisis it was, that he appointed for you this pledge of his dying love. And, that you might have a full feast,

In

In like manner, after supper, he took the cup, &c.

Now, communicant, you see, you feel, you taste what it is to be *made the righteousness of God in* Christ; and what is the unspeakable advantage of being *in him*. All the dainties of a sublunary world are not sufficient to constitute such a feast as that which you now enjoy. Nor can the hypocrite or the worldly man, amidst all their gains, and profits, and pleasures, and honours, and baubles of every kind, enjoy as much real happiness, as much solid delight and satisfaction, as you may have, in thus feeding upon the flesh and blood of a slain Redeemer. In this ordinance you have God's seal appended to that happy sentence, by which you was declared to *be the righteousness of God in* Christ. And as really as you have that bread and that cup among your hands, you have an inviolable security for all the fruits of Christ's purchase. You have no more reason to be afraid of condemnation than Christ himself has: He got up your discharge from the hand of divine justice, along with his own, in his resurrection from the dead.

You have full security for a complete and final victory over all your spiritual enemies, within you, as well as without you. When Christ was *made sin for* you, he *trode* those enemies " in *his* anger, and tram-" pled them in *his* fury." Their *blood*, as well as his own, " was sprinkled upon *his* vesture ;" and with it he " stained all his raiment." He now goes out against them, on your head, as *the Captain of salvation,* to subdue them all under your feet ; and to make you " conquerors, and more than conquerors, through " him that loved *you*." And surely, if he was a match for them all, when he had the wrath of an angry God to conflict with, and had *none to help* or *uphold* him; he cannot fail to be a match for them now, when he fits on the throne of his glory, and has all the hosts of heaven at his back.

You have security for the everlasting continuance of the love and favour of God towards you; for it was to procure a vent for this love, that Christ was *made sin for* you. And now, " this thing is as the " waters of Noah unto *God;* for as *he hath* sworn " that the waters of Noah shall no more go over the " earth, so *hath he* sworn that *he* will no more be " wroth with *you,* nor rebuke *you.*" He may be wroth, in the manner in which a loving Father is angry with offending children; and he will assuredly " visit *your* iniquities with the rod, and *your* sins with " chastisements." But he will never *rebuke* you *in* judicial *wrath, nor chasten* you *in* vindictive *displeasure.*

You have security for a competency of the good things of this life, while you continue in life; though you may, perhaps, be straitened in obtaining it. This also is contained in that covenant, of which the righteousness of Christ was the condition, and this sacrament is the seal. " Bread shall be given thee, and " thy water shall be sure."

You have security for the gracious presence of God with you, and the perpetual inhabitation of his Spirit in you; till your wilderness journey be finished, and your warfare wholly accomplished: for thus saith God the Father to Christ, " My Spirit which is upon thee, " and my words which are in thy mouth, shall not " depart out of thy mouth, nor out of the mouth of
" thy

"thy feed, nor out of the mouth of thy feed's feed, "from henceforth even for ever."

You have security for all necessary strength and grace, to enable you to perform all that is required of you; and to bear, in a becoming manner, all the trials and afflictions that shall be laid upon you: For thus saith he in whom you have been made righteousness, "My grace is sufficient for thee; and my "strength is made perfect in weakness."

You have security against the sting of death, and against a perpetual continuance in the state of the dead; for Christ, by that death which was the finishing part of his righteousness, and which you now commemorate, hath overcome and destroyed death itself; as well as "him that had the power of death, that is, "the devil." And now he himself has "the keys "*both* of hell and death."

You have security for the eternal and uninterrupted possession of "an inheritance, incorruptible, and "undefiled, and that fadeth not away;" of which Christ has taken possession in your name, and which is *reserved*, under his hand, *in heaven for you*.

You have security—But why should we attempt to enumerate the great things that are secured to you by your interest in the righteousness of Christ, and sealed over to you in this ordinance? The tongue of no mortal can recount them. The heart of no mortal can conceive them. "Eye hath not seen, "nor ear heard; neither have entered into the heart "of man, the good things which God hath laid up "for them that love him." Eternity shall be spent in recounting, to the praise of divine grace, the happy fruits of this righteousness which you shall enjoy.

And

And eternity itself shall never see the theme exhausted. God himself, an infinite, eternal, and all-sufficient God, is the portion of that inheritance which you shall possess, in consequence of the wonderful transaction mentioned in the text. And surely neither men nor angels, nor any creature, nor all creatures together, shall ever be able to declare the value, the extent, the pleasantness, nor the glory of such an inheritance. *Comfort ye* yourselves, and *one another, with these words*. And, in the faith of all this, go from the table where all has been sealed to you. And the God of all grace and consolation shall not fail to go with you.

An Ufe of Exhortation, delivered at the conclufion of the Solemn Action.

My Friends,

THE facramental table is now drawn. And we fhall conclude the work with a few exhortations, fuitable to what you have been employed about, and natively arifing from the fubject of which you were hearing in the forenoon. The words of exhortation fhall be addreffed, firft to communicants, and then to thofe who have been fpectators only.

As for you that have been communicants, we charitably hope, that moft of you have come to this folemn ordinance in obedience to the dying command of Chrift; and with a view to " feek Jefus who was " crucified." And fome of you, we truft, have not miffed your errand. Let fuch be thankful for their privilege, and remember to what they owe it. All has been beftowed upon you for his fake, who was *made fin for* you. And all is the fruit of your having been *made the righteoufnefs of God in him.* " Not " for your fakes, do I this, faith the Lord God ; be " it known unto you, but for mine holy name's fake." You have no reafon to be proud of your attainment: it is none of your procuring. All is the gift of free

and

and sovereign grace. "Where is boasting then? It " is *totally* excluded."

Beware of resting in your privilege, or fondly talking, like Peter, on the mount of transfiguration, of *building tabernacles*. It is but a transient visit that you can expect here. What you have attained, of this kind, will quickly be gone. Perhaps it is gone already; and you have begun to suspect that all was delusion. But your righteousness endureth for ever. You shall never be cut off from God's favour, nor shut out of his family. Never shall you want a share in his love, nor an interest in any of the happy fruits of this righteousness with which you are clothed. You must learn, therefore, to be denied to such manifestations, as well as to every thing else that you enjoy in this world; and to live always *by faith on the Son of God*. Even these you must count " but " loss and dung, for the excellency of Christ," and of his righteousness. Nor must you have any dependance upon them, or make any mention of them, as any part of the ground of your pleadings for after benefits. Yet you must not think yourself at liberty utterly to neglect what God has done for you, or to make what use of it you please. It is a part of the talent which he has bestowed upon you, and of which he will require a strict account. One end of all such visits is to encourage weak faith. And you ought to improve them as an argument, by which you may put unbelief to silence. You have seen the promise of God accomplished in part; let it embolden you to hope for a full accomplishment of it in due time. You have seen him present to-day in his ordinances; let it encourage you to depend upon him for his promised mifed prefence in every cafe. And fince he has begun to do this for you; truft in him, that he *will not fail* you, *nor forfake* you; *till* he *have done all for* you *that* he has *fpoken to* you *of.*

Some of you may be complaining, that hitherto you have not feen him, nor had any comfortable fellowfhip with him on this occafion. But beware of denying his goodnefs, and fo depriving him of any part of that praife which is due to him. He may have been gracioufly prefent with you, though you have not fenfibly perceived it. And he has been prefent, if your defire after him is increafed; if you are grieved for the apprehenfion of his abfence, and difpofed to perfevere in feeking him. Perfevere in feeking him; and in due time you fhall affuredly find him. Sometimes he "withdraws himfelf and is "gone," even when his prefence is moft confidently expected; that he may roufe his people from their bed of floth, and fet them to feek him in earneft. *Afk* then, till you *receive.* Continue to *feek, and you fhall find:* perfift in *knocking*, and it fhall be opened unto you. While you mourn for the want of his fenfible prefence, rejoice in the inviolable fecurity or the ground of your faith. The righteoufnefs of Chrift is of uninterrupted and perpetual efficacy. And therefore, if you are really clothed with it, the want of fenfible communion does not expofe you, in the fmalleft degree, to divine wrath; nor, in the leaft, invalidate your title to eternal enjoyment. The promife of God is as fure as ever; and the channel, through which promifed grace vents, is as open. "God "fpared not his own Son; but, *having* made him to "be fin, *he* delivered him up" to wrath and the curfe

for you : " And how shall he not with him also free-
" ly give *you* all things?"

You have all been witnessing a good confession before God, angels, and men, at the communion table. You have been saying, in the most solemn manner, " In the Lord have I righteousness and strength; " and in him alone will I glory: My beloved is mine, " and I am his." While you took Christ for your Lord and Husband, your Prophet, your Priest, your King, your All; you likewise gave away to him, yourself, and all that you possess, and all that you can do, either in time or through eternity. See that you never go back, nor turn from him at all. You will go back, and attempt to alienate what you have now devoted; if ever you employ yourself, your time, or your talents, in the service of another. You will be guilty of the same sin, if ever you find fault with the manner in which he shall dispose of you, or of any thing that is yours, in the course of adorable providence. Having given all over to him, you can have no right to dispose of any part, unless for promoting his glory in the manner that himself requires; nor can you have any right to repine, because he disposes of what you have called his own, in the manner that seems good in his sight. Nay, you have good reason to be pleased with his disposals; for he will assuredly manage all in the manner that shall tend most to your advantage. And you shall have a good account of all that is " committed to him against that day."

It is more than probable, that some of you may never have another opportunity of joining in this solemn ordinance. You may never " more drink of the fruit " of this vine, till *you* drink it new with *Christ* in *his*
" Father's

"Father's kingdom." But this need be no bad news to you. You shall have no reason to lament the loss of sermons or sacraments, when admitted to the table above, where you shall see and enjoy, and feed upon those things immediately, that are only seen darkly, and at a distance, through these glasses. Keep, therefore, your evidences always in view. I do not mean only those marks of a gracious state that you see, or have seen about yourself; but chiefly that full security which God has given you, in his word of grace and promise, for the enjoyment of eternal happiness; and that spotless righteousness which is the sole ground of your title to all. Being *made the righteousness of God in* Christ, you need neither be afraid to " walk through the valley of the shadow of " death," nor to stand before the tribunal of God, nor to enter upon an eternal and unchangeable estate; for still you are safe under that covering. In this " gar-" ment of wrought gold, *you* shall *infallibly* be brought " into the palace of the king;" even into his presence-chamber, and there you shall abide for ever.

As to you that have only been spectators of this solemn action, we likewise charitably hope, that many of you have come hither with the language of the Greeks in your heart, if not in your mouth, *We would see Jesus.* Let all such rejoice; he is really here to be seen. And you cannot be more desirous to see him, and to enjoy communion with him, than he is to be seen of you, and to hold the most intimate communion with you. If you wish to feed upon him in his word; there he has made " unto all people a " feast of fat things." And you shall have yourself to blame, if you go away without your errand. You

have

have reason, indeed, to beware, left you provoke him, by your sin, to with-hold from you the sense of his presence. And, particularly, you had need to beware, left your being mere spectators of this work be one reason why you have not seen him so clearly as you desire.

We know there are some of you who have joined in such work in time past, who yet for a good while bygone have not joined in it, either with us or with any other society. And surely, though such persons may be real friends of Christ, they act a very unfriendly part in this matter. Can it be your duty to continue in the neglect of the dying command of Christ? Is his death unworthy to be remembered? Or, are you satisfied, for your part, that the remembrance of it should be lost? Were every person to follow your example, this ordinance would cease in the church; and the public commemoration of Christ's death would cease with it.

I know there are others of you, who have not only attended with us to-day; but who attend ordinances in this congregation almost every Sabbath, unless when they go to join in sacramental work, perhaps once a-year, in another communion. Their conduct is not more reasonable than that of the others. If you can, with a safe conscience, receive the seals of the covenant in that communion, why should you leave it in other respects? If you cannot have satisfaction in your conscience, to attend other ordinances in that communion, how can you be safe in attending and partaking in this most solemn ordinance? Can they have a right to dispense the sacrament, who have no regular call to preach the gospel? Can you be justified

tified in receiving the fymbols of Chrift's body and blood, from the hands of thofe from whom you hear not, nor expect to hear the doctrines of the crofs of Chrift? Can you hope that they fhould be the inftruments of feeding your fouls in the facrament, who adminifter poifon to them in their doctrine? Or how can it be for the glory of Chrift, or of his Father, that you fhould receive the feals of the covenant of grace from thofe who would fend you back to the covenant of works for falvation; by teaching you to feek righteoufnefs, " as it were by the works of the law?" Is this an ordinance of lefs importance, or an ordinance that may be more fafely trifled with than any other? Nay, my dear brethren. While your conduct is fo inconfiftent with itfelf, you need not be furprifed that you have little fuccefs in feeking Chrift, either with us or with them. You even have matter of thankfulnefs, if he *make* not *a breach upon* you; for furely you feek him not " after the due order."

Some may, perhaps, have attended on this occafion, with no other view than to fatisfy a vain curiofity; from the fame motive which would have induced them to attend a puppet-fhow, or the tricks of a mountebank. Such have reafon to be thankful that they live under the mild and gracious difpenfation of the New Teftament. Such a curiofity might, one day, have coft you dear. The ordinances of God are of too much importance, God himfelf is a Being of too much majefty, to be waited on for mere paftime. You fhall find, in a little, that your attendance here was really a ferious matter, whether you meant it fo or not. It will either contribute to your eternal happinefs, or to your everlafting mifery. The word of God,

God, which you have heard, will not *return to* him *empty.* It will either be " the favour of life unto life, " *or* the favour of death unto death," in every perfon prefent.

But there is a method by which you may both obtain what you came for, and be accepted with God in your attendance. There has been fet before you fomething that as much deferves your attention, and is as much calculated to gratify a fanctified curiofity, as any thing in heaven or in earth. Come, then, behold a fight that never was equalled in God's creation, nor never will! The eternal Son of God *made fin for us ; that we might be made the righteoufnefs of God in him.* And this is fomething in which you are deeply interefted; it ought not to be looked upon with indifference. You, too, are a guilty finner in the fight of God, however little you ever thought about it. As fuch you ftand condemned, while in your natural eftate, by the dreadful fentence of the lawcurfe. And there is no other way to efcape the execution of that fentence, but by having an intereft in this amazing tranfaction. The facrifice of Chrift is exhibited to you, as a full atonement for all your fins. His righteoufnefs is in your offer, as a garment that will cover all the fhame of your fpiritual nakednefs, and effectually fcreen you from the tempeft of divine ire, to which you will otherwife ftand expofed through all the ages of an endlefs eternity. Take this righteoufnefs home with you: God makes you welcome to it for nought. And improve it in all your dealings with the great Judge of all the earth; for deal with him you muft, however little inclination you have for it; and you can never deal with him comfortably

fortably on another footing. In this way you shall never have occasion to attend upon divine ordinances, in time to come, without a better motive than that which brought you hither.

In one word, Whoever you are, whatever you have been, or whatever is the motive of your attendance; you are by no means unconcerned in what you have seen and heard to-day. Perhaps you may have " stood " all the day idle in the market-place;" but you were not your own friends in continuing so. The market of free grace is not yet over. And we conjure you not to depart, till you take *the righteousness of God* along with you. Perhaps you have never been sensible of your need of it; but you will assuredly be sensible of it another day. He, whom God *has made to be sin for us*, is likewise constituted, by the same authority, the final Judge of the quick and the dead. It is but a short time when he will " come with clouds; " and every eye shall see him:" and you shall see him among the rest. He will come to " take vengeance " on all that know not God," and a more dreadful vengeance on all " that obey not the gospel." Now he stands among you, with the arms of his mercy stretched out; making a free and full offer of his righteousness, and of all the rich fruits of it, to every son and daughter of Adam that now hears me. But then he will sit upon his " glorious high throne, *with his* weighty rod of iron" in his hand; ready to " break " in pieces, as a potter's vessel," every person who shall be found to have finally rejected his gracious offers.. Nothing else will then stand you in stead, if you are found without that righteousness which is now offered you. And you must appear without it

then

then, if you continue to defpife it *now;* for there are no offers of it in the grave, whither you are going. For any thing that you know, this may be the laft offer that ever you may enjoy. And how will you raife your guilty head, or look your inexhorable Judge in the face at that day, if you defpife it? Thus faith the Holy Ghoft, " Now is the accepted time: behold, " now is the day of falvation. To-day, if ye will " hear his voice, harden not your heart, as in the pro- " vocation." If you do, your blood fhall be upon your own head: God is free of it; I truft fo are his meffengers. And you fhall eternally curfe yourfelf, for your obftinacy in unbelief. But, whatever be the cafe with you then, be it known unto you, that " God's righteoufnefs *is* brought near, *even to* thofe " *among you* that are ftout-hearted and far from righ- " teoufnefs." And as truly as *God has made him to be fin for us, who knew no fin;* fo truly fhall it be your own fault if you are not, this very evening, *made the righteoufnefs of God in him.*

The God of all mercy grant that it may be fo; and to his name be praife.

SERMON III.

God's Covenant with the New Testament Church considered.

PART I.

Heb. viii. 10.

—I WILL BE TO THEM A GOD, AND THEY SHALL BE TO ME A PEOPLE.

ALL the genuine *saints* of God are persons that have *made a covenant with* him *by sacrifice.* And none but such shall be gathered to him, in that general assembly which Christ will summon to attend him at his final coming to judgment; though, alas! there are many of a very different character in the worshipping assemblies of his people here. I presume there are none present who are not in covenant with God by visible profession and appearance; all the members of the visible church are so. Many of us have professed to recognize and adhere to our covenant with God, in the most open and explicit manner.

ner. And this day we are met to have it ratified and confirmed, both on God's part and on ours, by a folemn facrifice. It is fit that, in the entry, we fhould take fome brief view of the tenor and fubftance of that covenant which fubfifts between God and us. You have it in the words of this text. God has gracioufly engaged, in this covenant, to be our God; and we, by our acceptance of it, become engaged, through his grace and ftrength, that we fhall be his people.

The fcope of the Spirit of God in this chapter is, to illuftrate the fuperiority of Chrift's priefthood to that of Aaron and his family. And this he does by two arguments.

The *firft* is taken from the place where his priefthood is finally exercifed; and he infifts upon it from the beginning to the fixth verfe. The fubftance of his reafoning is this: That muft needs be the moft excellent priefthood, which belongs to, and is exercifed in, the moft excellent temple or fanctuary. Aaron's priefthood was exercifed in a tabernacle which was made by the hands of men, according to a pattern given from heaven. But the priefthood of Chrift belongs to the heavenly fanctuary, of which the other was no more than a type, a model or figure: And therefore the priefthood of Chrift muft excel the Aaronical priefthood, as far as the houfe itfelf excels the model of it; as far as the type excels the antitype; as far as the " true tabernacle, which God pitched " and not man," is fuperior to the tabernacle which Mofes erected in the wildernefs.

The *fecond* argument, and that upon which he mainly infifts, is drawn from the difference between the two covenants, to which thefe two priefthoods did

did refpectively belong. Upon this he infifts from verfe fixth to the end of the chapter, and reafons in the following manner: No perfon will refufe, that the moft excellent covenant muft have the moft excellent priefthood. But the covenant to which the priefthood of Chrift belongs, is incomparably fuperior to that with which the priefthood of Aaron was connected; as being " eftablifhed upon better promifes," and as being introduced on account of the faultinefs of the other, to the utter fuperfeding of it. If the fecond covenant had not been fuperior to the firft, there had been no occafion to fet afide the one, and introduce the other. The priefthood of Chrift, therefore, muft be as much fuperior to that of Aaron, as the clear and fpiritual difpenfation of the covenant of grace, which obtains under the New Teftament, is fuperior to that typical, fhadowy difpenfation, under which the church of Ifrael lived; from the time that the priefthood was fettled in Aaron's family till the coming of Chrift.

In the illuftration of this argument, he introduces a quotation from the prophecy of Jeremiah*; wherein it is exprefsly foretold, that God would make a new covenant with the church in New Teftament days, widely different from that which he made with the people of Ifrael when he brought them out of Egypt, and incomparably fuperior to it; as being incapable of being broken or diffolved; of waxing old or fading away; and as containing promifes the moft excellent and precious.

In the words of Jeremiah, which are quoted by the Apoftle, we have the fubftance of the covenant, which
was

---
* Jer. xxxi. 31,—34.

was to be made with the church in gospel days, contained in various promises, which are recited in this and the two following verses; whereby it appears, that no other covenant is intended but the covenant of grace, which was originally made with Christ from all eternity; and is now exhibited in its naked simplicity, without types and shadows, and actually made with believers through Christ. These promises are four in number.

1. A promise of conformity to the law, and so to the image of God, of which his law is a transcript. " I will put my laws into their mind, and write them " in their hearts;" that is, ' I will have my law so in-
' corporated with their nature, that they shall run
' with pleasure in the way of new obedience. I will
' imprint the knowledge of these laws in their under-
' standings; and I will give them a disposition of will,
' sincerely to love, and cordially to obey them.'

2. A promise of a new and permanent relation to God; in the words of the text. By the Aaronic covenant he became related to the nation of Israel, as his *peculiar people:* but they cast him off from being their God; and he was, at last, provoked to say to them, *Lo-ammi, ye are not my people.* But by Christ's covenant, a relation is constituted between him and the members of the New Testament Church, as permanent as that everlasting covenant itself. Still he continues to be their God; and they shall never cease to be to him a peculiar and chosen people.

3. A promise of the saving and experimental knowledge of God; arising, not barely from human instruction, but from endearing intimacy, fellowship, and communion with him. " And they shall not teach
" every

"every man his neighbour, and every man his bro-
"ther, faying, know the Lord; for they fhall all
"know me, from the leaft even to the greateft of
"them:" That is, they fhall not need to teach one
another, as if any of them were totally ignorant of
God; for every one of them fhall attain, through
happy experience, fuch a knowledge of him as a man
has of his intimate friend, whofe face he frequently
fees, and with whom he converfes familiarly. Thus
they fhall have a knowledge of him much fuperior
to any thing that can arife from human inftitution or
inftruction.

4. As the foundation of all the reft, there is a promife of reftoration to God's favour; by the abolition
of all that guilt, which formerly feparated between
him and them. "For I will be merciful to their un-
"righteoufneffes; and their fins and their iniquities
"will I remember no more." It is manifeft that this
promife, though laft expreft, muft be firft accomplifhed. The particle *for*, with which it is introduced,
plainly imports fo much. It is the accomplifhment
of this that paves the way for the performance of
all the reft.

It is the *fecond* of thefe promifes, of which I propofe, through divine affiftance, to fpeak a little at prefent. It may be viewed as comprehending all the
reft: and, indeed, as containing the whole fubftance
of the covenant of grace; as it is exhibited to us in
the gofpel, and actually made with us, in the day of
our union to Chrift.

The promife confifts of two parts: for here we are
told, 1ft, What God will be to the church, and to
particular members of it, in New Teftament days;
I will

I will be to them a God: and, 2*dly*, What the Church, and her particular members, fhall be to God; *and they fhall be to me a people.*

Were we to attempt a more particular divifion of the words, we might obferve, in the firft part of them, the four following things.

1. The party fpeaking, or promifing, in the pronoun *I;* meaning God himfelf. He it is who propofes to make a covenant with us: And to him it belongs, to prefcribe and determine all the contents of it. It was an act of divine condefcenfion in him, to make a covenant with Adam in his innocent eftate: much greater is the condefcenfion that appears in his making a covenant with us. That ever he would condefcend fo far, none had a right to promife but himfelf.

2. The party fpoken of, or concerning whom the promife is made, in the pronoun *them;* referring to " the houfe of Ifrael and the houfe of Judah," mentioned in ver. 8. This is to be underftood of the New Teftament Church, of which the houfe of Ifrael and of Judah were typical. And of that privilege, which is here promifed to the church at large, every genuine member of the church is honoured to partake.

3. The relation in which God promifes to ftand to the church. He will be to her *a God.* He does not only mean, that he will always continue to be God; and to exercife fuch a dominion over the church, as his being the fupreme God entitles him to exercife over all the creatures. But he will be *her God,* in a manner peculiar to herfelf; and, as God, will ftand related to her in another manner than he does to any other part of the world.

4. The

4. The certainty of the event, intimated in the word *will*. God's words are not yea and nay. His promife, therefore, affords the moſt ample fecurity for the thing promifed. " Hath he faid, and will he not " do it ? Hath he fpoken, and fhall he not make it " good ?"

The other branch of the text might be divided in the fame manner. But, paffing this, we proceed to difcourfe a little more fully from the fubject, by enquiring,

I. What is imported in the words more generally ?

II. What is more particularly importd in God's promifing to be our God ?

III. What—in our being his people ?

Having briefly confidered each of thefe, we fhall conclude with fome improvement of the fubject.

I. WE return to confider the general import of the words. And the manner of expreffion here ufed, plainly imports the following things :

1. That a covenant fhall be made, and a covenant-relation fhall fubfift, between God and every member of the New Teftament church. At Sinai, God made a covenant with the whole family of Ifrael; not only with the generation then prefent, but with their pofterity " till the promifed Seed fhould come." In virtue hereof, every member of the Jewifh church was in covenant with God, in refpect of his outward and vifible ftate. In like manner, though the covenant of grace was originally made with Chriſt from all eternity, and all the terms of it fixed unalterably ; yet he gracioufly exhibits that covenant to all who are within the church, propofing to make the fame co-

VOL. II. G * venant

venant with every one of them. Hence that gracious promife; *I will make with you an everlafting covenant, even the fure mercies of David* *. And he actually makes it with every believer, by granting them an intereft in all that it contains; while they are faid to make it with him, by freely confenting to all the terms and articles of it, as they were fixed, and agreed upon, betwixt the Father and the Son from eternity. By virtue of the external difpenfation of the covenant, under which he lives, and of his own Chriftian profeffion, every member of the vifible church is externally and vifibly in covenant with God. But, alas! this will avail us nothing, when we ceafe to be members of the vifible church, as we muft all do at death, unlefs we are really and favingly brought " within the bond of the covenant;" and fo related to God as our God in Chrift.

This is it that God promifes in the text. Not only does he engage to make an offer of the covenant of grace to us; he likewife engages to enable us to embrace it. And in this light fhould the promife be confidered by all that hear the gofpel. You are not to apprehend, that when God has made the propofal of being your God, and taking you for one of his people, he has done all that to which he has bound himfelf by this promife. Neither muft you think, that it lies upon you, by any any ftrength or ability of your own, to lay hold of God's covenant; to embrace his gracious offer, and fo to enter into a faving relation to him. This would leave you in a condition as difmal as if the covenant had never been publifhed in your ears: for you are as incapable, of yourfelf, to exercife that faith by which you are interefted in God

as

as your God, as you are to perform all that obedience which the covenant of works requires. But God has engaged to make the relation complete, and to do all that is neceſſary, in order to your being intereſted in him as your God, or to your being accepted of him as one of his people. And you ought to truſt him for all that is included in your being brought within "the bond of *his* covenant."

Indeed there are many, to whom this promiſe is directed, who never enjoy any ſaving relation to God; being neither intereſted in him as their God, nor brought in among the number of his people. But, in this caſe, the promiſe is not accompliſhed to them. Nor is there any promiſe in the Bible that is accompliſhed to all to whom it is directed. Every promiſe is directed to all who hear the goſpel. All are equally welcome to embrace it. And God is ready and willing to accompliſh it to all. But, in the event, no promiſe is accompliſhed, ſave only to thoſe who receive it. So it is with this. In the diſpenſation of the goſpel, God is propoſing, offering, and declaring his willingneſs, to bring every ſinner into ſuch a relation to himſelf as the text expreſſes. And he will make good his offer to all but ſuch as obſtinately refuſe it. If there is any perſon among you, to whom this promiſe is not this day accompliſhed, it will be owing to one of theſe two things; either your unwillingneſs to be ſo related to him, or your attempting to bring yourſelf into that relation, by doing ſome part yourſelf of that work which God alone can do, inſtead of depending upon him for all. Your only method is to ſay *Amen* to the promiſe, as the word of God; and to look to him for the full accompliſhment of it. You should aim at taking God for your God, and giving yourself away to him as one of his people; but still you are to trust him for that faith by which you may do so, as well as for every thing else that you may expect from him, in the character of your God. " By grace are ye saved, through faith; " *but* that *faith is* not of yourselves, it is the gift of " God *." Yet, instead of deferring the exercise of faith, because it is *not of yourselves*, you ought rather to set about it with the greater confidence of success; as being assured, that seeing God has promised to complete the relation between him and you, he will not fail to give you that faith which is essentially necessary to such a relation; but will enable you to exercise it in such a manner that he shall really and eventually be your God, and you shall be one of his people.

2. The words import, that both parties, so related to one another, shall behave in a due and becoming manner, agreeable to the relation in which they stand. It is observable, that the LORD says not only " I will " be their God, and they shall be my people." The expression is much more emphatic: *I will be to them a God, and they shall be to me a people.* In the original languages it is still more so. Both here, and in the passage from which the words are quoted, it literally runs thus, *I will be to them for a God, and they shall be to me for a people.* If we compare this with other passages, where a similar mode of expression is used, we shall find it to mean, not only that he will be related to us as our God, and we to him as his people; but also, that he will be to us, and do for us, whatever

* Eph. ii. 8.

whatever may be juftly expected from a God, in behalf of thofe whom he acknowledges as his people; and that we, on the other hand, fhall behave towards him in a manner correfponding to the relation ; performing all that worfhip and obedience, and giving him all that honour and glory, that is due from any people to their God.

On God's part, there is no reafon to fufpect any failure as to the relation. It is impoffible for him to act inconfiftently with any relation in which he ftands. And therefore his engagement to be our God, affords unqueftionable fecurity that he will do all for us which that relation requires. But he knows our frailty; and, in condefcenfion to the weaknefs of our faith, explicitly binds himfelf to do all that for us, which is proper to be done by a God for his people. This was the more neceffary, becaufe he " knew that *we* would " deal very treacheroufly ;" and would fall egregioufly fhort of a regular performance of our duty to him. Though this can never provoke him to withhold from us any part of what he has promifed us, if once we are really in covenant with him ; yet it often proves an occafion of fufpicion on our part. When we are confcious that our behaviour towards him is undutiful, and juftly deferves that he fhould caft us off; we are in danger of apprehending that he will do fo. But to remove all fufpicions of this kind, and to encourage us, even when iniquity prevails againft us, to depend upon him for all the happy fruits of our relation to him ; he has bound himfelf to *be to* us *for a God*, and ftill to deal with us according to that character, even when we feem very

unlike

unlike his people, and behave in a very undutiful manner towards him.

Even this is not all, believer, that this promife warrants you to expect. You have in it likewife a full fecurity, that you fhall be enabled to walk in agreeablenefs to this relation; and to behave towards God as becomes his covenanted people. You are very fenfible that fuch a fecurity is neceffary. You are no Chriftian if you know not that you can neither behave dutifully to God nor to men in any relation in which you ftand, unlefs you are affifted by divine grace. And therefore to bring you into a faving relation to God, without affording you grace to be dutiful in that relation, would only be to afford you daily opportunities of difhonouring him more atrocioufly than you otherwife could have done. But neither your weaknefs, nor your remaining wickednefs, fhall ever be fuffered to prevent your behaving, in fome acceptable degree, as God's people. It is true, that, while you continue in this world, you will always have imperfections and corruptions about you. You will ever find, in your conduct towards God, much matter of mourning and humiliation before him. But he has gracioufly promifed to overlook all thefe, in his judicial procedure with regard to you. Having *forgiven* your *iniquity*, he *will remember* your *fins no more*, as the context affures you. It is equally true, that whenever you begin to be confident of your own ability, on the one hand; or, on the other hand, to be diffident of his promifed affiftance; he may, by fuch means, be provoked, to leave you to catch a fall; that you may learn to be the more dependent upon him for the future. But you may be affured, that he he will never fuffer you totally or finally to fall from your dutifulnefs. And, as often as you are enabled to renounce your own fufficiency, and to " go in the " ftrength of the Lord God ;" you fhall find yourfelf affifted and helped in fuch a manner, that you fhall perform the duties of your relation, with acceptance before God, and with comfort to your own foul. Having *put* his *fear into* your *heart*, himfelf will take effectual care, that you *fhall not depart from* him *.

3. The words import, that the relation itfelf, and the due behaviour of the relatives, on both fides, fhall be wholly the work of God. God hath promifed, without referve, both that *he will* be our *God, and* that *we fhall be* his *people*. And he does not fufpend his faithfulnefs, either upon the power, or upon the will of any other. Having made a promife, he does not leave the accomplifhment of it, in whole or in part, to any creature. What he has faid, himfelf will alfo do; and upon him only fhould be our dependance for all.

That he only muft accomplifh the promife on the one part, is apparent at firft view. None can make him our God but himfelf, neither can any other oblige him to act in agreeablenefs to the relation. It is matter of deep wonder, that he fhould condefcend to become your God, or lay himfelf under any engagements to that purpofe. But when he has come under fuch engagements, and is your God in confequence thereof; it is manifeft, that none can do that for you which correfponds to the relation, but himfelf. He has not engaged to be your God by proxy; nor will he leave it to any other to perform thofe

acts

---

* Jer. xxxii. 40.

acts of grace and goodnefs to you, which that relation warrants you to expect.

But what is moſt wonderful is God's engaging for your part as well as his own. When a man makes a propoſal of marriage to a woman, however advantageous the match be for her, he has not power to incline her to it; fhe may reject it, however ſtrongly he may preſs her to accept it. But when God propoſes to *betrothe* you to himſelf, he does not barely make the propoſal, and leave you to deliberate and determine upon it by yourſelf. Finding you ſo blind to your own intereſt, that you would certainly reject his offer, though the moſt advantageous that ever could be made you, and though it is enforced with the moſt cogent arguments; he powerfully inclines and determines you to embrace it. He does not oblige you to it againſt your will. Neither does he ſubdue your will only by ſuch force as would be neceſſary in dealing with " the horſe or the mule, that have no under- " ſtanding." He ſets before you thoſe motives that are proper to influence you in accepting his gracious propoſal. He opens your underſtanding to perceive the weight of them. He kindly ſubdues your will; at the ſame time, deſtroying that enmity which was in it, againſt himſelf, and againſt all that is like him. He thus makes you ſenſible what is your true intereſt; and, at the ſame time, determines you to fall in with it, in a rational manner. Thus it is, that *a willing people* is brought to Chriſt *in the day of his power*.*

When the marriage relation commences, the man engages to perform his duty to his wife, according to the

---

* Pſal. cx. 3.

the nature and intimacy of the relation. But, on the other hand, the wife alſo becomes engaged to perform her duty to him. And the performance of her engagements lies wholly upon herſelf, as much as the performance of his engagements lies upon him. It would be abſurd to expect that the huſband ſhould perform the wife's duties as well as his own, or that he ſhould lay himſelf under any engagements to that purpoſe. But here, in this wonderful covenant, God engages his faithfulneſs for the performance of our part as well as his own. Not only does he engage to do all that for us, that is agreeable to his relation to us, as he is our God; he likewiſe engages for all thoſe duties that we owe to him, as being his people. And he is as good as his word; for he both does all that for us that a God may be expected to do for his people; and enables us to do all that which a people ought to do for their God. In reſpect of the firſt of theſe, he does all by himſelf, and we do nothing; and, in reſpect of the laſt, though we labour and are active in the performance of our duty, ſtill " it is God " that worketh in *us*, both to will and to do of his ". good pleaſure." And when our duty is performed, the work is much more God's than our own. As Paul ſays of his life, ſo may every Chriſtian ſay of all the duties of his calling. *I live*, ſays he, *yet not I, but Chriſt liveth in me*. ' I do my duty,' may you ſay, ' as becomes one of God's people; yet not I, but my ' God does it in me, and by me; to him be all the ' glory.'

Chriſtians, indeed, when they enter into covenant with God, not only conſent that he be their God, and do for them what correſponds to that relation; they
                                                                                                                                                    alſo

also make a dedication of themselves to him as his people, and engage to perform to him all those duties that a people owe to their God. But then their engagements are founded, not upon any apprehension that they have of their own strength or sufficiency for the performance of them; but solely upon the grace and faithfulness of God, as pledged in his word of promise. They engage to nothing but what God has previously engaged to work in them and by them; and they engage only because God has engaged before them. Their engagements, therefore, are all on God's head, not their own; and may be considered as a profession of their faith, as well as a declaration of their resolution. They declare it as their resolution, only because they know and believe that God has given it as his promise, and will see to the accomplishment of it. As this is the exercise of every Christian, in the day of believing, so it is the open and explicit language of every acceptable covenanter. And it is this language to which every worthy communicant sets his seal at the Lord's table. Let this be the language of your heart, intended communicant, in the view of a solemn ratification of your covenant, by a symbolical commemoration of the sacrifice of Christ. And through your whole life, in all your endeavours to pay your vows, keep the same promise of God in your eye, as your only security for all that grace and strength, by which they may be paid acceptably. Trust him confidently for the communication of that grace in the moment of need. Stand not at a distance from any duty, on account of your inability to perform it; but go forward, at the call of God, to " break " through troops," however numerous, and to " leap

" over

"over walls," though high as heaven; go forward "in the strength of the Lord God, making mention "of his righteousness, even of his only *."

II. The next thing proposed in the method was, to enquire, more particularly, what is imported in God's being our God; or what we are to expect, as an accomplishment of this part of the promise? We shall only consider it, at present, as importing the two things following.

1. That God will graciously bring us to have a real and saving interest in him, as our God. This is far from being the case with all mankind. It is so with none but those who are brought " within the bond " of *this* covenant." Even they who enjoy this privilege do not comprehensively understand it. And, as for others, no language can give them any tolerable idea of. The person who has God for his God, has an interest in him, as the fountain of being, and of all blessedness; an interest in all that happiness which consists in, or arises from the enjoyment of him. He is interested in every perfection of the divine nature; and, therefore, whatever imperfections, corruptions, and infirmities, he finds about himself, he considers himself as complete in God. Though foolish and ignorant in himself, he fears not the effects of his own folly; for eternal Wisdom is his guide. Though he is weak in himself, and without any help of man, he can work, and fight, and conquer, like a champion; for his strength is omnipotence. He is disposed to " deal very treacherously, and was called " a transgressor from the womb;" hence he knows

himself

himself to be in continual danger of breaking God's covenant; and yet he is assured, that his covenant with God shall never be broken; he dare both vow and hope to pay his vows, because infinite faithfulness is his stay and his security. All the perfections of the divine nature are his; and it adds greatly to his happiness, that the improvement of these perfections for his advantage lies not upon himself. God, who has made a gift of all to him, has likewise engaged to employ and improve them all for him, in the manner that shall most effectually conduce to his spiritual and eternal welfare. All that God possesses is likewise made his, by virtue of this covenant; and God has bound himself to manage all for him to the best advantage. It is often but little that he commits into his own hand, and gives him the actual possession of for the present. But whatever the wide creation affords, God so disposes of it, that the person could not enjoy so much benefit by it, if he had it immediately under his own hand. Yea, the uncreated treasures of eternity are all his: "An inheritance, "incorruptible and undefiled, and unfading, is reser- "ved in heaven for *him*." God himself is this inheritance. And because he is *his God*, he will make him completely and eternally happy in the enjoyment of himself. *This honour, this hope, have all his saints.* Now, in order to our having such an interest in God, two things are necessary; both which are secured by this promise, and both are accomplished in behalf of every one who is brought within the bond of this covenant.

(1.) That God make a gracious grant and offer of himself to us, declaring us welcome to claim an interest tereft in him, and to look for the reft and happinefs of our fouls in the enjoyment of him. Without fuch an offer it would be impoffible that ever we fhould be interefted in him as our God. Such a happinefs is incapable of being purchafed by any creature. Much lefs can it be purchafed by any of mankind, in our prefent impoverifhed ftate. As it cannot be purchafed, neither can it be given by any other but God himfelf. Therefore, if he is to be our God, he muft firft make a free grant and offer of himfelf to us in that character. Such a grant he really makes in the difpenfation of the gofpel; not only to all who are within the covenant, but to every perfon who hears the gofpel, or has a Bible among his hands. This grant is fo often repeated in the Scriptures, that to produce particular inftances of it were fuperfluous. One is contained in the text. And every finner in this affembly may confider it as made to himfelf, as well as every faint. In giving you fuch an offer, God exhibits to you all that you need, all that ever you can poffibly enjoy; and infinitely more than you are able, or ever fhall be able, to comprehend. He is the infinite, the eternal, the immutable, and all-fufficient Jehovah; the heaven of heavens cannot contain him; the conceptions of angels cannot comprehend him; to that light in which he dwells, no created eye can approach: yet he makes you a free gift of himfelf! He is *the poffeffor of* HEAVEN and EARTH, yet along with himfelf he gives you all that he poffeffes! " He doth according to his will in the armies " of heaven, and among the inhabitants of *the earth;*" yet he freely engages to do all that he can do for your advantage! He is the only portion that is adapted ed to thofe extenfive defires that are implanted in every rational foul; and he engages to be our portion, to communicate himfelf to you in the higheft degree that your capacity will admit of; and to make you perfectly and eternally happy in the enjoyment of himfelf. You are not, indeed, to look for the full enjoyment of him in this world; becaufe, while fin hangs about you, you are not capable of it. But if you are determined to accept this wonderful grant, he will allow you even here, a foretafte of that enjoyment with which you fhall be bleffed hereafter. He will gradually *fubdue* your *iniquities*, and bring you gradually forward to a ftate of fitnefs for unreftrained enjoyment. And, as foon as you are capable of it, you fhall affuredly be " filled with all the fulnefs of " God *.

(2.) It is likewife neceffary that he enable us to accept this gracious offer, and really to chufe him as our God and portion. There can be no covenant without the confent of both parties. God has here engaged that there fhall be a covenant between him and us, by virtue of which he will be our God. And furely this contains an engagement, that both parties fhall give their confent to the happy compact. God gives his confent in this promife itfelf; and he likewife engages that we fhall give ours. This engagement cannot be founded upon any truft that God has in us, as being, of ourfelves, difpofed to give fuch confent: he well knows that we have neither power nor will to do fo. It is founded on his own gracious purpofe and refolution, powerfully and efficacioufly to determine us to do fo. Nor does he ever become

our

* Eph. iii. 19.

our God, till his promise is accomplished in this as well as in the former respect. Every person who is brought within the bond of the covenant, is, that moment, enabled to make choice of him as his God, on the footing of the condescending grant above mentioned,—and to take up the rest of his weary soul in him. The great Head of the covenant has set the example that is followed by all the members of his body. He is represented as saying, with unspeakable satisfaction, " God is the portion of mine inheritance, " and of my cup; thou maintainest my lot. The " lines are fallen unto me in pleasant places; and I " have a goodly heritage *." And the Scriptures afford various instances, in which this language has been imitated by the spiritual seed of Christ. Asaph, when recovered from temptation, expresses himself thus: " Whom have I in heaven but thee? and there none " upon earth that I desire besides thee. My flesh and " my heart faileth; but (adds he) God is the strength " of my heart, and my portion for ever †." In the same manner speaks the prophet Jeremiah, in the name of the church. When deploring the sad calamities that had befallen her, he introduces her as comforting herself with this consideration, " The " LORD is my portion, saith my soul; therefore will I " hope in him ‡."

Is there any soul in this company convinced of the vanity of all earthly things, and desirous to make choice of God as his portion; yet sensible of the deceitfulness of his own heart, and therefore hesitating whether to utter his desire, and speak out his choice or not? Let not any thing discourage you from attempting

---

* Psal. xvi. 5, 6.   † Psal. lxxiii. 25.   ‡ Lam. iii. 24.

tempting to make the choice, to exprefs it in words, and practically to abide by it. In this text he has promifed that he will be your God; and he cannot be fo unlefs you confent to it. You may, therefore, confider him as engaging that you fhall confent. And you ought to truft him for the accomplifhment of his engagements. In a dependence upon his promifed grace, aim at a prefent faying with your heart, "This "God is my God for ever and ever; and he will be "my guide even unto death." As an evidence that you wifh to fay it with your heart, be not afhamed to fay it with your mouth, or to fay it practically at the Lord's table. God will gracioufly ftrengthen you for the whole. If you have any doubt about the promife in the text, whether it warrants you to expect fuch a thing or not, you may find another more exprefs to the purpofe; a promife which has been accomplifhed in the Head, and in many of his myftical members already, and which God is prefently offering to accomplifh in you;

>Thou art my Father, he fhall cry,
>   Thou art my God alone;
>And he fhall fay, thou art the Rock
>   Of my falvation *.

2. This part of the promife imports, that God will do all that for us, that any people has reafon to expect, or ufually does expect from their God. He would be afhamed to be called our God, if he were not to act up to the character. And his allowing us to claim him in that character, may be viewed as an engagement that he will do for us whatever correfponds unto it. It is impoffible, Chriftian, to enumerate

---

* Pfal. lxxxix. 26.

rate all the great things that you may expect him to do for you, in confequence of his being your God. We fhall mention the four things following, as comprehending many of the reft.

(1.) He will fet you free from all fpiritual bondage, oppreffion, and mifery of every kind ; and put you in ample poffeffion of the glorious liberty of the fons of God. When Ifrael, God's chofen people, fojourned in Egypt, and were oppreffed with an intolerable yoke of bondage ; " God looked upon their affliction, " he heard their cry, and came down to deliver " them *." And when he fpeaks of what he wrought for them on that occafion, he very often joins his account of it with a declaration of his being their God. In this manner he fpake, with an audible voice, from mount Sinai. " I am the Lord thy God, which " brought thee out of the land of Egypt; out of the " houfe of bondage †:" plainly importing, that, in bringing them out of the houfe of bondage, he acted in a manner correfponding to his character as their God ; and that it would have been inconfiftent with that character to have fuffered them always to continue in that *iron furnace*. Ifrael alfo had fuch a perfuafion of the agreement and connection between that action and that character, that they feem to have thought it fhameful to acknowledge any other for their God, but him who brought them out of Egypt. Hence, when they turned afide from the true God, they ufually afcribed this deliverance to the falfe gods whom they worfhipped. When they made the calf at Horeb, they faid, " Thefe be thy gods, O Ifrael, which " brought thee out of the land of Egypt ‡." Hereby they

Vol. II.   H   *

* Exod. iii. 7, 8.   † Exod. xx. 2.   ‡ Exod. xxxii. 4.

they expreſſed a conviction, that it would be unreaſonable in them to worſhip any other but the author of their freedom; and that they could not pretend to juſtify themſelves in their abominable idolatry, otherwiſe than by aſcribing that deliverance to the calf that they worſhipped. The ſame method took Jeroboam, five hundred years afterwards, to perſuade their poſterity to worſhip the calves at Dan and Bethel *. That deliverance was ſo like an interpoſal of *their God*, that there was little more neceſſary to engage them to acknowledge even a gold calf in that character, and to give it that worſhip which was due to their God, but only to perſuade them that the calf was the author, or repreſented the author of that deliverance.

All mankind are naturally under bondage to ſin and Satan. And ſuch is the miſery of that ſtate, that the ſlavery of Iſrael in Egypt was but a faint emblem of it. From this bondage, and from all the miſery that ariſes from it, God gracioufly delivers all thoſe whom he takes into covenant with himſelf. There is ſuch an oppoſition between your natural eſtate of bondage, and a ſtate of covenant-union to him, that the one can never commence without the abolition of the other. He muſt bring you out of the one, that he may bring you into the other. So he ſpake concerning the deliverance from Egypt, and ſo he ſpeaks concerning your ſpiritual deliverance: " I am the " Lord, which bringeth you out of the land of Egypt, " to be your God. I am the Lord*." You cannot expect to be completely delivered from the tyranny of your oppreſſors, ſo long as you continue in the world.

* 1 Kings xii. 28. † Lev. xi. 45.

world. Though you are delivered from their reigning power, the moment that you obtain an interest in God as your God; they will doubtless pursue you as Pharaoh the Israelites, and attempt to *entangle you again* with the yoke of bondage. But your God will never suffer them to attain their purpose. And it is but a little, when you shall have occasion to sing, as Israel on the other side of the Red Sea, *Thine enemies whom thou hast seen to-day, thou shalt see them no more for ever.* Surely, if God's bringing you out of your bondage is necessary, in order to his being your God; you may safely consider his promise of being your God, as including a promise of complete deliverance from the house of your spiritual thraldom.

(2.) He will guide and conduct you through this weary wilderness, in every step of your journey towards the land of promise. When he had brought Israel out of Egypt, he led them through the wilderness of Arabia, for the space of forty years, by a pillar of cloud in the day, and a pillar of fire by night. Thereby he proved himself to be their God, in such a manner as to strike terror on all their enemies round about. To be our God and our guide are expressly joined together in Scripture. Yea, his being our guide is mentioned as one happy consequence of his being our God. " This God is our God for ever and ever;" and therefore we need not hesitate to promise ourselves that " he will be our guide, even unto death*."

You have many dark and dreary steps, Christian, in your journey through the wilderness of this world; many intricate paths, many hard and rocky passages. Many snares are laid for you by your enemies; it is " a land of desarts and of pits." There are many by-paths,

* Psal. xlviii. 14.

by-paths, tending to lead you afide out of the way; and many dangerous quick-fands, in which you will be in danger of being totally overwhelmed. You are ignorant and unfkilful in the way. You may have many dark nights before your journey be finifh-- ed. And, on all thefe accounts, your *foul* may be often in danger of being " much difcouraged becaufe " of the way." But fee that you give not up your- felf to unbelieving anxiety on any fuch account. God has appointed one to be your *Leader and Commander*, who is both acquainted with the way, as having tra- velled it before, and is likewife infinitely fkilful to conduct you in it. Yea, God himfelf confiders it as his own province, in confequence of the relation that fubfifts between him and you, to *lead* you *on fafely,* till you come " to the borders of his fanctuary, and to " the mountain which his right hand hath purcha- " fed." He is your God, and you are one of his peo- ple. And it is given, with juftice, as one effential branch of his ftanding character, that he " led his peo- " ple through the wildernefs; for his mercy endureth " for ever *."

(3.) He will lead you forth againft all your ene- mies, and make you completely victorious over them in due time. When Ifrael was fet upon by the Ama- lekites in the wildernefs, it was God that fought for them, and gave them the victory. Accordingly, " when Mofes held up his hands," in token of fupplica- tion to God for Ifrael, and as an emblem of the lifting up of God's Almighty hand in their behalf, *Ifrael pre- vailed;* but when the hands of Mofes were down, and God, of confequence, withdrew his affiftance,
Amalek

* Pfal. cxxxvii. 16.

Amalek prevailed.* In all their wars, not only did Ifrael depend upon God for fuccefs, when rightly exercifed; but even the neighbouring nations afcribed Ifrael's fuccefs to their God. And, in the fame manner, they looked for their fuccefs from the affiftance of the falfe gods whom they refpectively worfhipped; and to them they afcribed it when they were fuccefsful; as might be fhewed by various inftances were it neceffary.

Befides all the other dangers and difficulties of your way, believer, you have many enemies, both powerful and cunning, within you, and without you; who fet themfelves in oppofition to you, in your paffage through the wildernefs. You are always to march fword in hand. You muft fight every inch of your way. And, till your journey be finifhed, you muft never put off your armour. Of yourfelf, you are both weak and unfkilful. You are not a match for one of the leaft of thofe numerous enemies that fet themfelves in array againft you round about. On this account alfo, you are in danger of being caft down; and apprehending, as David with regard to Saul, that " one day *you* fhall fall by *their* hands." But your " Redeemer is *infinitely* ftrong; the Lord of " hofts is his name." Your covenanted God has all the armies of heaven under his command. Yea, he has all the hofts of your fpiritual enemies in his chains. He has promifed to fight your battles, and to bring you off the field " a conqueror, and more than a con- " queror, through him that loved you." This promife is exprefsly connected with his declaration that he is your God. And you are to look for the ac-

* Exod. xvii. 11.

complifhment of it, as a fruit of his relation to you. The " LORD thy God will drive out *all* thefe nations " before thee, by little and little."

4. In a word, he will bring you home, in the event, to the poffeffion of a plentiful and pleafant inheritance. When God chofe Ifrael to be his peculiar people, he not only promifed, but fware, that he would give them the land of Canaan, " a land flowing " with milk and honey." And when they obtained it, themfelves acknowledged to his praife, that it was not " their own fword *that* got them the land in pof- " feffion; neither did their own arm fave them; but " *his* right hand, *his* arm, and the light of *his* coun- " tenance; becaufe *he* had a favour unto them." Yea, it was ufual, even with the heathen nations, to afcribe to their idols, the putting them in poffeffion of the feveral countries which they inherited. This is manifeft from that heroic meffage of Jephtha, to the king of the children of Ammon. " The Lord God of If- " rael hath difpoffeffed the Amorites from before his " people Ifrael, and fhouldeft thou poffefs it? Wilt " not thou poffefs that which Chemofh thy god gi- " veth thee to poffefs? So whomfoever the Lord our " God fhall drive out from before us, them will we " poffefs."

But he has promifed and fworn to give us an inheritance, far more rich and glorious than that which he gave to the literal Ifrael in Canaan. Hence the covenant, by which he ftands related to us, when compared with that which he made with them, is preferred before it, as being " eftablifhed upon better " promifes*." To us he has promifed " an inheri-
" tance

* Heb. viii. 6.

" tance, incorruptible and undefiled, and that fadeth
" not away; *which is* referved in heaven for us *."
And this is fo neceffarily connected with his being
our God, that he would be afhamed to take that defignation to himfelf, if he had not provided for us fuch
an inheritance. This was the cafe, even with refpect
to thofe fathers to whom the promife of the typical
Canaan was made; for to them alfo was this inheritance promifed, and fecured by the pledge of the o-
ther. Though Abraham and his feed had the promife of the earthly Canaan, and God, as their God,
beftowed it upon them; yet that inheritance was
fo far below God's character, that, if he had provided no better for them, efpecially for the fathers
themfelves, who never obtained the poffeffion of Canaan in their own perfons; he would have been a-
fhamed to be called their God. But now, having
provided for them a " city that hath *everlafting* foun-
" dations," in the other world; he confiders this as
doing fomething for them that is worthy of himfelf,
and of that relation which he allows them to claim
to him; and therefore he is not afhamed to avow the
relation, or to fuffer himfelf to be called their God.
So reafons an infpired apoftle—" But now they de-
" fire a better country, that is, an heavenly; wherefore
" God is not afhamed to be called their God; for he
" hath prepared for them a city †."

And now, Chriftian, when he openly calls himfelf
your God, as in the text, you ought to confider it as
importing, that he hath provided for you a city; and
that he will affuredly bring you to the poffeffion of it
in due time. The city is the new and heavenly Jerufalem,

rufalem, where you fhall dwell for ever, in the prefence of God and the Lamb. The inheritance, which he will bring you in to poffefs, is no other than his own infinite felf. He will communicate and manifeft himfelf to you, even in this world, by means of thefe ordinances of his own appointment, in a manner far fuperior to any thing that he allows to the men of the world. And when death fhall have demolifhed this clay tabernacle in which you dwell, and thereby abolifhed and deftroyed the body of fin and death under which you groan; then he will admit you to the immediate and unreftrained enjoyment of all his fulnefs. You fhall dwell for ever in his prefencechamber. You fhall behold his glory in the face of Jefus Chrift, without any vail, or any glaffes intervening; you fhall have an opportunity, uninterrupted and undifturbed, to hold the moft intimate and familiar communion with him. You fhall bafk for ever in the rays of the Sun of righteoufnefs, who, without either fetting or being beclouded, enlightens that happy region. You fhall be fatisfied, not only with beholding, but alfo with enjoying, and being perfected in his likenefs. Eternally fhall you be ravifhed with that *fulnefs of joy*, which is *before* his *face;* and eternally have all your defires fatisfied, in the complete enjoyment of all thofe exuberant *pleafures* that are *at his right hand for evermore.* Have you not, even while thefe things are yet at a diftance, good reafon to join, with fatisfaction, in that fong which was fung by David, perfonating the glorious Head of that Covenant, by whom God has become your God:

God

>   God is of mine inheritance
>   And cup the portion,
>   The lot that fallen is to me
>   Thou doſt maintain alone.
>   Unto me happily the lines
>   In pleaſant places fell;
>   Yea, the inheritance I got
>   In beauty doth excel.

I thought to have proceeded to the next head in the method. But I ſee I cannot, without encroaching too much upon your time. I ſhall therefore conclude, at preſent, with a few inferences from what has been ſaid. And from it we may draw the following concluſions.

1. There is a clear warrant for the ſolemn work in which ſome of you have lately been engaged,—the work of covenanting with God. We are ſure it was practiſed, with divine approbation, under the Old-Teſtament diſpenſation; and it is not leſs warrantable under the New. One reaſon why ſo many are enemies to that work, whom yet charity obliges us to look upon as within the bond of God's covenant, is, that they do not attend duly to the nature of it, nor conſider wherein it conſiſts. They know that God is a Being infinitely ſuperior to us; that it is great condeſcenſion in him to enter into a covenant with us; and that, when he does ſo, it belongs to himſelf only to preſcribe all the terms of that covenant, by which he condeſcends to be related to us. They know that the Scriptures ſpeak of no covenants, properly ſo called, by which he propoſes to be related to ſinners, in New Teſtament days, but the covenant of grace; that everlaſting covenant, the ſubſtance of which is expreſſed in this text. And they juſtly conclude,

clude, that it muſt be the higheſt preſumption in ſinful duſt and aſhes, ſuch as we are, to propoſe entering into any covenant with God which is not of his own making. —' But,' ſay they, ' your covenant is al‐
' together different from the covenant of grace. It
' is wholly of man's contrivance. The terms of it
' are all of your own deviſing. And therefore the
' very propoſing of ſuch a thing is, in the higheſt de‐
' gree, preſumptuous.'

But all the force of this reaſoning will evaniſh, however plauſible it appears, if it is conſidered, that, by the duty of covenanting, we intend no more than an open, formal, and explicit acceptance of the covenant of grace, as it is offered in the goſpel, and is compendized and ſummed up in this text. Far be it from us to pretend to make another covenant with God, diſtinct from the covenant of grace, and independent upon it; or any covenant of mens deviſing. Thanks to the riches of divine grace, no other is neceſſary. This is abundantly ſufficient for all the purpoſes both of God's glory and of our ſalvation. But ſurely it muſt be proper, that we take hold of God's covenant in a manner correſponding to that in which it is offered to us. God has promiſed that he will be our God, and we ſhall be his people. And theſe are the gracious terms upon which he propoſes to "make an
" everlaſting covenant with *us*, even the ſure mercies
" of David." But while theſe are only the words of God to us, they are a promiſe which he makes to us; but no covenant between him and us; becauſe a covenant neceſſarily includes the conſent of both parties. It only becomes a covenant made with us, when we conſent that it ſhould be ſo; and ſay, upon the

credit

credit of God's promife, what he has faid before us, that " he is our God, and we are the people of his " pafture." This every believer fays in his heart the moment of his entering within the bond of the covenant; and public covenanters fay no more. We challenge all the enemies of covenanting to find a fentence in that bond, which was publicly fworn in this place three days ago, that is not comprehended and neceffarily included in a fimple confenting to what God promifes in this text. Every believer is materially a covenanter. And a public covenanter is no more than a believer, making an open profeffion of his faith; declaring his acceptance of God to be his God, and avouching his dedication of himfelf to God as one of his people; by that very covenant which God, fo long ago, promifed to make with the Church in New Teftament days.

'But,' may fome fay, 'what need is there for this 'open, public, and formal acceptance of the cove-'nant? Is it not enough that perfons be really and 'favingly in covenant with God? Surely every per-'fon that takes hold of the covenant of grace by faith, 'will be faved; and what do covenanters expect 'more? Public covenanting will not bring any per-'fon into a faving relation to God, unlefs he believes 'with his heart; and if he does this, he will have an 'intereft in God as his God, though he be no cove-'nanter. Why then fhould perfons bewray their hy-'pocrify and vain-glory, by thus openly telling all 'the world that they take hold of God's covenant; 'when perhaps they continue ftrangers to God ftill?'

'If any perfon joins in public covenanting in a way of continuing a ftranger to God, or to the covenant
of

of grace, he bewrays his hypocrify indeed ; and lies, in the moſt folemn manner, unto the God of truth. But is this a fufficient reafon why they who are really in covenant with God fhould not avouch him to be their God? When a man " believes with the heart " unto righteoufnefs ; is it not fit, that " with the " mouth confeffion be made unto falvation?" It is true that every believer will be faved, whether he be a covenanter or not ; and that no covenanter will be faved, unlefs he is a believer. But the fame will hold equally true with regard to communicating. Will any perfon argue, that therefore communicating is no duty?—If Chriſtians are to do nothing in obedience to the command of God, but that which is fo neceſ- fary that they cannot be faved without it, their duties will be reduced to a very fmall number; and the glo- ry of God, which fhould be the ultimate end of all, will be entirely out of the queſtion.

God's external revelation of his covenant of pro- mife, can have no efficacy for bringing any perfon within the bond of it ; unlefs he call them effectu- ally by the faving operation of his Spirit. And the working of the Holy Spirit will be effectual, even though the perfon had no external call. But dare any man therefore affirm, that the outward offer and propofal of the covenant of grace is unneceffary ; and that God might have contented himfelf with bring- ing us into covenant, by the fecret working of his Spirit, without it ? Such arguing would be manifeſtly blafphemous ; but it is not more abfurd or inconclu- clufive than the other. If God makes a public offer of his covenant to us, why fhould not we take hold of it in a manner equally public ? If his part of the
blefſed

bleſſed compact is openly avouched and ſworn to by him, is it not the leaſt that we can reaſonly do, to a-vouch our part of it, and ſwear to it in the ſame explicit manner.

When God's peculiar people covenanted with him ſo often under the Old Teſtament diſpenſation, did they make any covenant with him that was of men's deviſing? Or, if they had, would they have been leſs guilty than they who ſhould do ſo now? Surely that preſumption had been equally ſinful then as now. But they did no ſuch thing. God made a covenant with their " fathers, when he took them by the hand, to " lead them out of the land of Egypt;" and all their covenanting, while that diſpenſation continued, was no more than a ſolemn declaration of their acceptance of *that covenant*, and of their adherence to it. They did not make any new covenant of their own; but only took hold, in an open, formal, and explicit manner, of that covenant which God made with them at mount Sinai. And this was the only ſpecies of covenanting with God, that was lawful even at that time. Had they bound themſelves, by any of their covenants, to any thing that God had not required of them, in the publication of his covenant, they would have been guilty of ſin; much more, if they had pretended to bind God to any thing, to which he had not gracioully bound himſelf. And the ſame is the caſe with us now. Were we to make any covenant that God has not made, to add any new articles to that which he has made; or, in any reſpect, to change what he has already fixed; we would be chargeable with much ſin. But ſurely it can be no ſin, publicly to accept what God as publicly offers; nor to declare

clare our consent to *his* covenant in the same explicit manner in which he has declared his. As really as God made a covenant with the church of Israel in the wilderness, so really does he make this new covenant with the New Testament church, through the Lord Jesus Christ. He makes it in the same public and formal manner, though with much less pomp and terror. And if his open exhibition of *that* covenant to the church in that period, warranted her publicly to lay hold of it, by the duty of public covenanting; does not a similar exhibition of *this* everlasting covenant to us, afford an equal warrant for a similar acceptance of it? Thus, covenanting has the same warrant now that it had then. And the duty will ever be alike binding, while God continues proposing to make, with the New Testament church and her members, this new covenant which is compendized in our text.

Let the reasonings of men, or their practices, be what they will, covenanter, you have no cause to be ashamed of what you have done. God is not ashamed, either to call himself your God, or to call you his people, in the hearing of all the world; and why should you be ashamed to say what he has said before you. The covenant, by which he becomes your God, is publicly consented to and sworn on his part, and why should it not upon yours? Let others content themselves, if they will, with receiving him as their God in their hearts; but do you count it your honour, to avouch him to be your God before angels, men, and devils. Let others satisfy themselves with being night disciples, if so be that " they *really* love the praise of " men, more than the praise of God;" but let it be
consfiered

the New Testament Church.

considered as your glory and your happiness, to put honour upon Christ, by publicly " confessing *him* be-" fore men ;". in the faith that he " will confess *you,* " before *his* Father who is in heaven *."

2. We may see here a copious fund of encouragement and consolation, to all who either have been bringing themselves under *the vows of God* formerly or of late ; or are proposing this day to ratify their engagements at his table. Whatever there is about yourself, to occasion discouragement or down-casting, if you look up to God, through the glass of this promise, you shall see the prospect brighten before you, and shall be satisfied that you have abundant matter of confidence and joy. There are chiefly two considerations, that are apt to produce fears and discouragements on such an occasion as this. Against both you will find a sufficient antidote in this promise.

(1.) Some are afraid to venture upon a solemn approach to God, on account of their own felt unworthiness; fearing left God be thereby provoked to reject their claim, when they aim at calling him their God; and refuse to accept their offering, when they would devote themselves to him as his people. But why is it, O faithless and doubting Christian, that you suffer unbelief thus to deprive you both of your comfort and your confidence? Has not God already signified his consent to the covenant between him and you? And has he not exhibited and proposed it to you; inviting and calling you to give your consent to it? You would have good reason for your fears, if you were intending to deal with God by any other

covenant

* Matth. x. 32.

covenant than his own. But is it not your defire to be related to him only by the covenant of grace? Has not *he* already fworn and fubfcribed the covenant? Has he not delivered it to you, that it may likewife be ratified and confirmed on your part? Does he not earneftly call you to acknowledge him as your God, and to devote yourfelves to him as his people? Yea, has he not, in this text, engaged that you fhall do fo? And now, when you endeavour, through his grace, to do fo at his call; can you have any reafon to fear that you fhall not be accepted? After delivering his covenant to you, ratified and confirmed on his part; can *the God of truth* fo far belie himfelf as to refufe to ftand to it, when you return it to him, with your feal and fubfcription appended? You well know, that fuch conduct would render any perfon infamous among men; and dare you admit a thought fo blafphemous concerning God? " Shall not the " Judge of all the earth do right?" He knew all your unworthinefs, and all your finfulnefs, before he made an offer of his covenant to you; and furely he never would have offered it, if he had not been willing to receive you as you are. Nay, my dear brethren, give not way to any apprehenfions concerning him, fo egregioufly unworthy of him. Go, " eat *your* bread " with gladnefs, and drink *your* wine with a merry " heart; for the Lord accepteth *your* work."

(2.) The other confideration, by which I apprehend fome are prevented from joining in covenanting-work, and others may be difficulted about proceeding to recognize their former vows to God at his table; is, their own infufficiency to pay their vows. ' Alas!' fays the perfon, ' How fhall I come under the
' moft

'moſt ſolemn engagements to walk according to God's
'law, and to keep all his commandments, when I
'am ſenſible that I cannot keep one of them for a
'ment; and that, in every thing I ſet my hand to, I
'break them continually?' But conſider, Chriſtian,
where it is that your *great ſtrength lieth;* and then
you will find no reaſon to be diſcouraged. You ought,
indeed, to *count the coſt* before you ſet forward to a-
ny duty. Before coming under engagements to God
of any kind, you ought to conſider how they are to
be performed, and even to have ſome rational ſecurity that they ſhall be performed acceptably. But
you may wait long enough before you find any ſuch
ſecurity about yourſelf. Yea, though you wait to
your life's end, you never ſhall find it; for your ſtock
is not in your own hand. Your *ſtrength is God alone.*
He has engaged, as you were hearing, that you ſhall
not only be related to him as his people, but ſhall alſo be enabled to walk agreeably to that relation.
" He is faithful that hath promiſed; and he is able
" alſo to perform *it.*" It is, therefore, the ſtrength
and grace which God has promiſed to you, and has
laid up in the hand of Chriſt, to be communicated to
you according to your need, that you ſhould conſider
as your only ſecurity for the payment of all your
vows. And is it not ſecurity enough? However unable you are to keep God's commandments, God is
ſurely able to ſtrengthen and make you able to keep
them. And he will do it; for ſo he has expreſsly
promiſed. " I will ſtrengthen them in the Lord, and
" they ſhall walk up and down in his name, ſaith the
" Lord*." A ſenſe of your own weakneſs and inſufficiency,

* Zech. x. 12.

sufficiency, inſtead of being a bar in the way of your vowing to God, according to his commandment, ought rather to ſtir you up to it; as it ſhould lead you to take a believing view of God's omnipotence, as engaged to furniſh you with ſtrength, both to vow and to pay your vows. Thus, though you cannot go one ſtep on your own legs, you may confidently *go* to the Lord's table, or wherever elſe he calls you, " in the " ſtrength of the Lord God; making mention of his. " righteouſneſs, even of his only."

Who are they, then, that reproach us, as heaping coals of fire on our own head, and aggravating our own condemnation, by our covenanting; becauſe we engage to what we are unable to perform; and thereby lay ourſelves under a neceſſity of breaking our vows? Were the Jews, when they covenanted with God, any more able to obey his commandments than we are? Or was obedience eaſier under that burdenſome diſpenſation than it is now, when the yoke of legal ceremonies is broken? Are theſe men themſelves able to keep the commandments of God? or will they deny that they are bound to do ſo, by their vows in baptiſm and at the Lord's table, as really as we are by our covenants? Do they not then, by this argument, condemn all covenanting under the Old Teſtament as well as under the New? Yea, do they not condemn themſelves for joining in the ſacraments; becauſe their ſacramental vows contain more than they can perform?—But we never pretend to engage that we will keep God's commandments by any ſtrength of our own. We know that of ourſelves we can do nothing. Our engagements are only to be performed, as they ſhould be entered into, in the

ſtrength

strength of " the grace that is in Chrift Jefus." And dare any perfon fay, that his *grace is* not *fufficient for* us; or that we have no warrant to promife upon it? We do not expect to be fupplied with grace fufficient, in this life, to enable us to keep the law perfectly; neither do we engage that we will do fo. But furely we have reafon to depend upon him for all that is neceffary to enable us to keep it acceptably. And, in a dependence upon his promife, we need neither be afraid nor afhamed to fay, as does the Pfalmift, " I have fworn, and I will perform it, that I will keep " thy righteous judgments *."

We fhall now conclude with a fhort addrefs, firft to thofe who intend to be communicants; and then to thofe who, in refpect of the great work of *fhewing forth the Lord's death*, propofe to be fpectators only.

You fee in this text, communicant, how much you owe to Chrift, for that glorious and wonderful event which you are this day to commemorate. If Chrift had never died, you could never have heard fuch a promife as this; nor could the bleffing promifed in it have been enjoyed by any of you. Nay, the covenant itfelf, to which this promife belongs, could never have been made with you, nor offered to you, nor publifhed among you; unlefs Chrift, by his obedience unto death, had fulfilled the condition of it; and thereby made the promifes " fure to all the feed." You are therefore to remember the death of Chrift, as the fole ground of your claim and title to all the bleffednefs that you are to enjoy by the covenant of grace; and to all the fruits of your fœderal relation

* Pfal. cxix. 106.

to God, either in time or through eternity. While you remember it, see that you have all that dependence upon God as your God in covenant, and upon all the promises that the covenant contains, for which a sure foundation is laid by the death and satisfaction of Chrift. When you see the covenant ratified and confirmed by the sacrifice of Chrift, beware of giving way to unbelieving jealousies, as if God were unwilling to ftand to any part of the contents of it. Beware of that refined legality which would cause you doubt of God's acting up to his relation to you; because you are sensible of manifold fhort-comings, failings, and offences againft the laws of the relation on your part. Go forward to his table, in the exercife of all that holy boldness and confidence, that arife from the persuasion of his being a God " keeping co- " venant and mercy to a thousand generations." As this feaft was made for spiritual gladness, beware of difgracing it, by appearing at it with a sad or sullen countenance. But rejoice in God, as your God by covenant: exprefs your joy in him, and your gratitude to him, for condescending to enter into covenant with you, by a cheerful acceptance of all that he offers you, in word and facrament, and an equally chearful dedication of yourfelf and your fervices to him. Let your language, at his table, and in the near profpect of approaching to it, be an echo to his gracious declaration in the text. 'Lord, through thy ' grace, I consent to thy benign propofal; and am ' heartily fatisfied, that thou, and none but thou, be ' my God for ever and ever; and that I be confider- ' ed, in heaven and on earth, in time and through e-
' ternity,

' ternity, as one of thy covenanted people, though
' the moſt unworthy of them all.'

And you who are only to be ſpectators of the ſolemn action, beware of confidering yourſelves as mere ſpectators while you attend upon the difpenſation of the word. Unto you, as well as to thoſe who are to communicate, is this promiſe directed. The covenant of grace, which was originally made with Chriſt, and has been fulfilled, in its whole condition, by his obedience unto death; that covenant, now turned into a bundle of great and precious and free promiſes, is gracioufly offered and exhibited to you. Thus ſaith God to every perſon preſent, ſinner as well as ſaint; whatever be your age, ſex, condition, character, or relation; whatever has been the manner of your paſt life, or whatever is your preſent difpoſition: thus ſaith God to you, " Wherefore will ye ſpend " money for that which is not bread; and your la- " bour for that which ſatisfieth not? Incline your ear, " and come unto me; hear, and your ſoul ſhall live: " and I will make an everlaſting covenant with you, " even the ſure mercies of David*." If you would know what is the ſubſtance of the covenant that he propoſes to make with you, you have it in the words of the text. He will be your God, and you ſhall be his people. He requires no condition to be performed by you. He inſiſts for no qualifications on your part. Himſelf engages to make you whatever his people ought to be. ⁕ No objection can be ſuſtained againſt a preſent compliance with his call and offer. Even your inability to comply is no ſufficient excuſe;

* Iſaiah lv. 2, 3.

for God has engaged to enable you. And you shall assuredly have success, if you aim at saying *Amen* to his gracious proposal. While he exhibits the covenant to you, he engages that you shall consent to it. " I will say, it is my people: and they shall say, the " Lord is my God *."

* Zech. xiii. 9.

SERMON IV.

God's Covenant with the New Testament Church considered.

PART II.

HEB. viii. 10.

—I WILL BE TO THEM A GOD, AND THEY SHALL BE TO ME A PEOPLE.

UNDER the Old Testament dispensation there were different courts, in which different sorts of worshippers assembled. In the outer court, or court of the people, all clean Israelites were allowed to offer up their prayers, and to eat of the sacrifices which had been offered. But into the inner court, where the altar stood, and where sacrifices were offered, none were permitted to enter but the priests; and " the stranger that came nigh *was to* be put to " death *."

In like manner, under the New Testament our Lord Jesus Christ has instituted some ordinances in the

* Numb. xviii. 7.

the church to which every one of mankind may come, and in which every one has an immediate warrant to partake. Thus, according to an ancient promife, God has made " unto all people," in the mountain of the gofpel-church, " a feaft of fat things full of mar-" row, and wines on the lees well refined." This feaft is ferved up to you all in the preaching of the word. But there are other ordinances to which no perfon has any immediate warrant to approach, but they who, being of the family of the antitypical Aaron, are, through him, made kings and priefts unto God. And *the ftranger that cometh nigh* is in danger of fuffering eternal death. Such is the folemn ordinance which we propofe to celebrate in this place to-day.

For this caufe, " let a man examine himfelf; and " fo let him eat of that bread, and drink of that cup." If any perfon is defirous to comply with this exhortation, and would gladly know whether he be among thofe who have an immediate right to partake in this ordinance or not; he may find a fhort and eafy method of having the queftion refolved, if he looks into his own heart, and confiders attentively how he is affected at hearing this text read. You may come even to the holy table of the Lord, in the confidence of being welcome, if you are difpofed to confider this promife as relating to you in particular; if you fincerely believe that God is willing and ready to accomplifh the promife to you; and if you, on your part, are difpofed cordially to fay *Amen* to it; that he fhould be to you a God, and you fhould be, and, through grace, behave to him as one of his people.

Some

Some will probably remember, that we fpake from thefe words on laſt occafion of this nature; and, after taking a brief view of the Apoſtle's fcope in this chapter, we faw that the words contain the fecond of four capital promifes, mentioned by the prophet Jeremiah, and here recited by this Apoſtle, as expreſſive of the fubſtance of that new and well ordered covenant, which God makes with the church, and with particular believers in gofpel-days. Indeed we may confider this promife as a compend, or fummary, of the whole covenant, as it is exhibited in the gofpel, and confented unto by the Chriſtian in the day of believing, " I (fays JEHOVAH) will be to them a God, " and they fhall be to me a people."

The promife, as we formerly faw, confiſts of two parts. In it we have,

1ſt, What God will be to the New Teſtament church, and to the particular members of it,—*I will be to them a God.*

2dly, What the church and her particular members fhall be to God,—*And they ſhall be to me a people.*

In the *firſt* part of the text we obſerved four things more particularly; and we may take notice of the fame number in the fecond, *viz.*

1. The perſon fpeaking, in the pronoun *me*, referring to God himſelf. Ifrael of old was remarkable for a difpofition to idolatry. Though God had chofen them for his peculiar people, and they had confented to it; they were always backward to confider themfelves as his, in fuch a manner as to preclude all acknowledgement of any other God. The fame difpofition to idolatry, though perhaps in a more refined form, prevails, more or lefs, with all the members of

the

the gospel-church. Still we are prone to give away ourselves to another, even after we have been solemnly dedicated to him. But God himself has graciously engaged to subdue this disposition in us, and to make us heartily willing to be a people to him only.

2. The parties spoken of in the pronoun *they;* referring to the house of Israel and the house of Judah, which must be understood of the gospel-church. This promise belongs not only to the church at large, but likewise to all the genuine members of it. Not only is it directed to all the members of the church invisible; for to all such it is accomplished already: but to all who live within the visible church. To every person in whose ears this covenant is published, God becomes engaged, not only to receive them among his people, when they shall apply to him for that honour; but also, graciously to dispose and enable them to make such application, and really to become his people.

3. The happy relation to God, in which the New Testament church, and her individual members, shall be honoured to stand. They shall be to him *a people.* By nature they were so far degenerated, that they deserved not to be called a people at all. Yet God condescends to erect them into an organized society, and even to take them for a peculiar people to himself. Being related to one another, as members of the same body mystical, they all stand related to him, as the Sovereign Proprietor, the Lord, the Lawgiver, the God of the whole.

4. The freeness and stability of the promise, intimated in the word *shall.* It hangs upon no conditions to be performed by us. It admits of no peradventure,

ture, nor leaves room for any rational doubt. Were it only the word of a man, there would be reafon to doubt it. Had it been fpoken by a mere creature, though it had been the higheft angel in heaven, there would at leaft be a poffibility of its failing. But the words of God are not " yea and nay—He is not a " man, that he fhould lie; nor the fon of man, that " he fhould repent." What he *hath faid* he will af- furedly *do*. Having *fpoken in his holinefs*, he will not fail to *make it good*.

The method which we propofed to follow, in fpeaking from the fubject, was the following.

I. To take notice of a few things imported in the words, more generally.

II. To enquire more particularly what is implied in God's being our God.

III. To confider the import of our being to him a people. And then,

IV. To conclude with fome improvement of the whole.

Having attempted a difcuffion of the two firft heads in the method already, we now proceed, through divine affiftance, to

The *third*, which was, To confider what is imported in our being to God for a people. And I conceive this part of the promife imports the following things.

1. That God would gather together into one all the members of the New Teftament church; fo that in whatever place of the world they fhould have their refidence, from whatever nation they fhould fpring, whatever fhould be their kindred, tongue, or language; they fhould all be clofely united one to another, and conftituted one body myftical. The word *people*

is of a collective fignification; and ufually denotes a great number of perfons, regularly affociated and joined together in one fociety, or body-corporate.

Under the Mofaic difpenfation God did not only take every individual of Ifrael's feed into covenant with himfelf; but he feparated the whole nation from the reft of the world; erected them into an organical church; took them, in that united and joint capacity, to be his peculiar people; and married them to himfelf. In like manner under the New Teftament, though all who are brought within the bond of this covenant do not belong to one nation, or defcend from one family, but are fcattered through all the nations, families, and places of the earth; yet God, when he takes them into covenant with himfelf, does likewife unite them to one another, and make them all members of one and the fame body. Yea, the very fame covenant by which they ftand related to God, joins and unites them to one another; fo that they become one people, one church; and in that capacity they are efpoufed to God; who becomes a hufband, not only to every individual among them, but alfo to the whole catholic church. Now their union to one another arifes chiefly from two things.

(1.) They are all united to one Head, even Chrift. With him it was that this covenant was originally made: And ftill it is only in his right that any perfon can be admitted into it. Though the covenant is made with us in time, as really as it was made with Chrift from eternity; yet there are not three different parties contracting in the covenant, but only two—God the Father on the one fide, and Chrift and his fpiritual feed on the other. We enter into
covenant

covenant with God, by taking our place in Chrift; according to what was ftipulated concerning us in the original making of the covenant. As in the natural body all the members are really and jointly knit to the head; becaufe there all the nerves, from the different parts of the body, meet; and, in this way, the members are likewife knit and united one to another; fo alfo is Chrift. All the members of his body are united to him by faith, and enjoy communion with him. Confequently they are all united to one another in him; and enjoy a happy communion one with another, however diftant they be in point of place, or even in point of time. Yea, through him, thofe members of the church who are now in heaven, hold communion with us on earth, and we with them, as being all one body in him, and all partaking of vital influences from him, according to our different circumftances and conditions.

(2.) They are all partakers of one and the fame Spirit. The moment that they are united with Chrift, they "receive the Holy Ghoft;" and, from that time forth, are actuated by the fame Spirit that was, and ftill is in him. As no man can doubt that every limb, which is enlivened and actuated by his own rational foul, is a member of his natural body, and in union with all the reft; fo neither can we doubt, that the members of the church are all in union with one another, and conftitute a living whole, when we fee them all quickened and influenced by the felf-fame Spirit; even the Spirit of Chrift, who is as the foul of the body-myftical, and enables every member to perform its proper function in the body.

And as they are all united to one another, fo they
are

are united in the moſt regular and orderly manner. Every member has its own place and office in the body, in due ſubordination to one another, and in a proper ſubſervience to the good of the whole. He who makes them one body, has likewiſe aſſigned to every one his place; and eſtabliſhed rule, order, and ſubordination among them. He has given them laws, ordinances, and office-bearers, for the general edification of the whole; and thus has made them, to himſelf, not a ſavage or undiſciplined rabble, but a regular and orderly ſociety,—a well governed *people*.

2. The words import, that this dignified people, and every particular perſon among them, ſhall, in due time, be enabled to dedicate themſelves unto God, and chearfully to acknowledge themſelves to be his property. When God makes an offer of himſelf to us, to be our God,—he likewiſe makes a claim upon us; he calls us to give him our hearts, and our whole ſelves, to be his willing people. When we accept his offer, and ſay, "This God is our God;" we likewiſe admit his claim, and ſay, "We are the people "of his paſture." And as his promiſe to be our God includes an engagement to enable us to accept his offer; ſo his promiſe, that we ſhall be his people, muſt include an engagement to enable us to admit his claim; and ſo to devote ourſelves to him, and to acknowledge his ſovereign propriety in us.

Every member of the viſible church, is, by his appearance and profeſſion materially dedicated to God. This dedication, as well as our acceptance of God for our God, is ratified and ſealed, in a public and ſolemn manner, in baptiſm. It is openly recognized and renewed, by every communicant, at the Lord's table.

And

And every perfon, who, in partaking of either facracrament, enjoys the thing fignified, along with the outward and vifible fymbol, fincerely, and with the heart, gives himfelf away to God, as one of his covenanted people. This promife fecures, not only the outward, but alfo the inward and fpiritual part.

Every worthy communicant this day will have his heart concurring with his outward profeffion,—while he practically declares, before God, angels, and men, not only his acceptance of God for his God, but alfo his confent to be the Lord's, in time and through eternity; to be employed in his fervice, and difpofed of by him as he fees moft for his own glory, according to the tenor of his covenant. Some of you may be difcouraged, in the profpect of fuch work, from an apprehenfion, that your deceitful and defperately wicked hearts will not be got to join fincerely in the work ; and that you fhall be guilty of " lying to the " God of truth," while you profefs yourfelves his, and yet find your hearts cleaving to his rivals.

Indeed, if you look only to yourfelves, there is great danger that this will be the cafe, and no wonder that you be difcouraged. But if you look to the promife of God, the danger evanifhes, and all the grounds of your difcouragement. If you are to be God's people, it muft be with your own confent; for our glorious Mediator rules none but a willing people; and to him God commits the charge of bringing them within the bond of his covenant. If you are to give your confent to be his people, this is the very thing you wifh for, and are afraid you fhall not attain. And it is neceffarily included in the promife. Go forward, therefore, in a believing dependence upon his faithfulnefs
who

who has promised. Do not hesitate to say with the mouth, and likewise to say practically to Christ, what Amasai said to his type, "Thine are we, David, and "on thy side, thou son of Jesse *." Say it with chearfulness before this assembly, by chearfully taking your seat at the Lord's table. And aim at saying it to God with the heart at the same time. In this way you may be assured, that he who has given you the promise in the text will enable you to say it in sincerity, and so will make what you say to be a truth. As he will really be your God, so he will take effectual care that you shall be among his willing people. The one is the fruit of his gracious condescension; the other shall be the effect of his all-subduing grace. " Thy people shall be willing in the day of " thy power †."

3. They import, that having made such a dedication of themselves to God, the church, and her members, shall be preserved from ever attempting to *alienate what* they *have devoted*. While God makes an offer of his covenant to us, he has a multitude of rivals, who attempt to divert our attention from the advantageous offers that he makes us, and to engage our affections to themselves. When one is determined to hearken to God's gracious proposals, and to give himself away to him, those rivals do not cease to molest him with their importunities. Whereas formerly they endeavoured to prevent his being espoused to Christ, now they tempt him to commit adultery against him. After we have become his people, they set themselves to draw us off from our allegiance: and, alas! too often we are in danger of their prevailing,

* 1 Chron. xii. 18. † Psal. cx. 3.

vailing, to make us " change our God and our
" glory."

But that they shall never wholly prevail, this promise, Christian, gives you ample security; God engages, not only that you shall become his people, but that you shall continue to be so. He will still maintain that possession of you which he has obtained with your own consent; and will effectually prevent your being either able or willing wholly to alienate yourselves from him. Two ways you might alienate yourselves, and be guilty of revoking the dedication that you have made of yourselves to him. Against both you are hereby secured.

(1.) By employing yourselves in the service of any other, to the neglect of that work which he has put into your hands. If you are really his, it is doubtless your reasonable service to be always employed as he requires and appoints. You cannot continue his people unless this is the case. And his promise of making you his people, affords ample security that it shall ever be the case. While you remain in this world, you will always have a hankering after his rivals; still they will ply you with their importunities; and no wonder you be sometimes left to comply with them in part; and so to remit in your duty to God, and even to employ yourselves in their service. But as God will never give up with his property in you, so you shall never be suffered habitually to act inconsistently with it. His service shall still be your element. You shall never take the same pleasure in the service of his enemies, as in running the way of his commandments. He will keep you in that way, as far as you are enabled to trust him for it; and if, at any time, he permits you to go astray, he will be sure to

reclaim

reclaim you sooner or later—" Though you fall you
" shall not be utterly cast down ; for *still* the Lord
" upholdeth," and shall uphold you, " with his *al-*
" *mighty* hand."

(2.) By indulging yourselves in fretting or murmuring at the manner in which he sees meet to dispose of you in the course of his adorable providence. Resignation to the will of God under adversities, is one of the hardest lessons that a Christian has to learn. And yet resignation is a duty to which we are especially bound, by the dedication that we make of ourselves to God when we take hold of his covenant. If you give yourselves to the Lord, and consider yourselves as his property, surely you cannot expect to have the disposal of yourselves as if you were still your own. Nor can you reasonably complain, if he, to whom you have given yourselves, dispose of you as seems good in his own sight. Has he not *power to do what* he *will with* his *own?* Why is it then that you are so frequently guilty of *charging God with folly*, in his dispensations relative to you? And why are you displeased, because, in the use to which he puts you, and as to the lot which he casts into your lap, he does not consult your inclinations? 'Alas,' say you, 'I can assign no reason for it. I am sensible
' of the injustice and unreasonableness of my conduct ;
' but I find myself unable to help it. Still my un-
' circumcised heart will be rising up against God, and
' murmuring against his manner of dealing with me ;
' though I am convinced in my judgment, that his
' dispensations, like his law, are *holy, and just, and*
' *good;* while *I am carnal,* discontented, ungrateful,
' *and sold under sin.*' Well, here is your security a-
gainst

gainſt this atrocious fin. Refignation, like every other Chriſtian virtue, is the work of the Spirit of God in the foul. And God has engaged to perform it. He cannot make you his people, and keep you fuch, without enabling you, in fome degree, to fubmit to be difpofed of according to his fovereign will. Truſt him, then, for the accompliſhment of his promife, while you aim at the performance of the duty. And fo ſhall you be enabled to acquiefce in his difpenfations, as believing that he does *all things well.* At leaſt, you ſhall be determined, like the royal Pfalmiſt, to be *dumb, and not open* your *mouth* againſt any thing that befals you in providence, when you confider that it is *your God* who *does it* *.

4. The words import, that God will gracioufly accept the dedication that we make of ourfelves to him, and all thofe evangelical fervices which we perform in confequence thereof. This covenant, like all others, muſt have the confent of both parties. And both muſt confent to both the parts of it. While God declares himfelf willing to be our God, he likewife declares himfelf fatisfied that we ſhould be his people. And as he cannot be our God, till we confent that it ſhould be fo; much lefs can we be his people, unlefs he is gracioufly pleafed to accept us as fuch, and to admit us into that happy fociety. Nor can we ever ferve or worſhip him, as his people ought to do, unlefs he condefcends to accept thofe ferviees which we perform. If, therefore, he promifes that we ſhould be his people, it muſt include a promife of acceptance, both of our perfons and of thofe fervices which

* Pfal. xxxix. 9.

which we, through his grace, perform in that relation.

Is there, in this affembly, any poor dejected Chriftian, who dare hardly prefume to make an offering either of his perfon or his fervices to God, from a fenfe that he is altogether unworthy of acceptance before him? 'Alas!' may fuch an one fay, 'How fhall a
' worm, fo vile and finful as I am, adventure to make
' an offering of himfelf, or of any thing that he can
' do, to fuch a glorious and *holy* LORD *God?* Would
' an earthly Prince receive into his family a beggar
' from the dunghill, whofe rags were only fufficient
' to expofe his nakednefs, whofe body were all deformed, and covered over with a lothfome and infectious difeafe, and who could neither move hand
' nor foot without affiftance? Would he be pleafed
' with any fervices that fuch an one could perform?
' Or would it not be ridiculous for fuch a perfon to
' pretend to perform any fervices at all? How much
' more abfurd is it in me, to expect that the God of
' all glory, who is infinitely bleffed in himfelf, and
' ftands in no need of any of his creatures, or any of
' their fervices, who has *thoufands of thoufands*, of
' powerful and holy angels, *ftanding before him, and*
' *ten thoufand times ten thoufand miniftring unto him;*
' that he will receive into his fervice fuch a wretch
' as I am, or pay any regard to fuch unworthy and
' polluted fervices as I can perform; while I cannot
' but be fenfible that I am *all as unclean thing, and*
' *all my righteoufneffes are as filthy rags?*'

But beware that you give not way to the fuggeftions of Satan, nor hearken to the dictates of unbelief in this matter. You are in the fame condition with
every

every other Chriſtian in this reſpect. Never any of
Adam's loſt family was worthy to be a ſervant of
God. Never was there any piece of ſervice performed by the greateſt ſaint out of heaven that was, of itſelf, worthy to come up with acceptance upon his altar. Were we to judge of God by the ſtandard of
men like ourſelves, we could never look for acceptance with him. But his *ways are not* as our *ways,
nor* his *thoughts* as our *thoughts*. No man durſt ever
have thought of preſenting ſuch an unworthy offering to God, if himſelf had not required it. But now
that he has required it, the preſumption of refuſing it
is as great as that of offering it would otherwiſe have
been. He not only requires that you *preſent* your
ſouls, and even *your bodies a living ſacrifice* unto
him; but he promiſes that you ſhall do ſo; and that,
in ſo doing, you ſhall find acceptance, notwithſtanding all your unworthineſs. Yea, thoſe ſinful and imperfect ſervices, which you may perform, being pur-
ged and perfumed by the merit and interceſſion of
your glorious Surety, ſhall not only be accepted, they
ſhall even be graciouſly rewarded by him. Be encouraged, therefore, however unworthy you are,
chearfully to enter yourſelf among God's people, and
to aim at ſerving him in a manner becoming that character; for with ſuch ſacrifices God is well pleaſed.
Go forward, with holy confidence and alacrity, even
to the communion table; there to ſignify, before God,
angels, and men, that you count it your glory to be
devoted to his ſervice. At that table, " eat *your* bread
" with gladneſs, and drink your wine with a merry
" heart; for the Lord accepteth *both you and your*
" works."

5. The words import, that this chosen people, being thus brought into covenant with God, shall be enabled likewise to behave in a manner corresponding to that relation. Not only shall they employ themselves in his service; but the services which they perform shall be such as are due from a people to their God. Seeing he is not barely our Master, but our God; we must not satisfy ourselves with performing to him such services as are due to a common master; but must give him all that honour, glory, and worship, as well as all that obedience that is due to a master who, at the same time, is God, and our God. And that we shall do so, this promise is our security; for, unless this is the case, we cannot deserve the character of his people.

Here a large field opens to our view. We might go through all the duties required in the law of God; and shew, that by this promise, and others parallel to this, we have full security for the acceptable performance of them all. But we shall satisfy ourselves with naming a few of those which are essentially necessary in all who are the people of God.

1. We shall be enabled to give credit to his word of grace, and to trust in him for the accomplishment it. "He that believeth not hath made him a liar [*];" but he cannot be a liar, and yet be God; for it is an essential attribute of the Deity, that *he cannot lie*. He, therefore, who believes not, instead of acknowledging him as his God, or behaving towards him as one of his people, denies him to be God at all. Consequently, if we are to be his people, we must needs believe

---

[*] 1 John v. 10.

believe his word; and so give him that glory which is due to him as a God of truth.

Faith is so necessary in the duty of communicating, that every person who sits down at the communion-table without it, must be " guilty of the body " and blood of the Lord." Sensible of this, and conscious of the weakness of their own faith, or apprehensive of the want of it, some who have received tokens may be hesitating whether to make use of them or not. But why should you stand at a distance from a known duty for want of that faith which you may just now receive, and which God has promised to give you? Can you ever believe of yourself? And if faith is the gift of God, why should you not presently apply to him for it? It is utterly impossible that you should be his people without it. And it is equally impossible that you should behave as his people without the present exercise of it. Faith is as essential to God's people, as faithfulness is to God himself. And if he has promised to make you his people, you may safely trust him that he will give you this grace, and enable you to the exercise of it. If you think that the promise in the text is not explicit enough to this purpose, you may find a great many in the word of God, that more directly and immediately relate to this. Has he not said, for instance, " I will leave in the " midst of thee an afflicted and poor people; and they " shall trust in the name of the Lord*." Even in a sense of your utter inability to believe, set forward to your duty at his call; and, by the strength of his promised grace, you shall be enabled, in this as well as

in

---

* Zeph. iii. 12.

in other respects, to acquit yourself as becomes one of his people.

(2.) We shall be enabled to make him our refuge in every time of need, and always to call upon him for all necessary assistance and deliverance. " To " whom should a people seek but to their God." He who is the Author of this promise, represents it as absurd that they should seek to any other. And surely, when he engages that we shall be his people, it must include an engagement that we shall seek to him only, and not go *for the living to the dead*. Not only has he condescended to invite us to call upon him in the time of need; he has likewise pledged his faithfulness that we shall do so. The following promise looks both to the Head, and to all the members of the mystical body; " He shall call on me, and I " will answer him; I will be with him in trouble: I " will deliver him, and honour him*."

You, who know any thing about yourselves, will not be disposed to look upon this promise as unnecessary; though, perhaps, it may appear so to those who are strangers to that enmity against God, and that estrangement from him, which are natural to the human heart. Indeed, it is most unreasonable that any, who believes that God is both able and willing to help, should be backward to make application to him for that purpose. There was never occasion for many arguments to persuade the worshippers of false gods, to apply to them for help in time of need. But all the arguments that can be used are not sufficient to prevail with them who profess to worship the true God, regularly and seasonably to call on him for what they

* Psal. xci. 15.

they stand in need of. Are you not convinced, Chriftian, that you have often been foiled by your fpiritual enemies, have often come fhort in the performance of your duty, and often continued under fevere affliction, for want of a timely application to thé throne of grace for affiftance? And if you are left to yourfelf, it will be fo ftill. Such is the *folly* that is *bound up in* your *heart*, that you will never apply to God for any thing in an acceptable manner, till his grace determine and enable you to do fo. Such grace is fecured to you by promife. You *fhall* both *call upon* him, and he *will anfwer you*.

(3.) We fhall be enabled to perfevere in the performance of all that religious worfhip which is due to him as God, and our God. It has been taken for granted, in all nations, and in all periods, that religious worfhip is due to none but a divine object; till a generation arofe, who call themfelves Chriftians, to the difgrace of that honourable name, and yet prove themfelves the followers of antichrift, by this, among many other abominations, that they allow a kind of religious worfhip to various forts of creatures. And if religious worfhip is due to none but a divine perfon, they who believe that there is but one God, muft needs think it their duty to worfhip him only. So long as we continue to be the people of God, we muft perfift in worfhipping him only, and that in the manner which himfelf has appointed. We muft worfhip him with the heart, as well as with the outward man; "cafting all *our* idols," of every kind, " to the moles " and to the bats;" and carefully obferving all that God has commanded us, in this refpect, without " ad- " ding thereto, *or* diminifhing from it." When a
people

people ceases to do this, they behave not as the people of God. And if they persist in such a foolish course, he is, at length, provoked to disown them, and to refuse to be their God. So it was with the people of Israel. " Ye are not my people," says God to them ; " and I will not be your God *." The change of time, in this text, deserves to be carefully noticed. He does not say, " Ye are not my people ; and I am " not your God. *But* ye are not, and I will not be."
' You, by your idolatry, and corruption of my wor‑
' ship, have already ceased to be my people; and I,
' as a punishment for this, will also cease to be your
' God. The relation has been disowned, and the co‑
' venant dissolved, on your part; and it shall not much
' longer be maintained on mine.'

But such a thing shall never take place with the New Testament Church, nor with any of her genuine members. They shall always be to God for a people; always will he continue to be to them a God ; " and the idols will he utterly abolish." He will enable us still to maintain his instituted worship, and that in an acceptable manner; and still he will countenance and be present with us in it. His promise, considered in this view, has a partial accomplishment among us to‑day ; inasmuch as we have a regular dispensation of ordinances, and a number of persons brought together to celebrate them. Some, after all, may be afraid to take part in the solemn work before us, from a sense of the attachment of their heart to idols ; and its backwardness to go along with their outward man, when attending the worship of God. On this account they may be afraid, lest, by joining

outwardly

outwardly in the work, they subject themselves to the punishment that is due to those who " draw near *to* " *God* with the mouth, and honour *him* with the lip, " *while their* heart is far from *him.*" . But know you, not, poor soul, that the promise extends to your case also? You cannot be God's people unless you worship him only, in a way of renouncing all idols, and worship him with the heart as well as with the outward man. But he has promised that you shall be his people; and therefore you may trust him for grace to worship him, as becomes that character, both now and on every other occasion. Many other promises might be adduced for encouraging you to trust him for this. We shall mention but one, which God expressly designs as a testimony, both against your former idolatry and against your present unbelief. " Hear, O my people, and I will testify against thee: " O Israel, if thou wilt hearken unto me. There " shall no strange god be in thee : neither shalt thou " worship any strange god." He adds what is extremely suitable, both to this subject and to the work of this day. " I am the LORD thy God, who brought " thee out of the land of Egypt ; open thy mouth " wide, and I will fill it *."

(4.) We shall be enabled to be zealous for God, and to stand up in behalf of his truths and ways against all who set themselves in opposition to either. That such a zeal is one essential qualification of God's people, is manifest from that remarkable expression of the Apostle, " Jesus Christ gave himself for us; that " he might redeem us from all iniquity, and purify " unto himself a peculiar people, zealous of good " works.

* Psal. lxxxi. 8, 9.

"works *." God's peculiar people are to be zealous, not only in performing good works themselves, but likewise in promoting them among others: Consequently, in opposing and bearing testimony against all that is of a contrary nature and tendency; whether in those who are open enemies to God, or in them who profess to be of his people. And this, with every other necessary qualification belonging to the character, must be included in the promise of making us his people.

Beware, Christian, of indulging yourself in lukewarmness and indifference in the cause of God. Beware of going along with persons, or with churches, in any sinful course. Be not silent, or indifferent, when you see the authority of God contemned, his name profaned, his ordinances corrupted, his truths impugned, his people oppressed, or any part of his holy word perverted. By such silence, you should not only give reason to suspect, that hitherto you are none of his people; you should also cast a bar in the way of the accomplishment of this promise to you; and do what you can to render the death of Christ in vain, as far as it relates to you. God promises to make you his people, and Christ died to " purify *you* " a peculiar people, zealous of good works." Thus, in zealously promoting all that is agreeable to the will of God, and opposing what is contrary thereunto, both in yourself and in others, by every proper and habile mean, you may expect to be assisted by divine grace. You may even hope to be graciously rewarded. Remember what was the promise of God concerning Phinehas, " Behold I give unto him my co-
" venant

* Tit. ii. 14.

" venant of peace: and he fhall have it, and his feed
" after him; even a covenant of an everlafting prieft-
" hood; becaufe he was zealous for his God*."

(5.) In a word, being made the people of God, according to this promife, we muft needs be determined ftill to improve that fulnefs of grace and ftrength which is in the hand of our God, for enabling us to do every duty; and to do in his name and ftrength, whatever we attempt to do in his fervice. Even heathens trufted in their gods for affiftance in their enterprizes; and when they were fuccefsful, they afcribed it to *their* interpofal. The people of God of old are heard profeffing that they would do the fame. " All people will walk, every one in the name of his " God; and we will walk in the name of the LORD " our God, for ever and ever †." If it is a common thing for every people to walk in the name of their God, furely God cannot make us his people, without determining and enabling us to walk in his name; which is the fame thing with going always in his ftrength.

There are few who know any thing about Chriftianity, but can talk of doing things in God's ftrength. Many talk of it in a very ignorant and thoughtlefs manner. But they who know any thing of this matter by experience, are fenfible, that really to make ufe of divine ftrength, in the performance of duty, is a thing not eafily obtained. On this account it is neceffary, not only that you depend on divine ftrength in all that you do in God's fervice; but alfo that you depend on God's faithfulnefs, for enabling you to renounce your own ftrength, and to make a believing
improvement

improvement of *that* which he has laid up in the hand of Chriſt. For your encouragement herein, you have not only the general promiſe in the text, but likewiſe a variety of particular promiſes, more immediately relating to this matter. There is one very remarkable, in which God has engaged, not only to communicate ſtrength to you according to your day, but alſo to determine and enable you to make uſe of it. " I will ſtrengthen them in the Lord; and they ſhall " walk up and down in his name, faith the Lord*."

It is now high time to conclude with ſome improvement of the ſubject. We ſhall content ourſelves, for the preſent, with the following inferences.

1. From what has been ſaid, we may ſee one very remarkable difference between the covenant of grace, as it is exhibited in the goſpel, and actually made with every Chriſtian in the day of believing, a difference, I ſay, between this and all other covenants. In all covenants there are mutual engagements entered into by both parties reſpectively; and ſomething which they become bound to perform one to another, on both ſides. So far this covenant agrees with all others. God graciouſly binds himſelf to be our God, and to deal with us, in all caſes, according to that character. And we, on the other hand, by our acceptance of God's covenant, bind ourſelves to be his people, and to perform all that worſhip and obedience which we owe to him in that capacity; not as the condition of what he is to do for us, far from it, but as a teſtimony of our gratitude for it. But the amazing difference between this and every other covenant lies in this, that here one party binds himſelf for

* Zech. x. 12.

for the performance of the engagements of both. God obliges himself, by his faithful word of promise, not only to be our God, and to do all for us that this character may warrant us to expect; but also to make us his people, and that we, through his grace affifting us, shall behave dutifully in that relation.

Indeed, if it were otherwife, our entering into covenant with God would be to no purpofe. The covenant that God makes with the houfe of Ifrael and with the houfe of Judah, in New Teftament days, would be broken and diffolved, as quickly as was that which he made with the *firft Adam* in our name. We could no more perform the duties that we owe to God as our God, by our own ftrength, than we could perform the whole condition of the covenant of works. But, feeing God has engaged to work all our works in us and by us, as well as do all his own work for us, there is not a Chriftian fo weak, but, like Paul, he may do all things, through Chrift ftrengthening him. Let not, then, a fenfe of your own weaknefs, nor a fenfe of the difficulty of your work, caufe your heart to faint, or your hands to hang down. Be not afraid of the ftrength of your fpiritual enemies, nor let your courage fail, becaufe you feel that you are no match for them. But learn in the midft of weaknefs to be ftrong. Your ftrength is omnipotence itfelf. And, fo long as nothing is required of you that God cannot perform in you and by you, you have no reafon to be difcouraged, or to doubt of fuccefs. " Be ftrong, *therefore*, in the Lord, and in " the power of his might."

2. We may fee that all true Chriftians are really covenanters with God, however little relifh fome of
them

them may have for the name. God makes an open and free exhibition of the covenant of grace to all the hearers of the gofpel. He propofes to *make* this *new covenant* with every perfon who belongs to *the houfe of Ifrael,* or to *the houfe of Judah;* that is, to the New Teftament Church. Every Chriftian, in the day of believing, accepts God's gracious offer, gives his confent to the whole covenant, as fo exhibited; and thus *makes a covenant with God,* through the intervention of the facrifice of Chrift. Accordingly, he becomes engaged, in the ftrength of covenanted grace, not only to have and acknowledge God for his God; but alfo to confider himfelf as one of God's people, and, in all time coming, to behave himfelf agreeably to that character. And what is it that any formal covenanter does more? We difclaim all thofe impious and blafphemous attempts, with which we are charged by fome, to bind the great God to terms of our making. We difclaim all covenants with God, that are not of his own making, of his own propofing. We openly difclaim all that covenanting with God which amounts to any thing more, or to any thing lefs, than a formal and explicit declaration of our acceptance of God's covenant of grace, and of our hearty confent to the gracious offer and promife contained in this text. We are bold to challenge all the enemies of that defpifed work, to produce one fentence in our Bond, or what is ufually called our Covenant of Duties, that is not manifeftly included in fuch a confent; or any fentence that does not exprefs the genuine language of the heart of every believer, when he takes hold of the covenant by faith. And, though all the men on earth

earth fhould fet themfelves againft it, whether profeffors of religion or profane perfons, we hope never to be afhamed, to fay before angels, men, and devils, what God has gracioufly faid before us, and what every genuine Chriftian fays in his heart; that *he* fhall be to us *a God*, and we, through his grace, *fhall be* to him *a people*.

It is not ftrange to find all the open enemies of religion combined, as in fact they are, in the ftrongeft and firmeft manner, againft the duty of covenanting. They act in character. A thing fo manifeftly of God, cannot fail to meet with oppofition from his ftated enemies. But how *they* fhould join in that combination who are friends to God, and in their hearts approve the covenant of grace, and have laid hold upon it, is really unaccountable. Are you pleafed with God's covenant in your heart, and yet afhamed to avouch it before the world? Are you willing to be the people of God, but unwilling that any fhould know it? Have you really covenanted with God in fecret, or in your heart; and dare you condemn and revile thofe who do the fame thing in an open and explicit manner? In all this are you not felf-condemned? Being really the people of God, do you not openly take part with his enemies, in oppofing that work to which you have put your own hand, though in a fecret manner? " Tell it not in Gath ; publifh " it not in the ftreets of Afhkelon: left the daughters " of the Philiftines rejoice, left the daughter of the " uncircumcifed triumph."

3. From hence we may fee, that neither faith nor repentance, nor fincere obedience, nor any thing elfe wrought in us or done by us, can be the condition of

the covenant of grace. The whole fubftance of that covenant, as it is made with us, is expreft in this text; and all that is here expreft is to be performed by God himfelf. As made with Chrift from all eternity, this covenant had a very arduous condition; but, as made with us through Chrift, it is abfolutely free and unconditional. It is properly a *covenant of promife*. To us it is exhibited as a covenant already fulfilled by Chrift, in the whole condition of it. And in laying hold of the covenant, we give our confent to the fulfilment of its whole condition by Chrift, as well as to every thing elfe that it contains; renouncing our own righteoufnefs in every form, and difclaiming all right to any of its promifes, founded on any thing about ourfelves. We engage, indeed, to perform obedience to God's law, confidered as the law of Chrift, as becomes his people; but not with a view to found our claim to the accomplifhment of the promife, nor in a way of confidering what we engage unto as any part of the condition of the covenant. We have feen, that all that we engage to do is contained in the promife of the covenant. And it is only in confequence of the accomplifhment of the promife to us, that we can perform our engagements. When we perform them acceptably, it is only in the ftrength of promifed grace. Our fuccefs in fuch endeavours is folely owing to God's affiftance; and the work, when done, is much more properly his than ours. Thus, inftead of engaging to fulfil the condition of the covenant, we confent to have all our dependence upon Chrift's fulfilment of it for us; and we engage to do nothing, unlefs in the faith that God, according to the promife of the covenant, will work it in us and by us.

4. We

4. We may fee from this fubject, that real Chriftians are the only happy perfons in the world. All the things that men value or efteem, and in which they look for happinefs, riches, honours, power, pleafure, they poffefs in a fupereminent degree. They are the only perfons who deferve to be called rich; having an intereft in God himfelf, an infinite and inexhauftible good as their portion and inheritance. In comparifon of this, all other poffeffions are but drofs and dung. The fole heir of both the Indies would be a poor man without this. And, having an intereft in this, the beggar on the dunghill is richer than the owner of a world. They only are dignified and honourable perfons; being allied to heaven itfelf. To be married or adopted into the family of an earthly prince, is confidered as the fummit of honour and dignity in the kingdoms of this world. But Chriftians are efpoufed to "the Prince of the kings of the earth." They are adopted into the family of the Father of eternity. To exprefs all in few words,—they are in covenant with God. They only deferve to be confidered as powerful perfons. The man who rules the moft extenfive empire, whofe victories hold the whole world in awe, is liable to be overthrown in the midft of his fuccefs, and levelled with the meaneft of his flaves, the moment that God fees meet to ftrike the blow. But God himfelf is on the Chriftian's fide, and all the power of his almighty arm is ready to be exerted in his behalf. Hence Jacob, though but a *worm*, may "threfh the mountains *into* duft;" and, by faith in the power of God, the weakeft Chriftian, if called, may " fubdue kingdoms, and put to flight *whole* ar-
" mies of the aliens." None but they enjoy true and
folid

solid pleasure. God can and does make them *glad
with* his *countenance*, more than other men can be
when their corn and their wine are increased, and all
other sensual gratifications. They only have a valid
title to what they enjoy, and hold it by a sure tenure.
The covenant of God is their security for all that they
possess, and for all that they need, even of the good
things of the present life; and, while God is faithful,
they can want nothing. In a word, they only have
a comfortable prospect after death, and a *good hope*
for eternity. " The things that are not seen, *and* are
" eternal," are secured to them by covenant. They
have a " house, not made with hands, eternal in the
" heavens;" upon the possession of which they shall
enter, when " the earthly house of this tabernacle
" shall be dissolved." They have " an inheritance,
" incorruptible, undefiled, and that fadeth not away,
" reserved in heaven for *them*." Yea, they have " a
" kingdom that shall never be moved; prepared for
" *them* before the foundation of the world." This,
believer, is an inventory; a very general, and a very
defective inventory of what is yours, by virtue of this
covenant that subsists between God and you. All
this you either possess now, or shall possess in a little;
and inexpressibly more than this, more than ever
mortal *eye saw*, more than ever mortal *ear heard;*
yea, incomparably more than ever the *heart* of any
mortal could possibly *conceive*. Have you any reason, then, to be envious, or grudge when you " see
" the prosperity of the wicked?" What was Alexan-
der, amidst all his conquests, but a weak and contemp-
tible insect, crushed like a moth by the power that
is your Rock and Stay? What was Crœsus, amidst all
his

his treafures, but a bankrupt in comparifon of the pooreft of you? Haman, poffeft of all the honours that the ruler of *an hundred and feven and twenty provinces* could beftow, was lefs honourable than the meaneft of you. Yea, *Solomon in all his glory*, and amidft all the carnal delights by which his heart was drawn afide, enjoyed no pleafure fo folid, or fo exquifite, as one moment of real communion with God will afford you. Ye that are ftrangers to this covenant, what think you of the bleffed people who are interefted in all its contents? Do you not yet long to be among their number? Are you not conftrained to fay concerning them, " Happy is the people that is " in fuch a cafe: yea, happy is the people whofe God " is the LORD?"

I MUST come to a conclufion with a fhort word of exhortation.

" Let Ifrael be glad in him that made him; and let " the children of Zion be joyful in their *God and* " *King.*" Beware of fuffering any fublunary good to draw away your hearts from him. Beware of fuffering any temporal evil to diminifh, or, in the fmalleft degree, to damp your joy and rejoicing in him. Let not any fuppofed attainments of your own infpire you with one thought of living a moment without him; or of attempting the leaft duty, without an immediate dependence upon his ftrength and grace. Nor let any felt unworthinefs or infufficiency about yourfelf, influence you to ftand at a diftance from any thing that your God requires of you. Still go in the ftrength of the Lord God, making mention of his righteoufnefs, even of his only. In this way come forward to his holy table, over the belly of all difficulties and doubts from within; of all the fuggeſtions of Satan from without; of all difcouragement, and of all oppoſition, from hell or earth; and there avouch your covenant with God, your intereſt in him, your relation to him, and your voluntary dedication of yourſelf to his ſervice. God is ready to ſet his ſeal to the covenant on his part; and ſee that you be not backward to ſeal it alſo on yours. Let it be ſeen, by your conduct and appearance to-day, that you are not aſhamed to ſay before God, as a reply to his gracious promiſe; to ſay before his holy angels, who are preſent in the worſhipping aſſemblies of the church; to ſay in the face of devils, in a way of bidding them an open defiance; to ſay in the hearing of fellow Chriſtians, for their encouragement; and to ſay in the audience of thoſe who are ſtrangers to God's covenant, that, if poſſible, they may be ſtirred up to take hold of it; to ſay, in a word, before all the rational world, if you had an opportunity, what God has warranted you to ſay, by ſaying it before you, "He is our God; " and we are the people of his paſture, and the ſheep " of his hand; to-day if ye will hear his voice;"—

To-day, O ſinner, that continueſt under the broken covenant of works; " to-day, if ye will hear his voice, " then harden not your heart as in the provocation." What think you of the gracious invitation that is given you by God himſelf, that is repeated by his ſervants in his name, that is echoed from the mouths of all who now are " the people of his paſture; to-day, " if ye will hear his voice? The Spirit and the Bride " ſay come; and whoſoever will, let him take the " water of life freely." Let him take the Fountain
of

of life himſelf, as his God and portion, and that freely. He is preſently making an offer of himſelf to you, as your God. He is preſently declaring his willingneſs, yea, his earneſt deſire to have you for one of his people. He is willing to deal with you as ſuch, from this day forth; not in time only, but through an endleſs eternity. All the riches, dignity, power, pleaſure, and happineſs, of which you were juſt now hearing, are yours for the receiving. If you will but ſay *Amen* to God's covenant of promiſe, he will make no further account of all that you have done againſt him. It ſhall be, in his ſight, as if it had never been; and you ſhall be as if you had " never been caſt off." On the contrary, if you perſiſt in rejecting his offered covenant, this will bind down all your other ſins upon your head; and will itſelf be conſidered as the moſt atrocious of them all. As you love your own ſoul, therefore, and wiſh for its eternal happineſs, beware of rejecting your own mercy; and bringing upon yourſelf the curſe of the broken covenant of works, while God makes you welcome to all the bleſſings of the covenant of grace. This moment is God ready to " make with you an everlaſting covenant; even " the ſure mercies of David;" of which covenant, the ſum and ſubſtance is expreſt in this precious promiſe, *I will be to them a God, and they ſhall be to me a people.*

Let all the people ſay, Amen. Praiſe ye the LORD.

An

An Ufe of Trial, delivered in the Fencing of the Tables.

AMONG the many ineftimable privileges that God has beftowed upon his covenanted people, it is none of the leaft, that he " covers a table for them in " prefence of *their* enemies." He giveth meat unto them that fear him, as an evidence that " he is ever " mindful of his covenant." In the difpenfation of the word, he has been, and ftill is, making a feaft unto all people. But the feaft which we are now to celebrate is defigned for his own covenanted people only. And therefore you who have received tokens of admiffion, are called to examine yourfelves, whether you belong to that number or not. " Let a man " examine himfelf; and fo let him eat of that bread, " and drink of that cup."

The fubject from which we have been fpeaking affords a variety of interefting marks, by which you may try yourfelves. And, in agreeablenefs to what you have been hearing, we would afk you,—and we make bold to charge you, by the authority of this God whofe covenant has been exhibited to you,— that you afk your own confciences the following queftions.

1. What think you of the gracious promife that has this day been publifhed among you? Are you fatisfied that it is the word of God? Do you believe him

to

to be in earneft in what he fays? Do you confider it as faid to you? And is it your defire and aim, to truft in God for the accomplifhment of both parts of it? Is this the exercife in which you wifh to be employed, both now and at the communion-table; and are you grieved for that unbelief, which tends fo much to mar you in it? Then you are one of God's peculiar people; and we invite you to the holy table, where you may receive the feal of the covenant. But if you have only been receiving the promife as *the word of men;* if you regard it as an idle tale; if you confider it as a thing in which you have no perfonal concern; if you allow yourfelf to queftion the accomplifhment of it; if none of thefe things be matter of humiliation to you; or if you have no fincere defire that it were otherwife; then you are a ftranger to the covenant of promife, and, in that condition, can have nothing to do at the *Lord's table.*

2. What think you of your need of this covenant, and of your ruined ftate, while under the covenant of works? When God brings any perfon into the number of his people, he firft opens their eyes to fee their difmal condition, while under the curfe of Adam's broken covenant. They fee the juftice of God, armed with vengeance againft them; and all the divine perfections, engaged by covenant to bring them to endlefs mifery. The view of this makes them joyfully to welcome the glad tidings of another covenant, entered into for their relief. If this has been the cafe with you, we invite you to this holy table. But if you ftill live in fecurity within the flood-mark of divine wrath, and have never been affected with the dreadful curfe of the old covenant, which you faw, or

perhaps

perhaps never faw, hanging over your head; then you muft be a defpifer of God's Covenant, for you never faw your need of it; and, while this is the cafe, we debar you from the holy table of the Lord.

3. What think you of God's condefcending to enter into covenant with you? Job had fuch a view of his own vilenefs, and of the infinite glory and greatnefs of God; that he fpeaks of it as matter of wonder, that God fhould condefcend to chaftife him, or even to beftow a look upon him *. How much more reafon have we to wonder, when, inftead of *bringing us into judgment*, he brings us into covenant with himfelf? Does this confideration, then, fill you with holy amazement and adoration? And is it the language of your heart, " Doft thou open thine eyes up- " fuch an one; and bringeft me into *covenant* with " thee?" It is a comfortable fign that you are within the covenant, and are welcome to the feal of it. But if you have fuch low thoughts of God, or fuch high and conceited thoughts of yourfelf, as lead you to apprehend that you have any claim to fuch an honour, or prevent your being affected with wonder at fuch divine condefcenfion; then you know nothing experimentally about this covenant, and are utterly unfit for the holy table of the Lord.

4. What think you of the fcheme of the covenant; that wonderful plan, for the redemption of mankind finners, which was laid, in the original making of the covenant, from all eternity? No perfon can embrace this covenant, till he enjoy fuch a difcovery of the plan of falvation therein laid, as may convince him. of its exact fuitablenefs, both to his own neceffities,

and

* Job xiv. 3.

and to the glory of all the divine perfections. It is one article of this covenant, that all who are brought within it, being taught of God, and having an experimental acquaintance with him, know him and his will, in a better manner than they could attain by any human inftruction. If, therefore, you have feen the beauty, the order, the glory of the covenant; the harmony and due fubordination of the feveral parts of it, and the fuitablenefs of the whole, to promote the honour of God, and the happinefs of his covenanted people; fo as to be rationally convinced, that it is " ordered in all things and fure;" and to make choice " of it, as " all *your* falvation and all *your* defire;" then you are one of God's people, and are welcome to a fhare in their provifion. But if the covenant of grace appears to you, as the glorious Head of it once did to the prejudiced Jews, " like a root out of a dry " ground, *having* no form nor comelinefs in *it* why *it* " *fhould* be defired;" then you are a ftranger to the covenant, for you have no underftanding of its conftitution; and how can you be fit to partake worthily in the feal of it?

5. What think you of Chrift, the head of the covenant? All who are God's people, are favingly united to Chrift, and have been determined to embrace him, and unite with him, by a believing view of his love, his lovelinefs, the matchlefs excellency of every thing about him, and his exact fuitablenefs to every branch of their need. This has effectually convinced them that there is no *other beloved*, who deferves a comparifon with him; that no other can be worthy of their affections, when he lays claim to them. Is the language of your foul concerning him, the fame that is

exprefled

expressed by the Spouse, " My beloved is white and " ruddy; the chiefest among ten thousand. His " mouth is most sweet; yea, he is altogether lovely. " This is my beloved, and this is my friend, O daugh- " ters of Jerusalem!" Then you are invited to sit with him at the " banquet of wine." There will he *give* you his *loves*. But if you see not any thing to recommend Christ " more than another beloved;" if a view of his love has never constrained you to love him; if you think that you love him enough, or are not grieved, because your love corresponds so little either to his love or to his loveliness; then you are strangers to him whom God has given for a covenant of the people; and you cannot, in your present condition, be welcome to his holy table.

6. What think you of *the blood of the covenant?* The main design of that solemn ordinance, which we are about to celebrate, is to keep up the remembrance of the shedding of that precious blood; by which the covenant was confirmed, and still is *confirmed with many*. And surely they are unworthy to take part in this work, who do not consider that blood, or the shedding of it, as worthy to be remembered. Have you, then, been determined to consider the shedding of this blood, as the most glorious and wonderful event that ever the sun shone, or refused to shine upon? Is this blood the sole ground of all your pleadings with God, and of all your expectations from him? Does the love of Christ, evidenced by the shedding of his blood for you, appear to you as surpassing all description, all comprehension, all knowledge? Is it your motive, in going forward to the Lord's table, notwithstanding all the difficulties in your way; that
. you

you may caſt in your mite to keep up the remembrance of this love, and of the ſhedding of this precious blood, *till he come again?* And, as you go forward, are you aiming to learn and to ſing that ſong, " Thou art worthy to take the book, and to looſe the " ſeals thereof; for thou waſt ſlain, and haſt redeem- " ed us to God by thy blood ; and haſt made us kings " and prieſts unto our God; and we ſhall reign on " the earth ?" Then we are warranted kindly to invite you to eat the ſacramental bread, and to drink that cup which is " the New Teſtament in his blood, " which was ſhed for you." But if you are ſtill diſpoſed to " trample under foot the Son of God ; and " *to* count the blood of the covenant, wherewith he " was ſanctified, an unholy thing :" If you dare ſubſtitute your own ragged righteouſneſs, or any thing elſe, in the room of that atoning blood ; if you ſtill perſiſt in " crucifying *to yourſelves* afreſh the Son of " God," and putting him to an open ſhame, by habitual unbelief; or if you have never been humbled in the ſight of God, for the ſhameful treatment that you have formerly given, both to Chriſt and his blood, at his table and otherways; then your eating and drinking at the ſacramental table, in your preſent condition, would be to " betray the Son of man with " a kiſs," and make yourſelf " guilty of the body and " blood of the Lord." And therefore, in ſympathy to your ſoul, as well as in obedience to the command of Chriſt, we muſt debar you from this holy table of the Lord.

7. What think you of God's part of the covenant? Are you ſatisfied that he ſhould be your God, according to it? Have you ever ſeen the vanity of all earth-

ly

ly poffeffions? Are you convinced, that, by reafon of their paffing nature, as well as by reafon of their unfitnefs to yield fatisfaction in the time of enjoyment, they can never make you happy? Is it matter of rejoicing to you, that the eternal and all-fufficient God is offering himfelf to you as a portion, and engaging to be your God? And is it your defire, that the language of your heart fhould be the fame, that is fo fweetly fung by the royal Pfalmift, " This God is our " God for ever and ever; *and* he will be our guide, " even unto death*?" Then God is willing to take you at your word; and he invites you to have his gracious grant fealed to you at his table. But if you ftill prefer the trafh of this world to him; if you fuffer your defires to wander, without reftraint, among the vanities of time; and are not concerned to have them collected, and centring in him; if you fondly purfue that happinefs among the creatures, concerning which all fay, with one voice, It is not in me: If you allow the chief room in your heart to any thing below God; or if you was never humbled for your difpofition to choofe his rivals in preference to him; it is a fad evidence that you have no prefent intereft in God himfelf; and what have you to do at his table?

8. What think you of your own part of the covenant? Are you heartily willing, through his grace, to be his people? We call it your part of the covenant; not as if you were to perform it by your own ftrength; far lefs as if your performance of it was the condition of God's performing his part. Chrift, your Surety, has fulfilled the whole condition of the covenant;

* Pfal. xlviii. *ult.*

nant; and therefore, confidered as God makes it with you, it has no condition at all. But it is your part of the covenant, inafmuch as, by your acceptance of the covenant, you become engaged to perform it, in the ftrength of that grace with which God has engaged to furnifh you; and in the faith that he will effectually " work in *you*, both to will and to do of " his good pleafure." Are you fenfible that you are not your own, and defirous to be fatisfied that it fhould be fo? Are you aiming at a chearful fubmiffion to all the difpofals of God's providence, knowing that he has a right to ufe you as his own? Do you refolve, and through grace endeavour, to employ yourfelf always in his fervice, and to " be to the praife of his " glory?" And are you humbled for all that you feel about yourfelf, of a difpofition to alienate what you had devoted? Then thefe are the genuine marks of his peculiar people, and you are welcome to the table which he has covered for fuch. But if you ftill refufe to *give yourfelves to the Lord;* or, after pretending to do fo, indulge yourfelf in the fervice of Satan, of Mammon, or any other idol or luft; if you allow yourfelf in murmuring at his difpenfations. In a word, if you was never fenfible of a difpofition about yourfelf to revoke the dedication that has been made of you to God, nor humbled before him on account of it; then you are hitherto none of his people; and why fhould you appear among them at his holy table?

9. What think you of the law of the covenant? Do not ftartle at the expreffion. It is very proper, if rightly underftood. It is true, that, in a certain fenfe, the law is the direct reverfe of the covenant of grace;

and

and all who are within the covenant are delivered from the power of the law. But there is another senſe in which they are ſweetly ſubſervient to one another. The law was delivered to our firſt father, in the form of a covenant of works. And, in conſequence of the breach of that covenant, all the poſterity of Adam, in their natural eſtate, are ſubject to the law, as a cruel and rigorous huſband; breathing nothing but curſes and condemnation, becauſe of our diſobedience. From the law in that capacity, every one of God's covenanted people is delivered. But they are not delivered from the law in every form. " We are not without law to God, but under the law " to Chriſt." The law is now grafted into the covenant of grace; and every perſon who gives his conſent to that covenant, conſents alſo to the law, as the rule of his covenanted obedience. As he gives ear to Chriſt as the Prophet, and employs him as the Prieſt of the covenant; ſo he chearfully ſubmits to him as the King of it, and gladly receives the law at his mouth. He makes it his ſtudy to imitate the example of the Head of the covenant; in a regular obedience to every precept of the law; and reſolves, through divine grace, to perſiſt in that courſe, to the end of his mortal life.

We cannot now take time to give you a particular explication of the ſeveral precepts of the divine law: Such explications you have often heard, on occaſions of this nature. But, if you are God's people, you will pay a due regard to all the precepts of both tables; both in your outward life and converſation, and in the inward exerciſe and frame of your hearts. More particularly,

You will ufe every proper mean for attaining, and for growing in the faving knowledge of God; you will not be afhamed to acknowledge him as your God, in any cafe, in any place, or in any company; and, through his grace, you will be concerned to love, fear, obey, honour, and adore him, to believe and truft in him as your God. You will carefully maintain all that religious worfhip which you owe to him, in your clofet, in your family, and in the public affemblies of his people; and will contend, in your ftation, for the purity of all his inftitutions, relative to the doctrine, worfhip, difcipline, and government of his houfe. You will maintain a holy reverence for all that whereby he makes himfelf known; particularly for his written word, for all the titles and attributes that are there afcribed to him, and for all the ordinances there inftituted by him; fuch as oaths, religious vows, and lots. You will practically " call " the Sabbath a delight, the holy of the Lord, ho- " nourable;" and will honour him on that day, not doing your own ways, nor finding your own pleafure, nor fpeaking your own words.

Moreover, all who are God's people make confcience of performing their duty towards their brethren, and towards all men; as the fecond table of the law requires. They reverence their fuperiors, and fubmit to them in the Lord; they love and cherifh their inferiors; they give all due benevolence to their equals; and are patient towards all men. They abhor every thing that tends to take away their own life, or that of their neighbour, or to render it uneafy. They hate the garments fpotted with the flefh; and ftand at the utmoft diftance from all appearances of uncleannefs, cleanness, and all temptations to it. They take every method in their power, lawfully to promote their neighbour's wealth, as well as their own; and avoid carefully all that has an opposite tendency. They habitually " speak the truth in *their* heart; *being* " children that will not lie." And they abhor covetousness, in every form, as gross idolatry.

If these things be in you, and abound, we pronounce you the people of God; and invite you to communion, both with him and with your brethren, at the sacramental table. But if you dare follow an opposite practice, habitually neglecting any known duty, indulging yourself in any known sin, or being unconcerned when you are drawn aside from the way of God's commandments; whether by the temptations of Satan, or by the prevalence of indwelling corruption; if you pique yourself upon your obedience to the precepts of the first table, to the neglect of those of the second; or if you value yourself upon that morality, which consists in external obedience to the second table, in a way of overlooking the obligation that the first table lays upon you to perform your duty to God; if you have not seen yourself a debtor to the whole law, as having broken every precept of it, times and ways without number; or, if you have never been determined to flee to the blood of a crucified Redeemer, as the sole atonement for sin, and the sole ground upon which you expect the pardon of all your transgressions; then you are " yet " in the gall of bitterness, and in the bond of ini- " quity." While that is the case, you have " neither " part nor lot in this matter;" and it shall be at
your

your peril, if you approach the holy table of the Lord.

10. In one word, What think you of that inexhauſtible treaſure of grace and ſtrength which is lodged in the hand of Chriſt, according to the covenant; to be beſtowed upon all the people of God, as their circumſtances require? Are you ſenſible, that of yourſelf you can do nothing in God's ſervice? Do you aim at a continual dependence upon covenanted grace, for the performance of all the duties that are incumbent on you as God's people? Is it in this dependence, that you ſet forward to the duty of communicating; though ſenſible of your own unfitneſs, and inſufficiency for ſuch work? And is it, through grace, your fixed reſolution, always to " go in the " ſtrength of the Lord God; *making* mention of his " righteouſneſs, even of his only?" Then you are within this happy covenant, and may chearfully come forward to receive the ſeal of it. But if you have never been ſenſible, that, of yourſelf, you are incapable of any action ſpiritually good, being dead in treſpaſſes and ſins; if you think yourſelf able to perform the work, in which you propoſe to be engaged, without the aid of divine grace, or by any grace, which you have already received; if you are not willing to be indebted to the grace of God, venting through the imputed righteouſneſs of Chriſt, in the way of the new covenant, for all that you do, as well as all that you enjoy; you are hitherto none of God's covenanted people; 'and you can have no immediate right to intermeddle with this ſeal of the covenant.

Not to detain you longer, Let every intended communicant beware of eating and drinking judgment to himself; by approaching this holy table, either in a way of seeking happiness by the covenant of works; or, by unbelief, refusing to enter within the covenant of grace. And let every person who has said *Amen* to the promise in the text, or is willing now to say *Amen* to it, come chearfully forward to the communion-table, to have the covenant ratified and sealed between God and him; and the most ample security given him, for the everlasting possession of all that is included in the gracious declaration, *I will be to them a God, and they shall be to me a people.*

SERMON V.

The first Promise illustrated.

PART I.

Gen. iii. 15.

I WILL PUT ENMITY BETWEEN THEE AND THE WO-
MAN, AND BETWEEN THY SEED AND HER SEED.

WHEN our first parents were called to account for their sin, God addressed himself first to Adam. When he cast the blame upon his wife, God proceeded to examine her also. And when she accused the serpent as her seducer, he directs his discourse to it. Having thus convicted all the parties concerned in the transgression, he declares the consequences that should follow upon it; to the serpent, to the devil who influenced it; to the woman; and, last of all, to Adam himself, with whose examination he had begun.

The sentence passed against the tempter was dismal indeed. No ray of hope was left him; but he was irreversibly condemned to suffer the due reward of his deeds. It was otherwife with regard to mankind. Though terrible things were denounced againſt us in righteoufnefs; yet a door of hope was fet open before us, which fhall never be fhut while time remains. We were condemned to fuffer a variety of temporal miferies; but " life and immortality *were* " brought to light," and encouragement was given us to look for a happy eternity, by the words recorded in this verfe. This eternal happinefs was not to be enjoyed by all mankind, though they were all to be fubject to the miferies of this life; but only by a felect number, here denominated *the feed of the woman;* whom God would finally deliver from all the direful effects of Satan's power and policy.

And it deferves to be remarked, that this promife is addreffed to the old ferpent himfelf, as a part of his fentence. And thus the revelation of mercy to us is interwoven with the denunciation of wrath againſt our deſtroyer. This may have been the cafe for two reafons: 1ſt, To intimate, that as envy at the happinefs of mankind was Satan's motive for feducing them, fo the eternal gnawings of that fame envy fhould be a principal ingredient in his punifhment. God would place a number of mankind in fuch a ſtate, that he fhould have occafion to envy us for ever; and, by means of that nature which he had attempted finally to ruin, united to the Perfon of the Son of God, a punifhment fhould be inflicted upon him, more terrible than he could have fuffered if he had never drawn mankind into fin. 2*dly*, To allay the terror that had feized our firſt parents upon the appearance of the Judge. While God was paffing fentence againſt the ferpent, Adam and Eve ſtood trembling before him,

expecting

expecting a similar sentence to be past against themselves in their turn. In this sad condition, a ray of hope darted in upon them unawares. God prevented them, as he often does their posterity, " with the " blessings of *his* goodness;" and gave them a revelation of mercy, even sooner than they expected to hear the denunciation of wrath.

This merciful revelation consists of two parts. In the *first*, God denounces a warfare, to ensue betwixt the serpent and his seed on the one part; and the woman and her seed on the other. In the *second*, he foretels a notable victory, to be obtained by the latter party over the former. It is only the first of these, from which we intend a few thoughts at present; as we have it in these words, *I will put enmity between thee and the woman; and between thy seed and her seed.* In which words we may observe the following things.

1. The party speaking, in the pronoun *I*. It was Jehovah himself, in the person of the eternal Son; whom some take to be meant by " the voice of the " Lord God," mentioned in ver. 8. It was now that he began to act in his Mediatory character. He published his Father's will, relative to our salvation, as the Prophet of the new covenant; and, as our King, denounced war in his own name, and in name of all his spiritual seed, against Satan and all the abettors of his interests.

2. The parties spoken of; and here we find " the " company of two armies." On the one side stands Eve, our common mother, and all those of her posterity who should be partakers of like precious faith with her; under the conduct of that illustrious Person,

son, who is called, by way of eminence, *the seed of the woman*. And, on the other side is that *old serpent, who is called the devil and Satan*, at the head of all the forces of the bottomless pit; with whom are confederated all those of mankind who continue to bear the devil's image, and to do his works.

3. We have the disposition of these two parties towards one another. There is a mortal enmity between them; an enmity productive of a war that shall never be terminated, but by the total destruction of one of the parties; an enmity so violent, that the exercise of it has never been intermitted since these words were uttered; nor will it ever be abolished, through the remotest ages of eternity.

4. We have the origin of this enmity; or the spring from whence it arises. God put it between them. *Behold, we shew you a mystery.* The *very God of peace* becoming the Author of a mortal enmity. Satan, by the introduction of sin, put enmity into the hearts of men against God. And God, in the riches of his mercy to us, and in just indignation against the devil, hath put enmity between him and a chosen remnant of our family.

This subject we shall endeavour, through divine assistance, to elucidate in the following order.

I. We shall enquire into the general import of the words.

II. We shall consider, more particularly, whom we are to understand by the seed of the serpent, and by the seed of the woman.

III. We shall speak of that enmity which subsists between these two.

IV. We

IV. We shall consider in what sense it is that God puts this enmity between them. And,

V. Apply the whole.

I. THE words, among other things, plainly import.

1. That, in all futurity, there should be a remarkable aversion between the race of mankind and the whole *genus* of serpents. I am far from thinking that the words relate only, or mainly, to the serpent, literally considered. But I cannot think that they are without any relation to it; more especially, in regard that the preceding words are mainly intended of it. At first, all the creatures were made subject to man; and they all had an attachment to him as their master. And, as the serpent seems to have been remarkable for a sagacity approaching to reason; it is natural to think, that there would be such an attachment between it and its master, as we now see between mankind and some of those animals that are most sagacious and docile. But now, though there are various serpents of the most beautiful appearance and perfectly harmless in their natures; yet mankind have still a natural aversion to every species of these reptiles; and they to mankind. And, in this natural aversion, or antipathy, we have a visible proof of divine revelation, (particularly of that part of it which relates to the origin of evil,) before our eyes to this day.

2. As the words relate chiefly to the devil, who is called *the old serpent;* with regard to him they import, that, when they were spoken, there was at least a semblance or appearance of friendship between him and the woman; otherwise there could have been

no occasion to *put enmity* between them. A real friendship there could not be. The devil had a fixed principle of hatred against mankind. And this it was that influenced him to attempt their ruin. But he disguised his enmity, under a pretence of friendship. As for the woman, she could have no real friendship for Satan; for she knew him not. But what he appeared to be she loved and esteemed. Both she and her husband had acted a part the most friendly to his interests. It was with them, as it still is with all their posterity while in a natural estate. Whatever was their disposition towards the devil, they acted in the very manner in which they would have acted if they had been his hearty friends.

3. That this semblance of friendship could not be broken, nor open enmity introduced between the woman and the serpent, otherwise than by the immediate interposition of the hand of God. Satan had prevailed so far, by his first temptation, that our first parents were confederate with him in his rebellion against his Creator. And so firmly were they attached to his interests, that nothing but the power that made them could draw them off from the confederacy. A disposition to rebel against God was already become natural to them. In the same depraved state is their nature transmitted to their posterity. And nothing can ever make any of us real enemies to Satan's interests, but the efficacious operation of the Holy Ghost.

4. That, notwithstanding all this, an open and avowed enmity should take place between the woman and the serpent. All appearances of friendship should be laid aside, on the one part; and the falsehood of

all

The firſt Promiſe illuſtrated. 187

all ſuch appearances, on the other ſide, ſhould be clearly diſcovered. Thus, though Eve was the firſt ſubject of Satan's kingdom in this world; ſhe was likewiſe the firſt to ſhake off his yoke, and become a ſubject of the Redeemer, who is here promiſed under the deſignation of the woman's ſeed. Though ſhe was the firſt ſinner, ſhe was alſo the firſt ſaint. Not only was this enmity to ſubſiſt between the ſerpent and the ſeed of the woman; it is expreſsly ſaid, that it ſhould firſt be *put between* him *and the woman* herſelf. Thus David's Antitype gave an illuſtrious proof of what he would afterwards do, for the whole flock that his Father had committed to his charge; by ſnatching, in a ſudden and ſurpriſing manner, from the paw of the devouring lion, the very firſt lamb of which he expected to make a prey.

5. That the woman on the one ſide, and the ſerpent on the other, ſhould have each a *ſeed;* who might adhere to the intereſts, and eſpouſe the quarrel of their parents reſpectively. The devil, being a ſpirit, does not propagate his ſpecies by generation. He cannot, therefore, have a ſeed in a literal ſenſe. The words muſt be underſtood in ſuch a ſenſe as may be competent to a ſpirit. They are his ſeed who bear his image; and are partakers of the ſame miſchievous, wicked, and malignant nature with himſelf. As to the woman, ſhe had ſeed in a literal ſenſe; but it cannot be her natural poſterity, as ſuch, that are here intended. Many of them, alas! live and die in the confederacy with Satan; and are chief promoters of his intereſts. Even her firſt ſon, whom ſhe ſeems fondly to have taken for the *ſeed* of the *promiſe*, was ſo manifeſtly of the devil's party, that he *ſlew his brother;*

brother ; and that for no other reason, but *because his own works were evil, and his brother's righteous.* The seed of the woman, therefore, must also be understood in a spiritual sense,—of those who bear the woman's likeness, as being partakers of the same renewed nature that was communicated to her, in accomplishment of this promise.

6. That the same enmity, which should subsist between the woman and the serpent, should be propagated, and continue to subsist between their seeds respectively, to the latest posterity. The old serpent is an enemy to the seed of the woman, as well as he was to herself. No sooner is a child born to her, in a spiritual sense, than he opens his mouth to devour it. And every person who belongs to his seed bears his image in this, as well as in other respects. They always hate the seed of the woman; next to God himself, who is the supreme object of their enmity. And they are always disposed to seek their ruin. If there is any time, when they do not carry their rancour against them to the same height as on other occasions, it is not owing to any change in their disposition; but solely to those restraints that God lays upon them, for ends becoming himself. On the other hand, next to that *abominable thing which* God *hates,* Satan, who is the author of it, is the supreme object of hatred, abhorrence, and enmity, to all the genuine seed of the woman. They are in a state of perpetual warfare against him, and against all the interests of his kingdom. As for the seed of the serpent, though they love their persons, as the workmanship of God, and wish them as well as their own souls, both in this world and in the world to come; yet they are

mortal

mortal enemies to their ways. They hate the image of their father appearing about them. And they cannot but ftand up for God, in oppofition to them, when they fee them doing their father's works.

II. WE proceed to enquire, more particularly, whom we are to underftand by the feed of the ferpent, and of the woman. And,

Firft, As to the feed of the ferpent, they are diftinguifhed into two tribes, or families.

The firft comprehends all thofe wicked fpirits who joined with Satan in his rebellion; and are now joined with him in the fame condemnation. God is called *the Father of fpirits;* becaufe, being himfelf the fupreme, independent, and uncreated Spirit, all other fpirits refemble him in the immateriality and immortality of their natures; as children refemble their father. And on this account, as well as becaufe they bear the image of his moral perfections, thofe angels who kept their firft eftate are called *the fons of God*. On a fimilar account, fallen angels may be called the feed or children of Satan, *the old ferpent*. They all bear his image; are united into one fociety, under him as their head; and honour and obey him, as children do their father. Hence he may be called the Father, as well as the *Prince of Devils*. Perhaps there is no paffage of fcripture where they are exprefsly fo called: But as the enmity againft the woman's feed, which is mentioned in the text, is common to them all; and as they always give their affiftance in the warfare againft them, we cannot but look upon them as here included.

The

The other family of the serpent's seed, contains all those of mankind who continue in their natural estate. What our Lord said to the Jews of his time, may, with the same propriety, be said of all mankind, while they are strangers to the new birth; "Ye are of your "father the devil, and the works of your father ye "will do *." Though they are *the seed of the woman* in a literal, they are the *seed of the serpent* in a spiritual sense. And they may be so called on the following accounts.

1. Because as the natural father is the instrument of communicating existence to his children; so the devil is the author of their existence, considered as sinners. God is, indeed, the author of their being, properly speaking. And their immediate parents are the instruments of communicating to them human nature. But Satan is the author of their sin; he it is that communicated to the whole race, a share of his diabolical nature. As really, sinner, as you partake, through the instrumentality of your immediate parents, in a rational nature, whereby you are distinguished from the beasts that perish; so really do you derive that corruption, which is inherent in your nature, from the devil: and thus you partake of all those malignant qualities, by which he is distinguished from the unsinning angels. And though these qualities may be yet in their infancy, they will assuredly grow up, unless the grace of God prevent it, to perfection. And you shall be distinguished from the *old serpent*, your father, only by having less power, though no less will, to do mischief.

2. They all bear his image; and are as like him as children use to be like their father. Animals of every

---

* John viii. 44.

ry species bring forth others like themselves. The children of men not only partake of the same nature with their parents; they usually have some resemblance, in their dispositions, and in their features, to their fathers, more than to any other man. But never did you see a son bear a stronger likeness to his natural father in the features of his face, than every unregenerate person bears to Satan in his spiritual lineaments. The same enmity against God, and all divine things; the same hatred of the people of God, and the same disposition to seek their ruin, are common to them with him. The same love to sin is interwoven with their nature as with his; the same unsupportable pride; the same implacable malice; the same deceitful and lying disposition; and the same invincible obstinacy in all manner of wickedness. A very black portrait this of human nature in its lapsed state! but not less just than black.

3. They all submit to his authority, and do his work; as our Lord said of the Jews, in the passage lately quoted. Thereby they give to the devil that honour and obedience, which is due from children to their father. God complains of his ancient people, that while they acknowledged him as their father, they refused him that honour which was due to him in that relation. " If I be a Father, where is mine " honour; and if I be a Master, where is my fear *?" But Satan has no reason to complain, in this manner, of his children. Perhaps they deny him in words, and profess to be children of another family. This he values not; it is no way inconsistent with the law of his house. But they all confess him uniformly in
their

* Mal. i. 6.

their works; and declare themselves his children by doing his will. They do not all honour him in the same manner; for he has many pieces of work to do, and he gives a different employment to every different member of his family. But they are all employed willingly in his service, and thereby prove themselves to be his children.

4. In a word, They may be called his seed, because they are the natural and legal heirs of his inheritance. He can inherit nothing but consummate misery, in consequence of the curse pronounced against him, and recorded in the preceding context. This is not more justly due to him than to us. And every sinner of mankind shall as surely possess it, through all eternity, as he shall; unless they are prevailed with to quit his work, and leave his family. Hear the tremendous sentence that shall, in a little, be past against every impenitent sinner, from the supreme tribunal of the great Judge of all the earth, " Depart " from me, ye cursed, into everlasting fire, prepa- " red for the devil and his angels." God will not kindle one furnace for devils, and another for damned men; but the same unquenchable fire shall eternally consume them both. Let me, therefore, take occasion, now to intreat every sinner before me, " in " the bowels of Christ Jesus," to leave that cursed family. " Come out from among them, and be ye se- " parate. Touch not, *any more*, the unclean thing; " and God shall receive you." Consider the immense difference between inheriting eternal life, and eternal death; between " dwelling with devouring fire, " with everlasting burnings," and possessing " that ful- " ness of joy *that is at God's* right hand for ever- " more:"

" more;" between the fellowship of saints and angels, singing the praises of God, in the presence of their incarnate Redeemer; and the company of devils and damned men, howling, gnashing their teeth for rage and despair; gnawing their tongues for intolerable pain; and cursing God, themselves, and one another. Are you not convinced that the difference is great beyond conception? Sure I am, you will think so one day. " Hearken, *therefore*, O daughter, and " consider, and incline thine ear; forget also thy fa- " ther's house, and thine own people; then shall the " King," the King of glory, the King eternal, immortal, and invisible, " greatly desire thy beauty."

Secondly, With regard to the seed of the woman, they all belong to one family; yea, they are all members of one and the same body. Like Saul and Jonathan, they are *loving in their lives*, and *death* itself cannot *divide* them. They also shall have all the same dwelling; and shall, for ever, be blessed in the possession of the same inheritance. Yet there is a twofold seed here promised to the woman, both inimical to Satan's interests; though they are neither his enemies in the same degree, nor are they capable to prosecute their enmity with the same success.

1. The Lord Jesus Christ, who is also the eternal Son of God, is the seed here promised to the woman. That the words relate chiefly to him, is manifest from the following clause. *It*, or rather, " He shall bruise " thy head; and thou shalt bruise his heel." The words accordingly have been always understood, both by Jews and Christians, as referring to the Messiah. Now Christ may be called the seed of the woman on a twofold account.

(1.) In regard that he is the feed promifed to the woman. In this fenfe he is likewife called the *feed of Abraham*. The promife to Abraham was expreffed in the fame general terms as this; yet an infpired Apoftle limits it to Chrift. " Now, to Abraham and " his feed were the promifes made : he faith not to " feeds, as of many; but to thy feed, as of one, which " is Chrift*." Now, if Chrift was called *the feed of Abraham*, in a fenfe peculiar to himfelf; though the promife was fo expreffed as to include, in a certain refpect, all the peculiar people of God, who defcended from the loins of Abraham; why may not Chrift be here called the *feed of the woman*, in a fenfe that excludes all but himfelf; though there is likewife a fenfe in which the promife may and ought to be extended to many others, as we may fee in a little? Chrift, then, is that illuftrious perfon, who is chiefly intended in this promife. And in him it had its primary and moft remarkable accomplifhment.

(2.) In regard that he was miraculoufly conceived by a woman, without the intervention of a man. In thefe words, there was a dark intimation of what was afterwards more clearly foretold by Ifaiah : " Behold, " a virgin fhall conceive, and bring forth a fon; and " fhall call his name Immanuel †." Chrift is, indeed, often called *the Son of man;* becaufe he was an actual partaker of human nature, and was defcended really, though miraculoufly, from Adam. But he was the *feed of the woman*, fo as to be the immediate feed of no man. Adam ftood, in the covenant of works, as the reprefentative of all his natural pofterity. Confequently, all who defcend from him,

in

in an ordinary way, are conceived and born in fin. But it was neceffary that Chrift fhould be born without fin; and therefore his human nature was produced in a miraculous and extraordinary manner; being formed of a part of the virgin's body, fanctified and prepared for that purpofe, by the immediate agency of the Holy Ghoft. Thus, as in his divinity, he was *without mother;* fo in refpect of his human nature, he was *without father;* a complete antitype of Melchifedec, *after* whofe *order* he was *made a prieft.*

2. The promife includes all believers in Chrift; or all thofe of mankind, who, being delivered from Satan's power, and brought out of his family, are no longer of the number of the *feed of the ferpent.* Thefe may be called the feed of the woman, on the following accounts.

(1.) Becaufe they are the moft excellent part of the woman's natural feed, and therefore may be put for the whole. So they are exprefsly called by the fweet finger of Ifrael, perfonating Chrift himfelf: " My goodnefs extendeth not unto thee; but to " the faints, the excellent ones of the earth." All others have fo far degraded themfelves, and act fo inconfiftently with their rational nature, that they fcarcely deferve to be called men. Hence the people of God are often fpoken of in Scripture, as if they were the only men in the world. You may take for an example, that faying of Chrift himfelf. " I, if I " be lifted up, will draw all men unto me *." He does not mean all the race of mankind in general, or every individual of that family; but all thofe, who, by

* John xii. 32.

by divine grace, are enabled to act up to the character of men. All unbelievers are degenerated fo far, that they are even below the beafts that perifh. They are the children of the devil; and therefore are unworthy to be called the *feed* of the *woman;* efpecially after fhe was delivered out of Satan's family.

(2.) Becaufe they are the followers of her laudable example. Abraham is called *the father of the faithful;* becaufe he fet an eminent example of ftrong faith; which they endeavour, through the grace of God, to imitate. And, on the fame account, all believers are called the children of *the faithful Abraham.* In like manner, Eve was called *the mother of all living;* not fo much becaufe fhe is the natural mother of all that partake of temporal life, but rather becaufe fhe was, in a fpiritual fenfe, the mother of all who partake of a fpiritual life. Accordingly, the name *Eve* was given her, not on the back of her creation, but on the back of the publication of this promife. Adam and his wife had already felt themfelves fpiritually dead; and they looked for nothing but death in all the extent in which it was threatened. But, to their unfpeakable joy, " life and immortality " *were* brought to light," by this promife. A *feed* was promifed to the *woman,* who fhould be reftored to the poffeffion of that life which had been forfeited by the fall. As a pledge of the full accomplifhment of the promife, the *woman* herfelf was already made alive in Chrift. Thus, though fhe was the firft that died, fhe was alfo the firft that was raifed from the dead, in a fpiritual fenfe. Hence God himfelf had called the remnant who were chofen to eternal life

her

her feed; and Adam, who had been witnefs to all this, calls her their mother. Thus he gave her fuch a name as might, at the fame time, put her in mind of this promife ; and likewife of the honour God had done her, by making her the firft partaker of that new life which was revealed in the promife. This is the fenfe in which fhe was " the mother of all li- " ving." And in this fenfe all the fpiritually living are her feed.

(3.) Becaufe they alfo are the children of the promife that was made to the woman. Though Chrift was the feed promifed, in a fenfe peculiar to himfelf, they alfo are included in it. The fame promife that fecured God's fending " forth his Son made of a wo- " man, to bruife the head" of the ferpent ; fecured the exiftence of a number among thofe that fhould fpring from the woman, in an ordinary way, who fhould be partakers of the fame life that was now communicated to her; and fhould have the fame *enmity* put between them and the ferpent, that was now put between Eve and him. Thus, in relation to this firft promife made to Eve, as well as in relation to that which was afterwards made to Abraham, all Chriftians may fay to one another, as Paul to his Galatians ; " We, brethren, as Ifaac was, are children " of the promife*."

(4.) Becaufe they are all united to Chrift, the prime *feed* of the promife ; and made one in law, yea and *one fpirit* with him. Being vitally joined to Chrift, they are members of his body; and are fpoken of, both here and elfewhere, as if they were not diftinct from him. Though the word here ufed is fingular,

* Gal. iv. 28.

singular, and therefore is strictly applicable to no more than one individual; yet this individual, this one seed, comprehends both Christ and the church, and every genuine member of the church. It comprehends him as the Head, and them as the members of the same mystical body. For, " as the body is one, " and hath many members; so also is Christ," the promised *seed* of the *woman*.

III. We come now to speak of that *enmity* which subsists between these two parties. And all that we shall say concerning it, shall be comprized in the following observations.

1. This enmity is mutual and characteristic. Every person, who belongs to either society, has a rooted and natural enmity against the other party. Satan has an inexorable enmity against all the children of the promise. Next to God himself, there is nothing that he hates so much. And in this, as in other respects, all his children bear his image. On the other hand, Christ has such an enmity against Satan and his interests, that he became the seed of the woman, purposely to *bruise* his *head*, and *destroy* his *works*. And all his members, being under the influence of the same spirit, are of the same disposition. You cannot find a surer mark by which to try yourselves, to which of these societies you belong, than by considering who is the object of your enmity. If you have a real and predominant enmity against Christ, or against his people, for their likeness to him; or if you never felt the workings of such an enmity within yourself, so as to be humbled for them in the sight of God; you are yet among the serpent's seed. But if you have a sincere

cere hatred against sin, and are disposed on every occasion to set yourself in opposition to the interests of Satan's kingdom; then you belong to the seed of the woman, and may be welcome to partake in their provision.

2. There is a great difference between the manner in which this enmity works, and is exercised by the one party, and by the other; owing to the difference of their respective characters. The serpent and his seed have malice and envy for their ruling principles; and their enmity against the seed of the woman is still influenced by these. They hate their persons, as well as their manner of life. They are enemies to their happiness, as much as to their way. And nothing will satisfy them but their utter destruction. But the seed of the woman bear the image of the God of love. As they love God above all other objects, they not only love his image wherever it is, they also love and esteem all the workmanship of his hands. Even the devil himself they hate not, considered as one of God's creatures; nor do they take any pleasure in his misery, for itself. As to his seed among mankind, they are so far from being enemies to their happiness, that they wish them as well as their own souls. As an evidence of this, they pray to God for them; and they take every opportunity to do them good. Yea, when they find it necessary to oppose and fight against them in their sinful courses, they do it in such a manner as to shew that they wish well to their souls.

3. This enmity is, on both sides, altogether implacable. Satan can never be reconciled to any of the seed of the woman. He may put on a semblance of friendship,

friendship, as he did with the woman herself, and make many fair profeſſions. But beware of trusting him. He aims at nothing but your ruin. And if once you comply with his suggeſtions, you ſhall quickly find that he is not the friend that he pretends to be. The fairer his profeſſions are, the more dangerous are his deſigns. The ſame is, in a great degree, the caſe with all his ſeed. On the other hand, the ſeed of the woman can never be reconciled to ſin, nor to the interests of Satan's kingdom. They may, for a time, be ſo far prevailed upon by temptation, and by the remainders of corruption within them, as to take part, in a great degree, in promoting the interests of Satan's kingdom. But the principle of enmity againſt ſin, which the grace of God has implanted in them, ſhall never be totally eradicated; nor will they, knowingly and deliberately, take part with the ſerpent and his ſeed, in their oppoſition to Chriſt or his cauſe.

4. This enmity is effective. It lies not dormant in the heart, but appears in the whole tenor of the life and actions. Satan is abſolutely reſtleſs in ſeeking opportunities to wreak his malice upon the people of God. And if his ſeed are not equally buſy, it is not owing to themſelves. At any rate, their enmity will conſtantly appear by ſhunning the company of the oppoſite party; aſperſing their characters, injuring their perſons, or making their godly converſation an object of ridicule. And they who are the ſeed of the woman, will ſhew themſelves enemies to the ſerpent's interests; by conſtantly aiming at the mortification of ſin in themſelves; by teſtifying againſt it in others, as they are called in providence; by earneſtly praying

ing for the overthrow of Satan's kingdom; and by using their influence, in their several places and stations, to accomplish it. In vain do you pretend to be of this seed, unless this be the case with you. To no purpose is it that you profess to be enemies to sin, and to the kingdom of Satan, if you do not exert yourselves in maintaining a constant warfare against it. All they who are neutral in this war, are really on the serpent's side; for, thus saith the great Captain of the opposite army, " He that is not with me " is against me; and he that gathereth not with me " scattereth *."

5. This enmity is not always exercised in the same manner, nor is it always effective in the same degree. Armies, though always in the field, to oppose one another, are not always engaged in battle, nor always under arms. So it is in this warfare. Sometimes the serpent would seem to have laid aside his venom, and to live at peace with the *woman's seed;* so do his children. This takes place, either when they mean to lull the opposite party into security, or when God is pleased to shorten their chain, and restrain them from doing mischief. On the other side, the great *seed* of the *woman* appears, at some times, not only to make little opposition to the enemy's interests, but even to give up his own kingdom and interests into Satan's hand; till he sees it for his own glory to take the field. " Then *he* arises, as one that awaketh out " of sleep; and as a mighty man that shouteth by " reason of wine: He makes his stroke to fall upon the " hinder parts of his enemies, and puts them to a per- " petual shame." As to the followers of Christ, they
are

* Mat. xii. 30.

are zealous in his cause, or apparently neutral, or even active in promoting the enemy's designs; according as the grace of God in them, or their own corruption prevails.

6. In a word, This enmity shall be everlasting. Not only while time remains, but even so long as these two families exist, they will still be mutual enemies to one another. The war, indeed, which proceeds from that enemy, will not be eternal. It will be terminated in a manner the most glorious for the one party, and the most ignominious for the other. The seed of the woman shall finally prove victorious, and shall enjoy an everlasting triumph. The serpent and his seed shall all be taken captive by the conqueror, and shut up in the prison of hell; where they shall be effectually cut off from any opportunity to prosecute the war. But even when matters have come to that issue, this *enmity* will still remain. The people of God, though perfectly delivered from all the effects of Satan's malice, will be as much enemies to sin, and all the works of the devil, as ever. And both devils and wicked men will eternally continue enemies to Christ and to his people, to such a degree, that the rage of this enmity, together with the want of any opportunity to gratify it, shall undoubtedly constitute a great part of their torment.

IV. The last thing proposed, on the doctrinal part of the subject, was, To speak of the origin of this enmity, or to enquire in what respect God *put* it *between the serpent* and the *woman, and between* his *seed and her seed?* And here we must previously take notice

of

of the two or three things following, to prevent miſtakes.

1. Strictly ſpeaking, God is not, nor can be, the author of any kind of hatred or enmity. *God is love.* It is inconſiſtent with his nature to be at enmity with any of his creatures, unleſs that enmity begins on their ſide. When he made the world, an univerſal harmony ſubſiſted among all the creatures. As none of them were enemies to their Maker, ſo none of them were enemies to one another. God's law is a law of love. Love is the fulfilling of it. And he cannot approve, far leſs be the author of any thing that is contrary to his own law. Enmity was none of God's creatures, nor would it either have been produced or approved by him, if ſin had not introduced it into the world; at the ſame time that it produced an object, with which God himſelf behoved neceſſarily to be at enmity, and all that were friends to him.

2. The enmity that has been ſpoken of was already begun on the one ſide, when this promiſe was made. Satan's enmity againſt God, and againſt man, becauſe God's favourite, was the ſpring of the firſt temptation; and conſequently of our firſt ſin. There was, therefore, no need that God ſhould put enmity into the heart of Satan, againſt the woman or her ſeed; becauſe he was already full of it. Already had his enmity prompted him to plot, to attempt, and in all appearance to effect the final ruin of the whole human race. All his pretenſions of friendſhip were no more than a cloke for his enmity. Therefore,

3. All God's agency, in putting this enmity between theſe two parties, is confined to one of them. In accompliſhing this promiſe, he made no change

upon the serpent, nor does he make any upon any of his seed. He only leaves them to the perverse bias of their own nature; and permits them to exercise that *enmity* which they had before. It is far otherwise with the other party. Immediately before this promise was made, the woman herself was joined in confederacy with the serpent, against God and against herself. All her seed, the great Head of the body alone excepted, come into the world in the serpent's family. They have the same enmity against Christ and his followers, that is natural to all that cursed brood. And they would continue for ever to exercise it, if God did not accomplish the promise; by actually putting enmity between them and that family to which they formerly belonged.

4. The truth, relative to the rise of that enmity, is shortly thus. Satan having cast off subjection to God, became a mortal enemy to him. This was the first enmity that ever subsisted in the world; and it was introduced by sin, or rather by Satan, when he became a sinner. This was necessarily followed by enmity on God's part, both against sin, and against the author of it. He could not be other than an enemy to sin, without violating his holiness. Nor could he be a friend to Satan, without denying his justice. Satan's enmity against God had made him an enemy likewise to mankind. It was their duty to have repelled his enmity, and followed their Creator's example, in being enemies to him. But they knew him not; and therefore were imposed upon, by his pretensions of friendship, so far as to be joined with him in his enmity against God. But God, having a purpose of mercy for a number of mankind, resolved

resolved to bring them off from this confederacy; to turn away their enmity from him, as well as his wrath from them; and to direct it against their destroyer, who should have been the first object of it. This is it that he here promises to do; and his agency, in this matter, consists in the following things.

(1.) He pulls off the mask under which the serpent and his seed endeavour to hide themselves, and discovers to the other party, that they are really influenced by enmity, both against God and against them. As Satan pretended friendship for our first parents in the first temptation, so he does with all their posterity. He persuades them that happiness is to be found in the way of sin; and, as a friend, he pretends to advise them to seek it there. We are naturally disposed to believe him; and hence are all the vain attempts that are made to find happiness in sensual and sinful objects; and all the mournful disappointments that these produce. But, as God enabled our first parents to see through the vanity of Satan's first pretence; so, when he comes to deal graciously with any soul of their posterity, he discovers the cloven foot, under the assumed robes of light. He lets them see, through all his pretences, that enmity by which their seducer is influenced; convinces them, that happiness is not where he directs them to seek for it; and that he only allures them with the prospect of happiness, that he may bring them into irretrievable ruin. Thus the danger of sin is made to appear, and the deceitfulness of all its promises. And this is among the first things that the Spirit of God does for any person, when he comes to open their eyes; and to turn them from darkness unto light, and from the power of Satan unto God.

(2.) He discovers also the hatefulness of the devil's character, and of the characters and dispositions of his seed; and then represents them to us, not only as our enemies, but likewise as proper objects of our enmity. The leading branch of Satan's character is sin; so it is also with all his seed. This is like the black hue of the Ethiopian's skin; every part of the man, and every thing about him, is affected by it. And such is our folly, that we are in love with our blackness; and consider the purity and holiness of God as the most hateful thing. So far has Satan imposed upon us, that we may be said to love himself, while we are so deeply in love with that which constitutes the chief branch of his character. But this charm the Spirit of God breaks, in the day of the Mediator's power; and discovers the filthiness and odiousness of sin, as well as the danger of it. The person then sees the devil, and his whole family, to be really hateful and abominable, by reason of the sin that is about them. And, as he is sensible that himself has been a member of that family, and equally black and deformed as the rest; like Job, he " abhors " *himself*, and repents in dust and in ashes."

(3.) He implants in the soul a principle of sincere and rooted enmity against sin, and against all the interests of Satan's kingdom, both within him and without him. Such is the depravity of our nature, that no conviction in the understanding, relative to spiritual things, will have any proper influence, either upon our heart or upon our actions; unless a principle is implanted in the will, corresponding to the conviction

tion that is in the underſtanding. Our will and affections often carry us away, in direct oppoſition to the dictates of the underſtanding; ſo that, though we ſee and approve what is good, we really and practically follow that which is evil. And one main difference between the common operations of the Spirit, and thoſe which are ſaving confiſts in this; that the former produce convictions in the underſtanding only, while the others produce a correſponding difpoſition in the will. In relation to the ſubject under conſideration, it is not enough that we be convinced of Satan's enmity againſt us; and of the real hatefulneſs of ſin, which conſtitutes his character. All this we may be, and yet continue friends to ſin, and ſo to Satan, in our hearts. And it really would be ſo, if the Holy Ghoſt, after carrying his work thus far were to proceed no farther. But, having convinced the perſon of its hatefulneſs, he implants in his will a difpoſition correſponding to that conviction; and ſo enables him to hate it indeed. Thus he efficaciouſly *puts enmity* into the perſon's heart againſt ſin, againſt its author, and againſt its abettors, as far as they are ſuch; and thereby brings him in among the number of the *woman's ſeed*. The man is then in a condition to ſay from the heart, as ſays David,—" Do not " I hate thoſe, O Lord, that hate thee? Am not I " grieved with thoſe that riſe up againſt thee? I hate " them with perfect hatred. I count them mine e-" nemies *."

(4.) He directs, aſſiſts, and ſucceeds, the endeavours of the woman's ſeed, againſt the intereſts of Satan's family; ſo that they have ſome competent effect.

* Pſal. cxxxix. 21, 22.

effect. Such is the disproportion between us and our adversary, both in respect of strength and cunning, that our enmity against him could have no effect at all, unless God were to assist us in the prosecution of it. But it is he that " teaches *our* hands to war, and " *our* fingers to fight." This he does so effectually, that the " feeble *becomes* as David, and the house of " David as God; as the angel of the Lord before " him." Thus it comes to pass, that there is not a dwarf of all the woman's seed, (and God knows there are many silly dwarfs among them,) who is not a formidable enemy to the serpent's interests; and can perform exploits, that all the power and policy of hell are not sufficient to defeat. Such is the necessity of this assistance, and such its effect upon the Christian, that he who was incapable, when left to himself, to wield a weapon, but lay panting, and almost breathless, among the slain; shall be seen to rise up, in a moment, under the influence of this assistance, to fight " like a giant refreshed with wine,*and to* put to flight " *whole* armies of the aliens."

V. We are now to conclude with the following inferences from the subject.

1. We have here a dismal view of the condition in which all mankind are by nature. We are all the seed of the serpent,—the children of the devil; of the same hellish dispositions with our father, and employed in the same work. We are all under the same curse, and liable, every moment, to have our condition made equally desperate as his, by the final execution of our sentence. " Look," Christian, " to the " rock whence *you* was hewn;" and take an affecting
view

view of " the hole of the pit whence you was digged." Let this fill you both with ſhame and ſelf-abhorrence in the fight of God; and with unutterable gratitude to him who has wrought your deliverance, and made you what you are. " Conſider this and be afraid, ye " that forget the Lord." You are, by nature, a child of the devil; condemned, by the curſe of God, to the ſame puniſhment that he bears; engaged, under him, in a warfare againſt Chriſt, and againſt all the intereſts of his kingdom; and liable, every moment, to be *bruiſed* to pieces under the feet of him who is the prime *ſeed* of the *woman*.

2. We may hence learn, how much of the ſerpent's diſpoſition remains even about the *ſeed* of the *woman*, as long as they continue in this world. They who are the ſeed of the ſerpent, though they may have ſomething about them that bears a reſemblance to the diſpoſitions of the *woman's ſeed*, can never have the ſame diſpoſitions with them, in the ſmalleſt degree. But the ſeed of the woman, excepting only their glorious Head, were all the ſeed of the ſerpent once. The ſerpent's diſpoſitions are not inſtantaneouſly deſtroyed, nor the oppoſite habits perfected. Till death, the Chriſtian continues an antipode to himſelf. There are in him two oppoſite principles, continually at war with one another. There is in him an old man, a child of the devil, who wages war againſt the *ſeed* of the *woman;* and there is a new man, a child of God, on account of which the perſon may be called one of the *woman's ſeed;* and this is ever at war with the ſerpent and his abettors. According as the one or the other of theſe prevails, the ſame perſon is active in promoting the ſerpent's in- tereſts;

terests; or fights against him, under the banner of Christ, by turns. Let Christians mourn before God, not only in consideration of what they once were, but likewise on account of what they still are; while they cannot but feel in themselves the workings of that enmity against Christ, which are owing to the imperfection of *the seed of God abiding in* them; and to the remainders of the serpent's seed continuing about them.

3. We may see to what it is owing, that the serpent's disposition does not continue in its full force about all the posterity of Adam. It is owing to nothing about ourselves; to no endeavours of our own; to no improvement of our natural powers; nor to any thing that any creature did, or possibly could do for us; but solely to him who, according to this ancient promise, has put enmity between the seed of the serpent and that of the woman. As soon may a literal serpent be changed into a man, without any miracle, as a person may be translated from the one of these families to the other, by any thing inferior to creating power. Be not high minded, Christian, but fear and be thankful. Who maketh thee to differ from another? or what hast thou, that thou hast not freely received? And if thou hast received it, wherefore shouldest thou boast, as if it had been originally thine own, or a thing of thine own procuring?

4. We may see who they are that are like to be welcome guests at the Lord's table, on the ensuing solemn occasion. They, and they only, who have had a personal experience of the accomplishment of this promise in their own souls; into whose hearts God has put an irreconcileable enmity against sin, and against

all

all the interests of Satan's kingdom. The sacramental feast was provided, by the great representative of the woman's seed, for those that belong to the same family with himself. And surely it is not fit that any person should sit down at his table, with a principle of enmity reigning in his heart against the Master of the feast, and against all his friends. Wherefore, " let " a man examine himself, and so let him eat of that " bread and drink of that cup." Has God discovered to you the vanity and falsehood of all those suggestions, by which Satan would allure you to take part with him against Christ? Have you seen sin as a hateful thing, and been determined to hate it, and fight against it, wherever it is? Have you a sincere aversion at the devil's work? And is it your sincere desire to take Christ's side, in the war that he has so long been carrying on, against the dragon and his angels? Then, and then only, are you the woman's seed, and fit for a seat among them at the communion-table.

5. We may here see the duty of all who are, or sincerely desire to be, among the seed of the woman. Make a diligent search for all the remainders of the serpent's disposition about yourself. Mourn deeply before God for all of that kind that you discover. And give yourself no rest till it be mortified and destroyed. Let your enmity against the devil's interests be inflamed, by the sight of what abets those interests in your own soul. Give no quarter to any of the enemies of the seed of the woman within you. And make no truce with those without you. Continue to " quit yourselves like men, and fight" for the interests of the Redeemer; without being discouraged, either by the sense of your own weakness, or the power, the

policy, the numbers, or the apparent succefs of the enemy. Be careful, in the mean time, to maintain such a love to your glorious Head, and towards one another, as may influence you to mind the interests of the family, and to exert yourselves in maintaining and defending them. And be ever on your guard, against all the wiles, and all the fiery darts of the enemy. However indolent you may be, either in the offensive, or in the defensive part of the war; you may be assured, that, on the other side, no opportunity will be lost of doing you a mischief.

6. In a word, We may see what is the duty and interest of all that still continue in the devil's family. Be intreated, sinner, to "forsake your father's house, "and your own people;" and give over to prosecute your enmity against Christ or his followers. You cannot *harden* yourselves *against him and prosper.* All the efforts of your enmity against him will fall back, with redoubled violence, upon your own head. And he whom you now serve, and honour as your father, will be so far from pitying you, that he will help forward the affliction. Willingly shall he act as the executioner of the Mediator's vengeance upon you. And then you shall find, to your irreparable cost, that, however much you befriended his interests, he never was a hearty friend to you; but was, indeed, your greatest enemy. Why should you continue in league with your mortal enemy; and maintain a warfare against one who is able to befriend you in every case, and as willing as he is able? Christ is so far from wishing you evil, or having any pleasure in your destruction, that his heart bemoans you, when he sees you
running

running headlong to your ruin, and defpifing all his gracious invitations to the contrary; as he bemoaned Jerufalem of old, faying, " O Jerufalem, Jerufa-" lem, how often would I have gathered thee, as a " hen gathereth her chickens under her wings!" Oh! perfift not in giving him occafion to add concerning you, as he did concerning her children, " and " ye would not."

SERMON VI.

The first Promise illustrated.

PART II.

Gen. iii. 15.

—HE SHALL BRUISE THY HEAD, AND THOU SHALT BRUISE HIS HEEL.

MANY are the wars and fightings that sin has introduced into the world. Often is their success precarious, and their event doubtful. But there is one great warfare, which, though not properly the fruit of sin, is undoubtedly the consequence of sin's entrance; the event of which was infallibly determined before ever a blow was struck: I mean the war mentioned in the preceding part of this verse; between the woman and her seed on the one side, and the serpent and his seed on the other. Of this war, the final issue is foretold by God, who could not be mistaken, in the words of this text. Both parties must suffer in the course of the war; but the sufferings of the one are not comparable to those of the other.

The firſt Promiſe illuſtrated.

ther. The one ſhall have his *head*, which is the centre of life and motion, *bruiſed* to pieces; but the other ſhall eſcape, with only a ſlight *bruiſe* in the *heel*.

Having very lately ſpoken from the firſt part of this verſe, in the hearing of many preſent; we obſerved, that the whole verſe is part of what God ſaid to the devil, who ſtill continued to occupy the body of the ſerpent, as he had done while he managed the temptation that iſſued in Adam's fall. In it God foretels what ſhould be the continual ſtate of matters, between Satan and the unhappy family which he had now ſeduced, and what ſhould be their final iſſue. Accordingly, we took notice of two things, generally contained in the verſe: *viz.* 1. A denunciation of war, in theſe words, *I will put enmity between thee and the woman, and between thy ſeed and her ſeed*. Of this we have ſpoken already; and ſhall reſume nothing. 2. A promiſe of victory to one of the contending parties over the other, in the words of this text: *It ſhall bruiſe thy head, and thou ſhalt bruiſe his heel*.

In the words, in general, we have two things.

1. The ſucceſs of this war, on the ſide of the woman and her ſeed, in theſe words, *It ſhall bruiſe thy head*. And here, more particularly, we have four things noticeable.

(1.) An agent ſpoken of, in the pronoun *it*. In the original language, the word is maſculine; and ought to be tranſlated *he*, as it is in the margin of ſome of your Bibles. It manifeſtly refers to the *ſeed* of the *woman*, mentioned in the preceding clauſe; eſpecially to the great Head of that body, the Lord Jeſus Chriſt. Papiſts, indeed, render it *ſhe;* and underſtand

derstand it of the Virgin Mary. How she comes to be spoken of in this place, how she is spoken of in the masculine gender, and how she bruised the serpent's head, let the friends of that interpretation determine.

(2.) An action ascribed to him, or foretold, as about to be performed by him: *He shall bruise.* The word signifies to grind, or to break into very small pieces, as grain is broken under the millstone. It signifies also to darken, or hide in obscurity. Both senses may be here included. The substance of the meaning is, that Satan shall be shut up in utter darkness, by the power of Christ; and there subjected to a punishment, that may be compared to the grinding of one's head between two millstones.

(3.) The object of this action, or what it is that Christ shall so bruise,—*thy head.* Satan, that old serpent, being a spirit, has no bodily parts. But, as he still possessed the body of the serpent, God speaks to him as if he were literally that animal; and means, that he should be reduced, in the issue of this war, to a situation comparable to that of a serpent whose head is crushed to pieces.

(4.) The certainty of the event, exprest in the word *shall.* God himself has foretold it, and he cannot be mistaken. It is more than a bare prediction. It contains a positive engagement, in which the faithfulness of God was pledged, that it should be so.

2. We have the success of the war on the serpent's side. Here we have the same particulars as in the former. The agent here is the devil, exprest in the pronoun *thou.* The action is the same as before, that of *bruising.* But the object is very different—*his heel.*

heel. What the feed of the woman was to fuffer from the ferpent was as little, in comparifon of what the other fhould fuffer from him, as a bruife in the heel is, compared with a grinding of the head. The certainty of the event is the fame here as in the former. God could as certainly foretel what Satan fhould do to Chrift, as what Chrift fhould do to him; for, though the devil does nothing in obedience to God, he can do nothing without his permiffion. And he knew as well what he would permit to be done, as what himfelf would do.

The Jewifh Targum gives a very different reading of the words; which, though it may not exprefs the true fenfe of them, deferves not to be wholly overlooked. The word which we render to *bruife*, they underftand of *remembering.* And the words *head* and *heel*, they take figuratively, as referring to the beginning and end of time. They read the whole thus: ' It fhall remember thee in the beginning; and ' thou fhalt remember it in the end.' And they give us a paraphrafe of the text, to the following purpofe: ' Thou haft given a memorable ftroke to the family ' of mankind, in the beginning of time, at the com-
' mencement of the war. This the feed of the wo-
' man fhall not forget; but fhall take ample venge-
' ance for it in the end; by reaching thee fuch a blow ' as thou fhalt not be able to forget through all eter-
' nity.'

This, like all the reft of what we have in this and in the preceding verfe, may be applied literally to the ferpent itfelf, and to the fpecies that proceeded from it. It is well known that a ferpent's poifon lies in its head; and that the readieft method of deftroying it it is by a ſtroke upon that part. Hence men uſually ſhew their natural averſion to ſerpents, by endeavouring to cruſh their heads, either by treading upon them or otherways. It is alſo manifeſt, that, as ſerpents go upon their bellies, when a man walks upright, nothing but the lower parts of his body can be within the reach of the ſerpent's bite. And nothing is readier to happen than that the perſon who treads upon the ſerpent's head, and cruſhes it, ſhould, in that inſtant, receive a wound from it in the heel.

But, though the promiſe may have an accompliſhment, even in this reſpect; yet this is far from being the only thing, or the main thing here intended. The words, in their principal meaning, refer to Chriſt and the devil; and the other is included only as an emblem of this. It is as if God had ſaid, ' I tell thee, ' Satan, that a fixed antipathy ſhall take place between ' the race of mankind, and that ſpecies of creatures ' which thou haſt made uſe of as the inſtrument of their ' ſeduction; as an emblem of that mortal enmity ' which I will put between thee and a part of the ' woman's poſterity. And the ordinary iſſue of that ' antipathy ſhall likewiſe be a fit emblem of the iſſue, ' that matters ſhall come to, between thee and the re-' preſentative of that holy ſeed. For, as men ſhall ' take every opportunity of deſtroying ſerpents, by ' cruſhing them in the head; and as they who do ſo ' ſhall be in danger of receiving a wound in the foot, ' from the very animal which they kill; exactly ſo ſhall ' the conteſt iſſue between him and thee.' *He ſhall bruiſe thy head, and thou ſhalt bruiſe his heel.*

One thing farther deſerves to be taken notice of, before we leave the general explication of the words. I mean,

The first Promise illustrated.

I mean the inversion of the order, in which the two contending parties are mentioned in the beginning of the verse. In the declaration of war, the serpent and his seed are first mentioned, and then the woman and her seed; intimating that the war began on that side: and that they, being the aggressors, were to be accountable for all the blood that should be spilt on both sides; and for all the other consequences of the war. But in this text, where the issue of the contest is foretold, this order is inverted; the seed of the woman is first mentioned, and then the serpent. This may intimate, that, in the course of the war, Satan shall be proved inferior, both in power and wisdom, to the *Captain of our salvation;* that he who was last in taking the field shall prove himself the best warrior, and shall leave the field victorious and triumphant.

The sense of the text, as thus explained, may be summed up in the following proposition.

Though, in the grand contest between the serpent and the woman's seed, the former may be so far successful, as to bruise the heel of his opponent; yet God has given assurance, that the principal success shall fall on the other side: for the seed of the woman shall bruise the serpent's head.

The method to be prosecuted, in speaking a little farther from this subject, shall be, through divine assistance,

I. To consider a little the general import of the words.

II. To enquire, more particularly, what we are to understand by the *bruising* of Satan's *head*.

III. To

III. To speak of his *bruising* the *seed* of the woman in the *heel*. And,

IV. To conclude with some improvement.

I. In general, the words seem to import the following things, among others.

1. That the great warfare, mentioned in the preceding part of the verse, shall be chiefly managed by two individuals. The words used in the text are all in the singular number. Neither are they of a collective signification, as those in the preceding clause. It is true, that on each side there is a great army. All the forces of hell are on the one side, assisted by all those of mankind who continue in their natural estate. And on the other side, all the *nations of them that are saved*, with whom are joined all the hosts of elect angels; who, being *ministring spirits* to the church, in that capacity fight against the powers of hell. It is also true, that every person, in either army, bears his part in the contest; and every one shall be involved in the general issue. On the one part, all who fight under the old serpent, take part with him in *bruising* the *heel* of the *seed* of the *woman;* and every one of them, if they finally continue on that side, shall have his *head bruised*, as well as their leader. On the other part, every person belonging to the *seed* of the *woman*, and warring under Christ's banner, is enabled to take part in *bruising* the enemy's *head;* and every such person may lay his account with having his *heel bruised*.

But still the warfare is principally carried on by the leaders of the opposite armies; and the success on either side is chiefly owing to them. This is, in some degree, the case in every war. The conduct of the general is usually of as much importance as the courage of the army. It is peculiarly so here. In this war, the generals not only conduct their respective armies, and direct their motions; but, contrary to the ordinary course of things, they fight with their own hands more than all their soldiery. These two armies have each their champion, as it was with Israel and the Philistines, in the *valley of Elah*. And the two generals are the two champions, who, like David and Goliath, decide the controversy by single combat.

While David was engaged with the Philistine giant, both armies stood aloof as mere spectators, and neither took part in the struggle. But when the engagement was hotest between the two parties mentioned in this text, all the hosts of the uncircumcised assisted their champion; and joined in the fierce assault that was made upon David's antitype; while all the armies of the spiritual Israel shamefully deserted their colours, left their Captain engaged with all the combined forces of hell and earth, and turned their backs and fled! " Then *he* looked, and there was none to " help; *he* wondered;" and justly might he wonder, " that there was none to uphold. Then *his* own arm " brought salvation unto *him;* and *his* fury it upheld " him." Like Eleazar, the son of Dodo, " He smote " them till his hand was weary; and the people re- " turned after him, only to spoil."

And as Christ had the principal hand in managing the war, so he was principally concerned in all the events of it. None of his followers ever had their *heel bruised* by the enemy, in the same manner as his

was.

was. All that they suffer by the malice of hell, or by the enmity of the serpent's feed on earth, is nothing compared with what he suffered. And, on the other hand, none else ever gave such a *bruise* to the serpent's *head* as he did. None ever bruised it, none ever will bruise it, in any proper sense but himself. His people are conquerors only in him, and through him. It needs must be so. As he fought the main battle without assistance, the honour of the victory can, in no part, belong to any other.

Your glorious head, believer, encountered all the powers of darkness for you, when there was none to stand by or assist him. He submitted to have his *heel bruised*, in such a manner, that, to all appearance, the wound seemed incurable; and, without any assistance from you, he so *bruised the head* of his adversary, that he ceases to be a formidable enemy to you. Even this is not all. In every conflict of yours, he still goes forth on your head. Though all his brethren forsook him in the time of his conflict, he does not revenge their ingratitude, by turning his back upon them when the enemy assaults them. He is always present with you, he assists you in the prosecution of your warfare; and will finally *bruise Satan*, and all your other adversaries, *under your feet shortly*. See, therefore, that your dependence be always upon him, and of all the advantages that you gain over the enemy, see that you give him the glory.

2. The words import, That the principal aim of the combatants in this war, is to *bruise* one another. This is the success of the war on both sides; each party is successful in proportion as his opponent is bruised. The word, as you heard, signifies to grind, or break into

into very small pieces. And surely this must amount to utter ruin; as it is impossible for any person to live and be active, after this is the case with him. The old serpent hath his name in the Hebrew tongue *Abaddon**. The word signifies *destruction;* and so it is rendered, Job xxvi. 6. and elsewhere. He has this name, because the destruction of the whole human race, and especially of the seed of the woman, is his continual aim. In the beginning, he attempted the destruction of the whole family of mankind, in the person of the first Adam, and effected it. In like manner, he attempted the ruin of all the seed of the woman in the person of the last Adam; and, doubtless, he thought he had accomplished it, when the representative of the family was " brought to the dust " of death." In all his attacks upon particular members of the family, he aims at nothing less than their total ruin; and he would accomplish it, if the *Captain of* their *salvation* did not protect and defend them. On the other hand, it was Christ's errand in our world to destroy the devil and his works. And, however feeble their endeavours be, nothing less is aimed at by all that belong to that family. You are none of the *seed* of the *woman*, if any thing less can satisfy you than the total ruin of Satan's interests, both within you and without you.

3. That the success of the war should be various; sometimes one party prevailing, and sometimes another. In all wars, it is ordinary that battles are lost, and battles won, on both sides. Even in the same engagement, sometimes one party has the advantage, and sometimes the other. So it is here. Sometimes the

* Rev. ix. 11.

the serpent is suffered to carry all before him; his point seems almost gained; and there wants but one step to complete the ruin of the woman's seed on earth. At other times, Satan is bound, his interests in the world quite sunk, and the opposite family is almost undisturbed and triumphant. At some times, God " beats down *Christ's* enemies before his face, " and plagues them that hate him," according to his promise. And at other times, " the right hand of his " enemies *is* set up, and his adversaries made to re- " joice. The edge of his sword *seems* to be turned; " and *he does not* stand in the battle *." Look around you, Christian, and see. Alas! is not this the sad case in the day wherein we live? But you need not be too much cast down on this account. The enemy can have no success, unless the Captain of your salvation sees meet to permit it. Nor can any success be wanting to his followers, unless he sees it fit, that, for the time, it should be wanting. Never does the serpent prevail to the *bruising* of Christ's *heel*, unless when such bruising may contribute, both to the health of the body, and to the final *bruising* of the enemy's *head*.

4. The words import, That both parties might prove successful in some degree; at the same time, and by the same means. As a literal serpent is never more ready to sting a person in the heel, than when he is just about to crush its head, by treading upon it; so never is Satan more ready to bruise the heel of Christ, or of his followers, than when he is just about to receive a remarkable bruise in the head. And never has the *seed* of the *woman* given more remarkable

---

* Psal. lxxxix. 23. comp. v. 42, 43.

markable wounds to the enemy, than when he had juſt received an wound from him. Indeed, every degree of ſucceſs that Satan has enjoyed, has always coſt him ſo dear, that there is nothing that he has more reaſon to be afraid of than apparent ſucceſs. In his very firſt attack, before any war was proclaimed on the other ſide, he ſucceeded ſo far, that the bruiſe appeared incurable, and really was ſo to any created ſkill. Yet this very ſucceſs has expoſed him to all the bruiſing that ever he has ſuffered, or will ſuffer, from the *ſeed* of the *woman*.

But never was there any inſtance of this ſo remarkable as that which took place in the great and deciſive engagement that Chriſt had with him at his death. Then did the ſerpent *bruiſe his heel*, in a manner that he never could accompliſh before; nor ever ſhall accompliſh again. So eminent was his ſucceſs, that his antagoniſt lay dead at his feet. And yet this very ſucceſs hurt him more than any thing elſe that ever took place ſince the war commenced. Then was his *head bruiſed* in ſuch a manner, that he ſhall never recover the blow. Quickly did the *ſeed* of the *woman* riſe triumphant, even from the grave itſelf. *His* wound, though mortal, was ſpeedily healed. But at the ſame inſtant in which he received his wound, he gave another to his enemy, that ſhall never be healed through all eternity. Even *by death*, he overcame, " he deſtroyed him that had the power " of death; that is the devil. *Having* ſpoiled prin- " cipalities and powers, *he* made a ſhew of them o- " penly, triumphing over them in his croſs *." This

Vol. II.   P   is

* Col. ii. 15.

is the great event to which this text primarily refers; and in which it had its most remarkable accomplishment.

But it has an accomplishment in other cases also; and that in respect of the mystical body, and even of particular members of it. Hence is that remarkable saying of the Apostle Paul, " In all these things, we " are more than conquerors, through him that loved " us *." He is speaking of the various bruisings that the followers of Christ may suffer from the serpent and his seed; by which they are even " killed all the " day long, and counted as sheep for the slaughter." Yet he says not, *after all these*, or *notwithstanding all these;* but *in all these things we are conquerors.* Intimating, that even while we suffer we conquer; and that the enemy's success against us is the very means whereby we become victorious and triumphant over him. Take comfort all ye that are of the seed of the woman; such shall be the effect of all the success that Satan obtains, either against you or against the church in our day. Our glorious Captain may suffer him to prevail, till his heel be bruised in a cruel and shocking manner; but soon shall that old serpent find reason to repent his success. As Joshua caused Israel to flee before the men of Ai; so that the enemy said, " They are smitten down before us, as at the first ;" when all his design was to draw them into the ambuscade, and make their destruction inevitable; so does our Jesus, who is Joshua's antitype, in relation to the serpent and his seed. They may glory in their success for a little season; but their success shall prove the

---

* Rom. viii. 37.

the means of their eternal deftruction. Every wound which they inflict upon the *heel* of Chrift, or upon the loweft member in his body, fhall iffue in a proportionable wound in their own *head*.

5. The words import, That the victory fhall at laft be decifive on the fide of the woman's feed. A perfon whofe heel is bruifed may live and keep the field, even while he fmarts by his wound: And he may expect to fight after it is cured. But one whofe head is grinded, muft needs be totally ruined. And when this is the cafe with a whole army, there can be no occafion for any further ftruggle againft them. Such fhall be the final condition of the ferpent and all his feed. Though that party was the firft to take the field, the other fhall be laft on the field. None of them fhall efcape from the hand of the illuftrious conqueror. Eternally fhall they be bruifed in the *wine-prefs of the wrath of* Almighty God. They fhall be an everlafting prey to the *worm* that *dieth not*, everlafting fuel to the *fire* that *is not quenched*. Thus fhall the *feed* of the *woman* accomplifh his whole aim; he fhall fully execute all that he undertook to his Father, and all that he intended, when he entered upon the war. Every one of his followers fhall *fee* all their *defire upon* all their fpiritual *enemies*. Yes, believer, a troop may overcome you, and overcome you, and overcome you again; but you fhall be fure to overcome them all at the laft. You fhall reap, through eternity, the happy fruits of your victory; and, which is incomparably more, of the victory that your glorious Captain has obtained in your name. And eternally fhall you fing " the fong of Mofes and " the Lamb;" in an uninterrupted celebration of that

triumph,

triumph, which, in communion with your Captain, you shall enjoy, as the result of the victory; when those " enemies whom you see to-day, you shall see " them no more for ever." Comfort ye one another with these words.

II. We proposed to consider, more particularly, what we are to understand by the bruising of Satan's head. And, I apprehend, it includes the following things.

1. The total destruction of his works, and the abolition of all the effects of his infernal policy. A bruise in the head, you know, has a tendency to impair one's reason, and make him think and act like a fool. And if the bruise is severe, it totally destroys the exercise of reason. The devil's works are the fruits of his internal policy. And as the works of God must be supported by the same power and wisdom, that appeared in their creation; so the works of the devil must be supported by the same hellish policy that was exercised in their production. When his head is bruised, his policy is defeated, himself befooled, and rendered incapable of exercising his malicious cunning, either for accomplishing new works, or for the maintenance of the former. These works, of consequence, must fall into ruin; they shall be totally abolished. This was one great end of Christ's appearing in our world, in the character of the seed of the woman. " For this purpose was the Son of God manifested, " that he might destroy the works of the devil *." And this he will accomplish so effectually, that no effect of the devil's policy shall remain, which may

disturb

disturb or interrupt the happiness of any of that family of which he is the head.

The principal works of the devil are two: sin, which is his main work; and misery, which always accompanies or follows upon it. These Christ will destroy, and completely deliver all his people from them both. Yes, believer, from both these shall you be completely delivered in a little. The miseries that sin has brought upon you, the temptations with which you are now liable to be assaulted, shall, in a few years at most, give way to ",a far more exceeding " and eternal weight of glory." And, which is still more comfortable, sin itself, which is the just cause of all your sufferings, shall be totally routed out, and finally removed from you. And you shall continue, through eternity, as free from all the fruits of Satan's policy, as if none of them had ever been felt, or seen, or even heard of among you. You shall be as happy as your nature is capable of, and as holy as happy. Both in holiness and happiness, you shall be perfectly conformable to what Christ now is, at the right hand of God.

2. It includes the abolition of his power; that he may no longer be capable to hurt any of the *seed* of the *woman*. A serpent, you know, has its sting in its head; there is all its poison lodged. When once its head is sufficiently bruised, no person has any thing to fear from its bite. To this condition, Christian, shall your grand adversary be reduced in a little. Yea, such is his condition already; to such a degree, that it is beyond his power to do you any real injury. The great bruise that his head received when Christ triumphed over him in his cross, has utterly disabled

him from hurting any of the *woman's seed*. He is not yet completely slain, though the wound which he has received is mortal. Another bruise is wanting, to complete his destruction: and it shall be given him at the second coming of Christ. Till then, he may terrify you with his hissings; but he cannot touch you with his envenomed sting. He may wound you in the heel; but the wound shall never prove mortal. To you, even the serpent's bite shall be found medicinal. Why then should you be afraid of such a harmless enemy? What can you have to fear from the impotent threats of a foe reduced to such a condition? Indeed, your glorious Captain has secured you from any real injury from any quarter. *And who is he that will harm you, if ye be followers of that which is good* *?

3. The mortality, and incurableness of his wound. A wounded heel may be cured, even though it be much bruised, or bit by a serpent; if the cure is timeously undertaken, and properly managed. But the most skilful physician can never cure a person, whose head is grinded to pieces. So, all the injury that Satan ever did, or ever shall do, to any of the *seed of the woman*, admits of reparation; and it shall be repaired accordingly. But what Christ has done against him, and will further do in a little, is beyond all reparation or remedy. Christ himself, though his wound was the most dreadful that ever was made by the serpent's teeth, was completely cured in three days. And now he is for ever above the reach of his attempts. And his followers shall be cured as effectually, if they are not as speedily. *There is balm in Gilead,*

* 1 Pet. iii. 13.

The first Promise illustrated.

Gilead, Christian, and *a Physician there*, by whom every *wound of the daughter of* thy *people* shall be healed. But he who has undertaken your cure has himself infused poison into the serpent's wound; and who can pretend to extract it? Ah! sinner; to the same dreadful and desperate condition shall you be reduced in a very little, if you continue in the serpent's family, and take part with him in his warfare against Christ; till he be provoked, in just indignation, to *bruise* you also *in the head*. For, as all the *seed* of the *woman* are here included, together with their glorious Representative, on the one side; so all the *seed* of the *serpent* are included, along with their father, on the other.

4. The bruising of Satan's head includes the total destruction and overthrow of his kingdom. A kingdom without a head is incapable of subsisting. When a prince is slain in battle, his armies routed, and all his friends and abettors killed or taken captive; then a revolution in his kingdom is the necessary consequence. His dominions become the property of the conqueror; and all his power and authority is at an end, whether it was lawful or usurped. So, when Satan's head shall be finally grinded, the ruin of his kingdom shall be the necessary concomitant of his own; and all his usurped authority shall be made to cease. In this world, we often see the kingdom of Satan in a flourishing condition; his government cheerfully submitted to by the greatest part of mankind, and his interests thriving apace on every side; while the kingdom of Christ is proportionably low. But it shall not always be so. It is but a little, when the kingdom of Satan shall be ruined with himself;

and

and all the apparent glories of it shall become so many jewels in the Mediator's crown. His sin turned him out of his place in heaven; and the final punishment of his sin, executed by the hand of the woman's illustrious Seed, shall eternally dispossess him of all his usurped power upon earth. All his subjects shall either be brought to do homage to Christ, as his willing people; or else shall be for ever involved in the destruction of their master and his kingdom. Yea, that no vestiges may remain of his tyrannical usurpation, even the world itself, in which it was exercised, shall be burnt up. " Nevertheless, we look for new hea-
" vens, and a new earth; wherein dwelleth righte-
" ousness *."

III. It was farther proposed to enquire what we are to understand by Satan's *bruising* the *seed* of the *woman in the heel*. And I think the expression holds forth to us the following things.

1. That a suffering lot was appointed by God for all the seed of the woman, during the continuance of the war; at least during their continuance in the field. A wound in the heel may be very painful, especially when it arises from the biting of a serpent. Yea, it would be mortal if it were not skilfully managed. So would the wounds given by Satan to the followers of Christ. As it is, they are often very painful and uneasy. The first-born of this honourable family was himself " a man of sorrows and acquainted with grief," during his continuance in a state of warfare. From the womb of his mother to his grave, he was not a moment exempted from sufferings of one kind or other,

other. *He was wounded*, believer, *for* your *tranſgreſſions; he was bruiſed for* your *iniquities; the chaſtiſement of* your *peace was upon him*, that, *by his ſtripes* you might be *healed*. All his life through, we never hear of his ſmiling, but once of his rejoicing in ſpirit; though frequently of his weeping and being grieved. Towards the cloſe of his life, we hear him complaining, (and it was not uſual with him to complain); complaining in an agony, that forced the blood from every pore in his bleſſed body: " My ſoul " is exceedingly ſorrowful, even unto death!" And ſhall it be thought hard that his younger brethren alſo be partakers of a ſuffering lot, for the ſhort time of their continuance in this fighting world? Is *the ſervant* in any reſpect *above his lord?* Or can *the diſciple* expect to fare better than *his maſter?* Nay, Chriſtian, it is highly reaſonable, that through manifold tribulations you muſt enter into the kingdom. No warrior expects always to ſleep in a ſound ſkin. But be not diſcouraged on this account. You ſhall enter into the kingdom at laſt, when your warfare is accompliſhed. And your ſufferings, as they are a prelude, ſhall likewiſe prove an aggravation of your glory. " If you ſuffer with Chriſt, you ſhall alſo " reign with him." If, in this world, you are abaſed as he was; in the world to come, you ſhall alſo be glorified together.

2. That in the ſufferings, both of Chriſt and his followers, the old ſerpent and his ſeed ſhould have a principal hand. No doubt, trials are inflicted upon Chriſtians by the hand of God immediately, without the inſtrumentality of Satan or his agents. And we are ſure that the principal part of what Chriſt ſuffer-

ed

ed was from the hand of his God and Father. " It " pleased the Lord," not only to suffer him to be bruised by Satan, but also " to bruise him" with his own hand. He bruised him in a much severer manner than all the devils in hell, and all the devil's offspring on earth could ever have done. But it is likewise certain, that Satan and his instruments had a very deep hand in Christ's sufferings. The Jews were of their " father the devil;" and how much he suffered from them the whole gospel history evinces. And as for Satan himself, what agency he had in his sufferings is manifest from the two great instances which the scriptures have on record. First, he detained him in the wilderness forty days, hungry, thirsty, restless, and exposed; and all that while harrassed him with the most dreadful temptations. And then, towards the period of his suffering state, *the prince of this world came* upon him *like a ravening and a roaring lion;* though he could not but know that he *had nothing in* him. Thus did he *bruise his heel* in the estate of his humiliation.

The same is the case with all the friends of Christ. Some of them have suffered very much from the seed of the serpent in this world. They have " had trial " of cruel mockings, and scourgings; yea, of bonds " and imprisonments. They were stoned, they were " sawn asunder, were tempted, were slain with the " sword: they wandered about in sheep-skins, and " goat-skins; being destitute, afflicted, tormented." Though they were persons " of whom the world was " not worthy," they were yet constrained to " wan- " der in deserts, and in mountains, in dens, and in " caves

" caves of the earth*." Though they do not all suffer in the fame degree with thofe worthies, of whom the Apoftle fpeaks in the words now repeated; there is none of them but has fomewhat to bear from the hands, or at leaft from the tongues of wicked men. Becaufe they " are not of the world, but *Chrift hath* " chofen them out of the world; therefore the world " hateth *them.*" As to the devil, who is the " god of " this world," he is continually bruifing them in the heel; not only by violent temptations, and terrifying fuggeftions, which he throws into their minds; but even by bodily afflictions, and various kinds of outward troubles, which he is often permitted to lay upon them. Perhaps Satan's agency in thefe matters is often more than is apprehended, either by the afflicted themfelves, or by others around them. Had we been informed of Job's diftrefs, or only heard his own account of it, without being told what hand the devil had in it, we would fcarcely have afcribed fo much of it to him as the Scriptures do. And who would have thought that the poor woman, who was bound by an infirmity for eighteen years, was bound all that time by Satan, if our Lord had not plainly told us fo much †? Surely he is not lefs malicious now than in former ages; nor have we reafon to think that he is lefs concerned in the afflictions of the people of God now than he was then.

3. It imports, that, notwithftanding all thofe fufferings that the feed of the woman fhould be called to endure, their main interefts fhould ftill be fafe. The heel, you know, is far from the fprings of life; and therefore, a wound in the heel is far from being fo
dangerous

* Heb. xi. 36,—38.   † Luke xiii. 16.

dangerous as one in the vital parts. All the bruises that ever were, or ever shall be inflicted by the *old serpent*, upon any of the *woman's seed*, shall never destroy their spiritual life, nor hurt the dearest interests of their immortal souls.

With regard to Christ himself, it was expressly promised, and as expressly accomplished, that, notwithstanding all his sufferings, a " bone of him *should* not " be broken." The bones, you know, are the strength of the natural body. And this circumstance might be intended to signify, that even in death the strength of Christ was not diminished. While his body lay breathless in the tomb, he still had an *arm like God*. His own power was sufficient to raise his dead body from the grave ; and even to protect all his disciples from the rage of the enemy, while his human nature continued in the state of the dead. Thus, his main concerns were not affected by all that he suffered from the enemy's hand. His almighty arm was not shortened, his divine glory was not diminished ; nor was that infinite blessedness which he enjoyed in the bosom of his eternal Father, before all worlds, in the smallest degree impaired. But even when his *heel* was so *bruised*, that his humanity bled to death ; his divine life, glory, power, and felicity, were the same as they were and shall be, from eternity to eternity.

Something similar to this obtains in the case of all the followers of Christ. You have a mortal part, believer, which Satan may bruise, and, for a time, destroy; but you have likewise an immortal part, that he cannot injure. There is a life, a breath in your nostrils, that he may perhaps extinguish ; but you have a life, " hid with Christ in God," which he can in nowise impair. He may disturb the peace of your conscience; but he cannot interrupt your peace with God. He can mar your comfort; but he can never destroy the grounds of it. He may disturb the exercise of grace in you; but the habits he shall never be able to root out. Your covenant with God, your union to Christ; and consequently, your interest in all that fulness which God has laid up in Christ's hand, are things to which the power of your enemy shall never be able to extend. Thus, as it was with the head, so shall it be with every one of the members; God will " carefully keep all his bones, *so that* not one " of them shall be broken *."

4. This part of the text, especially when compared with the other, imports, that no wound which the serpent, or any of his seed, can inflict upon any of the opposite party, shall ever prove mortal. They shall all be completely cured, and the person restored to spiritual health and soundness. If a serpent's bite were so near the vitals, as that the poison might insinuate itself into the mass of blood before a remedy could take effect; the cure would be difficult, if not impossible. But, when the wound is only in the heel, the remedy may be applied before the poison can have time to diffuse itself; and there may be hopes of a cure, especially when the serpent is at hand with its head bruised. It is remarkable, that, if some naturalists may be believed, the most certain and effectual cure for the bite of a serpent may be found in the head of the animal itself; so that the person who has trode a serpent to death, and, in so doing, has been wounded by it in the foot, has a remedy at hand;

and,

* Psal. xxxiv. 20.

and, if he knows how to ufe it, may expect a cure. Whatever be in this as to literal ferpents, we are fure it obtains in the cafe under confideration. If Chrift had not bruifed the ferpent's head, when his own heel was bruifed by him, his bite would ftill have been mortal, both to Chrift himfelf, and to all the reft of the woman's feed. But now, from the effectual bruifing of Satan's head, arifes a fovereign and infallible cure for all that have been ftung by him; if they have but grace to ufe it. And with this grace all the genuine feed of the woman fhall be endued; and fo fhall infallibly be cured. Your wound, Chriftian, may fmart now, and fmart feverely; but you may reft affured that it fhall never prove mortal. You faw how fpeedily your glorious Reprefentative was cured; and you fee in what a happy and glorious condition he now is at his Father's right hand. Perhaps your cure may not be fo quickly accomplifhed as his was—And no wonder. The ferpent's poifon, with which he was not capable to be affected, has diffufed itfelf through your whole conftitution. And the cure muft be performed by degrees. But cured you fhall be, as certainly as Chrift is, and as completely too. And, together with him, you fhall enjoy fpiritual health and beauty; *i. e.* immortal happinefs and glory; in a much higher degree than you would have been capable of if your *heel* had never been *bruifed*.

IV. It is now high time to conclude with fome improvement of the fubject. It affords us the following inferences for our information.

1. There

1. There is no reason to be alarmed at the devil's success, in his opposition to Christ, and to the interests of his kingdom in our day. Alas! "the enemy has "entered *God's* heritage; he has defiled *his* house, "and laid *our spiritual* Jerusalem on heaps!" He has wounded the heel of Christ in a dreadful manner. He has diffused the poison of a delusive and contentious spirit, in that part of Christ's mystical body which is on the earth; so that it is bruised into a thousand pieces! this is a lamentation, and ought to be for a lamentation. But let us not sorrow as they that have no hope. Nor let us be alarmed, "as if some strange "thing had happened to us." This is the very thing that we had reason to look for. It was foretold as early as the day on which Adam fell. And, instead of being a breach of God's promise, it contains an exact fulfilment of it. When, therefore, we see the promise fulfilled in one part of it; let us not indulge an apprehension that God has forgotten the other. The work of Christ is going on, as really as the work of the devil. It is one great design of those ordinances which you, this day, enjoy; and of the whole dispensation of grace, which the goodness of God has still continued with us; that, by means hereof, Christ may carry on his great work of *bruising* the serpent's *head*. And he is here present to accomplish it. He will accomplish it in the soul of every believer. And it is but a little when he will accomplish it in the church, so as to make the enemy repent his success. Every bruise which he now gives to the *heel* of Christ, shall, ere long, be found a *bruise* in his own *head*.

2. Neither have we reason to be surprised at the malice which is continually vomited up by wicked men,

men, against Christ, his truths, his ways, his ordinances, or his people. They would act wholly out of character, and against their very natures, if it were otherwise. They are the seed of the serpent, and partake of his malignity. How can they be other than enemies to the seed of the woman? They naturally join with their father in bruising the heel of Christ and his followers—But wait a little. " The " day of vengeance is in *his* heart; and the year of " *his* redeemed is *as good as* come." He *will render* vengeance to his enemies; *and* an abundant *recompense to* all his *adversaries.* When Satan's own head shall be finally bruised, then all the heads of his seed shall be bruised along with his. And eternity itself shall never see their wound cured. " Consider " this and be afraid, ye that forget the Lord;" and maliciously set yourselves in opposition to Christ or his little ones. Consider it and repent of your conduct, " lest *he* tear you in pieces, when there *shall be* none " to deliver."

3. Nor is there any reason to stumble, or take offence at the cross of Christ. The people of God have no reason to be discouraged; nor have sinners any reason to stand at a distance from Christ or his cause, on account of any sufferings that are annexed to Christianity. There are but two classes, you see, into which all mankind are divided; and each of them may lay their account with *bruising.* If you belong to the seed of the woman, your heel may be bruised by Satan; but if you continue among the seed of the serpent, your head shall be bruised by Christ. It is true, these last enjoy a whole head in this world, while the heel of the others is sore bruised. But, in the other

ther world, their heads shall be bruised incurably, while those shall enjoy everlasting health and cure. Now, let the greatest enemy to Christ in this company be judge, which of the two is the most eligible condition. Whether is it better to have your heel now bruised by Satan, and afterwards healed by Christ; or to have your head bruised by Christ, in a manner that shall admit of no cure, through all eternity? Did not Moses, then, make a wise choice? And is it not your greatest wisdom to imitate him in it; "choosing rather to suffer affliction with the peo-
"ple of God, than to enjoy the pleasures of sin for a
"season?"

The subject might likewise afford us a variety of marks, to assist us in that self-examination, which is so necessary, as a preparative for communicating work. The seed of the woman are the only persons who have an immediate warrant to partake in this solemn feast. And they may be distinguished from the serpent's brood by the following marks; from each of which arises a question, fit to be asked at his own conscience by every intended communicant, and by every other person in this assembly.

1. What views have you of your natural estate, while a child of the old serpent? They who are still in Satan's family may apprehend that they are *Abraham's seed, and were never in bondage.* They think all is well with them; and therefore, as the manner of their *species* is, they *closely shut their ear* against every alarm, and refuse to flee for their life. But the seed of the woman are sensible, that, by nature, they are children of wrath, even as others; and that they

they juftly deferve to " fall into the condemnation of " the devil."

2. How do you go? A man is eafily diftinguifhed from a ferpent, becaufe he walks upon his legs, while the other goes always upon its belly. The feed of the woman have been raifed up, by divine grace, from the grovelling ftate in which they were by nature. They look up to heaven, in the exercife of faith, and of fpiritual meditation. Their hearts and their converfations are in heaven; and thitherward they travel, under the conduct of the elder brother of the family. But the ferpent's race continue to move on their belly. Their very hearts are in contact with the earth that is under them. And their eyes are never lifted towards heaven, unlefs it be to fuck a prey into their mouth; for God is not in all their thoughts.

3. What is your food? Do you feed upon the duft of the earth, or upon the corn of heaven? The ferpent's feed will ever be known by their licking the duft. They look for all their happinefs in the things of a prefent world. Some expect it in riches, fome in honours, fome in pleafures; fome in one thing and fome in another, but all in duft. But the feed of the woman have an appetite for the bread of life. They *hunger and thirft after* the imputed *righteoufnefs* of their Redeemer; after that inherent righteoufnefs which conftitutes their likenefs to him, and after God himfelf as their only fatisfying portion. The flefh and blood of the Son of God is the provifion, that, of all others, is moft fuited to their appetite. And this is it upon which they defire to feed, when attending divine ordinances.

4. Who

4. Who is the object of your enmity; Christ and his members, or Satan and his seed? Methinks I hear many saying, ' God forbid that I should entertain enmity in my heart against Christ. I hate the devil, and all his infernal crew. Surely I have this mark of the seed of the woman, if I have no more.' But be not too hasty. You are still an enemy to Christ, if you love or desire any thing else more than him; if you have no love to him, nor any enmity against Satan's interest, but what you always had; or if you do not shew your love to Christ, and your hatred of the devil's works, by the whole tenor of your behaviour. For all the seed of the woman have had enmity against Satan's interest, and love to Christ and his image, put into their hearts by the grace of God. And they evidence it by a constant endeavour to keep the commandments of Christ; and to fight strenuously against all the interests of Satan's kingdom, within them and without them.

5. To whom do you wish success in this war? Or how are you affected with the news of Christ's victory? It is Christ's great design to destroy the works of the devil; to abolish sin, and restore holiness in the world. Now say, as in the sight of God, whether would you desire that sin should be abolished in you, or would you rather wish that the law of God were abolished, and you allowed to sin on with impunity? If this last is the case, you are a child of the devil still; for all the seed of the woman are disposed to rejoice in Christ's victory, as a sure pledge of their complete deliverance from all the works of the devil.

6. In a word, Which are you most afraid of, and most studious to avoid; the bruising of your head, or

of your heel? This may feem a ftrange queftion to be put to rational creatures. And it would be a very needlefs queftion if all men were difpofed to act rationally. But who expects reafon among the ferpent's offspring? They are fo foolifh as to be really more afraid for their heel than for their head. They dare not be followers of Chrift, for fear of prefent fufferings. But they are not deterred, by the profpect of eternal mifery, from following the devil in a courfe of fin. They look only at the things that are feen, and at the prefent time; of the things that are not feen, and are eternal, they have no proper conception. But the feed of the woman are all refolved, cheerfully to fubmit to have their heel bruifed in the caufe of Chrift; in the faith, that, together with him, they fhall eternally lift up the head.

The fubject affords, moreover, a variety of ufeful directions to the Chriftian; both in relation to the work of this day, and in relation to all the duties of his after life.

As to the work of this day; you have come hither, intended communicant, with a view to commemorate the accomplifhment of this promife, by the hand of your glorious reprefentative, when he bruifed the ferpent's head at his death. And have you not good reafon, while you do fo, to mourn for all the bruifes that ever you have given to the heel of Chrift; either while you continued in the devil's family, or fince you was taken into the family of the woman's feed? While you was a ferpent, it was no wonder to fee you joining with all the reft, in oppofition to Chrift and his members. Yet even this fhould be matter of humiliation to you. Much more fhould you be grieved, becaufe, because, after you became a follower of Christ, instead of aiming your blow at the serpent's head, as duty and gratitude required, you should still continue to aim it at the heel of Christ. Come forward, therefore, to the Lord's table, in the exercise of humiliation; and let us eat the passover with " unleavened " bread, *and* bitter herbs." Come forward, likewise, in the exercise of mortification. Let it be your present aim to fetch a mortal blow at all the interests of Satan's kingdom within you. Bring forth every beloved lust; and let it be " hewed in pieces," like Agag, " before the Lord." Thus will you concur with, and promote the ends of Christ's death, while you cast in your mite to keep up the remembrance of it. In a word, Look forward, in the exercise of faith and hope, to the day when this promise shall have its full and final accomplishment. He who bruised the serpent's head, at the same time that his heel was bruised by him on the cross, shall come again to our world, in a little, to give him the final crush; and effectually to cure all the bruises that ever any of his followers have suffered in the combat. And be assured, that the Captain of your salvation will not leave his work unfinished; but will assuredly do all that for you, and against your spiritual enemies, *that he hath spoken to you of.*

As to the business of your after life, consider yourselves always as soldiers in the field. Lose not any opportunity of annoying the enemy, or of hurting his interests. Keep always on your armour, that armour which the Spirit of God has recommended *. Watch continually,

* Eph. vi. 13,—18.

continually, and be on your guard againſt the wiles of the enemy; he is a ſerpent, and ever noted for his infernal ſubtilty. Make no peace, no truce, no parley with him; nor give any quarter to any of thoſe luſts that are the abettors of his intereſts within you. Say not a confederacy with his ſeed, in any of their evil ways. Chooſe them not for your companions, nor ever truſt to their pretenſions of friendſhip. You are a *people* that ſhould *live alone*, and ſhould not ſuffer yourſelves to " be reckoned among the nations." Depend always upon your glorious Captain; that he may " teach *your* hands to war, and *your* fingers to " fight." Be always obedient to his orders; keep the poſt that he aſſigns you, and maintain it to the laſt extremity. Be not diſcouraged, though your heel ſhould be bruiſed in the conteſt; but wait patiently, and truſt confidently in him that hath promiſed, and who aſſuredly " will bruiſe Satan," and every other enemy, " under your feet ſhortly."

To conclude, This ſubject evinces how deeply every perſon preſent is intereſted in the work that we are going to ſet about. There ſhall be no mere ſpectators among us to-day. In the great event, which we are about to commemorate, this promiſe had an exact accompliſhment. Then was the deciſive engagement, in which the ſerpent " bruiſed the ſeed *of* " *the* woman in the heel, and he bruiſed *him* in the " head." And as we are all either the ſeed of the woman or the ſeed of the ſerpent; the ſymbolical commemoration of this event ſets before us, as in a glaſs, the object of our fear, or of our hope. Let every perſon preſent, then, take a view of the double

iſſue

issue of this combat. Let the feed of the woman mourn; their champion is " bruifed in the heel; " *and* he was bruifed for *their* iniquities." But let them alfo rejoice; he left the field victorious; having *bruifed* his enemy *in the head*. And he is now enjoying the moft glorious triumph in heaven. Let all the ferpent's family tremble. Your champion, O ye " generation of vipers," has received a mortal wound. His head is grinded; and he is rendered incapable of defending either himfelf or you. If he ftood not, in the day of battle, before " the Captain " of our falvation," how fhall you? Be affured, that, while you continue in the devil's family, you are an object of Chrift's enmity as really as your father is. And if you finally continue in it, your end fhall be the fame with his. Be exhorted, therefore, as you would not wifh to " fall into the condemnation of the " devil;" and to have your head bruifed eternally under the feet of Chrift; to leave the curfed family to which you belong. Caft away the weapons that you have hitherto borne in the ferpent's caufe. Embrace the gracious offers of peace and reconciliation, that are now made you in the name of our triumphant Redeemer. And take up arms, under him, againft your former mafter. He will doubtlefs rage againft you, and threaten you with terrible things, if you forfake his camp; but be not afraid of him. He who now invites you to his ftandard, will protect you with his Almighty arm; fo that you fhall never be hurt, by all that he, or any that take part with him, fhall be able to do againft you. And it is but a little, when he will make *you* alfo victorious over Satan himself, and all that espouse his interests. And you shall eternally share in that triumph, which all the seed of the woman shall obtain, when the contest shall be finally terminated; in the everlasting bruising of the serpent and all his seed, under the feet of Christ. " For he must reign, till all his enemies " be made his footstool."

SERMON VII.

The Invocation; or, *The Church's Prayer for the Influences of the Holy Ghoſt, to qualify her for Communion with Chriſt.*

Song iv. 16.

AWAKE, O NORTH WIND, AND COME, THOU SOUTH, BLOW UPON MY GARDEN, THAT THE SPICES THERE-OF MAY FLOW OUT.

THIS book, as you have had occaſion to hear be-fore, is a ſacred *epithalamium,* or marriage ſong. It was not compoſed on account of Solomon's marriage with any of thoſe women whom he loved; but to celebrate a ſpiritual marriage between one infinitely " greater than Solomon," and a bride apparently more unſuitable for him than any heathen princeſs was for the king of Iſrael. " This is a great " myſtery; but I ſpeak concerning Chriſt and the " church."

In the preceding part of this chapter Chriſt is introduced commending the church, and giving her
aſſurance

affurance of his love in the moſt ample, and the moſt condefcending manner. Among the other fimilitudes, which he ufes for fetting forth her excellencies, as ſhe is adorned and beautified with his falvation, he compares her to a garden, ver. 12. " A garden in- " clofed is my fifter, my fpoufe; a fpring ſhut up, a " fountain fealed." He recals the fame image, in ver. 15. " A fountain of gardens, a well of living waters, " and ſtreams from Lebanon."

With a peculiar eye to this part of his commendatory fpeech, does the church exprefs herfelf, as in the words of this text. For, though fome interpreters have confidered thefe as the words of Chriſt; yet, as there can be no doubt but the church is the fpeaker in the laſt claufe of the verfe, I fee no reafon why we ſhould not confider thefe alfo as her words.

What we have in this verfe is, then, to be confidered, as the whole of her reply to all that Chriſt fays, in commendation of her, in *fifteen* verfes before. A Chriſtian, hearing fuch ample praife, beſtowed by the Prince of life upon a finful worm, cannot help being filled with aſtoniſhment and admiration. It would not be confiſtent with his ſtation, or his character, to deny what his Lord had faid. But, allowing that his foul is a *garden inclofed*, he breaks forth in a fervent fupplication, that *that garden* may be rendered worthy of him that is the owner of it; and that he may be prefent in it accordingly.

The verfe confiſts of two parts. In the firſt, we have a prayer for the gracious influences of the Spirit of Chriſt; to make his church, and the fouls of his people, a fit place of abode for Chriſt himfelf. And

in

in the second, a prayer for the gracious presence of Christ; to hold communion with his church and people, in the fruits of his Spirit among them. It is only the first of these from which we propose to discourse a little at present, as it is expressed in the first clause of the verse.

In which, more particularly, we may observe the three things following.

1. To whom the spouse addresses herself in this supplication. It is to the Holy Spirit of God, under the designation of the *north* and *south winds*.

2. What she asks of him, in three particulars; viz. That he might *awake, come*, and *blow upon* her *garden;* i. e. that, by the communication of his gracious influences to her, he would make her like a garden through which the north and south winds blow freely.

3. The end that she had in view in this petition, and expected to attain by means of the answer of it; *that the spices thereof may flow out;* or that, by the drawing forth of the graces of the Spirit into exercise, she might be enabled to send up such a pleasant favour as might prove acceptable to her glorious Lord and Husband.

The farther explication of these particulars will fall in of course, while we prosecute the following doctrine; which we take to contain the sense of the words.

It is the duty of all Christians, especially in the view of a solemn approach to God, earnestly to pray for the influences of the Holy Ghost; that their graces may be drawn forth into proper and lively exercise.

THE

The method to be observed, in speaking from this subject, is suggested by the above division of the words. Accordingly,

I. We shall, through divine assistance, speak of the influences of the Spirit of God, under the denomination of the north and south winds.

II. We shall consider what it is that we are here taught to pray for; as represented by the awaking, coming, and blowing of these winds.

III. We shall enquire what advantage we may hope to enjoy by the answer of such a prayer; or what is meant by the flowing out of the spices, in the last words of the text.

IV. We shall conclude with some improvement.

I. The first thing proposed was, To speak of the influences of the Holy Ghost; as represented by the figure of the north and south winds. All that is proposed on this head shall be comprised in the following particulars.

1. The north wind, and the south wind, here invoked, are neither to be considered as emblematical of two different beings, nor of two distinct persons. It is one and the same person who goes by both designations. This is evident, among other things, from the consideration, that the word which we render *blow*, is in the singular number. She does not say, ' Awake, O north wind, and come thou south wind, ' blow ye upon my garden;' and yet it is evident she prays for the blowing of both. She only says, *Blow thou;* plainly intimating, that, under both figures, she had her eye to one and the same Spirit. In the natural world, the north wind and the south wind

wind are different, and oppofite one to another. They blow from oppofite quarters. But, in the fpiritual world, they blow from the fame point; they are both operations of one and the fame Spirit.

2. The perfon here addreffed is the Holy Ghoft, the third perfon of the ever bleffed Trinity. He is often compared to the wind in Scripture. " Come," fays the prophet, " from the four winds, O breath; and " breathe upon thefe flain, that they may live *." If there fhould be any doubt, whether the Holy Ghoft is meant in that paffage or not, there can be no fuch doubt relative to the words of Chrift to Nicodemus : " The wind bloweth where it lifteth ; and " thou heareft the found thereof, but canft not tell " whence it cometh, nor whither it goeth; fo is every " one that is born of the Spirit." The Holy Spirit, in his gracious operations upon the foul, is fitly compared to the wind, on the following accounts.

(1.) Becaufe the air, or wind, is the fitteft emblem that the material world can furnifh, for reprefenting any kind of fpirit. The wind is not vifible to the bodily eye. It does not fenfibly refift our touch. It has no fixed fhape or pofition. In all thefe refpects it refembles fpirit, which is an immaterial fubftance, and is not fubject to any of the bodily fenfes. Hence, in various languages, and particularly in the Hebrew, the fame word fignifies both *breath* and *fpirit*. Now, the Holy Ghoft, being an infinite Spirit, may furely be reprefented by this emblem, as fitly as any fpirit that is finite and created.

(2.) On account of the fecret and imperceptible manner of his working. Whatever knowledge of
the

* Ezek. xxxvii. 9.

the works of nature, and particularly of the caufes of winds, the learned of our day have to boaft of, beyond what was attained in former ages; ftill what our Lord faid to Nicodemus, in the paffage juft now quoted, continues to be true. No man has power either to raife the wind or allay it. It cannot be ftopt in its progrefs, nor refifted in its operations. In thefe refpects, it is a fit emblem of the working of the Holy Spirit. He worketh where, and only where he lifteth. His own fovereign pleafure is the only reafon that we can affign for his working upon one perfon, or at one time rather than another. Our refiftance to his motions may provoke him to withdraw them; but, when he has a mind to work efficacioufly, no created power can refift him. As we " hear the " found" of the wind, " but cannot tell whence it " cometh, nor whither it goeth;" fo the Holy Ghoft produces effects that may be perceived or felt; but his operation itfelf is feldom perceptible; for " the " kingdom of God," in the foul, " cometh not with " obfervation." And if at any time it is felt, the perfon may as foon determine at what place of the earth any guft of wind began to blow, or in what place it fhall ceafe, as explain, or fully underftand, what he feels.

(3.) The Holy Spirit, in his various operations, may, with fufficient propriety, be compared both to the north and to the fouth wind. Interpreters have juftly confidered the north wind here, as expreffive of the awakening and convincing influences of the Holy Ghoft; and the fouth wind, as reprefenting his quickening and comforting influences.

His

His awakening and convincing influences may be compared to the north wind on the following accounts.

[1.] The north wind is ufually pinching and fevere; fo that a perfon expofed to it feels no fmall pain and uneafinefs from its cold. In like manner, the convictions of the Spirit, however falutary, are far from being pleafant to the perfon who is under them. On the contrary, they often fill his mind and confcience with fuch uneafinefs, that nothing on this fide hell can equal it. You can bear witnefs to the truth of this, who have had all your fins laid open before you; all the danger of your condition difcovered unto you; all the thunders of Sinai roaring above your head; and hell itfelf appearing to yawn beneath your feet; while your confcience roared under a fenfe of the curfe of God that lay upon you, and under the dreadful apprehenfion of divine wrath purfuing you at the heels! Surely the north wind had never fuch influence to congeal the waters under the pole, as thefe convictions had to freeze your fpirits.

[2.] As " the north wind driveth away rain * ;" fo do thofe convictions difpel the ftorm of divine wrath, to which all mankind are expofed in their natural eftate. There is, however, this remarkable difference; the north wind drives away the rain, by purging the air of thofe vapours by which it is engendered; fo that a perfon, without changing his pofition, finds himfelf relieved from any apprehenfions on account of the fhower that formerly hung over him. But convictions free us from the apprehenfions of divine wrath, not by driving away the fhower from the place where

* Prov. xxv. 23.

where we were; but by driving us into a place where no shower of that kind ever falls. When they come to be sanctified, they drive us to Chrift, our city of refuge. And then, like thofe Egyptians who "feared the word of the Lord," we feel no harm from that hail-ftorm, which brings inevitable death on every perfon who is found without.

[3.] Though the north wind, while it continues, tends to harden the earth, and render it unfit for the purpofes of vegetation; yet, by means of it, the foil is pulverized, and fitted to receive the feed from the hand of the hufbandman, againft the return of the fpring. In the very fame manner, while convictions laft, and are not accompanied with the comforting influences of the Spirit in any degree; they have no tendency, but to irritate corruption, and render the hard and ftony heart ftill harder. Yet convictions are the means through which the foul comes afterwards to be mollified; the ftony heart turned into a heart of flefh; and the perfon prepared to receive the good feed of the word of God, fo as to bring forth fruit; " fome thirty, fome fixty, and fome an hun-" dred fold."

[4.] The north wind kills thofe weeds with which the ground is infefted; and which are peculiarly noxious in gardens; fo that the foil is left clear for thofe plants that are nourifhed by the care of the hufbandman. In the garden of the church, and in the fouls of particular believers, a variety of corruptions fpring up of their own accord, as noxious weeds; and are in danger of choaking that good feed which the great hufbandman has fown in it. But a blaft of this fpiritual north wind fo nips thofe corruptions, that they
wither

wither and die apace; and the heart is left free, for the cultivation of thofe graces that the Spirit of God has implanted. - Hence it is that convictions are neceffary, not only in the day of regeneration; but through the whole courfe of life, till corruption be wholly mortified. And, however unpleafant they are in themfelves, the Chriftian who knows his own intereft will always defire and pray for them, as in the text: " Awake, O north wind, blow upon my gar-" den."

The quickening and comforting influences of the fame Spirit are compared to the *fouth wind;* and that on the following accounts.

[1.] As the fouth wind revives the decayed face of nature, and reftores to plants their former verdure; fo thefe quickening influences of the Holy Ghoft reftore frefhnefs and vigour to the Chriftian, after a time of fpiritual withering and decay. It is not more natural for a winter to fucceed a fummer, in the material world, and another fummer the winter; than for the child of God to have his times of fpiritual withering, fucceeding his times of refrefhing, and again fucceeded by them. Thefe witherings always take place when the quickening influences of the Spirit are withdrawn; and as foon as they are reftored a frefh fpring enfues. In the natural world, though the blowing of the fouth wind may reftore the verdure of thofe plants whofe life remained in them, it can do nothing for fuch as are really dead. But thofe influences of the Spirit, of which we fpeak, can give life to dead fouls, as well as livelinefs to thofe that are fickly. Though you be *twice dead,* and *plucked up by the root,* a blaft of this wind will revive you effectually; fo that there shall not be a plant in all " the garden of God," more vigorous or more fragrant than you shall become.

[2.] As the breathing of the south wind tends to revive the spirits of those who were melancholy, and disposes them to cheerfulness and gaiety; so these influences of the Spirit raise the drooping heart of the Christian, and fill him with holy joy and consolation. Many times he is made sad and melancholy,—by a sense of sin, by his Lord's withdrawing, by the reproach of the enemy, by outward afflictions, and often by all these together; so that, like David, he cries out, " O my God, my soul is cast down in me." Yet, on the back of such a season, he is enabled to " re-" joice in the Lord, and be joyful in God *his* Savi-" our." His *harp* is taken down from the *willows;* and he " sings the Lord's song, *though still* in a foreign " land." Yea, even while afflictions continue, he finds them all so much overbalanced by the blowing of this wind; that, like Habakkuk, he can " rejoice in the " Lord," though all the springs of earthly comfort run dry. Or, like the primitive Christians, though " in heaviness through manifold temptations," he can yet " rejoice, with joy unspeakable and full of " glory*."

[3.] As the south wind usually dispels the cold with which the face of nature was formerly benumbed, and brings heat and warmth along with it; so these refreshing influences of the Holy Ghost restore spiritual warmness to the soul, and set all the frozen affections a-flowing towards God and spiritual things. Then the Christian's zeal, (which was so lukewarm, that

* 1 Pet. i. 6, 8.

that he had reason to fear, left God should " spue *him* " out of his mouth)," is kindled to such a degree, that he neither fears the face of man, in bearing testimony for God, nor spares the most beloved lust, when making war against God's enemies. His love, which was frozen almost to death, is now so far invigorated, that " many waters cannot quench it," nor can any " floods drown it." A sight of the matchless love of Christ, joined with his equally matchless loveliness, has made him sick of love. And he finds himself much at a loss, either how to express, or how to evidence his love to him; who so undeservedly, so transcendently, so efficaciously, so incomprehensibly, " first " loved us!"

[4.] In one word, As the south wind, blowing freely through a garden, causes all the plants to spring up apace; diffuses their pleasant smell on every side, and brings forward their respective fruits unto perfection; so these quickening influences of the Spirit make " those who are planted in the house of God, " to grow up and flourish in the courts of our God; " *so that*, even in old age, when others fade, they still " bring forth fruit;" and continue " fat and flourish- " ing." It is when God " pours out *his* Spirit upon " *Zion's* seed, and *his* blessing upon *her* offspring, " *that they* grow up as among the grass, and as wil- " lows by the water courses *." By this means, the image of God is gradually perfected upon the soul; the person " grows in grace, and in the knowledge of " the Lord Jesus Christ." He sends out a fragrant perfume in the nostrils of God, and of all who have
their

* Isa. xliv. 4.

their spiritual senses exercised. His *fruit* comes to be " unto holiness, and *his* end everlasting life."

II. It was next proposed, To enquire what we are here taught to ask, as represented by the *awakening*, *coming*, and *blowing* of the north and south winds. For clearing of this we may observe the following things.

1. The Holy Spirit of God, though always present in his church, and in the hearts of his people, often seems, in their apprehension, like one asleep. His work appears then at a stand. He seems inattentive to his own interests, and to those of his people. His enemies are permitted to sow their tares, even in his garden. And many things take place, on account of which both friends and enemies are in danger of concluding, that there is not " in the Most High *any* " knowledge of the things that are below." Sleep, indeed, being a thing that implies imperfection, is altogether incompetent to God. But in such cases, he seems as if he were asleep. The same things take place in the church, that might be expected to happen in a garden, while the keeper thereof was asleep. On this account we may warrantably pray for his awaking; while our meaning and desire is, that he would shew himself awake, to the comfort of his people, and to the conviction of his enemies. So prays the sweet singer of Israel: " Awake, why sleepest " thou, O Lord; arise, cast us not off for ever *." This is the meaning of the first part of the prayer in the next.

2. God may not only seem to be asleep, and so inattentive

* Psal. xliv. 25.

attentive to what paffes in the church; he may even feem to be abfent from her, and to have forfaken her altogether. His gracious prefence can never be withdrawn from her; but he may often be abfent to her fenfe. Zion, in fuch a cafe, is oft in danger of faying, "The Lord hath forfaken, and my God forgotten "me." And no wonder that fhe longs for his return. Nothing is more common than to find the people of God, under fuch apprehenfions, crying to him for this, and faying, as David, " O when wilt thou come " unto me *?" Yet the meaning of fuch a petition is not that he would really be prefent where he was not before; but that he would grant new difcoveries, manifeftations, and difplays of his gracious prefence, by carrying on his work in the church or in the foul. Thus, when we adopt the fecond part of the prayer in this text, our meaning fhould be, that he would accomplifh his work among us, in fuch a manner, that every friend and every enemy may fee his hand at it; and all may be convinced, that " there is a God " in *our* Ifrael."

3. As to the laft branch of this petition, which is expreffed in thefe words, " Blow upon my garden;" for the better underftanding of it, the following things muft be attended to.

The *garden* here mentioned is the church herfelf. Chrift had compared her to a garden in ver. 12. " A " garden inclofed is my fifter, my fpoufe." To thefe words, as we have feen, fhe alludes in this text. Her garden is herfelf. And the meaning is the fame as if fhe had faid, ' Blow upon me.' Neither is there any abfurdity in calling the church of Chrift both his

* Pfal. ci. 2.

spouse and a *garden*. Both expressions are metaphorical; and both metaphors together do not exhaust the subject. Now, the church is fitly compared to a garden on the following accounts.

(1.) A garden is usually fenced about, and inclosed with walls or hedges; to prevent its being hurt, either by men or beasts. So the church of God has her fence, which secures her more effectually than walls of adamant. She has a hedge of government and discipline, which Christ has planted about her; and which her office-bearers are called to keep in repair. By this, profane persons may be prevented from " devouring that which is holy;" and her fruits are nourished till they ripen. But she has likewise a wall of divine protection around her, by which she is secured against all the depredations of thieves and robbers; so that none of them can enter her borders, far less can they do her any injury, without a divine permission. This was the hedge that God set about Job, and about all that he had. He sets it, in the same manner, about all his people in every age. And even Satan himself is not able to break through it. This is it of which the church elsewhere sings, " We " have a strong city, salvation will God appoint for " walls and bulwarks *."

(2.) A garden is a place of pleasure. A man usually takes more delight in his garden than in any other part of his possessions. He plants it with the choicest flowers and fruits. He repairs to it from time to time, to amuse himself with its agreeable verdure, and with its pleasing variety. He plucks the most fragrant of its flowers; and tastes those fruits that are

in

---

* Isa. xxvi. 1.

in feafon. In like manner, the church is Chrift's pleafure ground. In her are his flowers, his lillies, and the " trees of his right hand; the planting of the " Lord, that he may be glorified." In her he takes pleafure and delight, more than in all the creation befides. To her he always reforts; " to feed in the " gardens, and to gather lillies *." And hence fays God, concerning his church of old, " The vineyard of " the LORD of hofts is the houfe of Ifrael, and the men " of Judah are his pleafant plants †."

(3.) A garden is ufually well dreffed and highly cultivated. The hufbandman beftows more care upon it than upon any other fpot. So it is with the church of Chrift. " In that day, fing ye unto her, A vine- " yard of red wine. I the LORD do keep it; I will " water it every moment; left any hurt it, I will keep " it night and day ‡." The Lord Jefus Chrift, being appointed to drefs this garden, and to keep it, as the firft Adam was fet to drefs the garden of God in Eden; he has fuch a peculiar care of it, and of every plant in it, that he takes the very method with each that is beft calculated to promote its growth, and bring it forward to perfection. Yea, even thofe plants that continue fruitlefs, he will not fuffer them to be dug up, or thrown over the hedge, till all due pains have been taken with them. To fpeak without allegory; as, in all his dealings with his own people, he follows that method which is beft calculated to promote their fpiritual growth in faith and holinefs; fo even hypocrites and falfe profeffors have a fhare of that fpiritual culture which he beftows upon his church and people, by means of his ordinances. And,
with

* Song vi. 2.   † Ifa. v. 7.   ‡ Ifa. xxvii. 2, 3.

with regard to such in this congregation as have never hitherto brought forth any acceptable fruit, he is presently saying, in his providence, " Let *them* alone " this year also, till I dig about *them* and dung *them*."

(4.) A garden is, of consequence, a profitable spot. It brings forth much fruit meet for the Master's use. Indeed, no man, nor any society of men, can, in any proper sense, " be profitable unto God ; as he that is " wise may be profitable to himself." He stands in no need of any advantage by us; nor is it possible that he should receive any from us. But in the church are produced those fruits of holiness in which God takes pleasure; while the rest of the world is over-run with the weeds of corruption, and brings forth nothing but briers and thorns. These fruits that are produced in the church, are of real usefulness in the house of God.

Now, as every true believer is a member of the church, all that has been said of her may be applied to every one of them in his measure. They all have the benefit of that inclosure that God has set about the church. They are all confidered by him as his *pleafant plants*. They all share in that spiritual culture which he bestows upon his garden; and have their " fruit unto holiness." Hence, what has been said of the church is applicable to the soul of every Christian. Each has a garden of his own ; and, with relation to his own soul, may pray, as in the text, " Blow upon my garden."

If any should ask, Why the church speaks of this garden as her own, when her Lord and husband is the rightful proprietor of it? We answer she may justly do so, on the following accounts.

[1.] It

[1.] It cannot poffibly be his, without being hers alfo. By virtue of her union to him fhe has an intereft in all that he poffeffes, as well as in himfelf; while he has a fovereign propriety in her, and in all that fhe can claim as hers. This is ufually the cafe in marriages among men; and it is happily the cafe in this fpiritual marriage. It cannot be his garden without being her's alfo.

[2.] She has a charge of the garden, and is appointed to keep it under him. Eve was joined with Adam in the charge to keep the garden of Eden; and, by this means, fhe had an intereft in it as well as he. In like manner, though Chrift is the chief keeper of this fpiritual garden, his fpoufe alfo has a charge of it. And feldom does any injury befal it, but through her neglect. She has a charge of that hedge of difcipline by which it is inclofed; of all thofe truths which are as the food of the plants; and of the plants themfelves, of every ftature. Yea, every Chriftian has a charge of his own foul in particular. And in whatever manner he has been bufied otherwife, he will find it a heavy matter, if he have reafon at any time to fay, " Mine own vineyard have I not kept."

[3.] Her hufband has given her the garden for her poffeffion. Though he bought it at an immenfe price; though himfelf takes fuch pleafure in it, and has fo much care about it; he has made a gift of it to her. All the fruits of it are for her ufe; and fhe may warrantly confider every thing that it contains as her own. To fpeak more plainly, believer, Chrift, though he redeemed your foul by his own precious blood, has made a free gift of it to you; and you fhall have it " for a prey in all places whither you go."

All

All the fruit that you bring forth unto God shall redound to your own advantage. And all that pleasure which God has in the works of his own hand about you, shall flow back to you in rivers to swim in, through all eternity. The same is the case with the church in general.

Now, from all this it is manifest, that, by the blowing of the north and south wind upon her garden, the church means the actual communication of the influences of the Spirit to herself, in agreeableness to her need. As the wind, in blowing freely through a garden, touches every plant, and every part of the soil; and, in this way, communicates its influences to the whole; so she prays that the Holy Ghost may communicate, both his convincing and comforting influences, to every part of the church, and to every one of her members; so that the whole body, and the whole man in every member of the body, may be subject to their efficacy.

III. We come now to enquire what is the happy effect that the blowing of this spiritual wind will produce; or what may be expected to follow upon the answer of this prayer, as it is expressed in these words, *That the spices thereof may flow out.*

The word which we render spices is meant of those aromatic or sweet-smelling herbs, that are usually planted in gardens, and diffuse an agreeable perfume all around them. These, in this passage, are emblematical of all that God has instituted in his church, or bestowed upon her; which is pleasing and acceptable to him, as the fragrant smell of such plants is to the owner of the garden where they grow. Thus it comprehends

hends all the ordinances of divine appointment in the church; all the office-bearers that Chrift has given her; all the gifts beftowed upon them or others, for the ufe of edifying; all the graces of the Spirit in her members; and all their exercife of thefe graces; together with all that holy obedience which Chriftians daily offer up, as their " fpiritual facrifices, holy " and acceptable to God, through Jefus Chrift."

To *flow out*, ftrictly fpeaking, is not the property of fpices; but of waters, or fome other liquid. Here, then, is a metaphor within a metaphor; and it feems to be ftrongly expreffive of two things. 1. The abounding of thofe things that are acceptable to God in the church, to fuch a degree, that they may be compared to waters, which *flow out* fpeedily and plentifully when a fluice is opened. 2. The abundant acceptablenefs of all thefe. As a gentle breeze upon the flowers and plants in a garden, caufes them to fend forth, in abundance, thofe aromatic *effluvia*, which, affecting the organs of fmell, produce the fenfation of a pleafant perfume; fo the fpoufe expects, that, when the wind of divine influences blows upon her, all the fpiritual gifts beftowed upon her by her head fhall be improved and occupied, in fuch a manner as to afford fuitable entertainment to the royal gueft, whofe prefence fhe invites in the next claufe of the verfe. Her ordinances will then be difpenfed in purity as well as in plenty. Her gifts and graces will be drawn forth into lively exercife. Her members will be animated for running their Chriftian race; many fpiritual facrifices of a fweet-fmelling favour will be offered in her to God. And every thing will
be

be in such a condition as may prove most acceptable to her Beloved.

Now, for producing this effect the influences of the Spirit are abfolutely neceffary. When thefe are withheld, though the difpenfation of ordinances may be continued, they will ftill be dry and taftelefs, unacceptable to God, and unprofitable to men. There may be fpiritual gifts; but they will not be improved for the edification of the body. Yea, the graces of the Spirit themfelves will never be fo exercifed as to fend up any pleafant favour in Chrift's noftrils. But, when this fpiritual wind does actually blow, there cannot fail to be a proportionable flowing out of the fpices in this garden. The blowing of the fouth wind, accompanied with the cherifhing influence of the returning fun, does not more naturally revive the winter-beaten plants, and caufe them give forth their balmy odours in the fpring; than the influences of the Holy Ghoft, communicated to the church, and to the particular Chriftian, revive the decayed face of religion, and fet every thing to rights in this fpiritual garden. Then ordinances become a pleafure to God and to his people. Then gofpel minifters are a " fweet " favour of God;" not only " in them that perifh," but efpecially " in them that believe." The graces of faith, love, joy, hope, zeal for God, and all the reft, become lively and vigorous in their exercife. And the whole church, like the garments of Efau on his brother's back, has " the fmell of a field which the " Lord hath bleffed." In proportion as thofe influences are communicated, this will always be their effect. An affurance of this is plainly imported in the expreffion which we are now confidering. It runs
literally

literally, in the future time, thus: " Blow upon my
" garden, and the fpices thereof fhall flow out." ' I
' am fure the effect cannot be wanting, if once I en-
' joy the caufe.'

IV. WE fhall now conclude with fome improvement of the fubject. And it affords us information in the following particulars.

1. All the three perfons of the adorable Godhead are alike the object of divine worfhip. And we may fafely addrefs our fupplications to any of them, provided we duly attend to the unity of the divine effence. When we afk for thofe bleffings, the beftowing of which is more particularly afcribed to the Father, according to the œconomy of our redemption, we may addrefs ourfelves to him. When we pray for thofe gifts which Chrift, as Mediator, is exalted to beftow; we may fpeak to the fecond perfon, as did Stephen in his dying moments. And when we fupplicate, as we are here taught to do, for thofe fpiritual bleffings that are more immediately the gifts of the Holy Ghoft, we may lawfully direct our prayer to him.

2. Whatever *diverfities of gifts* there are in the church, they are all the fruits of the *fame Spirit*. Yea, however oppofite the confolations may be, by which the Chriftian is made happy, beyond any thing that can arife from the enjoyment of earthly things, to thofe convictions by which he was warned to flee from the wrath to come; ftill both are the work of the fame ever bleffed Spirit. The north wind and the fouth wind are here addreffed as one.

3. There

3. There is nothing in the church, or about any particular member of it, that is truly acceptable to God, or can afford suitable entertainment to Chrift; unlefs it is the fruit of the gracious operation of the Holy Ghoft. There is a manifeft connection between this and the following part of the verfe. What the fpoufe here prays for, is intended as a mean of preparing her garden for the reception and entertainment of her Beloved. And here fhe plainly enough infinuates, that it would be impoffible to have it fo prepared, unlefs the wind of divine influences fhould gracioufly blow upon it.

4. All the fruits of the Spirit are pleafant and defirable unto Chrift. Every grace in the foul is, to Chrift, like a fweet-fmelling plant in a garden; fo is every degree of conformity to the will of God in the church. It affords him the higheft fatisfaction and delight. When the fpices of your garden, believer, flow out, by the blowing of this fpiritual wind upon them; then your *Beloved* will take pleafure to " come " into his garden." Oh! pray earneftly for the influences of the Spirit, that your graces may be drawn forth into exercife, you that wifh for the prefence of Chrift with you in his own ordinances.

5. The prefence of the Spirit of God, and his gracious operation in the hearts of his people, are not lefs neceffary, in order to the regular and acceptable exercife of their graces, than they are for the implantation of thofe graces at the firft. The fpoufe of Chrift has a garden already, and that planted with fpices; yet fhe prays for the blowing of the wind, as neceffary to make her " fpices flow out." If ever you wifh to be exercifed, as becomes a gracious perfon, let your

dependence

dependence be always upon him that gave you grace, that he may enable you to exercife it.

6. As thofe operations of the Holy Ghoft which are painful to the Chriftian, are not lefs ufeful and falutary than the others; fo they ought not to be lefs welcome when he is pleafed to fend them. Nay, on the contrary, every Chriftian fhould pray for thefe as well as for the others; and be thankful for them when they come. You need the piercing blafts of the north wind, to wither your corruptions; as well as the gentle breezes of the fouth wind, to cherifh your graces. Both together will make you both fragrant and fruitful.

THIS fubject likewife affords matter of trial; and may affift us in the duty of felf-examination. If you are efpoufed to Chrift, and capable of being welcome at his table; then,

1. Being fenfible that you have a garden, and are intrufted with the keeping of it, it is your concern to keep it carefully and faithfully. Knowing that God has given you an immortal foul, for which you muft be accountable to Chrift at his coming, you are careful to mind the things that belong to its everlafting peace; and allow not yourfelf to prefer the vanities of a prefent world, in your heart or in your practice, to the concerns of eternity.

2. This garden of yours is planted with fpices. The great Hufbandman, by the faving operations of his Spirit, has implanted in your foul thofe graces in which conformity to the image of God confifts. You have fome degree of faith in Jefus Chrift, of repentance unto life, of love to God and to the brethren, of

joy

joy in the Holy Ghoft, of refignation to the divine will, and of all the other fruits of the Spirit; and you earneftly long for more.

3. It is your earneft defire, that the fpices of your garden may flow out. Many there are who have fome kind of defire to have grace, becaufe they know that they cannot be faved from hell without it, who yet have little or no concern about the exercife of it. But as for you, it is not enough to you that you be faved from wrath, or that you get to heaven at laft. You wifh to be acceptable to your Beloved, to put honour upon him, and to have fellowfhip with him by the way. You know that this cannot be attained without the actual exercife of grace, and the practice of evangelical holinefs. Thefe you, therefore, earneftly defire; thefe you conftantly aim at; for thefe you daily pray.

4. You are fenfible that your fpices can never flow out, unlefs the north and fouth winds blow upon your garden for that effect. You know, by experience, that of yourfelf you can do nothing; that no grace already received can do your bufinefs; and that all your endeavours to exercife grace will be as fruitlefs as were your endeavours to implant it; unlefs you are affifted by the Holy Ghoft. In all your endeavours to this purpofe, you " go in the ftrength of the " Lord God," and in his only.

In a word, You heartily join with the fpoufe in the prayer of this text, and fay, " Awake, O north wind, " come thou fouth *wind*, and blow upon my garden; " that the fpices thereof may flow out." Not only do you profefs to fay fo, now that you are put in mind of it; this is the habitual language of your heart. In the

the view of the folemn work before us, you have been praying already, in your families, and in your clofets; if not in thefe very words, in words of the fame import, for the gracious influence of the Holy Spirit; to draw forth grace into exercife in your foul, and fo to prepare you for a feat at the holy table of the Lord.

If thefe things be in you and abound; if you really defire that they fhould abound, and are grieved becaufe they abound fo little; then you belong to the fpoufe and bride of Chrift; and, if your prayer is anfwered, you may be welcome at his table. Otherwife you are an enemy to him; and, while this is the cafe, you have no right to partake in the folemn feaft in view.

WE conclude with a fhort word of exhortation.

Let the fpoufe of Chrift, and every one of her members, pray as in the text. Pray for fuch a blowing of this fupernatural wind, as may be fuitable to your condition, whatever it is. Pray for his blowing in the church at large; as the only mean of reviving her decayed face, and reftoring " the beauty of the " LORD *her* God upon *her*." Pray for this congregation; that he may fo blow upon us, as to make ready, among us, a people prepared for himfelf. Pray for thofe who are fo carelefs about all fuch matters, that they pray not for themfelves. Pray for your brethren, who may join with you in the work of the enfuing occafion. Pray for God's fervants of the miniftry, who may affift in the work; that this wind may fo blow upon them, as to make them a fweet favour of God among you. In this manner pray for me.

Let thofe who are ftrangers to Chrift, be exhorted to confider their ways. You alfo have a garden, finner; but it is the garden of the fluggard. Inftead of being planted with thofe fpices that it ought to produce, it is wholly " grown over with thorns; nettles " *have* covered the face thereof, and the ftone-wall " thereof *is* broken down." Corruption reigns where grace ought to grow. There is nothing in your foul acceptable to God, nothing that can be profitable to yourfelf. Nay, your foul is in danger of being totally loft; and then, though you could gain the whole world, it would profit you nothing. Nothing can better your condition, without a blaft of this myftical wind. As you would avoid the dreadful fate of that ground which is "nigh unto curfing, whofe end is to be " burned," do you alfo pray, as in this text, " Awake, " O north wind," &c.

In one word, Let all that hear the gofpel beware of neglecting and overlooking, of interrupting or refifting, this myfterious wind when it blows. Thus faith the Lord, " Quench not the Spirit." Refift not his motions, when he blows upon your fouls by his inward and fecret admonitions. " Harden not your " hearts," when he blows upon you by the external difpenfations of his grace. The Spirit of God is fpeaking to every one of you in this gofpel, as really as I am. He calls, he befeeches, he prays you to " be re- " conciled unto God ;" and to be ready to meet the Bridegroom, the beloved of fouls, when he cometh. Prepare to meet him, and to give him a becoming reception, when he comes into his garden, as we have reafon to expect he will, on the enfuing occafion. And fee that you be ready to meet him, and to

go

go in with him, when he comes to confummate his marriage in a little; left, when you come afterwards, you find the door fhut. This you may confider as the advice of the Spirit of God to you. And you fhall be guilty of quenching the Spirit as far as you refufe it. " Wherefore, as the Holy Ghoft faith, " to-day, if ye will hear his voice, harden not your " hearts, as in the provocation; in " the day of the temptation in the wildernefs."

SERMON VIII.

The Invitation; or, *A Prayer of the Church for the Presence of Christ, and for his gracious acceptance of the Fruits of his Spirit in her.*

Song iv. 16.

—LET MY BELOVED COME INTO HIS GARDEN, AND EAT HIS PLEASANT FRUITS.

WE now proceed, through divine assistance, to consider the last clause of the verse. In which we have four things deserving our attention.

1. The person spoken of by the church; and by her called *My Beloved.* This can be no other than Christ himself, her glorious Lord and Husband, whom she frequently calls by this designation in this book.

2. His interest in the church acknowledged; she calls herself *His garden.* What she called her own garden in the preceding clause, she now calls his. Indeed, so close is the union between them, that she has nothing that is not devoted to him; neither has

he

he any thing which he has not gracioufly given to her.

3. His prefence in the church requefted: "Let him come into his garden." In refpect of his Godhead, Chrift is prefent every where. When this book was compofed, he had not yet affumed human nature. Now his prefence, in that nature, is confined to heaven, "till the time of the reftitution of all things." But ftill there is a fenfe in which he might be invited to come into his church both then and now.

4. His entertainment in the church fpecified; let him "eat his pleafant fruits." If fhe invites him into his garden, fhe has provided fomewhat; at leaft fhe defires to have fomething ready for his entertainment; even the fruits of his own Spirit and grace wrought in her, and beftowed upon her, by means of the blowing of that wind, which fhe prays for in the preceding claufe.

The fenfe of the words may be fummed up in the following propofition:

As all they who are efpoufed to Chrift, love him above every other object; fo they earneftly defire that he may be prefent in his church, to hold communion with her, and with them, in the fruits of his Spirit and grace.

CONCERNING the defignation here given to Chrift, we have fpoken at large on a former occafion*; and fhall not now detain you with any thing on this part of the fubject. But fhall only fpeak a few words.

I. Of Chrift's intereft in the church, as his garden.

II. Of

---

* See Vol. I. p. 67,—74.

II. Of his prefence in the church, which is here invoked.

III. Of the entertainment that his fpoufe is willing to give him, or of his " eating his pleafant fruits." And then,

IV. We fhall conclude with fome improvement.

I. In difcourfing from the firft head, we fhall not need to inform you why the church is compared to a garden, nor why fhe calls herfelf her own garden. Both thefe we have confidered already. All that we have now to do, is only to enquire why fhe is called *His garden?* And fhe may be fo, with propriety, on the following accounts.

1. He received her, as his inheritance, from his Father. Every plant in the garden, and every part of the foil, is included in that declaration which he makes to his Father: " I have manifefted thy name unto " the men whom thou gaveft me out of the world ; " thine they were, and thou gaveft them me*." From all eternity, when God took a view of that deplorable eftate into which all mankind were to bring themfelves by their fin, he paffed by the far greateft part of them, determining to leave them to perifh in their fin, and under the punifhment of it. He was infinitely juft in fo doing; for furely none had any right to be delivered by him, from that mifery which they had wilfully brought upon themfelves. But the church, and every genuine member of it, he gave to Chrift, his eternal Son; that he might " redeem *them* " from all iniquity, and purify *them* to himfelf a peculiar

* John xvii. 6.

"culiar people, zealous of good works." And by virtue of this gift she becomes his garden.

2. He bought her at an immenſe price. Though ſhe was given him by his Father, ſhe was conſidered, when ſhe was given him, as in a ſtate of alienation from God; ſo that Chriſt could not obtain the poſſeſſion of her, unleſs in the way of paying a ranſom for her. And it was upon the expreſs condition of his paying this ranſom, that the deed of gift was made. Accordingly, when the appointed time came, he paid down the price of her redemption into the hands of divine juſtice; not in ſuch " corruptible " things as ſilver and gold." Theſe, however much they are valued among men, are not current in heaven. Nay, he paid it in his own " precious blood." A ranſom this infinitely more valuable than ten thouſand worlds. Every man conſiders that as his own property, which he has purchaſed with his own money. And ſurely Chriſt has a juſt right to the church, as his garden, ſeeing " he purchaſed *her* with his own blood *."

3. He redeemed her from the hand of the enemy by the power of his almighty arm. You will remember, that Jacob gave to his ſon Joſeph " one portion " above his brethren, which *he* took out of the hand " of the Amorite, with *his* ſword and with *his* bow †." This is thought to be the ſame piece of ground which he is elſewhere ſaid to have purchaſed of the ſons of Hamor, for an hundred pieces of ſilver ‡. Though he bought it from the Amorites, yet they reſumed their poſſeſſion of it when he left that part of the country. And he found it neceſſary to redeem it " with *his* ſword and with *his* bow." In this, as in many

---

* Acts xx. 28.   † Gen. xlviii. 22.   ‡ Gen. xxxviii. 19.

many other things, Jacob was a type of Chriſt. Though he paid for the church, which is his garden, that immenſe price which has been mentioned; even this was not ſufficient to obtain him the peaceable poſſeſſion of her. Satan had uſurped poſſeſſion of this garden; and, beſides the ranſom that he paid for it, Chriſt found it neceſſary to redeem her from that enemy by the power of the ſword. And ſurely this muſt greatly enhance the right by which he claims her as his garden.

4. She is a garden of his planting. When ſhe came into his hand, ſhe was a mere waſte, entirely grown over with briers and thorns. It was he that incloſed it, planted it with thoſe ſpices that are to be found in it, and made it a garden for himſelf. So much has he done for it in this reſpect, that he can appeal to any rational perſon if any more was neceſſary, or even if more could have been done. This garden is the ſame with the vineyard of which the Prophet Iſaiah ſpeaks: " My beloved hath a vineyard, in a very " fruitful hill. And he fenced it, and gathered out " the ſtones thereof, and planted it with the choiceſt " vine, and built a tower therein, and alſo made a " wine-preſs in it. What could have been done more " to my vineyard, that I have not done in it *?"

5. Himſelf takes care of the garden, and cultivates it with his own hand. Indeed he may be ſaid, in one ſenſe, to have " let it out to keepers †;" in as much as he has committed the external management of it into the hands of men, who are called to dreſs it for him, and to return him the fruits of it. But ſtill himſelf preſides among them, directs them in all that they

---

* Iſa. v. 1, 2, 4.   † Song viii. 11.

they should do about his garden, makes their endeavours effectual; and accomplishes, with his own hand, what none of them has power to do. He dresses it, he keeps it, he watches over it, he defends it, he waters it; and neither night nor day does he remit in his care of it. Concerning this garden it is, that himself is represented as saying, " In that day, sing ye " unto her, A vineyard of red wine. I the Lord do " keep it, I will water it every moment; lest any hurt " it, I will keep it night and day *."

6. He takes pleasure in it, as a man does in his own garden. He feeds with satisfaction upon the fruits of it. He plucks the flowers of it, and transplants them to a better soil; and is never wholly absent from it. If ever you wish to find him, or to enjoy communion with him, it is there that you must seek him. If ever you enquire after him, you will be sure to hear of him in this garden. For thus saith she, who, of all others, has best opportunity to know his retreats; " My be- " loved is gone down into his garden, to the beds of " spices; to feed in the gardens, and to gather lil- " lies†." Surely these things, all taken together, confirm his property in her; so that she cannot, with half the justice, be ascribed to any other; but is fitly called *his garden*.

II. Concerning the presence of Christ in the church, or his *coming into his garden*, which is here invoked, we shall only take notice of the following things.

1. There is a fourfold coming of Christ mentioned in scripture. *First*, There is his coming in the flesh, which

---

* Isa. xxvii. 2, 3. † Song vi. 2.

which the Apostle mentions as a thing past: "Whose are the fathers; and of whom, as concerning the flesh, Christ came, who is over all, God blessed for ever *." This coming was an object of ardent and longing desire to the church under the Old Testament. And for this she earnestly prayed. It was the matter of that capital promise, in the faith of which all the saints of that period died; and which, if it had not been accomplished in its appointed time, all their faith had been vain, and ours to. *Secondly*, There is his coming, in just displeasure, to execute judgment upon a rebellious and gainsaying people or church. In this sense, we often hear of his coming to the church of the Jews. And in this sense he threatens to come to the church of Pergamos, unless she repented of those evils for which she is reproved. "Repent, (says he) or else I will come unto thee quickly; and will fight against them with the sword of my mouth†." This coming is never an object of desire to the church in any period. She always deprecates it, and is grieved at the prospect of it. *Thirdly*, We read of his coming, in the dispensation of his grace, to manifest himself as " the desire of all nations, *and to* fill the house *of God* with *his* glory." Of this must the Apostle be understood, when he says, concerning Antichrist, that " the Lord will consume him with the spirit of his mouth; and destroy *him* with the brightness of his coming ‡." This cannot be meant of the second coming of Christ at the last day; for the scriptures represent the downfal, or destruction of Antichrist, as about to take place a considerable time before the end of the world; and

assure

assure us, that the church will enjoy a pretty long season of peace and tranquillity; which shall, at last, be disturbed by the conspiracy of Gog and Magog, between the fall of Antichrist and the coming of Christ. But we know, that the fall of Antichrist shall be accompanied by an universal spreading, and an universal success of the gospel. In this way Christ shall come, and be present in his church, in such a remarkable manner, that it is said the saints shall then " reign with " him on the earth a thousand years." And this coming of Christ shall be the very mean by which the destruction of the man of sin shall be accomplished. We have reason to think that it has begun to be so already; and it is but a little, when it shall be completed, by the same means by which it has been begun. This coming of Christ may be understood, either of a more clear, and full, and extensive dispensation of the gospel externally; or of a more plentiful inward communication of his grace to the souls of his people. Or rather, both these take place together, as often as Christ comes to his church in this respect. Such a coming is the most desirable thing that the church can enjoy in this world. For this she prays continually, and so does every one of her genuine members when rightly exercised. *Fourthly*, We read of his coming to the general judgment at the last day. Concerning this he testifies, saying, " Surely 1 come " quickly." And his church, when acting like herself, will still reply, " Amen, even so come, Lord Jesus." For this also we ought all to pray, that the Lord may hasten it in his time. I apprehend it is the third of these that the spouse has an eye to in the text. She prays

prays that Chrift may gracioufly maintain a clear, extenfive, and regular difpenfation of his own ordinances; and may fo communicate himfelf to the fouls of his people, by thefe means, that their communion with him may be intimate, and the effects of it upon them lafting and evident.

2. We may not expect the perfonal prefence of Chrift, in human nature, in the church, until his final coming to judgment. Once he came in that refpect; but fo were the men of the world infatuated, and even the profeffed members of the church, that they knew him not; and therefore " crucified the Lord of " glory." After his refurrection " he afcended up in- " to heaven, and fat on the right hand of God." There he muft continue till he come to bring home his fpoufe into the " palace of the King," there to abide for ever. Even when he fhall reign on the earth, after the total downfal of Antichrift, during the more eminent glory of the latter days, his bodily prefence fhall be confined to heaven. In that refpect, he will never come into his garden on earth, till that awful day when " every eye fhall fee him." It is only by his Spirit, working in the church, and in the hearts of his people, that we can expect him now to come into his garden. Yet,

3. The coming of the Beloved into his garden, which is here prayed for, is not the fame with the blowing of the wind, mentioned in the preceding claufe of the verfe. There the church prays for thofe influences of the Spirit, by which fhe may be fitted to hold communion with Chrift on her part. Here fhe prays for thofe fruits of the Spirit, by which Chrift manifefts
himfelf

himself as graciously present with his people, and by which he maintains the communion on his part. All real fellowship must be mutual. Whenever communion with Christ is enjoyed, the person maintains it on the one side, by pouring out his heart into Christ's bosom; and cheerfully giving himself, and all that he can claim any interest in, to his beloved. For this we can never be qualified, unless by the communication of the influences of the Spirit. And therefore, whenever we wish to do so, we must pray for the blowing of the wind. But then, at the same time that we are thus exercised, Christ, on the other side, maintains the communion with us; by graciously accepting what we offer to him, and intimating his acceptance of it, by discovering to us his glory, and imparting to us out of that infinite fulness, which God has laid up in his hand, what he finds agreeable to our need; thus he makes us happy, beyond what any unrenewed person is able to conceive, in the enjoyment of himself. And this is it for which we are taught to pray in this clause of the verse.

III. WE are now to speak a few words concerning that entertainment, which the spouse of Christ is willing to give him in his own garden; or concerning his "eating his pleasant fruits." And here it will be necessary that we enquire, What are those *fruits* that she wishes him to eat? Why they are called *his fruits?* Why they are denominated *pleasant-fruits?* And what we are to understand by his eating them?

1. If it is asked, What are those fruits which Christ is here invited to eat? We answer, They are of two sorts. The *first* comprehends all those benefits that

Christ has bestowed upon his church and people. All those external privileges that accompany or flow from our membership in the visible church; whatever they are to others, to real Christians they are the fruits of Christ's mediation. More especially, all those inward and spiritual blessings that are peculiar to a state of grace; justification, adoption, sanctification, and all the benefits that justified persons enjoy by Christ, are to be considered as *his fruits*. They are always to be found in his garden, and they proceed from himself. Hence, when Christ is compared to the apple tree, these fruits are said to grow upon him; for of these is the spouse to be understood, when she says, "I sat down under his shadow with great delight; "and his fruit was sweet to my taste *."

The *other* sort contains all those graces which the Spirit of Christ has implanted in the hearts of his people; comprehending the exercise of those graces, and all that course of holy evangelical obedience which they produce. These are called, even in the language of the New Testament, " the fruits of the Spi-" rit †. And these are mainly intended, by the fruits of Christ, in this text. Against this, it is no sufficient objection that they are called the spices of the garden, in the preceding part of the verse; seeing it is well known, that nothing is more usual in Scripture, especially in this book, than to represent the same thing under various metaphors; the further to illustrate, and set forth the excellency of it. As the spices of a garden are fit emblems of the graces of the Spirit, on account of their fragrant smell; so are likewise the
fruits

---

*. Song ii. 2.   † Gal. v. 22.

fruits that grow in a garden, on account of their a-
greeable tafte and flavour.

2. If it is enquired, Why thefe are called Chrift's fruits?
We fhall only mention the following reafons for it.—
They are all the fruits of his mediation. The graces
of the Spirit are fo, as well as the benefits that accompany a gracious ftate. It was as impoffible for
us to have been conformed to the image of God, as
it was that we fhould be reftored to his favour, or admitted into his family, unlefs upon the footing of the
payment of our ranfom in the " precious blood of
" Chrift." They are the fruits of his cultivation.
Chrift is appointed by his Father, to drefs and keep
the garden of the church. And it is folely owing to
his diligence and activity in this work, that her members enjoy either the benefits, or the graces that are
here comprehended under the fruits of Chrift. They
are fruits that fpring from himfelf as their root. How
this is the cafe, as to the benefits derived from him,
is not dubious. It is as truly the cafe with regard to
all the graces, and all the holy obedience of his people. Upon him, as the living ftock, they are all in-
grafted; and all the fruit that they bring forth is in
confequence of their union to him. Hence his exhortation to his difciples: " Abide in me, and I in
" you; as the branch cannot bear fruit of itfelf, ex-
" cept it abide in the vine; no more can ye, except
" ye abide in me*." In a word, they are fruits prepared for his entertainment, and devoted to his ufe,
by his fpoufe. And it is to eat thefe fruits that fhe
invites him into his garden. Whatever a Chriftian
enjoys from Chrift, he is concerned to improve it for
Chrift's

* John xv. 4.

Chrift's glory. All his graces, and all his gracious exercifes, are dedicated to Chrift. And it is always his higheft ambition, that, in his endeavours after obedience, he may be accepted of him.

3. Why thefe are called *pleafant fruits*, we need not be at a lofs to know. They are things really pleafant and defirable in themfelves; and every Chriftian feels them to be fo. All the things that this world can afford, yield no pleafure comparable to what the child of God enjoys in the poffeffion, or even in the believing profpect of the fruits of Chrift's purchafe. Nor is there any other employment in which he could enjoy half the fatisfaction, as in bringing forth the fruits of holinefs, under the influence of the Spirit of Chrift. Thefe fruits are alfo pleafant to Chrift himfelf. He takes pleafure in beftowing upon his people thofe benefits that are the the fruits of his love to them. And he takes no lefs pleafure in obferving about them thofe graces, and thofe exercifes, that are the fruits of his Spirit in them.

The word which we render *pleafant*, fignifies alfo *precious;* and the phrafe might be read, ' the fruits of ' his precious things.' According to the idiom of the Hebrew language, this may be put for his *precious fruits*. And all that is comprehended under his fruits is as precious as it is pleafant. The leaft valuable of thefe fruits could not be purchafed with all the " gold " of Ophir." But I apprehend the expreffion imports fomething more than this; namely, that all that the fpoufe had, or expected to have ready, for the entertainment of Chrift in his garden, was only the fruit of thofe precious things which himfelf had done for

her

her and given to her. It was all his own that she proposed to give him.

4. The last enquiry here proposed was, What we are to understand by Christ's *eating* those precious and pleasant fruits, which are here mentioned? To this, it will, perhaps, be unnecessary to answer, that the whole passage is allegorical; and, therefore, this expression cannot be meant of literal *eating*. Though Christ, in *the days of his flesh*, had occasion to eat and drink, for the support of nature, as other men do; this neither was the case when this book was composed, nor is it the case now in his glorified estate. Neither are the fruits here mentioned capable of being eaten in a literal sense. The expression includes the three things following.

(1.) His graciously accepting, at the hand of his spouse, what she has provided for him, and offers to him; as a man who is invited to an entertainment, receives what is set before him, that he may feed upon it. As Christians make an offering to Christ of all the benefits that they receive from him, and of all that they can do through the assistance of his grace in his service; so Christ is graciously pleased to accept the spiritual sacrifice. And that he may do so, is the matter of their earnest prayer and supplication.

(2.) His taking pleasure and delight in those fruits of his garden, as a man does in the food that he eats. Not only does Christ accept the offering that his spouse makes unto him, he accepts it with divine pleasure and satisfaction. The most sumptuous feast cannot afford such pleasure to the greatest sensualist, as Christ enjoys, in observing the fruits of his Spirit about his people; in taking notice of the improvement that they make of his gifts and benefits to his glory; and in gracioully accepting all from their hand.

(3.) His holding communion with his people in all thefe; as a man holds communion with his friend, when he fits at his table, and feeds upon what he had provided for his entertainment. If ever friends have comfortable intercourfe with one another, it may be expected when one entertains and feafts the other with the beft that his houfe can afford. When the fpoufe invites Chrift to an entertainment in his garden, fhe means not that he fhould eat his morfel alone. She wifhes to partake with him. That fhe may enjoy communion with him in it, is one principal part of her defign, in preparing him fuch a repaft. And, whatever provifion fhe makes for him, his company and fellowfhip fhe always confiders as the beft part of her cheer.

V. We are now to apply the fubject, in the following inferences.

1. Though the gracious prefence of Chrift is always in his Church; there are feafons when he may be faid to come to her, and to be prefent in her in a peculiar manner. Otherwife fuch a prayer as this would never be requifite, nor proper. The fame is the cafe with particular perfons among his people. From the moment, Chriftian, in which your happy union to him commenced, you never have been without his prefence, and never will. Nay, your communion with him has never been wholly interrupted. You have, at leaft, had communion with him in his righteoufnefs: which can never ceafe to be yours, for

all

all the purposes of your salvation. But your mournful experience can testify, that he has oft been absent to your apprehension; and oft have you wanted the comfortable sense, both of your union to him and of your communion with him. On the other hand, there are times when he enlightens your eyes to see him present with you; when the effects of his presence are so visible, that you have no room to doubt of it; and when he maintains communion with you in such a manner, that you cannot choose but be sensible of it. Of this also, some of you, I trust, have had experience. And you are all warranted to pray that it may be so.

2. There is nothing in the Church of Christ, suitable for his entertainment, but what proceeds from himself. His spouse can only invite him to eat his own fruits. In your natural estate, Christian, you had nothing about you that was not an abomination unto Christ. And now, if you differ from what you was before, or differ from what the world is, that lieth in wickedness, you owe it solely to the love and grace of Christ. If there is any thing that you enjoy, any thing that belongs to your nature, or any thing that appears in your practice, capable of acceptance in the sight of God, or capable of being viewed with pleasure by Christ, it is all his own. And when you offer it to him, you should say, as David on another occasion, *Who am I, and what is my people, that we should be able to offer so willingly? For all things come of thee; and of thine own have we given thee* *.

3. The blowing of the wind of divine influences upon the Church, or upon any particular believer, may

---

* 1 Chron. xxix. 14.

may be confidered as a happy earneft of Chrift's gracious coming to hold communion with that Church, or with that perfon. As the laft words of the firft claufe, fo the whole of this claufe of the verfe, may be read indicatively. *Blow upon my garden, and the fpices thereof fhall flow out:* then *my beloved fhall come into his garden, and eat his pleafant fruits.* If you have enjoyed to-day, or formerly, any roufing blaft of the north wind of conviction, fucceeded by any warming and cherifhing breeze of the fouth wind of divine confolation; you may confider it, and plead it as a pledge of his coming into your *garden* to *eat his pleafant fruits*, on every proper occafion.

4. Every perfon who invites Chrift into his garden, ought to be concerned about having fome proper entertainment ready for him. When Queen Efther invited her hufband, fhe did not fet him down at a table uncovered. She had her banquet of wine prepared. Indeed no wife man would invite any friend to be his gueft, without having fomewhat ready for his entertainment. And how fhall your glorious Hufband take it well, if you give him an invitation, and yet have nothing ready for him? The fpoufe here invites the wind to blow, that her fpices may be ready, before fhe invites her beloved to come and eat his fruits. Her fpices and his fruits are the fame thing, under different names. You who have been inviting Chrift, or wifh now to invite him to be prefent among us, be careful, as you would avoid his difpleafure, as you would not affront him openly, to have fome of thofe pleafant fruits, that his garden produces, ready to fet before him, when he condefcends to accept your invitation.

5. Here

5. Here alſo we may find various marks, by which intended communicants may try themſelves, about their fitneſs for a ſeat at the Lord's table. All who are in a capacity to feaſt with him, are perſons diſpoſed to invite him to an entertainment with them, as in the words of this text. More particularly, (1.) They readily acknowledge his rightful propriety in them, and the whole Church, as his garden. (2.) They confider him as their beloved, in preference to all other objects. As none ever loved as he did, they do not entertain a thought that any other ſhould be loved as he ſhould. (3.) They earneſtly defire his prefence, with themſelves, and in the Church; and long for communion with him in his own ordinances. If they have a proſpect of attending ordinances, they will not fail to invite him to meet with them in his own garden. (4.) They will be concerned to have their ſpices flowing out, *i. e.* their graces in exerciſe; and to have the fruits of holy and evangelical obedience ready for his entertainment. (5.) The fruits of Chriſt will all be pleaſant and precious in their fight. Not only will they find pleaſure in enjoying the precious gifts and benefits that are the fruits of Chriſt's purchaſe, they will find an equal pleaſure in being enabled, by his grace, to bring forth the fruits of holineſs to Chriſt, in their life and converſation. In a word, (6.) They will be careful to have every thing removed out of the way that may render his garden diſagreeable to him; and ſo provoke him either to refuſe their invitation, or to reject their entertainment, or ſpeedily to withdraw, after condeſcending to be preſent. They who are not diligent in " purging out the old leaven," are very unfit to

keep our New Testament *feast,* as it ought to be kept, " with the unleavened bread of sincerity and truth."

6. We may here see the indispensible duty of all that wish well to the interests of Christ in the Church, or are concerned about the eternal interests of their own souls. It is earnestly to cry for the presence of Christ, in the Church, and in their own souls; and, in order that we may be capable to give him a proper reception, to pray for the wind of divine influences to blow upon our garden. Let all persons who attend ordinances pray in this manner; for themselves, and for all their brethren. Unless he be present among us, we can have no feast. Unless he feast with us, our provision cannot be blessed; and therefore it cannot be profitable to us. Invite him then, tenderly and earnestly invite him to " come in- " to his garden and eat his pleasant fruits." Consider your garden as his garden, your spices as his fruits. Pray for his presence with you in particular: and see that you have some fruits ready for his entertainment. Unless he is present, there will be no satisfaction, no advantage enjoyed in an outward attendance upon his ordinances. He will not be present, unless there is something prepared for him. There will be no suitable preparation made, unless a blast of this spiritual wind spread abroad the fragrance of our spices, and ripen our fruits for Christ. And we have no reason to expect, either that the wind will blow, or that our Beloved will come, unless in the way of our asking it. But we know who has said, " Ask " and ye shall receive; seek and ye shall find; knock " and it shall be opened unto you." Let us, therefore,

fore, now join together, in a public manner; and let us all feparately exercife ourfelves, in our families and retirements, from this day till the day when *our folemn feaft is appointed;* in lifting up the prayer which is taught us in this verfe, and faying,

"Awake, O north wind, and come thou fouth
" *wind*; blow upon *our* garden, that the fpices there-
" of may flow out: Let *our* beloved come into his
" garden, and eat his pleafant fruits."

SERMON IX.

The Invitation accepted and returned; or, *Christ's gracious Presence vouchsafed to his Church, in Answer to her Prayer.*

SONG V. I.

I AM COME INTO MY GARDEN, MY SISTER, MY SPOUSE: I HAVE GATHERED MY MYRRH WITH MY SPICE; I HAVE EATEN MY HONEY-COMB WITH MY HONEY; I HAVE DRUNK MY WINE WITH MY MILK: EAT, O FRIENDS, DRINK, YEA DRINK ABUNDANTLY, O BELOVED.

WE are met for the celebration of a great feast: a feast made by the Redeemer and Husband of souls, for the refreshment of his spouse, whom he kindly invites to partake in it with him: and yet a feast kept by the spouse of Christ, for the entertainment of her *Beloved;* in which she humbly, yet tenderly, invites him to be graciously present with her.

We

We may attain a pretty diſtinct view of the nature of this feaſt, of the gueſts who partake in it, and of the proviſion upon which they feed, if we duly attend to what is ſet before us in this text.

There can be no doubt that theſe are the words of Chriſt. They contain his gracious anſwer to the requeſt of his Church, which is expreſſed in the laſt verſe of the preceding chapter. He ſays to her; yea, he ſays to every perſon in this aſſembly who has been eſſaying to pray for his preſence, as ſhe there does; " I am come into my garden, my ſiſter, " my ſpouſe," &c.

In the words we may obſerve three things, in general.

1. An intimation of the gracious preſence of Chriſt in his Church. " I am come into my garden, my " ſiſter, my ſpouſe." ' O thou my loving and affec-
' tionate bride, who ſo ardently longeſt, and ſo loudly
' calleſt for my preſence, in the garden of my Church;
' I tell thee that I am preſent, according to thy wiſh:
' *I am* already *come into my garden*, agreeably to
' thine invitation.'

2. An account of Chriſt's employment in the Church. " I have gathered my myrrh with my " ſpice; I have eaten my honey-comb with my ho- " ney; I have drunk my wine with my milk." ' I
' am not only preſent, ready to partake of that en-
' tertainment which thou haſt provided for me; I
' have taſted of it already. The fruits of my Spirit
' in the thee, and of thy love to me, are ſavoury as
' myrrh and the moſt fragrant ſpices; they are ſweet
' as honey in the comb; they are cheering as wine,

' and

' and delicious as milk. I accept and take pleasure
' in them accordingly.'

3. An invitation, tendered by him to his people, to partake with him in his repast. " Eat, O friends; " drink, yea drink abundantly, O beloved."· ' I ne-
' ver took pleasure in eating my morsel myself alone;
' thou didst kindly invite me to eat with thee; and
' I, in my turn, invite thee, my spouse, and all you
' my friends, the objects of my love and delight, to
' eat and drink plentifully with me.'

The words, thus divided and paraphrased, afford us the following doctrinal proposition.

All the friends and lovers of Christ may be assured that he is present in his Church, according to their desire; feeding, with pleasure, upon the produce of his garden; and graciously inviting them to feed, and feast with him.

In speaking from this subject, we shall, through divine assistance, take a brief view,

I. Of the presence of Christ in his Church, as here intimated.

II. Of the provision upon which he feeds.

III. Of his feeding upon that provision.

IV. Of the kindly appellations which he gives to his Church and people in this text.

V. Of the gracious invitation that he gives them to feast with him.

And then we shall conclude with some improvement.

I. That

I. THAT you may underſtand the intimation that is here given, of the preſence of Chriſt in his Church, it muſt be obſerved,

That Chriſt is not now preſent in his Church in human nature, nor in any corporeal manner. Once he came into his garden in this ſenſe; and, though he was *the heir*, the keepers did not heſitate to *kill him*, as this day's work evinces. But in this manner he returns no more, till *the time of the reſtitution of all things*. It is a fooliſh and abſurd notion, that Chriſt's body and blood are corporeally preſent in the *ſacrament* of the *ſupper;* equally repugnant to ſcripture, reaſon, and common ſenſe. Nay, Chriſtian, your expectations muſt not be ſo groſs or ſenſual. It is his ſpiritual preſence, by his Spirit working graciouſly in your hearts, that you are to look for in this ſolemn ordinance. And this may be enjoyed in every ordinance, at every time, and in every place. Concerning this, beſides what was ſaid upon the preceding verſe, we may obſerve the following things.

1. The gracious preſence of Chriſt, by his Spirit, is always in the Church, and with every one of his people. And, when their faith is in exerciſe, they will always ſee it to be ſo; that is, they will always believe him to be preſent, becauſe himſelf has ſaid it. ' When you pray for his preſence, you ought always to guard againſt hearkening to the ſuggeſtions of unbelief, ſo far as to apprehend that he is really abſent. This miſtake his people too often fall into. And if we conſider the ſpouſe as labouring under this miſtake in her prayer, theſe words contain a gentle reproof for her unbelief. ' Why ſhouldſt thou
' intreat me, O my deareſt ſiſter, my beloved ſpouſe,

'to come into my garden; as if I were now abfent
'from it, or ever could be fo? I am come into it
'once for all; and have ever continued in it fince it
'was firft planted. If thou didft not fee me, the
'fault was thine own. Thou didft not look where I
'was. Look, by the eye of faith, into my word of
'grace and promife, and thou canft not but perceive
'that I am always prefent with thee.'

2. He fometimes condefcends to be prefent, even to the fenfe of his people; fo that their own feelings may convince them that he is *come into* his *garden*. Though his ufual method is to carry on his work in a fecret manner, and to difcover himfelf only to the eye of faith; yet, when his people have any peculiar trial to undergo; when they have any piece of work uncommonly difficult to perform; when their faith is fo weak as to need a prop to lean upon; or when any other peculiarity in their condition makes it neceffary, he fometimes condefcends to manage his work fo vifibly, that they cannot choofe but fee it, and fee his hand at it: he difcovers himfelf to them fo clearly, that they can no more doubt of his prefence, than they can doubt of the fhining of the fun at noon day. Thefe manifeftations, as they are ufually very fhort, fo they are often balanced, either by fome trial that went before them, fome ftroke that accompanies them, or fome *meffenger of Satan* that follows them. Hence, though we may pray for them, we fhould always do it with much refignation. And we have no reafon to be diffatisfied when we want them. When he comes into his garden in this fenfe, he needs not tell his fpoufe that it is fo. Her own eyes inform her of it. But,

3. There

3. There is another sense in which he may be present in his Church at one time more than at another: I mean, in respect of his efficient, or operative presence. He may be said to be present, most remarkably, where he works in the most effectual and obvious manner. Sometimes his work, in the Church, or in the soul, is apparently at a stand. In such a case, he may be said to be absent in a great degree. But when he plucks his hand out of his bosom, and sets forward his work with speed and vigour, he may then be said to return, and come to his garden anew. Many instances might be produced from Scripture, in which his coming, or his being present, is to be understood in this sense. One very remarkable, you have in these words of the Psalmist Asaph: "Before Ephraim, and Benjamin, and Manasseh; stir up thy strength, and come and save us *." To this coming, the prayer of the Church in the preceding context refers. And to this also refers the declaration in the text. When any person is truly desirous of his coming in this way, and prays for it in faith, it may be considered as a token for good, not only that he will, come according to their request, but that he is come already, and his work is going forward in them, whether they be sensible of it or not. The same thing may be said of any church, or of any particular congregation, or society in the Church. He is really present with you, and his work in your soul is making progress, if you do but sincerely desire, and believingly pray for it. And if the body of this congregation has been offering such a petition this morning, or is presently entertaining such a desire, then he

is

* Psal. lxxx. 2.

is really come into his garden among us; and, whether his hand be seen at his work on this occasion or not, the happy effects of it shall both be seen and felt among us many days hence.

II. We proceed to speak of the provision upon which Christ feeds; as himself gives us his bill of fare, in the text. Concerning it we shall only take notice of the following things.

1. The provision here mentioned is of various kinds; for, *1st*, There is myrrh and other spices for perfume. Common people, at their meals, satisfy themselves with what is necessary to eat and drink. But kings and great men have their banquetting houses sprinkled with the richest perfumes, that the smell of their guests may be regaled as well as their taste. And the feast at which Christ is present must be according to the state of so great a King. *2dly*, There is *honey-comb with honey*, for the nourishment of the guests. Honey, as it is one of the most pleasant, is likewise one of the most nourishing things in nature. And when eaten in the comb, it is both most pleasant and most wholesome. Jonathan did but taste a little of it upon the top of his staff; and his *eyes*, which were ready to fail through weariness and fasting, *were enlightened*. Of such nourishing provision there is plenty in Christ's garden. *3dly*, There is *wine and milk*, for refreshment. At feasts, there must be somewhat to drink, as well as to eat. And here is drink of various kinds. Here is wine, for cheering and exhilarating the spirits; and milk, for restoring the decayed constitution. Strong men

may

may here be refreshed with wine; and babes may be suckled with milk.

If it should be asked, What spiritual things are represented by all this variety? We answer, in general, it represents all the fulness of the new covenant. But if you ask, more particularly, What is meant by each piece of this provision? For instance, what are we to understand by the *myrrh* and the *spices?* what by the *honey-comb* and the *honey?* &c. I can only reply, that I do not apprehend any one spiritual blessing to be represented by each of these. It seems rather the design of the Spirit of God, by all these together, to exhibit the various excellencies of that provision which stands upon Christ's table, and upon which he feeds with his people. This provision has a sweet favour to God, to Christ, and to all that feed upon it, like that of myrrh and other spices. It is sweet and nourishing, like honey in the comb. It serves to revive the drooping spirits, like the best wine; and to restore the soul, when in a weak and declining condition, as milk does the bodily constitution. In a word, it is suitable to the weakest, and within the reach of the poorest, as milk is in the world of nature; and yet, like wine, it is adapted to strong men, and to those who are rich and honourable.

2. The provision here mentioned, though the very best in nature, is yet the most plain and simple. We hear of no rich sauces, none of the refinements of cookery. These may please the palate; but they tend to ruin the constitution, and destroy the wholesome and nourishing quality of the food. In the natural world, that food is ever most wholesome which

is

is ufed as it comes from the hand of the God of nature; much more is this the cafe in the fpiritual world. All the refinements of human art, in dreffing out the food of fouls, tend to fpoil the relifh of the provifion; and are hurtful to the fpiritual conftitutions of the children of God. The garden of Chrift is like the land of Canaan; it " flows with milk and " honey." But all thofe pretended delicacies, that are the effects of human art, ought for ever to be banifhed from it. If they are introduced, Chrift does not feed upon them. He *eats* but the *honey-comb with the honey; he drinks* only the *wine* and the *milk*. And if ever his people tafte what he rejects, it muft be to their hurt. Thofe *enticing words of man's wifdom*, which many affect to ufe in difpenfing to the people of God their fpiritual food, may gratify thofe *itching ears*, which God, in his juft judgment, has made the plague of this generation; but they muft always prove hurtful to the interefts of genuine religion in the Church, and are often no better than a gilding to fome dangerous pill. That fublime and elegant fimplicity of ftyle for which the Holy Scriptures are fo remarkable, will ever be the moft ornamental, as well as the moft ufeful, in fpeaking or writing about divine things.

3. The provifion upon which Chrift feeds is all his own. It is fo in a twofold refpect. 1ft, It is all his own property: " I have gathered MY myrrh with " MY fpice, eaten MY honey-comb with MY honey, "·drunk MY wine with MY milk." Though Chrift will feed with his Church and people, fo as to hold communion with them in their folemn feafts, he will not feed at their coft. Nay, all that he feeds upon

is

is his own; fo is all that upon which they are invited to feed with him. It is all the produce of his own garden, the purchafe of his own blood. 2*dly*, It is all of his own providing. The *myrrh* and the *fpice* are of his own gathering. The fame may be faid of the other articles. All human inventions, in the worfhip of God, are an abomination. All human endeavours, in the fervice of God, when they are not affifted by the Spirit of God, are incapable of acceptance. It is only what the working of his own Spirit prepares, that can be fuitable entertainment for this Divine Gueft. And is it not matter of praife, believer, that when Chrift propofes to feaft with you, he does not leave it to you to make the provifion? Alas! If he did, God knows there would be little, either for his entertainment or yours. But, when he comes into his garden, he brings his whole feaft along with him. And, though you can, of yourfelf, provide nothing, you fhall find abundance on the table, if he is prefent, both for him and you.

But does Chrift, then, make no ufe of what was provided for him by his fpoufe? Did fhe not, when inviting him into his garden, plainly enough intimate, that fhe intended to prepare an entertainment for him, both of fpices and fruits? Was it not for this purpofe, that fhe fo earneftly requefted the blowing of the north and fouth winds? And is all her labour now in vain? Will he affront her fo egregioufly, as to tafte of nothing that fhe had prepared? Nay, he means not at all to affront her; nor does he rejeét her provifions. The myrrh and the fpice which he gathers, are the very fpices of her garden, which the blowing of the wind has caufed to flow out. The

Vol. II.   U   *   *honey*,

honey, the *wine*, and the *milk*, are the fame with thofe pleafant fruits which fhe had provided for him, and which fhe invited him to eat. But how can thefe things be prepared for him by his fpoufe, and yet be all of his own providing? They who are acquainted with the *myftery* of the Chriftian life, will fee no inconfiftancy here. The truth is, the fpoufe of Chrift muft ftill be active, and ever diligent, in making provifion for him. But all her activity, as well as all her fuccefs, is his work; for he it is that works all her works in her. So much fhe plainly acknowledges, when fhe prays for the blowing of the wind: and he again puts her in mind of it, when he calls the provifion *his.* Keep this ever in mind, Chriftian, on this, and on all after occafions; Chrift's feaft is all of his own providing. And yet you muft always exert yourfelf, in making preparation for him. You muft be as diligent in your preparation, as if you were to provide all: and yet, if he is pleafed to feaft with you, you muft be as humble, and as thankful, as if you had done nothing; knowing, that whatever was on the table, capable of entertaining either him or you, he brought it all along with him.

III. WE were next to fpeak of Chrift's feeding upon this provifion, In this we are much prevented by what was faid, when we fpake of his *eating his pleafant fruits;* as requefted in the laft verfe of the preceding chapter. To what was then obferved, we fhall only add the two following obfervations, arifing from the manner of fpeech ufed in the text.

1. Chrift, in defcribing the fatisfaction that he takes in the fruits of his own grace about his people, mentions
all

The Invitation accepted and returned. 307

all the actions of one that feeds plentifully and deliciously. *I have gathered, I have eaten, I have drunk;* intimating the fullest acceptance of what was offered to him, and the fullest satisfaction in it. As he is not scanty or churlish in what he bestows upon his Church, but allows her a full feast; so neither is he sparing or scrupulous in feeding upon her provision. He likewise enjoys a full feast with her.

2. He speaks not, by way of promise, in the future; but he speaks in the past time. Or, according to the Hebrew idiom, it may be read in the present time. ' I am come, I have gathered, I am eating, I am ' drinking.' No sooner had his spouse said, " Let " my beloved come, and let him eat," than he instantly replies, " I am come, I am gathering, I am " eating, I am drinking." Believing communicant, you cannot be more desirous of a feast with Christ than he is of a feast with you. You cannot be more earnest in inviting him than you shall find him ready in accepting your invitation. *As soon* as you *call* he will *answer;* and *whiles* you are *yet speaking* he will *hear* *. Yea, we dare affirm, that if you have been inviting him into his garden on this occasion, and to his own table, then he has heard you already, and granted your request. Already is he present in this assembly, feasting with you at the Gospel table; and taking pleasure in the fruits of his Spirit about you. For thus faith your beloved, and you know he cannot lie, " I am come into my garden, my " sister, my spouse: I have gathered my myrrh with " my spice, I am eating my honey-comb with my " honey, I am drinking my wine with my milk; eat,

" O

* Isa. lxv. 24.

" O friends; drink, yea drink abundantly, O belo-
" ved !"

IV. THE next thing propofed in the method was, to fpeak of thofe endearing appellations that Chrift here makes ufe of, when addreffing himfelf to his Church and people. They are, in number, four; two of them applicable to the Church in general, and two more directly applicable to particular believers.

The two that more directly apply to the Church, are,

1. *My fifter.* This intimates that the Church is related, not only to Chrift, but likewife to his God and Father. She is " the daughter of the King * ;" of the fame eternal and almighty King whom Chrift acknowledges as his Father; and all her genuine members belong to the fame family with him. God has made him is *firft-born;* and he is the " firft-born " among many brethren;" for all Chriftians are his brethren and fifters, being gracioufly adopted into that family of which he is the Head. Hence " he " is not afhamed to call them brethren †." Nor is God afhamed to call them children. He fays to them, " I will be to you a Father; and ye fhall be " my fons and daughters, faith the Lord Almighty ‡." This happy relation is likewife acknowledged on their part. Being endued with *the fpirit of adoption*, they learn to cry *Abba*, *Father*. Among the Jews, it feems to have been ufual to give the defignation of fifter to one's wife; but the Church is a fifter to Chrift, not only as fhe is efpoufed to himfelf, but likewife

* Pfal. xlv. 13.   † Heb. iii. 11   ‡ 2 Cor. vi. 18.

wife, as she is adopted, and acknowledged for a daughter by his Father.

2. *My spouse.* The former is expressive of the relation in which she stands to God; this expresses the relation by which she is joined to Christ himself. And this, on many accounts, may be compared to that which subsists between husband and wife. Like the marriage relation, it is constituted by virtue of a mutual engagement, or voluntary covenant, between those who formerly were not related by blood. Like the other, it subsists while the parties continue to live; and that shall be through all eternity. The glorious Bridegroom was once dead; but he is now *alive, and behold* he *liveth for evermore.* And, by virtue of her relation to him, his spouse also is secured against dying. *Because* he *lives,* she *shall live also.* The marriage relation is closer than any other upon earth; so that *a man* ought to *leave* his *father and mother, and cleave unto his wife.* This is still nearer than the marriage relation itself. And with this ancient law of marriage Christ has literally complied. He left his Father's bosom, when he came into our world, to lay the foundation of his union with the Church. And he left his mother, weeping and disconsolate, at the foot of his cross, when he was about to leave our world and return to his Father. All this he did, that he might cleave unto his Church; that she, and all her members, might continue, through eternity, to enjoy the closest union, and the most intimate communion with him. In a word, as the marriage relation is usually prolific, having been instituted for the propagation of mankind; so, in consequence of this relation, a numerous and holy seed is brought forth

forth to Christ in the Church. It comes to *be said of Zion*, and of particular churches,—I hope it shall be said of this place, " that this man and that man was " born there; and the highest himself shall establish " her *."

But, though these two designations, as here expressed, apply most directly to the Church in general, it is manifest that they likewise apply to every particular believer; as they are all adopted into God's family, and espoused to Christ by faith. In like manner, those appellations may be understood of the Church in general, which are more immediately directed to particular believers. These also are two; for,

1. He calls them his *friends*. *Eat*, says he, *O friends*. The reason of this compellation our Lord himself intimates, when he says to his Apostles, " Henceforth I call you not servants, but I have call-" ed you friends; for the servant knoweth not what his " Lord doth; but all things which I have heard of " my Father have I made known unto you.†." A person may sometimes have secrets, which he finds it improper to reveal, even to the wife of his bosom. But if he has a trusty friend, he can tell him all that is in his heart. Thus does Christ with his people; for " the secret of the Lord is with them that fear " him; and he will shew them his covenant ‡." He hath given them such proofs of a constant, an extensive, and unalterable friendship, as the world never heard of in any other instance. And he expects that they, in return, should maintain and give evidence of a faithful and inviolable friendship to him; for " he

* Psal. lxxxvii. 5. † Jo. xv. 7. ‡ Psal. xxv. 24.

"he that hath friends muſt ſhew himſelf friendly;"
"and *this is the* friend that ſticketh cloſer than a
"brother *."

2. He calls them his *beloved*. Concerning this word, as it ſtands in the original, two things are to be obſerved. (1.) It is in the plural number; and may be read, *my beloved ones*. Frequently does Chriſt addreſs the Church, in this book, as his love, or his beloved, in the ſingular number. Here the word is plural; intimating, that in the love which Chriſt bears to the Church, every particular Chriſtian has his ſhare. (2.) It is of the maſculine gender. All earthly marriages muſt take place between perſons of different ſexes; and this difference of ſex enters into the ground of all conjugal love among men. But the love between Chriſt and his people has no ſuch foundation. And when we think of the ſpiritual marriage between Chriſt and his people, we are carefully to abſtract from all ſuch carnal views. Here the bridegroom and the bride are both expreſſed by words of the ſame gender, intimating what an inſpired Apoſtle more fully expreſſes; *As in Chriſt there is neither Jew nor Greek, circumciſion nor uncircumciſion,* ſo neither is there *male nor female; but in Chriſt Jeſus all are one,* both head and members.

Now, as every member of the Church allows the higheſt place in his heart to Chriſt, and loves him above all other objects; ſo Chriſt has a love to them, that infinitely more than correſponds to their love to him. He loves them more than he does all the creation beſides. He loves them to ſuch a degree, and has given ſuch evidence of his love to them, that the

* Prov. xviii. 24.

the world never afforded, nor ever will afford any fimilar, or any comparable example. The tongues of all the angels about the throne, joined with thofe of all the redeemed from among men, though eternally employed on the fubject, fhall never be able, Chriftian, to tell how much he loves you; or with what propriety he calls you his *beloved.*

V. WE now come to the laft thing propofed on the doctrinal part of our fubject; which was to fpeak of the gracious invitation which Chrift here gives to his Church and people, to feed and feaft with him. Concerning this we fhall only take notice of the following things.

1. He invites them to a full feaft. " Eat, drink, " yea drink abundantly." Here is not only food for nourifhment, but alfo drink for refrefhment. In a fpiritual fenfe, hunger and thirft may be the fame thing: hence our Lord fpeaks of both as terminating upon the fame object, " Bleffed are they that hunger " and thirft after righteoufnefs *." Confequently eating and drinking, in a fpiritual fenfe, may fignify the fame thing. But this variety of expreffion is not ufed in vain. It fignifies, that whatever be the Chriftian's defires, if they are fuch as he ought to encourage, he will find that on Chrift's table which will gratify them. As that feaft would not be complete where either meat or drink fhould be wanting, fo Chrift would not think his table fufficiently furnifhed, if there wanted any thing that any of his guefts could ftand in need of, or could reafonably wifh for. The feaft, believer, to which you are invited, is full and

* Matth. v. 6.

and complete. Whatever is adapted to your various neceffities, you may have it for the ufing. If you are *ftraitened*, therefore, it muft be *in your own bowels;* in your Hufband you cannot be ftraitened. Whether you are ftrong or weak, a babe in grace or a grown Chriftian, a difconfolate mourner or one that fhouts for joy; you will find on Chrift's table all that is fuited to your condition, and that in exhauftlefs plenty.

2. He invites them to a fulnefs in feafting. As he is not fparing in his acceptance of what his fpoufe, under the influence of his Spirit, provides for him, but takes and feeds upon the whole; fo neither does he wifh any of his friends to be fparing, in their acceptance and ufe-making of what he has provided for them. He invites, not only to eat, but to eat plentifully. He fays, not only *drink*, but he adds, *drink abundantly*. The original word literally fignifies, *drink and be drunken*. This, in our language, carries an idea, that is far from being comely; and therefore our tranflators have rightly paraphrafed it, *drink abundantly*. But, in the firft language, the world conveys no fuch image. It means, that you are invited to drink of the *cup of falvation*, as deeply as they drink of wine and ftrong drink, who are thereby ftupified and made drunken. The wine and milk that are here provided do not intoxicate. The more you drink of them, the more active and vigorous will all your fpiritual fenfes be. Drink, therefore, and drink abundantly, of all that is brought to hand. Here there can be no excefs. Though all the fulnefs of the New Covenant is fet before you, there is nothing to which you are not welcome. Take not fparingly;

sparingly; take all that is on the table. You will not leave the less to your brethren; nor will you ever find the less served up for yourself on any after occasion. Appropriate to yourself by faith, all that you can need in time; and all that is sufficient to make you happy in perfection through eternity. " The liberal deviseth liberal things; and by liberal " things shall he stand."

3. He invites in the most pressing and importunate manner; *drink*, says he, *yea drink*. Nothing can be more disagreeable to Christ, than to see any person at his table with *his hand in his bosom*. Not only they who are his genuine friends, but all who hear the invitation, provoke him egregiously if they eat not. Think not, sinner, that you have no concern in this matter, because you are none of his friends. You appear *as* his friends, while you sit around his table attending a gospel dispensation; and to you also is his invitation addressed. The invitation in this text is indeed tendered, in a peculiar manner, to his friends. But the feast that he makes *on this mountain* is *a feast unto all people*. We, as the servants of the great King, are commanded to invite, to press, yea, even to *compel* you *to come in; that* his *house may be filled*, and his table furnished with guests. Oh! that the guests were as numerous, as the provision is ample and various! " We then are ambassa- " dors for Christ: As though God did beseech you " by us, we pray you in Christ's stead," to eat and drink abundantly of his provision. *Eat*, and be the bridegroom's *friends*. " Drink, yea drink abundant- " ly;" and so shall you be among the number of his

beloved

beloved ones. If you refift all his importunity, yourfelves, and not he, will be the lofers.

4. He invites them to feaft with himfelf. Chrift tells you that he is prefent in his garden; that he has eaten and drunk; or, as we told you the words might be read, that he is now eating and drinking. At the fame time, he invites you to eat and drink in company with himfelf. It is not in your hufband's family, as it was in Jofeph's; where they behoved to eat at different tables, becaufe one part of the company were an abomination to the other. Here all the guefts are reputed the friends of the mafter of the feaft. He fits at the fame table with them, and entertains them in perfon; while himfelf is entertained by them and with them. As Abfalom was not content with being at Jerufalem, without feeing the king's face; fo no real Chriftian will be fatisfied with eating of Chrift's provifion, if he be deprived of his own company. His prefence at the table makes the principal ingredient of the feaft. And you need not fear but you fhall have it. He is not fo inhofpitable or unfriendly, as to invite his friends to an entertainment and never *come in to fee the guefts.* Nay, he fits at the table during the whole repaft. Himfelf taftes of every difh. And he it is that diftributes to every one his portion. Not only will he fend meffes to each of you, as Jofeph to his brethren; himfelf will lay your mefs in your difh. Yea, his own condefcending hand will put every morfel into your mouth. For thus faith your beloved, " Open thy " mouth wide, and I will fill it."

5. In a word, He invites them to a feaft upon the fame provifion upon which himfelf feeds. You may

eat

eat the same honey-comb which he eats. You are to drink the same wine and milk of which he drinks. And the same myrrh and other spices, which give a smell to his own garments, shall both gratify your spiritual senses, and cause you to send up a pleasant savour in the nostrils of God. The same fruits of his Spirit, that constitute a feast to him, you also may feast upon them; for if he takes pleasure in them, all the profit of them accrues to you. And the same fruits of his purchase, which himself enjoys in his exalted state, are really served up to you, on his table, both in word and sacrament. Those very blessings which God, according to the tenor of his covenant, hath bestowed upon him as the first-born of the family of grace, he also bestows upon you; and exhibits to you in the gospel-feast. These are the gifts which he *received for men*, when he *ascended on high ;* and it is thus that he gives them unto men, in a gospel dispensation. You are called to take them, to use them; and to unite with them, as a man does with the food that he eats. Yea, a chief part of the satisfaction that Christ has in them, arises from your participation of them with him. You know, it is long since he said, " My meat and my drink is to do the " will of my Father, and to finish his work." This is the case in his exalted state, as really as it was in his humiliation. And the work which his Father now employs him in, is to bestow upon his people those benefits which he purchased by his obedience unto death. Thus every blessing that you receive from the hand of Christ is a feast, both to him and to you. You feed upon the same provision that he eats. You do so now at the table below. And, through

all

all eternity, you fhall do fo, at the table in the upper houfe.

VI. We fhall now draw to a conclufion, with fome practical improvement of the fubject. For the prefent, we fhall fatisfy ourfelves with the following inferences. From what has been faid, we may fee,

1. How highly the Chriftian is dignified and honoured. Barzillai the Gileadite, notwithftanding all his wealth and greatnefs, counted it a very great honour to fit at the table of an earthly prince. So did Mephibofheth, though himfelf the grandfon of a king. How much greater is the honour to which you are advanced, Chriftian? You are permitted, nay you are commanded, to fit always at the table of the *King of Glory;* and to eat and drink in his prefence! Even this is not all. You are admitted into the family of God. You are acknowledged, by Chrift, as his brethren and fifters. You are called his friends, and allowed to fhare the fecrets of his bofom. You are even efpoufed to himfelf, and made the objects of his love, that wonderful *love that paffeth knowledge.* Oh! difhonour not yourfelf, nor affront your hufband, by whom you have been fo dignified, by a conduct unworthy of yourfelves, or of him.

2. How richly the Chriftian is fed and provided for. Your food, you have heard, is all the fulnefs of God's covenant, " the fatnefs of his ' ʳ· " You have even the flefh and blood of his feed upon. Is not this *meat indeed deed?* What a glorious difference ; this and thofe withered *hufks, that* world *eat;* and with which you

ut

to fill your belly! Since your provision is so exquisite, is there any danger that ever it should become loathsome? Since it is so plentiful, can there be any danger that ever you should want? Nay, " the young " lions may lack, and suffer hunger; but they " that truly seek the Lord shall not want any good " thing *."

3. How comfortably Christians are matched. Even the honour of being espoused to *the Prince of the kings of the earth* is not all that makes your marriage comfortable, Christian. Such is the character of your Husband, and his disposition towards you, that you can think of nothing about him which may not afford you comfort and satisfaction. He is a Husband that treats you as a *sister*, and as a *friend*. He is ever ready to come to you at your call; for he takes pleasure in your company. Though he has all the affairs of heaven and earth on his hands, yet he is ever at leisure to wait upon his beloved, when she calls upon him, or has need of his presence. He has made such provision for you, that you can never want. And he never desires you to take a meal without his presence. He loves you as never another husband loved the wife of his youth; and it is impossible that ever his love should change. To crown all, he never dies; nor will he ever suffer you to die. That grim messenger, which dissolves all earthly marriages, will only bring you home to the everlasting consummation of your marriage with him. And where, in heaven or in earth, can you find another husband like him? Or who are they that are such strangers in Israel, as to say, or have any occasion

* Psal. xxxiv. 10.

sion to say concerning him, " What is thy beloved, " more than another beloved? O ye that are still married to the law, that tyrannical, oppressive, and cruel lord, see that you lose not a moment, but presently sue for a divorce, and rest not till you obtain it; that you may be married to this better, this incomparably best of husbands.

4. How little reason the people of God have, at any time, to complain of Christ's absence; and how groundless all such complaints must needs be. Be not surprised, Christian, at the assertion. Methinks I hear you saying, ' What! shall I not complain ' when my husband withdraws himself? Surely ' if such a complaint be groundless, there is no- ' thing in hell itself a sufficient ground of complaint. ' Is not his absence the principal ingredient of the ' misery of that dismal place? And why should not ' I complain heavily when my Lord is away?' Yes, poor soul, thou shouldest have reason to complain indeed, if it were possible that ever he should be absent from thee. But sooner shall " the mountains depart, " and the hills be removed," than any such thing shall take place. You shall see these " heavens roll- " ed together as a scroll, the earth and the works " thereof burnt up, and the *very* elements melting " with fervent heat; *but never shall you, nor any " other for you, see* Israel forsaken, nor Judah of her " God; though her land *should* be filled with sin a- " gainst the Holy One of Israel:" Aye, and filled with blood too, on account of that sin. The same is equally true of every particular believer. He may withdraw from you the sense of his presence; or you, by reason of your unbelief, may lose sight of him.

But

But the declaration in the text is, and ever will be, a current truth. He has said, and who ever heard him say an untruth? " I will never, never, never " leave thee, nor forsake thee." His gracious prefence shall never be withdrawn from you; nor shall you ever want his operative prefence, when you sincerely defire it. Therefore, all complaints of his abfence, in this refpect, muft be worfe than groundlefs. They are fo many flanderous lies, to the prejudice of his faithfulnefs and love.

5. What encouragement they have, who continue ftrangers to Chrift, prefently to match with him. You have heard, finner, that every fuch perfon as you are, has an invitation to partake in the feaft of fat things that ftands on the gofpel table. But you cannot partake in it, without clofing with Chrift himfelf. Along with an invitation to his marriage-fupper, he gives you an offer of himfelf, as your Lord and Hufband. And declares himfelf willing to *betrothe* you to himfelf *for ever.* In a way of accepting this offer, you are welcome to all that ftands upon his table, either in word or facrament. But while you refufe himfelf, you cannot tafte of his fupper; for himfelf and his benefits can never be feparated. If, therefore, you wifh well to your own foul, if you defire to feed eternally upon the fatnefs of God's houfe, if you would not ftarve within fight of plenty; if you wifh to efcape all the feverity that you muft otherwife fuffer, from that fiery law which is your prefent hufband; if you would fhun thofe gnawings of confcience, that muft eternally be the refult of a final rejection of this offer; I befeech you
consult

consult your own happiness; and let me, this day, have the honour of espousing you, *as a chaste virgin unto Christ.* Then all the great things that his spouse enjoys, as the fruits of her union to him, shall be yours. He will count you his *sister,* his *spouse,* his *friend,* his *beloved.* He will hearken to your calls; and be ever present with you, at your desire. He will graciously accept the provision that you make for him, however unworthy of him it may appear. Himself will make ample provision for you, in every case. You shall be nourished at his cost, while you continue in this world; and it is but a little when you shall be set down with him at the table that shall never be drawn. And what objection can you have against such a match? Can you ever be as happy in the arms of any of his rivals? Surely no. He *is fairer than the children of men.* All created beauty disappears, like a glow-worm before the meridian sun, in his presence. You may despise him, because you never knew him. But surely there was never one who saw him, that could think of a comparison between him and any other; nor one who was not ready to join in the declaration of the spouse concerning him—" My beloved is white and ruddy, " the chiefest among ten thousand. His mouth is " most sweet, and he is altogether lovely. This is " my beloved." Oh! that every person in this assembly would join, this moment, in saying, " This is " my beloved, and this is my friend, O daughters of " Jerusalem."

6. In a word, we may see from this subject, what plentiful encouragement they have, who wait upon divine

divine ordinances with a defire to fee Jefus, and to have fellowfhip with him in them; particularly, what encouragement we have, to fet forward, with cheerfulnefs, in the great work of this day. You have been wreftling, I truft, for the blowing of the *wind* of divine influences, to make the *fpices* of your garden to *flow out.* You have been endeavouring to provide an entertainment for your beloved, in his garden. And you have been giving him repeated invitations to come and feed upon it. After all, you are fenfible that your provifion is unworthy of him; and perhaps you are doubtful whether he will accept your invitation or not. But we come, in his name, to affure you, that all your doubts are groundlefs. The unworthinefs of your provifion fhall be no bar in his way; for he will bring his provifion with him. Yea, he is already prefent among you; his provifion is in his hand; and it is richly fufficient, both for him and you. Already is he begun to feaft upon it; and he is tenderly inviting you to feaft with him. Set but the eye of faith to the glafs that is prefented to you in this text; look through it to the head of his own table; and you fhall affuredly fee him prefent, feeding and inviting. Let us, therefore, fhow ourfelves as ready to accept his invitation, as he has been to accept and comply with ours. And let us go forward, with cheerfulnefs and joy, to meet him, to adore him, to commemorate his dying love, and to feaft with him at his table. It is the voice of our beloved! Hear him juft now faying, and faying it to every perfon among us, that fincerely defires his prefence,

" I

" I am come into my garden, my fifter, my fpoufe;
" I have gathered my myrrh with my fpice ; I am
" eating my honey-comb with my honey ; I am
" drinking my wine with my milk : eat, O friends,
" drink, yea drink abundantly, O beloved."

An Use of Trial, delivered as the Fencing of the Tables.

AS we are now to set forward to the celebration of the sacramental feast, which Christ has instituted in the New Testament Church, for the entertainment of his friends and beloved ones; and as none but such can be welcome to this table, it is necessary that every person, who has received a token of admission, should bring himself to the test of the word of God; that he may know both his state and his exercise, how far they do, or do not, correspond to the character of the bride of Christ. Your having essayed the duty of self-examination before, does not render it unnecessary now, whatever reason you then had to consider yourselves as among the friends of Christ. On the contrary, the nearer you come to the solemn action, the more strict and impartial should you be in your scrutiny; that you may be in a condition to make use of your provision, in a manner adapted to the present necessities of your soul. To assist you in this duty, the text will furnish a variety of questions; which we go on to put to every conscience among you, in the name of the Great Master of this feast. And we charge you, that you do not satisfy yourself with any answer, but such as will be sustained at the tribunal in a little.

1. Are you a member of the same family with Christ, and a child of the same Father? In our natural estate, we are all the children of the devil. And you

you ſtill belong to that accurſed family, if you bear the devil's image, delight to be employed in his work, and ſeek to fill your belly with thoſe huſks which are the only proviſion that his houſe affords. In that caſe you cannot be welcome at the Lord's table; for you *cannot drink of the cup of the Lord and of the cup of devils.* But if you have been determined to forget your own people, and your father's houſe; if you have been taken into the family of God, and endued with the ſpirit of adoption; if you wear the robe of righteouſneſs, with which all the family are covered; and have taſted of the proviſion of the family, ſo as to be now appetiſed for a new feaſt upon it; then you are a brother or a ſiſter of Chriſt, and himſelf invites you to his table.

2. Are you truly eſpouſed to Chriſt? She whom he invites is his ſpouſe, as well as his ſiſter. And there are no ſingle perſons, in a ſpiritual ſenſe. You are all married, either to Chriſt or to the law. The laſt is the cruel huſband, to whom we are all joined in our natural ſtate. And they all continue ſo joined, who ſeek *righteouſneſs as it were by the works of the law;* who allow themſelves in having any dependence upon any thing wrought in them, or done by them, as any part of the ground of their acceptance with God; who indulge themſelves in making free with Chriſt or his benefits, becauſe they think themſelves ſo and ſo qualified; or yet in ſtanding at a diſtance from him, becauſe they find thoſe qualifications wanting about themſelves. If you are of that number, you cannot be a welcome gueſt at this table, in your preſent ſtate. But we are warranted to invite you to it, if you *through the law* are become *dead to the law,*

law, that you might be married to Chrift; if you are fenfible that your own righteoufnefs is but *filthy rags*, and are willing to " count *it* lofs and dung for " the excellency of Chrift Jefus *your* Lord;" if you have heard Chrift engaging to *betrothe* you *to* him- felf *for ever*, and have been determined to confent to the happy match; if you are prefently difpofed to fay concerning him, as the fpoufe does, in a former part of this book, " My beloved is mine, and I am " his;" for, in this cafe, you are confidered in hea- ven as efpoufed to Chrift, and we invite you to his table accordingly.

3. Are you really the friends of Chrift? They are fuch, and fuch only, whom he invites in the text. And the friendfhip between him and them is mutual; while all the reft of the world are enemies to him, and objects of his enmity. More particularly here,

(1.) What evidence has ever he given of his friendfhip to you? He calls his people friends; be- caufe he *fhews* them *all that he has heard of* his *Father*. Has he, then, made known the myftery of his Fa- ther's will to you, and admitted you to know the fe- crets of his covenant? I do not mean it of external revelation only; this you all enjoy; for I fee Bibles in your hands. Neither would I be underftood of any new revelation, not contained in the Bible; this none of you can reafonably expect to enjoy. But has he brought home his written word, with power and efficacy upon your heart and confcience, fo as to let you fee and feel that in it, of which no carnal mind was ever apprized? Have you felt *the word of God* to be *quick and powerful, fharper than a two-edged fword;* feparating between you and thofe

corruptions,

corruptions, that were as clofely united with your nature as *the foul* is with *the fpirit*, or *the joints* with *the marrow?* Has he brought you to fee the plan of falvation, which is revealed in the word, as in every refpect worthy of that infinite wifdom which laid it down; and every way fuitable to the neceffities of your foul? Then he deals with you as friends; and you are welcome to a new proof of his friendfhip at his table.

(2.) What evidence can you produce of your friendfhip to him? "He that hath friends muft "fhew himfelf friendly; and *this* is the friend that "fticketh clofer than a brother." Are you difpofed, like John the Baptift, to rejoice at the hearing of his voice? Do you rejoice at feeing him increafe, though you fhould decreafe? Are you happy to fee his work profpering, though it fhould be at the expence of your reputation, or of all that is deareft to you in the world? Do you ufe that familiarity with him which a man ufes with his intimate friend? Is it your ordinary method, to take the firft opportunity to impart to him all your fecrets; to acquaint him with all your perplexing cafes; and to unbofom yourfelf to him, in another manner than you could do to any perfon on earth? Do you always take his part behind his back; and bear your teftimony againft all the flanderous afperfions that are caft upon him, all the indignities that are done him, and all the treafonable confultations that are held againft him in your fight? Are you concerned about all his intetereft, and ready to put to your hand for maintaining and promoting them; and for rectifying all that you fee amifs in his houfe? In a word, Are you friends to

thofe

those who are his friends, and enemies only to his enemies? Do you *hate all those that hate* him? Are you *grieved with those that rise up against* him? But are they who bear his image the objects of your delight, the companions of your choice; and, as occasion offers, the chief objects of your beneficence? Then, all these are undoubted evidences of friendship to him; and himself invites you to his holy table.

But we must debar you from this table, while you neither have any genuine friendship for him, nor have enjoyed any saving communications of his friendship. All ye to whom the Bible continues to be a sealed book; you who have never seen any beauty, nor felt any power or efficacy in the word of God, serving to convince you, more than a thousand arguments, that it is no mere human composition; you to whom the plan of salvation, through a crucified Redeemer, still appears to be foolishness, you are hitherto enemies to Christ. So are all ye who wish yourselves to encrease, though Christ should decrease; who can use more freedom with any other than with him; who have no concern about the dishonour that is done him in the world, unless when you apprehend yourself liable to be punished for it; who cultivate the friendship of his enemies, or entertain hatred and enmity against his friends. Such persons can have no business at his table; unless it be, that, while they *eat* his *bread*, they may the more successfully *lift up* their *heel against* him.

4. Are you among the number of his *beloved ones?* These are they whom he invites to a feast with him. 'Alas!' may some say, 'This is the main thing that 'I am at a loss to know. Could I be sensible that I
'was

' was chosen in him, and was an object of his love
' before the foundation of the world, this would set
' my heart at ease; and I could go forward with
' cheerfulness to the work of the day.' But you
should take care not to begin at the wrong end of
your work. It is not electing love that was exercised from eternity, but his love of complacency that
terminates upon his people just now, that is directly
intimated in the text. And it is this, not the other,
about which you are called, more immediately, to
examine yourself. If once you find yourself to be
an object of this, then you may likewise be sure, that
you was an object of the other. Nor have you any
other method of attaining such assurance. Now you
are presently the objects of his love, if you bear his
image, and are daily pressing after more conformity
to him ; for he loves all that are like himself. He
really loves you, if you have ever been enabled to
appropriate to yourself those intimations of his love,
that he makes to his people in his word; and to trust
in his love, so intimated, for all those fruits of it that
you need. You may certainly conclude that he
loves you, if you feel, or ever have truly felt, the
constraining power of his love; if a view of his unmerited love to you, has kindled in your heart a flame
of love to him that many waters cannot quench;
and if this love operates, as an invincible cord, in
drawing you after him, in a course of evangelical
obedience to his law, and in a diligent attendance in
those places where his presence may be expected; if,
in a word, it is your earnest desire, and, through
grace, your fixed resolution, to *live henceforth, not
to yourselves, but to him that loved you* in such a degree,

gree, that he *died for* you. All these may likewise be considered as sure evidences that he loved you from all eternity, when he struck hands with the Father, in the making of the covenant of grace; that he had you, in particular, on his heart, when his love affixed him to the accursed tree; and that he had a special eye to your spiritual nourishment, when he instituted this feast, in the *same night in which he was betrayed.*

But if you are strangers to his image, and neither desire to be like him, nor to walk as he walked; if you have always considered the offers and intimation of his love as things in which you had no personal concern; if you have never felt the constraining influence of his love, nor consider him as deserving your affections, more than any other beloved; then you have nothing about you that can appear lovely to him. You are still an abomination in his sight; and your appearing at his table, in your present condition, would only tend to expose you to his wrath.

5. Have you seen him present on this occasion, ready to feed you, and to feast with you? It may be thought hard to exclude all from his table, who have not already seen him since they came to the place. And, doubtless, it would be hard to exclude all who have not seen him in a sensible manner. But surely none can be welcome to it, who have not seen him by faith. He has been setting himself before you, in the clearest manner, in the text; as already *come* into his *garden*, as *gathering*, as *eating*, as *drinking;* and as inviting his friends to eat and drink with him. You have all heard him making that declaration; and you have either believed him or not.

If you believe that he speaks the truth, you must have seen him present; for this act of believing is that seeing of him, which we require as a mark of your fitness for his table. If, therefore, you have not seen him, it must either be, because you do not consider these as the words of Christ to this assembly, or because you consider him as speaking a falsehood when he says so. In either case, you have called him a liar to his face, as often as you have heard the text repeated; you continue to do so still; and surely, while that is the case, you cannot be fit for a seat at his holy table. But if you have seen him present, according to his word; if you consider these words as the words of Christ to you; if you believe that he brings no false report concerning himself; if you propose to go forward in his work, trusting that you shall find him present according to his promise; if it is your sincere desire thus to believe his word, though you may be sensible of a sad prevalence of unbelief, then you are invited by Christ himself, in the text; and we should contradict our Master, if we should take upon us to keep you back. We, therefore, invite you kindly, to your seat at the holy table of the Lord.

6. What think you of the provision that stands upon Christ's table, in word and sacrament? Are you pleased with the perfume of that myrrh and those spices which Christ has gathered? Is his honey-comb sweet to your taste? Do you consider his wine and milk as nourishing and delicious? Is the flesh of Christ meat indeed, and his blood drink indeed, in your esteem? To speak without allegory; the righteousness of Christ, and all the fruits of his righteousness,

righteousness, to be enjoyed in grace here and in glory hereafter, even to full conformity to the image of Chrift, and a complete enjoyment of all his fulnefs; this is what you are now called to feed upon. And does your foul lothe it as light bread? Is your own righteoufnefs better than Chrift's, in your efteem?—Would you rather be conformed to the prefent world, than transformed into the image of God? Would you choofe to poffefs a few handfuls of white and yellow duft, rather than to inherit all the fulnefs of God? Then you need not go to the Lord's table; it will afford nothing fuited to your tafte. But if you are weary of thofe empty hufks which this world affords, and long for the bread of your Father's houfe; if you confider the food that Chrift exhibits to you, as comparable to honey for fweetnefs, to wine for richnefs, and to milk for its pleafant fimplicity and fuitablenefs to your weak condition; and if the whole difpenfation of grace, in which this provifion is exhibited, fmells to you like aloes, myrrh, and caffia;—then your tafte refembles Chrift's, and you are welcome to a feaft with him.

7. Are you difpofed to accept Chrift's invitation, and to eat and drink *abundantly* at his table. He is much difpleafed to fee his guefts, like the fluggard, putting their hand in their bofom, and grieving to bring it to their mouth. If you mean to fatisfy yourfelf with an outward attendance, or with a bare participation of the external elements, you will but mock Chrift, and befool yourfelf by coming to his table. But if you truly hunger and thirft after Chrift's righteoufnefs; if you refolve, through divine grace,

grace, to receive, appropriate, and ufe all that Chrift brings to hand, and fets before you; if you are prefently endeavouring, by the exercife of faith, to do fo, then you are a hearty gueft, fit for the table of fuch a liberal giver; and we invite you to your feat among his beloved ones.

8. How long do you wifh the feaft in Chrift's garden to laft? Are you, like Doeg, detained before the Lord, already weary of attending public ordinances; and faying, when will the Sabbath be over, that we may return to our bufinefs, and to our gain? Is it enough to you that you feed upon Chrift's provifion, while a facramental occafion lafts, though you return afterwards to the devil's fare? Then you had better keep at a diftance; for you cannot drink the cup of the Lord and the cup of devils. But, on the contrary, all you are welcome to this table, who come forward faying, as did the Jews of Capernaum, " Lord, evermore give us this bread;" who, though you know the facramental table will foon be drawn, refolve every day to *keep the feaft* upon the fame provifion, as it ftands always ready on the gofpel table; longing for that happy period, when you fhall be fet down at the table above, which fhall ftand covered for ever.

9. In a word, What returns do you propofe to make to Chrift, for all this ample and rich provifion that he has made for you? Is all this infufficient to make you afhamed of difhonouring him by fin? Are you ftill difpofed to perfift in breaking all the commands of both tables of his holy law? Do you love and worfhip and ferve the creature, more than the Creator? Will you ftill defpife, neglect, or profane the

ordinances

ordinances of divine appointment? Can you think of polluting his holy name among his enemies; or defiling his sanctuary in the same day, and profaning his Sabbaths? Dare you live in the neglect of relative duties; or persist in lying, stealing, killing, committing adultery; or any other practice, inward or outward, tending thereunto? And is your heart still going after your covetousness? Then surely you were never apprised of the value of what Christ brings to your hand, nor affected with gratitude for what he has done for you. And while this is the case, we cannot but debar you from this holy table.

But if the consideration of his undeserved and inestimable goodness fills you with shame and self-loathing, on account of your past sins; and makes you resolve to *take the cup of salvation, to call upon the name of the Lord*, and to *pay your vows unto the Lord, now* and in all time coming, *in the presence of his people ;* if you sincerely resolve upon a constant, regular, universal, and evangelical obedience to all the laws of Christ ; in the inward, as well as in the outward man ;—if you are determined, through divine grace, that Christ's God, and he alone, shall be your God ; that Christ's ordinances shall be carefully observed by you, without addition or diminution ; that his name, and his Father's, shall be objects of your habitual reverence, and his Sabbaths your delight ; if you resolve to imitate your husband's example, by a dutiful and affectionate behaviour towards all your relatives, natural, civil or religious ;— if you are disposed, not only to abstain from every thing injurious, but even carefully to maintain and watch over the life, the chastity, the outward estate,

and

and the good name of all your neighbours, as well as you own; and if you hate covetoufnefs as idolatry; —if fuch is your prefent difpofition, however oppofite your former practice has been, then you are the very perfons to whom our Lord addreffes himfelf in this text. He moft tenderly and importunately invites you to his table, promifing his gracious prefence with you there; yea, declaring that he is prefent already, with all his rich provifion in his hand, kindly to welcome, and liberally to entertain you. Thefe are the words of your Beloved, and he fpeaks them to every one of you, " I am come into my garden, my " fifter, my fpoufe, I have gathered my myrrh with " my fpice; I have eaten, I am eating my honey- " comb with my honey; I am drinking my wine " with my milk: Eat, O friends; drink, yea drink " abundantly, O beloved."

SERMON X.

Ifrael's Power with God; or, *The Bleffing of God upon his People, a happy Confequence of his gracious Interviews with them.*

Gen. xxxii. 29.

——AND HE BLESSED HIM THERE.

IT is a great happinefs to be allowed to attend upon the ordinances of God, as we do this day. And it is matter of thankfulnefs, that fuch a number of perfons, as I fee before me, are brought up, in providence, to keep the folemn feaft which we have in view. Yet all this will avail us nothing, unlefs Chrift himfelf be prefent among us, to blefs our provifion, according to his promife, and to blefs us. But it will be a day much to be remembered unto the Lord, if there be reafon, in the iffue, to fay concerning us, in this place, as it was faid of Jacob at Peniel, in the words of this text,—" He bleffed him there."

From

From the 24th verſe of this chapter, we have an account of a very remarkable interview that Jacob had with *the angel of the covenant*, at the ford of the river Jabbok. It may not be improper to take a view of the happy iſſue of this wonderful conteſt; in Jacob's obtaining that for which he wreſtled ſo powerfully, while the angel *bleſſed him there*.

Beſides the conjunctive particle *and*, by which the text is connected with what goes before, it conſiſts but of four words; each expreſſive of ſomething deſerving our attention.

1. A glorious agent is ſpoken of, in the pronoun *he*; the man who wreſtled with Jacob. This was no other than Chriſt himſelf, putting on an appearance of that humanity, which he afterwards really aſſumed.

2. We have an action aſcribed to him, in the word *bleſſed*. The bleſſing was that for which Jacob had wreſtled long. And it was beſtowed upon him at the laſt.

3. The object of this action is expreſſed, in the pronoun *him*; referring to the patriarch Jacob. Though the angel had disjointed his thigh, and hitherto ſeemed to refuſe him what he ſought, yet he prevailed at laſt.

4. We have the place where this tranſaction happened, in the particle *there*; including alſo the time of it. At the place where Jacob had wreſtled ſo long, at Peniel, by the ford of Jabbok, juſt as the day began to dawn, when Jacob's preſence could no longer be wanted with his family, then and *there he bleſſed him*.

Vol. II.   Y   *   It

It would afford little edification, and would be in a great degree foreign to the work of this day, to speak of the text barely as recording an attainment of the patriarch Jacob, near four thousand years ago. But Christ is still ready to deal with us as he did with him; we need the blessing as much as he did. And, in the way of wrestling for it, after his example, we have the same reason to expect it; for,

Wherever our blessed Lord condescends to meet with his people, and allows them to wrestle with him for that effect, there is the fullest encouragement to expect that he will bless them there.

IN discoursing from this text and doctrine, we propose, through Divine assistance, to enquire,

I. What it is that we are here encouraged to expect?

II. From whom we are taught to expect it?

III. Who they are that may look for it?

IV. When a person may be said to receive it?

V. Where there is ground to expect it? And,

VI. What improvement should be made of the whole?

I. IN general, what we are here taught to expect is *the blessing*. For understanding hereof, you will do well to attend to the following things.

1. As *blessing* is every where opposed to *cursing*, so the blessing which we may expect from Christ, is opposed to that curse under which all mankind lie, in their natural estate. That curse, you know, is the sentence of God, the supreme Judge of all the earth, condemning the sinner to undergo the punishment
which

which is juftly due to him, as a tranfgreffor of the Divine law. The bleffing, therefore, muft alfo be *a judicial fentence, paft by a fimilar authority, fetting the perfon free from all the effects of the curfe; and adjudging him to the enjoyment of a happinefs, worthy to be beftowed by him that paffes the fentence.* Hence,

2. To *blefs*, in a ftrict and proper fenfe, can be the work of none but a divine Perfon. God alone can effectually curfe; becaufe none elfe has power to execute the fentence of eternal condemnation. In like manner, God alone can blefs; becaufe none but he can execute the fentence of bleffing, by putting the perfon in poffeffion of that happinefs to which he is thereby adjudged. Befides, all mankind being naturally under the curfe, a fentence of bleffing, relative to any of them, muft needs include an abrogation of the curfe. But the curfe which God has pronounced, no other can have authority to reverfe. What Balak faid of Balaam, can only be faid, with propriety, concerning the fupreme God. *He whom thou bleffeft is bleffed; and he whom thou curfeft is curfed* *. Yet,

3. The act of *bleffing* is fometimes afcribed to men in Scripture. And they are faid either to blefs God, or to blefs men like themfelves. When a man is faid to blefs God, it can only be meant of an afcription of bleffednefs to him; including a declaration of our perfuafion, that God is infinitely bleffed, or happy, in himfelf; and is the fole fountain of all happinefs to his creatures, together with our holy and humble acquiefcence in him as fuch. In this fenfe muft we underftand

* Numb. xxii. 6.

understand the frequent exhortations to bless God, which we have in various places of Scripture.

When one man is said to bless another, it either means no more, but his praying to God for a blessing upon him; so it is to be understood in this expression, "We bless you in the name of the Lord *;" which is thus paraphrased in the verse translation:

"We in the name of God the Lord
"do wish you to be bless'd."

Or otherwise, it must be understood ministerially, of a person having a commission from God for that purpose, pronouncing, in the name of God, a blessing which none but God can execute. Thus the patriarchs, under the inspiration of the Spirit of God, blessed their children. Thus the priests, of old, were authorised to bless the people. And thus the ministers of the gospel are warranted to do still.

4. Sometimes the word is used, to signify the actual communication of that happiness, to which the person had been previously adjudged by a sentence of blessing. To this purpose, God is said to have "blessed "us with all spiritual blessings, in heavenly places, in "Christ Jesus †." Not only has he, by a judicial sentence, appointed us to enjoy all those spiritual benefits that are laid up in the hand of Christ, in heaven; but, in consequence thereof, he hath given to every genuine Christian a real and personal interest in the whole. And, even while they continue in this state of mortality, he distributes to them, out of that fulness, according to their necessity, *even grace for grace.*

5. It

---

* Psal. cxxix. 8.   † Eph. i. 3.

5. It is impoffible for any of mankind to enjoy a bleffing, in any proper fenfe, unlefs through the Lord Jefus Chrift. When our firft parents were created, God was pleafed with the workmanfhip of his own hands; and he *bleffed them*. But when fin entered, that bleffing was forfeited; and a curfe was denounced againft them, which is entailed upon all their pofterity. And fo ftrictly juft is the great *Judge of all the earth*, that none of them can get free from the punifhment to which they are adjudged, till their fentence has been fully executed, and the law fatisfied for their offence. This can never be accomplifhed in the finner himfelf; but it was accomplifhed in Chrift, when he " was made a curfe for us, that " the bleffing of Abraham might come upon us " through him." It is, therefore, in his right only, and in confequence of the imputation of his righteoufnefs to us, that any of us can inherit a bleffing. And in this way only it is promifed to us. For *men shall be bleffed* only *in him; and all nations shall call him bleffed* *.

6. They who are thus bleffed *in* Chrift, muft alfo be bleffed *by* him. What he purchafed for us, by his blood, as the furety of the covenant, he likewife beftows upon us as the adminiftrator of it. This leads us to enquire,

II. From whom it is, that we are here taught to expect the bleffing. It is from no other than Chrift himfelf.

We fhall not need to infift in proving, that it was *he* who bleffed Jacob on this occafion. He who wreftled

---
* Pfal. lxxii. 17.

wreftled with the patriarch, though in appearance a man, very plainly calls himfelf God, when he fays, " As a prince haft thou power with God *." Jacob was fenfible that he was a divine Perfon, as appears from his faying, " I have feen God face to face ; and " my life is preferved †." The prophet Hofea plainly determines that he was an *angel*, and yet *the* LORD *God of Hofts,* whofe *memorial is* JEHOVAH ‡. Surely all thefe characters can belong to no other perfon but Chrift. He is God, equal with the other divine Perfons. Yet he is the Angel, or Meffenger of God's covenant. Now he is alfo truly man; and, though he had not then actually taken upon him our nature, it was fit that he fhould appear as a man, to furnifh, both to Jacob and others who fhould hear of this interview, a happy pledge and prelude of his actual incarnation.

Neither fhall we detain you long, in proving that it belongs to him to blefs his people, in the manner above explained. If we view him as God, equal with the Father, he has the fame authority to blefs, and the fame power to execute his fentence, that the other perfons of the Godhead have. If we confider him as Mediator, it belongs to him to perform this, and every other act of judgment, in the Church. For himfelf informs us, " the Father judgeth no man, " but hath committed all judgment unto the Son ‖." He had power, even when he was on earth, to forgive fins. That power he actually exercifed. And, now that he is in heaven, it is one fpecial end for which " God hath exalted him a Prince and a Savi- " our, to give repentance unto Ifrael and the for-
" givenefs

---

* Ver. 28.   † Ver. 30.   ‡ Hof. xii. 3, 4, 5.   ‖ John v. 22.

" givenefs of fins." The forgivenefs of fin cannot be given, without giving the bleffing at the fame time; for both are only parts of the fame fentence of juftification, which it belongs to Chrift, as a branch of his kingly office, to pronounce. Yea, the actual communication of that happinefs, to which believers are adjudged by this fentence, is likewife his work; as he is the adminiftrator of God's covenant, or the executor of his own teftament. Were we to fpeak at large concerning this glorious Perfon, time would fail; yea, eternity fhould be too fhort, to number up all his excellencies. The following confiderations concerning him, ferve greatly to enhance the value of every bleffing that he beftows upon us.

1. He is one, from whofe hand, inftead of deferving the bleffing, we had amply deferved the curfe. That he gives the bleffing freely, is matter of wonder and of praife. But even the freenefs of this gift is not the moft wonderful circumftance concerning it. Adam, in innocence, was bleffed freely, without any merit on his part; for, even according to the tenor of the covenant of works, Adam merited nothing, till the condition of that covenant was fulfilled. But to us, Chrift gives the bleffing not only without, but againft merit. We have merited the curfe, though he gives us the bleffing. We deferve death in its utmoft extent,—he gives us eternal life. We deferved to have funk for ever in the bottomlefs abyfs of mifery,—he exalts us to an inconceivable height of glory and happinefs. Yet all the fin, by which we had deferved this, was committed againft him. And he was as much difpleafed with it as he poffibly could be. But his difpleafure againft the fin

does

does not ſtop the egreſs of his mercy to the ſinner. He gives *pardon* and the bleſſing to us, though he neceſſarily muſt *take vengeance on* our *inventions*.

2. He is one who actually had curſed us, condemning us to ſuffer all the puniſhment that our ſin ſo richly deſerved. King Darius was reduced to a ſad *dilemma*, when he had bound himſelf by a law, which the conſtitution of his kingdom rendered unalterable, to caſt Daniel, his principal favourite, into the den of lions. From this he could not extricate himſelf; though *he laboured*, for that purpoſe, *till the going down of the ſun*. At laſt he was obliged to execute his own ſentence, though he did it with the utmoſt reluctance. But ſuch a ſituation proved no *dilemma* to Chriſt. He had paſſed a ſentence much more unalterable than the *laws of the Medes and Perſians*; condemning all his elect, among the reſt of mankind, to be caſt into the den of that *roaring lion*, who *goes about* inceſſantly, *ſeeking whom he may devour*. But infinite wiſdom, prompted by infinite love, found out a method to maintain his faithfulneſs inviolate; and yet to deliver his people from the puniſhment which they had been condemned to ſuffer. Their ſentence is reverſed, and yet executed to the full. The firſt ſentence is not altered, and yet an oppoſite ſentence is both paſſed and executed upon them. He who formerly curſed you, believer, in the moſt dreadful manner, now bleſſes you in moſt ample form. This he does without any change at all on his part; and without any previous change to the better on your part.

3. He is one who is infinitely beyond either enjoying any advantage, or ſuffering any diſadvantage,

by

by any thing that ever could have taken place with regard to us. He was from eternity, he will be to eternity,—he unchangeably *is* from eternity to eternity, incomprehenſibly bleſſed in himſelf. He can neither be more nor leſs ſo, whatever take place among his creatures. Neither our bleſſing nor our curſe can add any thing to him, or diminiſh any thing from him. In all the beneficence that one man ſhews to another, there is uſually a great mixture of ſelf. But no ſuch principle could have influence with Chriſt, in any part of what he did for us. However ample the bleſſing is which he beſtows, nothing could move him to beſtow it, but pure, unmerited, and diſintereſted love. Oh! that it did but meet with ſuitable returns, from thoſe who are the happy objects of it.

4. He is the ſame who endured the curſe for us; and bare all that puniſhment, which that curſe denounced, in our room and ſtead. Our ſentence of curſing was incapable of being wholly reverſed. All that could be done was to divert the execution of it, from the ſinner to a ſurety. But where ſhould a ſurety be found, that was, at the ſame time, willing to underly the puniſhment in our ſtead; and able to ſatisfy divine juſtice, by ſuffering all that was contained in our ſentence? All the creatures, though joining their power into one, had been for ever unequal to the mighty taſk. Neither heaven nor earth could furniſh a proper perſon, below the throne of God. But the eternal Son of God, in his love to our family, undertook, from all eternity, to be our Surety, and to bear our curſe. This undertaking he cheerfully executed, *when the fulneſs of the time was come.*

Thus

Thus he shed his precious blood, that we might be capable of enjoying the blessing. Had he given us what cost him nothing, however valuable it was to us, there had been no such display of love or grace on his part. But now his love shines, in the whole transaction, beyond all parallels, beyond all comparison, beyond all expression, beyond all finite comprehension. It shines with a lustre that will astonish heaven, and confound hell, through all the ages of eternity. And what is it, Christian, that you may not expect from this love? He *gave himself for* you, to procure your right to the blessing. And he gave himself to you, as your Lord and Husband, when he met with you, in the day of espousals, and *blessed* you *there*. And dare you, after all, pour disgrace upon his love, and upon himself, by your unbelieving doubts about his willingness to give you any thing that you need?

5. He is the same person who is to execute the sentence of blessing, by putting us in full possession of all that happiness to which we are thereby adjudged. He who gave him authority to pronounce the blessing, gave him likewise a commission to make it good. And he gave into his hand, for that effect, all that infinite fulness which himself possesses. For " it hath pleased the Father, that in him should all " fulness dwell *." Neither is there any thing in his commission, that he has not sufficient power to execute; whatever opposition he may meet with from enemies, in bringing us forward to the state of promised blessedness. Already have we seen him assaulted by the powers of hell and earth, combined

to

to prevent his procuring the bleffing for you, believer; and that in the very inftant when he had the full flood of divine wrath to conflict with, and none to help or uphold him; yet his *own arm brought falvation* unto him; and his enemies were trodden down in his anger. Surely they will never again attack him at fuch a difadvantage. And, feeing he was then victorious, you may be affured that he will be fo on every occafion, till he have brought you, and all your brethren, home, to the full poffeffion of all that to which you are entitled by virtue of the fentence which he has paffed upon you.

III. We now proceed, through divine affiftance, to inform you, who they are to whom Chrift gives this bleffing. Upon this head we mean not to infift. Only, that every perfon prefent may know what right he has to expect a bleffing from Chrift, we fhall here obferve the two things following.

1. He offers and exhibits the bleffing to all that hear the gofpel indifcriminately. Whatever is your character, or whatever it has been; whatever it was that brought you hither, or in whatever manner you are juft now employed, *life and death* are *fet before you, the bleffing and the curfe;* and you are at full liberty to choofe for yourfelves. As really as Chrift ftood in the temple, on the laft and great day of the laft feaft of tabernacles, " and cried, If any man " thirft, let him come to me and drink," fo really is he prefent in this affembly, on this great day of our gofpel feaft, crying, by the mouth of a finful worm like yourfelves, and faying, ' If any man, or any wo-
' man, young or old, rich or poor, faint or finner, pro-
' feffor

'fessor of religion, or profane person; if any descen-
'dant of Adam, sensible of his misery under the curse,
'wishes to be delivered from it, let him come unto
'me, and I will bless him.' Yea, though you are
not sensible of your condition, nor have any desire
after Christ, nor after any blessing that he can bestow, even this stupid insensibility does not exclude
you. Nothing on this side death can shut the door
of access upon you, which Christ himself has opened.
For he *opens and none can shut*. Come to him, then,
whatever you are. If you cannot come of yourself,
he will draw you; and, as he draws, he will bless
you. He will bless you so as none in heaven, earth,
or hell, shall ever reverse it. He will bless you this
very moment. He will bless you here.

2. He actually bestows the blessing; he has bestowed it already, upon every person who is but
willing to receive it. In the moment of a person's
union to Christ, he undergoes a twofold change.
There is a real change made upon his nature and
disposition; by virtue of which he loves Christ, whom
he hated before; becomes willing to embrace those
gracious offers which he formerly rejected; willing
to be blessed in Christ, and cheerfully to call him
blessed. There is likewise a change made in his relative state, or in his standing before the law and justice of God; by which he is set free from the curse,
and made to inherit a blessing. Now, as these two
always go together, the person who has undergone
the first change can never want evidence that he
has undergone the other. Consequently, he who is
really willing to receive the blessing, in the way in
which it is offered, is blessed indeed. At what time
soever

foever it was, or in whatever place, that you found yourfelf made truly defirous to be bleffed in Chrift, or fincerely willing to receive the bleffing from him, you may be as fure, as you are of the prefent fhining of *that* fun, that *he bleffed* you there.

IV. IF it is enquired, When Chrift may be faid to blefs a perfon, as Jacob was bleffed at Peniel? We anfwer, in the following particulars.

1. He does fo, when, by a fentence of juftification, he abolifhes the curfe under which the perfon lay in his natural eftate, and adjudges him to the enjoy: ment of the favour of God, and of all that happinefs that proceeds from it. Then it is that the man *receives the bleffing from the Lord, and righteoufnefs from the God of his falvation* *. In what place foever you was, Chriftian, when fuch a fentence paffed in your behalf; it may be faid, with the greateft propriety, that *he bleffed* you *there*.

2. When, by a new intimation of that fentence, he gives eafe to the troubled confcience, and allows the perfon a comfortable view of it, that he is bleffed. When the fentence of juftification is paft in heaven, it is ordinary for God to intimate it in the court of confcience, by a word of grace. The fentence itfelf will ftand for ever ; nor can there ever be occafion for any renewal or ratification of it. But the intimation of it to the confcience is in danger of being forgotten. The impreffion of it wears gradually off. And the perfon is in danger of being perplexed with apprehenfions, however groundlefs, of the curfe ftill hanging over his head. To remove thefe apprehenfions,'

* Pfal. xxiv. 5.

fions, and to reftore that comfort and joy in the Holy Ghoft, which are among the fruits of juftification, the fame word of grace, by which the fentence was intimated at the firft, or another of the fame import, is fent home upon the confcience with the fame power as before. The perfon's faith is drawn forth into exercife; fo that he gives credit to the divine teftimony contained in that gracious word. His foul is, by that means, filled with joy and peace in believing. And he is enabled to confider himfelf as a bleffed perfon. If ever you have had experience of fuch a thing as this; if God has brought home upon your confcience fuch a promife as this, " I will be " merciful to their unrighteoufneffes, their fins and " their iniquities will I remember no more," enabling you to make a believing application of it to your own foul; then you furely felt a bleffednefs, that nothing fublunary could equal. And you may be affured that you ftill are, and ever fhall be *bleffed of the* LORD *that made heaven and earth.*

3. When, in a time of peculiar neceffity, he difcovers to them the applicablenefs of their fentence of bleffing to their prefent condition; the fecurity it affords them againft any danger that they fear, or the encouragement it affords them to expect any benefit which they need. It was fuch a bleffing as this that Jacob infifted for, and obtained, on this occafion. God had appeared unto him at Bethel, and had bleffed him twenty years ago *. The bleffing which he had then received ftood in the fame force now as before; fo that he did not now need to be bleffed, as one that had always been under the curfe hitherto. Yea, what

---

* Chap. xxviii. 13, 14, 15.

what God said to him at Bethel, included all the blessing that he now either received or sought for. But at this time a peculiar danger hung over him; his brother was coming against him with *four hundred* armed men. The aspect of Providence was peculiarly dark before him. On this account his faith began to stagger; and he was ready to doubt whether the blessing formerly granted him, was any security to him in his present case or not. Therefore he sought, and the Lord granted him, such an explication and enlargement of his former blessing, as convinced him that it was applicable to his present circumstances; and determined him to set forward in his journey, at the call of God, despising all the dangers that threatened him. The same, Christian, may often be the state of matters with you. The blessing that was past upon you, in the day of your justification, extended to every case that ever you can be in. But, when the aspects of Providence begin to darken, when all seems going to confusion, within you and around you; and when, to crown all, God himself seems to deal with you as if he had become your enemy, then you begin to apprehend, that no promise, upon which you was caused formerly to hope, has any relation to your present condition; and you are ready to give up all for lost. In such a case, has not the great angel of the covenant sometimes paid you a new visit? Has he not discovered to you some other promise, whose application to your present condition you could not dispute? Has not this been a happy mean of clearing up all your doubts, relative to former experiences; and convincing you that your former blessing extended also to your present

sent case? And, wherever this happened, you will surely acknowledge, that *he blessed* you *there*.

4. When, from time to time, he communicates to them, according to their necessity, those benefits which the blessing ensures. This happy sentence begins to be executed the moment that it is past. The happiness to which Christians are thereby adjudged, begins that moment to be enjoyed. And what they enjoy here, is, for substance, the same with what they shall enjoy hereafter; though much inferior, both in the degree, and in the manner of enjoyment. All the fulness of God is theirs, in consequence of the blessing which Christ pronounces upon them. To bestow upon them of this fulness, is one main design of every visit that he pays them. And he sometimes bestows so largely, that they enjoy a foretaste of heaven. And, oh! how they then *rejoice, with joy unspeakable and full of glory!* Such communications are usually allowed them, during their attendance upon divine ordinances, of one kind or other. And this is one thing that strengthens their attachment to the courts of God's house. If this has contributed to bring any of you to this assembly today, you may consider it as a token for good, that he will *bless* you here.

In these four consists that blessing, which the Christian may expect, at the ford of Jabbok, during his pilgrimage on the wilderness side of the river. But something incomparably better shall be enjoyed, when once he has past the ford of Jordan. Then will Christ meet with you, believer, never to part again. And he will bless you in a manner corresponding to such a meeting. He will then bring you

home,

home, to the full, immediate, and eternal enjoyment of all that your sentence bears. He will then say to you, as himself assures us, " Come, ye blessed of my " Father, inherit the kingdom prepared for you be- " fore the foundation of the world." But how he will bless you then it is impossible for us to tell. Though an angel from heaven should attempt it; though one of your brethren, who is already in possession of that blessedness, were to return to this world for the purpose of describing it, they would find it impossible to do it in any language that mortals could understand. Your own happy experience will inform you in a little, to better purpose than any words can, in what manner he will *bless* you *there*.

V. WE hasten to the next enquiry proposed; namely, Where it is, that such a blessing may be expected from Christ? The sentence of blessing is always past in heaven. But, as to those communications of divine goodness that are the fruits of it, they may be enjoyed any where. But, as particular notice is here taken of the place where Jacob obtained this blessing, I apprehend it is done with a special design to encourage others to expect a similar blessing, when they come to be in circumstances similar to those in which Jacob was at Peniel. For the encouragement, therefore, of such as desire the blessing, we shall observe, that Christ blesses his people,

1. Wherever he condescends to meet with them. In a proper sense, he and they never have a meeting but one; and then they meet, so as never totally to part again. I do not speak of the day of death, nor of the day of Christ's second coming, but of the day

of their effectual calling. Then an union commences, between him and them, that shall never be diffolved. And from that time forth his gracious prefence is continually with them, while they remain in this world. Surely, wherever they are, when this happy meeting takes place, it will not be doubted that he *bleſſes* them *there*. But there is another fenfe, in which there are many meetings between him and them, and many partings. I mean, in refpect of his fenfible and comforting prefence. Though he is ever with them, *their eyes*, like thofe of the two difciples, are often *holden*, *that they* do *not know him* to be prefent. They can perceive no evidence of his being with them; and therefore they not only think him abfent, but doubt if ever he was prefent with them, or ever will. Then they fore lament his abfence, and *go mourning without the fun*. When he finds their faith in danger of failing, and that they can no longer bear the apprehenfion of his abfence, then he is pleafed again to draw afide the viel, and open their eyes to fee him prefent with them. Now they can truft him, that he never will be abfent; and, perhaps, are convinced that he was prefent, when their complaints of his abfence were loudeft. Then their mouths are opened, their hearts are enlarged. They find themfelves fupernaturally affifted in wreftling for the bleffing. And they prevail. If ever you enjoy fuch a vifit, it will be a difappointment to him, as well as to you, if you do not refufe to let him go, except he blefs you.

2. He does fo wherever they wait upon him in the believing expectation of enjoying a bleffing. Jacob, on the occafion to which the text refers, could have

have no reason to stay behind his company, unless to seek an opportunity of holding communion with God, in the duty of secret prayer. For this he had a loud call in providence; and in this exercise he met with the blessing. The ordinances of divine grace are trysting places; where Christ has engaged to be present with his people, and bless them. What he said to Moses long ago, he as really says to us: " In all " places where I cause my name to be recorded, I " will come unto you, and I will bless you." And when any person attends upon his ordinances, in the faith of this, or any such promise, it is impossible that that person should go away without the blessing. Is there, then, any person in this assembly, attending ordinances, under the influence of a sincere desire to meet with Christ, and to receive the blessing from him? We are warranted to assure such a person, that he shall not lose his errand. Nay, *the* LORD, *whom ye seek, shall suddenly come to his temple.'* Yea, he is come already; for the appointment cannot be broken on his part. He is come to bestow upon you whatever blessing is suitable to your present condition. And, whether you are sensible of it or not, we dare assure you, that he will *bless* you here.

3. Wherever they wrestle with him for the blessing. This was Jacob's exercise at the ford of Jabbok; and the text informs us of his success. Our Lord gives nothing to his people for their asking; but he loves to give them all, in the way of their asking it of him. It is no wonder that they have not, when they ask not, or when they ask amiss. But we have an express command to ask, accompanied with a promise equally express, that, in so doing, we shall receive.

And we may be assured, that he who hath made the promise will accomplish it. Consequently, when any person asks, according to the command; he shall be sure to receive, according to the promise. Perhaps you may not receive the very thing that you asked. Or, if you do, it may not come at the precise time, or in the exact manner in which you looked for it; because the infinite wisdom of God knows much better how to give, than you know how to ask. Besides, he often delays the answer of your prayers, that he may lead you out to wrestle with him for it, in a persevering and importunate manner. But, if you ask any thing that is contained in the covenant of grace, and persist in wrestling for it, as Jacob did for the blessing, you shall assuredly receive it, or else something better instead of it, in God's good time and way.

4. He often blesses them even where he seemed to deny their request, and made as if he intended to leave them without the blessing. This was the case with Jacob here, as the context informs us. The woman of Canaan is another memorable instance of the same thing. At first he seemed utterly to neglect her. When the disciples applied to him to dismiss her, he gave them an answer that seemed to import a refusal of her petition. When she still continued to cry, he gave her not only what any other would have construed into a flat denial; but, along with this, he seemed to call her a dog, and to spurn her from his footstool. Yet, after all, when her faith, supported by secret communications from himself, surmounted all these difficulties, and wrestled on; he was pleased to make her own will the measure of his bounty

bounty towards her *. " Go and do likewife." Then, before you leave the fpot, where he feemed to give you the refufal, you may confidently expect that he will *blefs* you *there*.

5. In a word, He often bleffes them in the fame place where he had pled a controverfy with them, and touched them feverely with his afflicting hand. The *angel* wreftled againft Jacob, while Jacob wreftled with him. Yea, fo far did he carry his teftimony againft the fins of the patriarch, that he left upon him a ftanding mark of his difpleafure, in the diflocation of his thigh. Yet, after all, he granted him the bleffing that he prayed for. There is much fin about the beft Chriftian in this world; and, though Chrift loves their perfons, he cannot but hate their fin, and teftify againft it. When he beftows any bleffing upon them, he often does it in fuch a way as to recal their fin to their remembrance; and make them fenfible how much they deferve the curfe. As foon as he has laid them low enough in humiliation, and made them, like Jacob, confefs what is their true name, he begins to raife them up; gives them a new name and a bleffing.

I know there are various perfons prefent, upon whom the Lord has been laying his hand of late, by various kinds of trials. On this account their heads hang down, perhaps, and their hearts are heavy. ' Alas!' fay they, ' how fhall I expect the bleffing? ' God has a controverfy with me; and he has been ' pleading it with much feverity. He has laid afflic- ' tions on my body, deprived me of my deareft rela- ' tions, fubjected me to the fcourge of the tongue; ' and,

* Matth. xv. 22,—28.

'and, which is worſt of all, left me to walk in dark-
'neſs, with regard to my ſpiritual caſe. And what
'can I expect, but that he will continue to plead his
'controverſy even at his table, if I ſhall venture for-
'ward to it? I am convinced that he will be juſt in
'ſo doing. And I dare not expect,—I ſcarcely dare
'aſk the bleſſing.'

But, "O thou afflicted, toſſed with tempeſt, and
" not comforted; *he* will *yet* lay thy ſtones with fair
" colours, and thy foundations with ſapphires." What
do you know, but it was one principal deſign of his
paſt contendings, that his controverſy might be happily taken up; and might not ſtand in the way of your
receiving that bleſſing which he intends this day to
beſtow upon you? The chaſtiſements that he lays
upon his people are influenced by fatherly love, as
well as by fatherly diſpleaſure. And the ſame love
which moved him to chaſten you before, may now
influence him to bleſs you. However ſeverely he has
chaſtened you of late,—yea, though his hand be ever
ſo heavy upon you at this moment; inſtead of doubting his willingneſs to bleſs you, you may even draw
an argument from your afflicted condition, and plead
with him, that proportionable to the ſeverity of the
touch that he has given you, may be the value of
the bleſſing with which he will bleſs you here.

VI. We are now to conclude with ſome improvement of the ſubject. At preſent we ſhall but name
the following inferences.

1. There is a happy difference between the people
of God and the reſt of mankind. All the poſterity
of Adam, having ſinned in him, and fallen with him,
come

come into the world under that curfe which the law of God denounces againſt every tranſgreſſor. By that fearful ſentence, they are bound over to a puniſhment which they can never fully bear. And it is every moment in danger of being executed. Thus the ſinner hangs continually over the mouth of the *bottomleſs pit;* ſuſpended by the bare thread of life, which is liable to be broken by every accident. But the people of God, having met with the angel of the covenant, have obtained the bleſſing from him. Their ſentence of condemnation is reverſed. They have an intereſt in all that fulneſs which God has cauſed to dwell in Chriſt. They are entitled to have their journey-charges defrayed out of it, while they are here; and have ſecurity for the full poſſeſſion of the whole in due time. Thrice " happy is the people " that is in ſuch a caſe. Yea, happy is the people, " whoſe God is the LORD."

2. We here ſee the real importance of a meeting with Chriſt; and the improvement that Chriſtians ſhould make of ſuch a privilege, when allowed to enjoy it. If the bleſſing of God is a thing of any value; if the curſe of God is terrible, in its nature and its conſequences, then a meeting with Chriſt muſt be a thing of the greateſt moment; for wherever he meets with his people, he bleſſes them there. Strangers to Chriſt may now ceaſe to wonder, why Chriſtians are ſo anxious in ſeeking him whom their ſoul loveth. They have good reaſon to ſeek him above all things. Oh! that they were more ſenſible of their duty and intereſt in this reſpect. You whoſe buſineſs it is really to ſeek him in his ordinances to-day, ſee that you deſiſt not till you find him. Having found

found him, wreftle with nim; and let him not go till he blefs you. Wreftle for a bleffing to your families and relatives, to your brethren in Chrift, to the Church of God. If you are enabled to do fo, he will certainly blefs you here.

3. We may here fee the true value of gofpel ordinances, thofe means of grace which we enjoy. Thefe are the places where Chrift has appointed to meet with his people, and to blefs them. And furely an opportunity of attending, where Chrift has promifed to come, muft be precious. Good reafon have the people of God to *love the habitation of* his *houfe, and the place where* his *honour dwelleth.* However much divine ordinances may be defpifed by thofe who are ftrangers to Chrift, and to that bleffing which he beftows, the time is haftening on, when one of thefe *days of the Son of man* will be confidered, even by the moft profane, as more valuable than a thoufand worlds. So foon as the finner is beyond a poffibility of enjoying fuch a privilege, he will begin, alas! too late, to be fenfible of its true value. " Tremble *at* " *this,* ye that are at eafe in Zion; be *fore* troubled, " carelefs ones." Thofe things which you efteem, and upon which your hearts are fet, are no more than empty bubbles, mere *vanity and vexation of fpirit.* The things which you defpife, and turn to ridicule, are much more precious than diamonds. Oh! be not fo foolifh, as ftill to contemn *the things that belong to* your *peace,* until they be *hid from* your *eyes.*

4. We here fee good encouragement to perfeverance and importunity in prayer, however little fuccefs we may have for a long time. In the days of his flefh our Lord taught, " that men ought always
" to

" to pray and not to faint." He taught the same thing, by his manner of dealing with this patriarch long before. Jacob had wreſtled long; he was detained the whole night, even to the breaking of the day; he had met with many apparent refuſals; the Lord had teſtified his difpleaſure againſt his former ſins, and even ſeemed to ſhew difpleaſure on account of his preſent importunity; yet, after all, his importunity prevailed, and he obtained the bleſſing which he ſought. Let neither delays, nor ſeeming refuſals, nor rebukes in Providence, nor any thing in God's manner of dealing with you, nor any thing in your paſt conduct towards him, nor any other conſideration whatſoever, prevail with you, to deſiſt from pleading with him for any bleſſing that you find neceſſary. If you are enabled to follow Jacob's example, by continuing to wreſtle in faith, we dare promiſe you an anſwer of peace in the iſſue.

5. We may hence learn the true character of all genuine Iſraelites. They are perſons who are ſenſible that they are, by nature, under the curſe; and that deliverance from that dreadful ſentence can only be obtained through Chriſt. They are perſons who not only deſire freedom from the curſe, but earneſtly wiſh for communion with Chriſt, and with God through him; and embrace every opportunity of ſeeking after it. They are willing to bleſs themſelves in Chriſt; and to be indebted to him for every bleſſing here, and for all bleſſedneſs hereafter. They are endowed with a wreſtling ſpirit; and, like princes, have power with God, and prevail. They have ſome experience of the anſwer of prayer; and of being bleſſed, in conſequence of their wreſtling for it.

it. And they are difpofed to manifeft their gratitude for what Chrift has done for them, by cheerfully calling him bleffed; and by yielding a willing and univerfal obedience to all his commandments. By thefe things you are called to try yourfelves. If this character fuits you, it is a comfortable evidence that you may be welcome to the Lord's table; and an encouragement to hope, that, according as your circumftances fhall require, he will blefs you there.

6. We may here fee both what we have to do, and what we have to expect from the hand of Chrift to-day. The folemn ordinance, which we are about to celebrate, is one place of meeting, where Chrift has promifed to be prefent, and to blefs us. Come forward, then, to his table, with the prayer of faith in your mouth, and you fhall find Chrift prefent, with bleffings of all kinds in his hand, to be diftributed to every wreftler according to their defire. If you hefitate to come forward, from an apprehenfion that you are ftill under the curfe, apply to him now for a previous bleffing; and you may receive it, even before the communion-table be covered. If you are fenfible of the deficiency of your preparation, apply to him alfo for that bleffing. And when you come to the banquet of wine, be not fhy in prefenting your petition. If what you defire is included in that fulnefs which God has made to dwell in Chrift, you may be certain that it fhall be given you, *even to the whole of the kingdom*.

7. In one word, We may here fee how precious is the opportunity that is now enjoyed by every perfon in this affembly, and in what manner it fhould be improved. You have heard that Chrift has engaged
to

to be prefent wherever his *name* is *recorded;* and to blefs thofe who are employed in recording it. We are met here for this exprefs purpofe; and, by profeffion, we are employed in that work. Can there, then, be any reafon to doubt of his being prefent to blefs us? What Peter once faid to the Jews, we have an equal warrant to fay to every perfon prefent. " Unto you God, having raifed up his Son Jefus " Chrift, hath fent him, to blefs you, in turning e-- " very one of you away from his iniquity *." Is there, then, any perfon prefent, groaning under a fenfe of his juft fubjection to the curfe, and defirous to obtain the blefling? Is there any fenfible that the things of this vain world cannot yield happinefs, and defirous to be bleffed with all fpiritual bleffings? Is there any who has found himfelf difappointed in all his purfuits after happinefs hitherto, and knows not where to go next in queft of it. Let them all come to Chrift and be bleffed. Yea, let thofe alfo come, who never had a ferious thought, either about the blefling or the curfe. Chrift is now prefent among you, with the blefling in the one hand, and the curfe in the other. Every one of you has an opportunity of choofing for yourfelf. And, for any thing that either you or I know, the choice that you now make may be confirmed for eternity. The difference between thofe who are under the curfe, and the who enjoy the blefling, is apparently fmall in this world. But in the world to come it fhall be as wide as the diftance between heaven and hell; between the height of confummate happinefs, and the depths of intolerable mifery.

And,

* Acts iii. 26.

And, which is still worse, there will be no possibility of passing from the one to the other. By refusing the offered blessing, and continuing to do so till death surprise you, you bind yourself irrecoverably under all that wrath which the curse denounces. And Oh! how *fearful a thing* it is *to fall into the hands of the living God!* Perhaps this may be your last opportunity of escaping. But if you come to Christ, at his call, however little you deserve it, however much you deserve the contrary, you shall find him ready to do with you as he did with the little children of old; he will *take* you *in his arms, and bless* you.

SERMON XI.

The returning Prodigal's Attire; or, The Robe of imputed Righteousness actually put upon every penitent Sinner.

LUKE XV. 22.

—BRING FORTH THE BEST ROBE, AND PUT IT ON HIM.

THE parable recorded from the 11th verse of this chapter, is one of the moſt ſignificative that our Lord delivered in the days of humiliation. In it, under the ſimilitude of a prodigal ſon, returning penitent to his father, and kindly received by him, he repreſents the gracious reception that God gave to the Gentiles, when returning from the vain ſuperſtitions of paganiſm; and ſtill gives to every ſinner, when ſincerely returning from the evil of his way. Having been informed of the prodigal's folly, ver. 11, 12, 13.; of the miſery to which his folly reduced him,

him, ver. 14, 15, 16.; and of his refolution to return to his father's houfe, ver. 17, 18, 19. We hear, in ver. 20. of his actual return, in purfuance of that refolution; and of the kindly reception with which his father furprifed and prevented him. And, in ver. 21. we are informed of the free and voluntary confeffion that he made of the fin and folly of his paft courfe of life.

The tender and affectionate father, having heard his confeffion, makes no direct reply. But, that he might evince his defign of receiving him into the family, not as a hired fervant, but as a fon, he calls his fervants, and gives them injunctions to do every thing for him that was neceffary to make him appear like a child of the family; as we fee in this verfe and the following. Thus, when any finner returns to God, by faith and fincere repentance, he is received among the number of the fons of God And, as one confequence hereof, all the fervants of the family receive a charge concerning him. And they all contribute their endeavours to fit him for his place and ftation in his father's houfe. The orders given by the father to the fervants, relative to his fon, now reftored to him, confift of four particulars.

1. As his clothing was worn to rags, they have orders to *bring forth the beft robe, and put it on him*.

2. As his jewels were forfeited, even to the ring that contained the family feal; they are commanded to *put a ring on his hand*.

3. His fhoes being worn out, and his feet fore bruifed with the fatigues of his journey; they are ordered to *put fhoes on his feet*.

4. To

4. To relieve him from that famine, by which he was ready to perish; and to give opportunity to the whole family, and the friends of the family, to partake in the joy that was felt by his father at his return; he enjoins them to *bring the fatted calf, and kill it*, that they might all *eat and be merry*.

We only propose to consider the first of these at present; as we have it in these words, " Bring forth " the best robe, and put it on him." In which words we have the following things deserving notice.

1. The piece of clothing appointed for the returning prodigal, a *robe*. Critics observe, that the word signifies a long loose garment, like a cloak, or mantle, that was worn above all the rest of the clothes. This piece of dress no slave was permitted to wear; but it was so necessary to free men, that it was a shame for any person of character to appear without it. The prodigal had reduced himself to the shameful necessity of appearing, like a slave, without a robe. But his father, that he might be habited like a free man, and like a son of his family, orders him to be furnished with one.

2. The quality of the robe that he was to wear; it was *the best robe*. In the original, it is the *first robe;* and may either be understood of the same robe that he wore at the first, before he left the family, or of the first in point of quality, that is, the best in the wardrobe. The last of these seems the proper meaning; as it is manifest that the robe which he formerly wore had been carried into the far country, and worn out.

3. The orders that were given concerning this robe; the servants were required to *bring* it *forth,* and

and *put it on him.* He who was formerly employed in the meanest drudgery, is now served like a prince. He is not allowed to put on his own clothes, but has servants appointed to dress him. Neither was he first taken home, and then adorned with the robe. It was brought forth and put upon him where he was, that he might not enter his father's house in a garb unbecoming a son of the family.

The spiritual meaning of all this may be summed up in the following proposition.

It is the express will and pleasure of God, that every sinner of Adam's family, returning from that dissolute course of life in which we are all naturally engaged, be covered with that robe of righteousness, which is incomparably the best in all the wardrobe of heaven.

WHAT we propose on this subject, is only, through divine assistance,

I. To speak a little of the best robe here mentioned.

II. To explain the orders here given concerning it.

III. To endeavour some improvement of the whole.

I. ALL that we have to say concerning the *best robe*, shall be comprised in the following particulars.

1. That spiritual blessing, which is here represented by the best robe that was to be put upon the prodigal, is no other than the imputed righteousness of Jesus Christ. This will clearly appear, by comparing

The Robe of imputed Righteousness.

ing the text with these words of the Prophet: "I will greatly rejoice in the Lord, my soul shall be joyful in my God: for he hath clothed me with the garments of salvation, he hath covered me with the robe of righteousness *." Some, indeed, understand both passages of that inherent righteousness, with which the child of God is endued, by the working of the Holy Ghost. But this deserves not to be called a robe. It is only our inner garment, which is covered; and stands in need to be covered by another. It is so far from being the *best robe* that our heavenly Father has to give us, that, while we continue in this world, it is no better than *filthy rags*. Besides, it is never completely put upon us, till we come to heaven; whereas the robe here mentioned is put upon the returning prodigal before he taste of his father's provision, or enter the door of his house. It is, therefore, the surety righteousness of Christ, imputed to us in the day of our union to him, that we are to consider as our *best robe*.

2. This righteousness is fitly compared to a robe, on various accounts. It hides our spiritual nakedness in the most perfect manner. To cover shame is the principal use of all garments. Other garments cover but a part of the body; but the robe covers the whole. And this righteousness actually covers the whole man in every Christian, so that no part of his shame appears: it covers every member of the mystical body of Christ. Hence he is represented as "clothed with a garment down to the foot †."—It covers all the defects of our other garments, so that our filthy rags appear not to our confusion in the sight of God. It

Vol. II.   A a   *   is

* Isa. lxi. 10.   † Rev. i. 13.

is obfervable, that the fervants are not here commanded to ſtrip the prodigal of all his rags; and to clothe him, from head to foot, in change of raiment. They are only to put a robe upon him, which may cover all the defects of the reſt of his clothing; till the whole might be changed at leiſure. This is a lively repreſentation of God's method of dealing with penitent ſinners. He will have them at length made "all glorious within;" being covered with a garment of inherent holineſs that ſhall be abſolutely perfect. But this he does not all at once. And while it is gradually accompliſhed, it is neceſſary that the defects of this inner garment, as well as all that ſhame which cannot be hid by theſe rags, be covered by the robe of imputed righteouſneſs; ſo as to be hid from the piercing eye of divine juſtice.—This rightouſneſs, like an impenetrable robe, ſcreens us from every ſpiritual ſtorm; whether we ſuppoſe it to blow from heaven, earth, or hell. Hence it is ſaid concerning Chriſt,—" A man ſhall be an hiding place from the "wind, and a covert from the tempeſt; as rivers of " waters in a dry place, and as the ſhadow of a great " rock in a weary land *."—Like a robe, it ſerves to keep our other garments clean. Yea, it excels every other robe in this; that, after our other garments are defiled, it ſerves to make them clean. Hence the diſtinguiſhed company, who ſtand before the throne, are ſaid to have " waſhed their robes, and made them " white in the blood of the lamb †." The robes which they are there ſaid to waſh, cannot be the ſame that is mentioned in this text. It is incapable of defilement; and therefore can ſtand in no need of waſhing.

* Iſa. xxxii. 2. † Rev. vii. 14.

washing. Besides, this robe is the same with "the "blood of the Lamb," in which the others are washed. The meaning of the passage is, that the inherent righteousnesses of the saints, which are liable to frequent defilements, while in this world, are gradually cleansed and made white through the efficacy of this imputed righteousness; which is the spring of their sanctification, as well as of their justification. —This righteousness, like the robe of old, is a badge of freedom. It is worn by none but free-men. So long as a person continues enslaved by Satan, and is employed in feeding his swine, he can have no such robe. But Christ having redeemed us by power, at the same time that he redeemed us by price, the moment that we are covered with that righteousness, which was the price of our redemption, we are also made partakers of that liberty which is the fruit of his victory. And while we wear the robe, we can never be " entangled again with the yoke of bon- " dage."—In a word, as no person of character used to be seen abroad without his robe; so none of the family of God, none of the citizens of the new Jerusalem, ever appear without this righteousness. From the moment that it is put upon them, in the day of their union to Christ, it is never more put off; nor will be through eternity. They are peculiarly careful to have it on at public feasts, and on days of spiritual solemnity. Hence they endeavour, by renewed actings of faith, in the prospect of such occasions, to comply with the Apostles exhortation; by " putting on the Lord Jesus " Christ, and making no provision for the flesh, to ful- " fil the lusts thereof."

3. This righteousness is fitly denominated the best robe.

robe. Heaven itself cannot afford a better. Nor was ever any comparable to it worn in the family of God; as might be shewn by various considerations. It is, by far, the most precious and expensive robe. The goodness of things ought to bear a proportion to their price. By this rule, this robe is infinitely better than all others; as being purchased at a higher price. Indeed, it is often lightly esteemed among men; but it bears such a value in heaven, that it could not be purchased by any thing less than " the blood of " God."—It is the most beautiful, sumptuous, and magnificent robe. It is called, by the inspired Psalmist, " a garment of wrought gold." Such is the beauty of it, that angels gaze upon it with admiration. Yea, such is the beauty of it, that God himself is well pleased with it, and with all who are clothed with it.—It is a garment universally esteemed, by all the members of God's family, beyond all others whatsoever. You may take the Apostle Paul for an example. He counted all " things but loss and dung, that " *he might* win Christ; and be found in him," covered with this robe.—It is a robe of most universal usefulness. It serves the best purposes, and that in the best manner. You have heard that it covers our shame, screens us from the storm, and keeps our other garments clean. We may add, it recommends us to the favour and blessing of God; as the smell of Esau's garments recommended Jacob to Isaac his father. It makes us fit to appear in the house of God, and among his children. It serves as a wedding garment; in which even thieves and robbers, the inhabitants of the high-ways and hedges, may be welcome at the marriage-supper of the lamb. It serves as an armour of

proof,

proof, to defend us "on the right hand and on the "left," againſt all the wiles, and all the "fiery darts "of the wicked one." Yea, it ſerves to reconcile us to ourſelves; and to introduce that peace into our conſciences, to which we muſt ever have been ſtrangers without it.—It is, of all others, leaſt ſubject to injuries of any kind. It can neither be torn nor worn out. Though it keeps our other garments clean, itſelf is incapable of pollution. It needs no reparation; nor can it ever wax old. It will ever be as new, and as perfect, as in the day it was firſt put on. Conſequently, it is the moſt durable and laſting of all robes. It is infinite in duration, as well as in value; for it is an "everlaſting righteouſneſs." And every perſon upon whom it is put in time, ſhall continue to wear it through all eternity.

We might likewiſe have ſhewn it to be the *beſt robe*, by comparing it with all others that are worn, or have been worn, in the family of God. It is better than the robe of original righteouſneſs, with which our firſt parents were covered, before they played the prodigal, and left that family. That robe was pure indeed, but it was never complete; for the covenant of works was never perfectly fulfilled. And the event ſhewed how ſubject it was to decay. But this, you have heard, is perfect, everlaſting, and incapable of decay.—It is better than the garment of inherent righteouſneſs, which is put upon the ſaints by the ſaving operation of the Holy Ghoſt. While they are in this world, that garment is both imperfect and defiled. And even in the other world, it will only be capable of ſuch a perfection as is competent to a finite ſubject. And all its perfection will be wholly owing to the other. But this robe is infinitely perfect, and it derives none of its excellencies from any other. It is better than the robe which is worn by confirmed angels—Their righteousness is no more than commensurate to the demands of their Creator's law; nor can it be profitable to any but themselves. Their robe is too narrow to wrap any other person in. But this is a righteousness that no law could ever have demanded, if Christ had not voluntarily made himself under the law for us. It is more than answerable unto the natural demands of that law to which he was made subject; for it " magnified the law, and " made it honourable." This robe is also broad and large enough to cover all the members of the mystical body of Christ. In a word, it is even better than the robe of immortal glory, that shall eternally be worn by the children of God in the upper house. The robe here mentioned is the cause of the other; and the cause is always more excellent than the effect. That robe, however magnificent, had never been half so glorious, if it had not been " washed and " made white in the blood of the Lamb." When all these things are considered, it appears to be a truth indisputable, that this is the *best robe*. The wardrobe of heaven affords none like it. The treasures of eternity cannot purchase a better. Nor can the hand of omnipotence, directed by infinite wisdom, work out one more excellent.

II. We now proceed, as was proposed in the entry, to attempt some explication of the orders here given, for arraying the returning prodigal in this best robe. All that we intend on this head, is only to set before

you

you the few following things, which we confider as imported in the words.

1. They import, that finners, while they continue without God's houfe and family, ftand much in need of this robe. Had the prodigal been fent to feed fheep, he might have expected to clothe himfelf with their fleeces; but his fwine afforded nothing to cover his nakednefs. And when his garments were worn out, he had no means to repair them. Not only was he ready to perifh through hunger, he was alfo reduced to the laft extremity for want of clothing. Hence, his father's firft care was to have him provided with a becoming robe. In like manner, the finner is as much at a lofs for clothing as for food, in a fpiritual fenfe. Our own "righteoufnefs are filthy rags." In the houfe of our tyrannical mafter, there is neither food nor clothing. Our nakednefs is expofed to every eye. Ourfelves are obnoxious to every ftorm. And, fooner or later, we muft feel ourfelves miferable, without fuch a robe as this.

2. That fuch a robe is actually provided, and ready for the putting on. The father fays not to his fervants, go buy a robe, or make one, and put it on him; but go and bring it forth. There was not fo much as occafion for any alteration of it, to make it fit for the ftature of the prodigal. It was juft ready to be put on. The robe of righteoufnefs was prepared by Chrift, during his humiliation on earth. It lies ready in the wardrobe of our heavenly Father. It fuits the meafure of every returning prodigal. Come, then, prefently, and be covered with it. You fhall find nothing ado but put it on. If you are unable to do this, it will be done for you. Already it is brought

forth,

forth, and God has given commandment to put it on you.

3. That no sinner can be admitted into the family of God, nor suffered to enter his house, without it. The prodigal's father says not, Take my son home, introduce him to the family, and then clothe him with change of raiment. He was to be clothed with the best robe, before he entered the house, or was seen of any that were in it. So God first clothes the returning sinner with the robe of righteousness in his justification; then he brings him into his family, and admits him to all the privileges of his children. In point of time, there is no difference between our justification and our adoption. But we must view the one as following the other, in the order of nature. Surely none can be suffered to enjoy a place in the house of God, till he is first clothed with this robe.

4. That the righteousness of Christ must become ours in possession, and be actually put upon us; otherwise we can have no real advantage by it. No man can be the better for having a garment within his reach, unless it be actually put upon him, or applied to his body in such a manner as to cover his nakedness. So neither can any of mankind have any benefit by this righteousness, even though it is brought forth, and offered to him in the Gospel, unless it is actually made his, for the purposes of salvation. Now, in order hereto, three things are necessary. (1.) It must be received by faith. The person must consent to receive it, on the footing of the offer, as made to him in particular; and say, " in the Lord have I righ-
" teousness." (2.) It must be actually given us of God. The gospel offer gives every man a right of access to it; but the Christian, when he receives it by

faith,

faith, obtains a right of poffeffion in it, a real property of it; founded on the deed of gift in the gofpel offer. What God offers in the gofpel to all without diftinction, he actually gives to the believer, when he is made willing to receive it. (3.) It muft be imputed to us, or judicially *fuftained* as ours in law. This act of *judicially fuftaining* it is the confequence of both the former. This differs from the giving above mentioned, as a judicial fentence differs from an act of fovereign bounty; and it neceffarily prefuppofes the other. Without fuch a deed of gift, this righteoufnefs could not be ours indeed. And unlefs actually ours, it can never be juftly fuftained, or declared to be ours in law. And unlefs it is both ours indeed, and ours in law, it will avail us nothing to have an offer and exhibition of it made to us in the gofpel.

5. The words import, that finners are utterly infufficient, of themfelves, to put on this robe, after it is brought to hand. If the prodigal had not laboured under fome inability to put on the beft robe upon himfelf, there had been no occafion for others to put it on him. So far are we from being able to work out a righteoufnefs for ourfelves, which may anfwer the demands of the law of God; that, even when fuch a righteoufnefs is brought to our hand, we might perifh, we certainly would perifh for ever, before we could make fuch an appropriation of it as is neceffary to our having an actual intereft in it. Even that faith, by which we " put on the Lord Jefus Chrift, " *is not of ourfelves*, it is the gift of God." If it were true, as fome affert, that faith in Chrift were the condition of the covenant of grace, and that condition to be performed by us, without any fupernatural affiftance;

ance; then we would be for ever incapable of salvation, and Christ would be dead in vain.

Finally, The words import, that all the servants of God, each in his proper station and place, are to use their utmost endeavours, that sinners may be clothed with this precious robe. The father of the prodigal does not bring forth the robe himself, and put it on; but orders the servants to do both. This shews plainly, that, though no creature can put the robe of righteousness upon any sinner, without the efficacious agency of God himself; yet every servant in God's family should be some way active about it. Angels, who are ministring spirits to God's adopted children, deal with them, in a manner of which we have very little knowledge, persuading them to " put on the "Lord Jesus Christ." And even private Christians should take every opportunity of commending Christ and his righteousness to those around them: that, if possible, they may be the happy and *wise* instruments of *winning* some *souls*. But, in a special manner, it is incumbent upon ministers of the gospel to be active in this matter. The following things are expected of them to this effect.

(1.) They must employ themselves, " in season, " out of season," in explaining the method of salvation by the imputed righteousness of Christ; in commending this righteousness to their hearers, as every way suitable to all their necessities, and to all the purposes of God's glory. This should be the main subject of all their preaching; the main scope and tendency of all their ministrations. Empty harangues of morality, such as might have been admired if coming from a Pagan philosopher, will not do. We cannot

cannot fulfil our miniſtry, by pompous declamations about the dignity of human nature, or the extenſive powers of the human mind. We forfeit the name of goſpel miniſters, if we attempt to perſuade men, that piety and virtue, faith, repentance and ſincere obedience, all performed by our own natural abilities, are the proper means of recommending ourſelves to God's favour. Every perſon, who takes upon him to preach the goſpel, had need to be determined, like Paul, " to " know nothing among *his people*, but Jeſus Chriſt, " and him crucified." (2.) They are to make a free and unconditional offer of Chriſt and his righteouſneſs to every ſinner, without exception; inviting every one to receive it, and, by faith, to *put it on*. We muſt not tell the world, that Chriſt " came not to call " *ſelf*-righteous *perſons*, but *ſenſible* ſinners *only to* re- " pentance." The words of Chriſt to the Phariſees bore never ſuch a meaning. We have no authority to require any previous qualifications about any of mankind, in order to his being welcome to come to Chriſt. This were to deſire men to heal themſelves, and then to come to the phyſician. Nay, the *righteouſneſs* of God muſt be *brought near*, even to thoſe " that are " ſtout-hearted and far from righteouſneſs." We are to conſider ourſelves as the *maidens* of divine Wiſdom; and to publiſh the goſpel offer, in the ſame univerſal and unlimited manner as ſhe does. " Unto " you, O men, I call: and my voice is to the ſons of " Adam *."

This call we are to enforce with all the arguments that the ſcriptures of truth, or the neceſſities of periſhing ſouls, can ſuggeſt. We ſhould ſet every motive

---

* Prov. viii. 4.

tive to the duty of embracing this call, in the cleareſt light; and inſiſt upon it in the moſt preſſing manner. This we are to do, not in any vain hope, that ſinners are capable of being prevailed upon by moral ſuaſion only, to put on the Lord Jeſus Chriſt ; but as knowing that the Spirit of God deals with men as with rational creatures, draws them efficaciouſly to Chriſt by means of ſuch exhortations and arguments: making theſe the vehicles of that almighty power, by which alone they can be enabled to put on this *beſt robe.*

(3.) When exhorting ſinners to believe in Chriſt, as *the* LORD their *righteouſneſs,* we are to direct them to the only method in which it is poſſible for them to do ſo. As ſoon may a dead carcaſe riſe out of its grave, at the call of ſome diſconſolate friend who waters the ſepulchre with his tears, and repeats the name of the deceaſed, as any ſinner can exerciſe faith, or perform any other duty acceptably, without divine and ſupernatural aſſiſtance. All exhortations to duty, in which no eye is had to the ſtrength of *the grace that is in* Chriſt Jeſus, as alone ſufficient to enable us to perform duty, are no better than Pharaoh's tyrannical edicts, that demanded the " full tale of bricks," but allowed no ſtraw. When, therefore, we exhort them to believe, we muſt teach them to eſſay it, in imitation of the father of the lunatic, ſaying, " Lord, " I believe, help thou mine unbelief."

Accordingly, we muſt publiſh thoſe gracious promiſes, in which God has condeſcended to bind himſelf, actually to put this robe upon us; not only by imputing the righteouſneſs of Chriſt to us, but likewiſe enabling us to receive it. We muſt commend
the

The Robe of imputed Righteousness. 381

the faithfulness of a promising God, and his ability to perform his engagements; and shew, that " he is not " a man that he should lie, nor the son of man that " he should repent."

(4.) We must, upon every proper occasion, put on this robe declaratively; intimating to the disconsolate Christian, that God has actually put it upon him. We are to lay before men those marks of a justified state which the word of God furnishes; that, by comparing themselves with these, the people of God may see themselves to be justified persons. This is not all. Nothing is more frequent than for real Christians, through the prevalence of temptation and of unbelief, not only to question their present interest in the righteousness of Christ, but even their access to it. They are ready to apprehend, like Cain, that their sin is greater than can be forgiven; and hence are in danger of giving themselves up to despair. A minister of the gospel, in dealing with such a person, may be able to discern about him those marks of a justified state, that he cannot, for the present, discern about himself; so that he may have no doubt of the person's being presently under this robe. In such a case, we may, and ought to say to the dejected soul, what the Prophet was commanded to say to Jerusalem; that his *warfare* is as good as *accomplished;* for his *iniquity is pardoned**. By this means peace may be restored to the troubled conscience, and the person may be helped to see that the *best robe* is already put upon him.

Here it must not be overlooked, that Christ, God's honorary servant, does much more, in execution of the

* Isa. xl. 2.

the order of the text, than any created fervant can do, or all created fervants together. He, in the exercife of his prophetical office, *brings forth the beſt robe*, by a full and free exhibition of it to finners. This he did in his own perfon, while he was on earth; and he ſtill does it by his written word, and by the voice of his fervants. And, in the exercife of his kingly office, he both beſtows the gift of faith, by which his righteoufnefs is received, and paſſes that fentence of juſtification, by which it is judicially declared to be ours. Thus he who, by way of eminence, is called *God's ſervant*, does, in the fulleſt and propereſt fenfe, *bring forth the beſt robe*, to every returning prodigal, *and put it on him.*

III. WE now draw to a conclufion with fome practical improvement of the fubject. It affords us information in the following particulars.

1. It fets forth the fhameful and deplorable condition in which mankind are by nature. We are all at a diſtance from God, enflaved by the devil; and employed in the bafeſt drudgery, the feeding of our luſts. We are ready to perifh for fpiritual hunger; and when we think to fatisfy ourfelves with the hufks of fublunary enjoyments, find nothing but difappointment upon difappointment. We likewife ſtand expofed to every ſtorm, and to the fcorn of all obfervers; without a rag to cover our nakednefs, or to hide our fhame. To crown all, we are utterly infenfible of this laſt and greateſt mifery of our condition. It is remarkable, that notwithſtanding all his complaints, whether of his condition or his conduct, whether uttered with himfelf in the far country, or to his father

at

at his return; we never hear a word from the prodigal about his nakedneſs, or the unſeemlineſs of thoſe rags with which he was covered: though this was a principal thing that affected his father, and the firſt thing that he provided againſt. A ſinner, in a natural eſtate, may be ſenſible of his dangerous and periſhing condition. He may ſee the folly of ſeeking happineſs among ſenſual objects; and even be ready to acknowledge that he has ſinned againſt Heaven and in God's ſight: but never, till he is actually intereſted in the righteouſneſs of Chriſt, having this *beſt robe brought forth* and put upon him, will he be properly ſenſible of the filthineſs of his own righteouſneſs; and convinced, that what he formerly counted his *glory* is really *the ſhame of* his father's *houſe*.

2. We have, in this ſubject, a clear diſcovery of the wonderful love and goodneſs, both of God the Father and of his eternal Son. The love of God appears wonderful, in that he deals with us, as the father of this prodigal is repreſented as dealing with him. Not only does he give us what we aſk, and relieve us from all thoſe miſeries which we either feel or fear; but he begins with arraying us in the ſpotleſs robe of imputed righteouſneſs, which is among the laſt things that a convinced ſinner wiſhes for, or apprehends to be neceſſary for him. This robe he had provided and kept ready for us, before we had a thought of returning to him. The love of Chriſt is not leſs conſpicuous in preparing ſuch a robe, and working it out for us; at the expence not barely of the ſweat of his face, but even of his heart's blood. The elder brother of this prodigal is repreſented as envying the reception that his father gave him; and ſo fondly ſelfiſh

were

were the Jews, in their religion, that in them this figure had its antitype. But the glorious elder Brother of God's family is so far from being of this disposition, that when he saw us in our far country, rioting among harlots, and feeding the devil's swine, his bowels yearned upon us; himself undertook to bring us back to our Father's house: and, that we might appear in it, in a manner becoming the character of children, he purchased for us this robe, with his own precious life. Oh! what returns of gratitude and love are due for such unparalleled goodness!

We here see the brutish folly of legality; of all attempts " to establish *our* own righteousness, not sub-" mitting to the righteousness of God." Should not this prodigal have acted a foolish part, if, when he heard his father give out these orders, he had replied, ' There is no occasion for it; I am very well pleased ' with the clothes I wear, and am resolved that I will ' neither part with them, nor have them covered with ' any other: if I cannot be admitted into thy house ' in my present dress, I will not enter it at all; rather ' will I take my hazard of all the miseries of my for-' mer condition, than submit to be clothed with that ' *best robe* which thou hast ordered me?' But this is the very manner in which every person behaves, who unbelievingly rejects the righteousness of Christ; and persists in seeking righteousness, " as it were by the " works of the law." And does not such a person justly deserve to be taken at his word, and given up to that ruin which would undoubtedly be the fruit of his mad choice? Oh! sinner, persist not in your folly, till God be provoked to do so.

4. We

4. We may here see when our humiliation for sin becomes so deep, as to be capable of acceptance in the presence of God. Never till our own righteousness be considered as serving to expose our shame, and we be convinced of the necessity of being arrayed with heaven's *best robe*. It is not enough that you be sensible of the sin and folly of your past course of life, and of the danger that you are in of perishing by the effects of it; you must consider your very *righteousnesses* as *filthy rags*. You must view all your obedience, whether performed before or after conversion, as serving to expose you to the stroke of God's wrath, instead of recommending you to his favour. You must learn to mourn before God for your righteousness, as a part of your sin; and for your trusting to your own righteousness, as one of the greatest sins that ever you committed, or ever were capable to commit.

Lastly, We may here be informed how inconsistent it is, for a Christian to allow himself in any act of sin; to indulge any corruption, or to stop short of perfection in conformity to the image of Christ. What son of a king would satisfy himself with being covered with a magnificent robe without, while his other garments were nothing but rotten and stinking rags? You, believer, are a son of the King of heaven. The righteousness of Christ, as you heard, is your robe, or outer garment; your inner garment is your own personal inherent righteousness. And is it not fit that the one should correspond to the other? Every spot that remains upon your inner garment, is so much dishonour done to the robe that you wear. If you wish to appear

pear like the family to which you belong, you muſt labour inceſſantly after perfection in holineſs. You muſt *waſh* your *robes* daily, *and make them white in the blood of the Lamb;* and give yourſelf no reſt, till you be *all-glorious within;* as your garment, your robe *is of wrought gold.*

This ſubject may likewiſe aſſiſt us in the duty of ſelf-examination. There is nothing about which you have more need to try yourſelf, than whether you have on this precious robe or not. That you may know it, aſk your conſcience the following queſtions.

1. Are you ſenſible that your own righteouſneſs is but *filthy rags;* and cannot ſerve you for a robe in the preſence of God? Are you convinced that you cannot deal with God in the way of the covenant of works; and yet ſenſible of your ſinful attachment to it? Are you diſpoſed to mourn for your legality; while you ſincerely deſire to renounce all dependence upon your own righteouſneſs; and count it but dung that you may win Chriſt, and be clothed with the ſpotleſs robe of his righteouſneſs? So was the Apoſtle Paul diſpoſed; and ſo will every Chriſtian.

2. Do you, indeed, conſider this righteouſneſs as the *beſt robe?* Have you ſeen its exact ſuitableneſs to your neceſſitous condition? Have you got a view of it, as ſecuring the honour of all the divine perfections in the ſalvation of ſinners? Is the method of free juſtification, through a crucified Redeemer, " the wiſdom " of God, and the power of God," in your eſteem? So it is " to every one that believeth." And ſo it is to you, if you have any intereſt in it.

3. Have

3. Have you seen, with holy wonder, admiration and joy, this robe brought forth, in the difpenfation of the gofpel, and offered to you in particular? It is not enough that you have feen it in general, brought near to the ftout-hearted, and them that are far from righteoufnefs. If it is really put upon you, you have feen this to be your genuine character; and you have feen it brought near to you, as truly as to any other of the fame denomination. And it has filled you with joy unfpeakable, with unutterable wonder, that you, in particular, had accefs to have your nakednefs covered by fuch a robe.

4. Are you prefently difpofed to receive it and to put it on? You have heard that it is to be received by faith. And the queftion that our Lord put to his difciples before his fufferings, he may be confidered as putting to you, in the view of a folemn commemoration of his fufferings; "Do ye now believe*?" If ever you believed before, you doubtlefs have on this robe; and it fhall never be put off again. But, if ever you have believed, the habit will continue with you, and you will be difpofed to aim at the renewed exercife of it. Befides, it is not mainly your former attainments, but your prefent difpofition and exercife, that you are called to examine. And if you are clothed with this robe, the prefent language of your heart will be, " In the LORD have I righteoufnefs and " ftrength."

5. In one word, Are you ever ftudious to have your inner garment more and more correfponding to this robe? Do you labour to have your own perfonal righteoufnefs more and more perfect; that it may have

* John xvi. 31.

more and more refemblance to the all-fufficient righteoufnefs of your Surety? The beloved Apoftle tells us, that " he who faith he abideth in him, ought him-" felf alfo to walk even as he walked." If you are in him indeed, you will be fenfible of the propriety of this; and will ufe your endeavours accordingly. That fame law, in obedience to which Chrift " fulfilled all " righteoufnefs," will conftantly be the rule of your actions. The example of Chrift will be confidered as your pattern. And it will be your continual aim, to obey at all times, and to fuffer when called to it, in the fame manner as Chrift did. If this is the cafe with you, it is the fureft evidence that you can have, that this *beft robe* has been actually *put upon* you.

THE fubject likewife affords matter of exhortation.

Let me therefore conclude, by executing the commiffion, which the great Father of the heavenly family has condefcended to give me, in the words of this text. In the name of the God and Father of our Lord Jefus Chrift, I, though the moft unworthy fervant in the family, have the honour to bring forth this beft robe; and make a free offer of it to every prodigal in this affembly. It is offered to young finners, that are but fetting out in their prodigal courfes. It is offered to gray-headed finners, who have grown old in the arms of harlots. It is offered to thofe mad finners who ftill perfift in their riotous living, without any concern about the confequences; and to thofe who begin to be in want, and to feel that univerfal famine, which prevails in the far country. It is offered to thofe who ftill continue to feed the devil's fwine, employing themfelves in making provifion for the flefh, to fulfil

it

it in the lufts thereof; as well as to thofe who begin to entertain thoughts of returning to their father's houfe. It is not only brought forth, and ready to be put upon all thofe who are already returned; it is brought abroad, even to the far country, to be put upon thofe who never yet had a thought of returning. If there is any other defcription of finners, that has not yet been mentioned, if they only belong to the pofterity of Adam, and have rational fouls in union to their bodies; it is brought near to them alfo; and it fhall be their own fault, if it is not juft now put upon them.

As you tender your own happinefs, or the glory of the God that made you; as you wifh to have your fhame covered, or to efcape the ftorm and tempeft of God's anger; as you defire to be admitted into his family, or to partake in the privileges of his children; if you are in earneft about appearing in a proper garb at the table of God now, or at the tribunal of God in a little; Oh! beware of rejecting or refufing it. Let every perfon that hears me be concerned, *now* to put it on. You who intend to be communicants, put it on: it is the only garment, in which you can be accepted, when *the King* fhall come *in to fee the guefts.* You who wifh to partake in that *feaft of fat things* which ftands on the gofpel table, put it on: this is the marriage-fupper which the King of heaven has made for his Son; and this *beft robe* is the wedding-garment, which the Bridegroom himfelf has provided. You who have been adorned with it heretofore, put it on anew, by renewed actings of faith. And you who continue ftrangers to it, be perfuaded to put it on; it is the only garment in which you can ftand with acceptance before God. Even you, who care for none of thefe things, are invited to put it on: a time is faſt approaching, when you muſt either be clothed with this robe, or clothed, as enemies to Chriſt, with everlaſting ſhame.

Oh! that I had the tongue of an angel, to commend this robe unto you; and to perfuade you to confult your own happinefs, by putting it on. Rather, Oh! that he who has " the tongue of the learn-" ed," would himfelf commend it to your hearts; and make me the happy inſtrument of conveying his powerful voice to you! Confider your naked and expofed condition without it. Confider the excellency of it; it is heaven's beſt robe. Confider the ufeleffnefs of every other garment; all other coverings are too narrow for a man to wrap himfelf in. Confider the abſolute impoſſibility of entering the houſe of God without it. Confider the deplorable condition, to which you muſt be reduced in a little, if you perfiſt in rejecting it. All the ſhame of your nakedneſs will be difcovered, before an aſſembled world; and, when God " ſhall rain fire and brimſtone, and an horrible " tempeſt upon every impenitent finner;" that dreadful ſtorm will irrecoverably fweep you into " the lake " which burneth with fire and brimſtone, which is the " fecond death." In one word, confider that indefeafible right which you will have, if once this robe is put upon you, in " all the fulnefs of God, *as it* dwells " in Chriſt bodily." It will entitle you to God's protection from all your enemies; to God's bleſſing upon all your temporal, and all your fpiritual privileges; to God's prefence with you, under all the trials of life; to

a com-a complete deliverance from the fting of death; and to a dwelling " in the houfe of the Lord for ever." For thus faith he, who prepared this robe for you, and by whofe authority we bring it near unto you,— " Seek firft the kingdom of God, and the righteouf- " nefs thereof; and all other things fhall be added " unto you."

SERMON XII.

The returning Prodigal's Hand adorned.

LUKE XV. 22.

—AND PUT A RING ON HIS HAND.

AS all mankind are, by nature, in a ſtate of diſtance from God, and are the children of the devil; ſo we have all caſt off the badge of God's children, and openly bear the mark of the family to which we belong. But when ſinners are brought back to God's family, they receive his ſeal in their foreheads. The ſpirit, under whoſe influence they act, gives a manifeſt indication to what family they belong. This is what our Lord intimates in theſe words; which contain the the ſecond branch of thoſe orders which were given, by the father of the prodigal, to the ſervants of the family, concerning him. In them we may obſerve, more particularly,

1. The ornament which was appointed for the returning prodigal, *a ring*. When perſons of rank are reduced to ſtraitening circumſtances, the laſt things

that

that they ufually part with are their jewels; efpecially fuch as are peculiar to the family of which they fpring, and ferve to illuftrate their pedigree. This unhappy man had forfeited even his jewels; and had not fo much as referved the family ring.

2. The place where this ornament was to be worn; *on his hand.* As early as the days of Abraham, it was ufual to wear rings, or bracelets on the hand; for his fervants put a pair of bracelets on the hands of Rebekah *. Neither were they worn by women only; but alfo by men: as is plain from the inftance of Judah, who left his bracelets with Tamar †.

It feems to be agreed, among interpreters of found reputation, that the ring here fpoken of is emblematical of the *gift of the Holy Ghoft;* which every finner receives in the day of his reftoration to God; and which is of the fame ufe to them as fuch rings were to the children of great men in thofe days. Hence we take the fenfe of the text to be, that

Every penitent finner, upon returning to the houfe and family of God, is fealed with the Holy Spirit of promife.

All that we now propofe is only to enquire, Why the gift of the Holy Spirit is compared to a ring on the hand; and then to conclude with a few inferences.

The Holy Spirit, which they who believe on Chrift receive in the day of their reftoration to God's family, may be compared to a ring on the hand, on the following accounts.

1. The

---

* Gen. xxiv. 22.   † Gen. xxxviii. 18.

1. The rings which were worn in those eastern countries were considered, by persons of distinction, as their principal ornaments. So is the Holy Ghost to the Christian. In our natural estate, every thing about us is filthy and polluted. Ourselves are lothsome in the sight of God, and incapable of appearing with acceptance in his presence. But when the Holy Spirit is given us, the comeliness of God is put upon us; we are freed, in some degree, from our natural defilement, and made fit for standing in God's holy place. Not only is the Spirit himself an ornament to us; he is the author of all those graces, which are as so many jewels, with which the Christian is adorned, " as a bride is adorned for her husband."

2. Those rings were only worn by the rich and great. The poor, however fond they may be of ornaments, are obliged to repress such desires; and either to be content with necessaries, or else to satisfy themselves with ornaments of a coarser kind. Gold rings and bracelets are not within their reach. So while persons continue in that impoverished state in which they were by nature, they are strangers to the inhabitation of the Spirit of God. This privilege is, to the Christian, a sure sign that he is enriched for eternity. He could not have enjoyed it, unless he had hearkened to the call which infinite wisdom addresses to all who hear the gospel. And all who comply with this call are convinced, by their own happy experience, that " riches and honour are with *her:* even " durable riches and righteousness."

3. Such rings were oft given by princes to their prime ministers, and chief favourites, as a pledge of their favour, and of the trust that they reposed in them.

them. Thus, when Pharaoh advanced Joseph to be lord of all the land of Egypt, he "took his ring off "his hand, and put it on the hand of Joseph *." On the same account did king Ahasuerus, long afterwards, give his ring to Haman; and upon his disgrace, to Mordecai the Jew †. In like manner, the Holy Ghost is bestowed, by God, upon none but favourites. The moment that a person is delivered from that wrath and curse under which he formerly lay, and restored to the favour of God, this unspeakable gift is bestowed upon him; and not before. Every person who has it, may consider it as an inviolable pledge of God's love. And every fruit of the Spirit appearing about him, he may look upon as an incontestible evidence that he is a person in favour at the court of heaven.

4. These rings usually contained the armorial bearings of the person who bestowed, or of the person that wore them: these, you know, are the honours of a family, the badges of its nobility. And the Holy Spirit, given to the Christian in the day of his conversion, is the badge of his spiritual nobility; the sign of his restoration to all the honours of God's family. When a man is attainted for any crime, the arms of the family are broken; he is stripped of all his honours, and his blood is rendered infamous in all after generations. This is the very case with all Adam's posterity, in a spiritual sense. Our first father, being "in honour, abode not." By his unprovoked rebellion, he forfeited all his honour, as well as his happiness. His blood was attainted; and all his posterity are covered with dishonour and infamy. But, upon our return to God, we are not only restored to all the honour

* Gen. xli. 42.   † Esth. iii. 10. & viii. 2.

honour that we forfeited, we are even invested with new honours, of which none of our family would have been capable, if the forfeiture had not taken place. We are admitted to be members of God's family. He gives us his own ring, when we receive the Holy Ghost; and he dwells in us, as a sure evidence that we are advanced to all the dignity, and entitled to all the honours that belong to the sons of the Most High.

5. These rings usually contained the seal which was used by the person to whom they belonged. It is still usual, you know, for persons of distinction to have their coats of arms cut upon a seal, which they use in transacting business; and annex to such deeds as they intend should be pleadable in law. So it was as early as the reign of Ahasuerus king of Persia. Accordingly, the ring which he gave to Haman contained the king's seal; and when he wrote the bloody decree, for exterminating the Jews, he had no more to do, for rendering it authentic, but to seal it with " the " king's ring," which he wore. In like manner, the Holy Spirit is the seal of God's family. By it is every deed stamped, that God intends to be pleadable in law; and nothing pretending to contain any declaration of the will of God, can be considered as authentic without it. By it is every thing marked that truly belongs to God, and every person; so that nothing that wants this mark can be considered as any of his. By this are the children of God distinguished from all others. The sacraments are the outward and visible seals of God's covenant; and by them his people are confirmed in faith and holiness, and in respect of their interest in all the benefits of the covenant. But the
Holy

Holy Spirit is the inward and invifible feal, without which the others can have no faving efficacy. It is only by the "Holy Spirit of God," that Chriftians are effectually "fealed unto the day of redemption *."

6. When a ring is worn on the hand, it will fcarcely be poffible for the perfon to do any piece of work, or to handle any thing, without touching it with the ring that he wears. And, if the materials are capable of receiving it, the impreffion of the ring will probably be left upon what the perfon has among his hands. In this refpect alfo the comparifon holds juft. The Holy Spirit, who is given to the Chriftian in the day of his union to Chrift, influences all the work of his hands. And it is only in proportion as they are fo influenced, that his works are capable of being accepted in the fight of God. Every act of acceptable obedience is a fruit of the Spirit. What the Chriftian puts his hand to, is ftamped with the impreffion of this fpiritual ring. It afcends to God, through the mediation of Jefus Chrift, bearing his own feal upon it; and hence it becomes a "fpiritual facrifice, holy "and acceptable, through Jefus Chrift." As the Holy Ghoft renews the nature of the Chriftian, after the image of him that created him; fo it is under *his* influence that he is enabled to conform his practice to the law of God, and to "walk in newnefs of life."

THIS fubject affords us the following practical inferences.

1. The doctrine of juftification by imputed righteoufnefs is far from encouraging licentioufnefs, as its enemies falfely fuggeft. Indeed, this doctrine, like every

* Eph. iv. 30.

every other, is capable of being abused by the corruption of men. And it has been abused to the encouragement of licentiousness. As early as the days of the Apostle Jude, there were some who turned " the grace " of God into lasciviousness." And no wonder that there should be some such in the world still. But they who allow themselves to make such an use of this doctrine, must be persons who continue strangers to any experimental acquaintance with the truth of it. Every person who is clothed with the robe of imputed righteousness, has his hand adorned, at the same time, with God's family-ring; that is, he is endued with the gift of the Holy Ghost. By his saving operation, the person is gradually cleansed from all filthiness of the flesh and spirit. Not only is he restrained from licentious courses, but his disposition towards them is gradually rooted out; and he is made holy in heart, and " in all manner of conversation." The man who vainly hopes to be saved by his own works, is restrained from outward acts of sin by the force of arguments; and experience may teach him, that arguments have very little force against the corrupt bias of nature in its lapsed state. But the man who is " justified freely by *God's* grace, through the redemp- " tion that is in Christ Jesus," is restrained from all licentiousness by almighty power. And he cannot sin habitually; because " the seed of God abideth in " him."

2. Even in the communication of the gift of the Holy Ghost, the servants of God may be some way instrumental. You see the servants are ordered to " put a ring on *the prodigal's* hand;" as well as to " bring forth the best robe, and put it on him." And, though

though we muſt not look upon every circumſtance in any parable as ſignificative; yet this ſeems evidently to point out both the duty and the privilege of thoſe who are honoured to be ſervants in God's family; eſpecially of miniſters of the goſpel. We ſaw that there is much incumbent upon them, relative to the clothing of ſinners with the robe of righteouſneſs. And they have not leſs concern with their being brought to receive the Holy Ghoſt. Indeed, the actual beſtowing of this gift muſt be the work of God; but ſo muſt the actual imputation of Chriſt's righteouſneſs. And it is the deſign of the goſpel, which we are called to diſpenſe, to exhibit to every ſinner the gift of the Spirit, as well as the gift of righteouſneſs; to invite ſinners to receive it; to declare, that, as men, " being evil, " know how to give good gifts to *their* children, much " more will *our* heavenly Father give the Holy Spi- " rit to them that aſk him;" and to publiſh all thoſe ſalutary truths, and precious promiſes, which the Spirit of God makes uſe of as vehicles for conveying himſelf, (if the expreſſion may be allowed), into the hearts of his people. Paul appeals to the Galatians, if they had not " received the Spirit by the hearing of faith." And if the hearing of faith is the mean by which the Spirit is received; ſurely they who are employed in publiſhing the doctrines of faith, muſt have ſome kind of inſtrumentality in this matter.

3. The beſt mark of a juſtified ſtate is the perſon's being endued with the ſaving inhabitation of the Spirit. In vain does any perſon pretend to be clothed with the *beſt robe*, unleſs he has alſo this ſpiritual *ring on his hand*. For " if any man have not the Spirit " of Chriſt, he is none of his *." On the other hand, it

* Rom. viii. 9.

it is equally vain and groundlefs for any perfon, who enjoys the inhabitation of the Spirit of Chrift, and lives under his influence, to be afraid of condemnation; or to look upon himfelf as a ftranger to imputed righteoufnefs; for it is given as the diftinguifhing characteriftic of " them who are in Chrift Jefus," and to whom " there is no condemnation, *that they* walk not " after the flefh, but after the Spirit *."

But perhaps it may be confidered, and not without fome juftice, as a pretty difficult matter, for a perfon to know whether he has the Spirit of Chrift or not. If you really wifh to examine yourfelf in relation to this matter; we are warranted to inform you, that you are hitherto ftrangers to this privilege; unlefs you are difpofed to confider the inhabitation of the Spirit, as your chief ornament, as the feal of your union to Chrift, and as the pledge of the heavenly inheritance. If the holy Spirit really dwells in you, you have enjoyed his falutary influences; as a fpirit of wifdom and underftanding, enlightening your minds in the knowledge of God, of his Son Jefus Chrift, and of the method of falvation through him; as a " fpirit of " grace and fupplication;" enabling you to *look upon* Chrift as *pierced* by your fin, and " to mourn for " him;" as a fpirit of prayer, making *interceffion* within you, and enabling you to pour out your hearts before God, " with groanings which cannot be utter- " ed;" as a fpirit of adoption, enabling you to cry to God, *Abba, Father:* and as a fpirit of holinefs, powerfully inclining you to prefs after more and more conformity to the image of God; to die more and more unto fin, and live unto righteoufnefs. If this
is

* Rom. viii. 1.

is the cafe, the fruits of the Spirit will appear about you; in the exercife of the graces of faith, love, joy, in the Holy Ghoft, and all the reft, which he implants in his people; and in the practice of all thofe holy duties, by which you may glorify God in the world. You will be concerned, not only to be much engaged in thofe duties of religious worfhip, which you owe to God himfelf; but alfo to have " holinefs to the " Lord" infcribed upon all the duties of your ordinary calling, and upon every part of your conduct towards fellow-creatures. Thus, upon every thing that you put your hand to, you will leave the impreffion of this precious ring, which your Father has put upon your hand.

4. To conclude, We may fee how much it is the intereft of every perfon who hears the gofpel to have this ring on his hand; or, in other words, to enjoy the prefence and inhabitation of the Spirit of Chrift. If you wifh to enjoy this blefling, and therein to have a pledge of your reftoration to God's favour, of your advacement to the dignity of fonfhip in his family, and of your intereft in the family inheritance; pray for it. Chrift himfelf has affured us that no earthly father can be fo willing to " give good gifts to his " children, as *our* heavenly Father *is to* give the Holy " Spirit to them that afk him." If you cannot afk him, do but give him admittance. He " ftands at " *your* door and knocks," in the difpenfation of the gofpel, ready to enter, and to dwell with you, if you do not keep him out by your unbelief. Beware of refifting his motions, and thereby provoking him to withdraw them. Woe will be to you indeed, if he

Vol. II. * C c finally

finally depart from you. But if you are enabled to give him admittance, he will continue to dwell in you; and will be " as a well of water ſpringing up to " everlaſting life." He will " guide you into all " truth," while you continue in this world. And he will not leave you till he has finally brought you home to the place where Chriſt is, that ye may behold his glory.

SER-

SERMON XIII.

The returning Prodigal's Feet shod; or, The Penitent Sinner furnished with the Preparation of the Gospel of Peace.

LUKE XV. 23.

—AND PUT SHOES ON HIS FEET.

THESE words contain the third branch of the orders, which were given to the servants of the family, concerning the prodigal, at his return. His shoes, as well as every thing else that he possessed, had been forfeited in the *far country*, to satisfy a luxurious appetite. He had accomplished a long journey, in returning to his father's house. And now his feet were sore beaten with the way, and miserably scorched with the heat of the sun, so that he could neither walk nor stand. To remedy this, his affectionate father gives orders to " put shoes on his feet."

That we may understand what our Lord means to represent by the emblem of the shoes that were ordered for the prodigal; we may compare this text with that of the Apostle Paul, where he exhorts his
Ephesians,

Ephesians, to have their "feet shod with the preparation of the gospel of peace *:" by which we are to understand that habitual preparation, or readiness for every thing that we have to meet with in the course of providence, which the gospel of peace recommends, and with which it furnishes every one that believes it. We are all engaged in a spiritual journey. The people of God are so in a peculiar sense. There are a variety of difficulties to be surmounted, a variety of hardships to be endured, while we are in the way. By reason of these, the Christian is often in danger of becoming like a person whose feet are so beaten, bruised, and wounded, that he cannot prosecute his journey. To defend us against all real injury by those hardships and difficulties; to ease the smart of those wounds which we may have already received; and to enable us to prosecute our journey, however rough the way may be; nothing can have such a tendency, under the influence of the divine blessing, as "the preparation of the gospel of peace." This, therefore, is the shoes intended in this text, as well as in the parallel text just quoted. And the sense of the words may be summed up in the following proposition.

It is the express will and pleasure of God, the Father of the whole family of grace, that every returning prodigal have his feet shod with the preparation of the gospel of peace. Not only has he commanded us to provide ourselves with such shoes. This he knows we cannot do of ourselves. He has them ready in his house; he has given commandment to bring them forth,

* Eph. vi. 15.

forth, and put them upon us; and the moment that we return to his family we shall find ourselves furnished with them.

In speaking from this subject, it is only proposed,

I. To enquire, a little more particularly, What is that preparation which is represented by the shoes that were appointed for the prodigal's feet?

II. To consider how these shoes are to be put on? In other words, How this preparation may be attained? And then,

III. To apply the whole.

I. In relation to the first of these, we may observe, that there are, in general, four things for which we stand in special need to be always ready.

1. We should always be prepared for the acceptable performance of every piece of work that God calls, or may call for, at our hand. Every Christian has some piece of work assigned him, for the glory of God in the world; in the performance of which he must occupy his talents, in view of the Master's coming. And this is comprehensive of every duty required in the law of God, and every thing to which we have the call of God, in the course of providence. We should therefore live in constant readiness, not only to perform every religious and moral duty in its proper season, but also to follow every call of Providence; and so to accomplish every piece of work, however difficult, that our God and Father may see meet to employ us in.

In order hereunto, the following things are continually necessary: (1.) A proper acquaintance both
with

with the word of God and with the *language* of Providence; that, by comparing both together, we may be in cafe to fet forward to our work, in the firm perfuafion that we do our duty. When a perfon does any thing, even though it be lawful and warrantable in itfelf, without a well-grounded perfuafion that it is fo; to him it is fin. A due refpect to the authority of God requiring it, is a neceffary ingredient of all acceptable obedience; for " whatfoever is not of faith " is fin *." (2.) A due fenfe of the importance of the work in which we are engaged, and of the difficulty of performing it acceptably. As nothing lays us more open to temptation to the commiffion of any fin, than an apprehenfion that it is a little one; fo nothing has a greater tendency to make us remifs in the performance of any duty, than our entertaining a thought that the duty is of fmall moment, or is eafily accomplifhed. (3.) A deep fenfe of our own weaknefs, and utter infufficiency for the acceptable performance of any duty. Confidence in his own ftrength, is almoft a conftant prelude to a Chriftian's fall. (4.) Some acquaintance with that inexhauftible fulnefs of grace and ftrength, which is lodged in the hand of Chrift, and of our accefs to it. No perfon can rationally fet about any enterprize without fome probable hope of fuccefs. And, feeing we can have no hope of fuccefs in any duty from our own ftrength, it is neceffary that we have fome competent knowledge of that ftock of fpiritual ftrength which God has laid up in Chrift: And, (5.) Such dependence upon that fulnefs, and upon the faithfulnefs of him who has promifed to furnifh us with fupplies from thence,

as

Rom. xiv. *ult.*

the preparation of the Gospel of Peace. 407

as may encourage us to set forward, under a sense of our being capable to do nothing of ourselves. Every Christian, in setting about every duty, is to consider himself as going to perform what is to him an impossibility. But he knows, that what is impossible to him, is possible and easy with God. He knows who has said, "My grace is sufficient for thee, and my strength " is made perfect in weakness *." And, though he does not yet feel the promise accomplished, nor himself possessed of the promised strength; yet he dares set forward, in the faith that this strength shall be communicated to him in the moment of need. Like the man with the withered hand, he sets himself to obey the divine command; though sensible, that, in present circumstances, it is beyond his power; trusting, that he who has given the command will also give power to obey it. Unless this is habitually the case with *you*, you cannot be rightly prepared for any piece of work or duty; you are hitherto a stranger to the shoes mentioned in the text.

2. We should likewise be in a state of constant readiness for prosecuting our spiritual warfare, either by way of defence or assault, according to whatever orders we may receive from the " Captain of our salva- " tion." Shoes are peculiarly necessary for a soldier, not only to preserve his feet from cold and from bruises, in marching and counter-marching; but also to secure them from those weapons that the enemy may straw in the way, purposely to wound his feet, and disable him for the service. Every Christian is a soldier; and the shoes mentioned in the text are expressly recommended as one branch of his armour.

And

* 2 Cor. xii. 9.

And unlefs we are in a ftate of habitual preparation, and readinefs for every event of the war, it is impoffible that we can profecute it to advantage.

For this purpofe, it is neceffary, (1.) That we have a rooted principle of enmity againft Satan, and all the interefts of his kingdom, within us and without us. When this war was firft proclaimed, God promifed to put fuch an enmity into the hearts of all the feed of the woman. And while the love of fin remains, or where a perfon is not a fincere enemy to Satan's interefts, it is impoffible that ever he will exert himfelf in the war. (2.) That we have a fuperlative love to Chrift, and the interefts of his kingdom. Unlefs a man's love to his king and country be fo ftrong, as even to balance the principle of felf-prefervation, he will never willingly expofe himfelf to danger for their fake; confequently he is unfit for the foldier's calling. And we can never exert ourfelves, in behalf of Chrift or his interefts, againft the common enemy, till we love him to fuch a degree, as to be willing to expofe ourfelves to any poffible hazard for his fake. (3.) That we be duly fenfible of the enemy's ftrength and cunning, and of our own weaknefs and folly. Nothing is more dangerous for a warrior, than to defpife his enemy, or to be confident in the fuperiority of his own ftrength. Much more is this the cafe in this warfare; where the foldiers of Chrift are a compofition of weaknefs and folly, while all the power and policy of hell are employed againft them. (4.) That we be ever watchful. So Chrift himfelf exhorts, " What I fay unto you, I fay unto all, watch *." In every army fome are appointed to watch and keep guard,

* Mark xiii. 37.

guard, while the rest sleep. But in times of extreme danger, the whole army must watch, and every soldier must rest on his arms. This is always the case in the camp of Christ. " Let us not, *then*, sleep as " do others; but let us *always* watch and be sober." (5.) That we have always our armour on. As our Lord sends not any a warfare on his charges, so neither does he send any to the war without armour; ~~both~~ offensive and defensive. We are presented with a complete set by the Apostle Paul; and, if we would war succesfully, we must comply with his exhortation, by putting and keeping it on *. (6.) We must daily endeavour to learn the use of our armour; that, when we are called to use it, we may not find ourselves like David, who could not go against the Philistine in the king's armour, because he had not proved it. Even in time of peace, soldiers exercise themselves to the use of their arms. And we will never be expert in repelling the assaults of the enemy, unless we live daily in the exercise of those graces that are peculiarly necessary in a time of temptation. (7.) Our eye should be continually upon our colours; that we may be ready to follow them, or to defend them, as circumstances require. The colours, you know, are the principal means of directing the motions of an army in the time of action. And for this, among other reasons, the enemy's attacks are chiefly directed against them. We also have our colours; the *banner* which God has " given to be displayed " because of truth." Our eye should be continually upon the *present truth*, the testimony of the day; that we may keep the word of Christ's patience; for

against

---

* Eph. vi. 12,—18.

against it particularly are the enemy's attacks directed. (8.) We should be ever attentive to the motions of our Captain general, and to the orders that he issues; that we may be ever ready to obey him, and to " follow him, whitherfoever he goeth." In a word, We muſt have a conſtant dependence upon him for making us fuccefsful in the war; and a continual aſſurance that he will bring us off conquerors at the laſt. A man would not hefitate to expofe himfelf to the greateſt danger, or to undertake the hardeſt piece of fervice, if he were affured of fuccefs before hand. This cannot be the cafe in any other warfare; but fuch affurance we have. The faithfulnefs of God is engaged to " bruife Satan under *our* feet fhortly;" and to " drive out *all enemies* before us, by little and " little." Were this always in our eye, there is no piece of fervice, to which our Captain might appoint us, for which we would not be habitually ready.

3. We need to be always ready for a profitable enjoyment of our privileges, and of the benefits which God beſtows upon us, whether in the difpenfations of grace, or of common providence. We are as much in danger of mifcarrying in profperity as under adverfity. And when 'we are loaded with God's benefits before we are duly prepared for them, they often prove a curfe in the event rather than a bleffing. With regard to fpiritual benefits, there are fome of them for which we are no otherwife prepared than by our extreme need of them; fuch are regeneration and juſtification. But there are others of fuch a nature, that we can neither be profited by them, nor can we glorify God in the ufe of them; unlefs we are, in fome meafure, prepared for them before hand.

This

This is the cafe with many of thofe bleffings which are conferred upon Chriftians in the progrefs of fanctification. It is peculiarly fo with regard to thofe precious interviews with God, which they are allowed to enjoy in their attendance upon divine ordinances.

To prepare us for thefe, and for every other branch of profperity, fpiritual or temporal, the following things will be found of fpecial ufe. (1.) A deep and humbling fenfe of our own fin and unworthinefs; that we are "lefs than the leaft of all *God's* mercies." That he may not give his *glory to another*, the Lord will always have his people convinced, that what he does for their advantage he does not for their fakes. "Not for your fakes do I this, faith the Lord God: "be afhamed and confounded for your own ways, O "houfe of Ifrael *." When a perfon imagines that his own merit or induftry has procured what he enjoys, he will ever be difpofed to affume to himfelf a part of the praife that is due to God. And therefore, when God beftows any thing in mercy, he firft brings the perfon to be fenfible that he muft owe it to mercy and free grace only. (2.) Some degree of refignation and denial, not only to thofe benefits that are merely of a temporal nature, but even to thofe fpiritual enjoyments which are to be attained in this life. When young David was anointed to the kingdom, he was doubtlefs elated with the hopes of his future advancement, and thought himfelf fomewhat. But before he was put in poffeffion of it, God, by cafting a variety of difappointments in his way, and fubjecting him to various reverfes of fortune, brought his foul to be "even as a weaned child;" capable of living

* Ezek. xxxvi. 32.

ving content and happy, either with the kingdom or without it, as God faw meet. To the fame difpofition muft every Chriftian be brought, with regard to all that can be enjoyed in time. And if he is brought to that temper before the enjoyment of what he feeks and hopes for, he will find an unfpeakable advantage in it. (3.) Some competent degree of mortification. As far as pride, or any other corruption, remains unmortified, even Chriftians themfelves will be in danger of abufing their privileges, and turning them to be food for their lufts. Uzziah, Hezekiah, and others, have left us mournful evidence how far worldly profperity is liable to be fo abufed. And that fpiritual attainments are not lefs fo, the example of Paul himfelf may convince us. His exaltation *to the third heavens*, and the *abundance of revelations* which he there enjoyed, made a *meffenger of Satan*, and a fevere buffeting neceffary; otherwife he was in danger of being *exalted above meafure*. The more that corruption is mortified before enjoyment, the lefs buffeting will be neceffary after it. (4.) The fetting of our hearts and affections upon the things that are above, in preference to all that can be enjoyed on the earth. So far as this is wanting, we will always be in danger of refting in what we enjoy here, and acting as if we thought this our home. This is one reafon why the profperity of the people of God in this world is often fo fhort-lived. They become fecure, and dream of building tabernacles, as if their journey were ended; and they need a new trial, to put them in mind that this is not their reft. But if our hearts and our converfation were in heaven, as they ought; if we confidered " the things that are not feen, *and*
" are

"are eternal," as our only portion; and were daily preffing forward in the hope of enjoying complete happinefs *there only;* we would often be in lefs danger of abufing our profperity; and a ftate of adverfity would be lefs neceffary.

4. We need to be always prepared for thofe trials and afflictions, that God may be pleafed to lay upon us in this life, and for death itfelf in the end. No man can expect to be without afflictions in this world. Neither can any man forefee what trials are awaiting him, or from what quarter they fhall come. The people of God have a double fhare of them. Their heavenly Father will not fuffer them to be without chaftifement, fo long as they are not without fin. The world hates them, becaufe they are not of the world. And Satan will ever do them all the mifchief for which he can obtain a permiffion. Thus they are often " plagued all the day long, and chaftened eve-" ry morning;" while wicked men are fuffered to profper at their will. When public trials are inflicted, they feldom efcape a fhare in them; yea, " judge-" ment *often* begins at the houfe of God." And every Chriftian, as well as every ftranger to Chrift, has death to meet with in the event; for " there is no " difference in that warfare." But it is impoffible to bear any trial, fo as to reap fpiritual advantage by it, or to give glory to God under it, unlefs we are fome way prepared for it before hand. As you may all lay your account with perfonal trials, and more efpecially, as God is loudly threatening to vifit us with public calamities; you may confider him as addreffing every one of you, in the words which he fpoke to Ifrael by the prophet Amos, " Becaufe I will do this unto thee,

" prepar

"prepare to meet thy God, O Ifrael." What preparation is neceffary in the profpect of coming trials, we fhall endeavour to point out, in the form of an exhortation, in the following particulars.

(1.) Above all things, be concerned to be in Chrift, and fo in a ftate of peace with God. Then, however fevere your afflictions may be, they fhall neither be faftened upon you by the curfe of God, nor fhall they be imbittered by vindictive wrath. Chrift is that hiding-place, without which no man can be fafe in a time of the greateft profperity; and in which every perfon is fafe in the time of the foreft adverfity. Here you can never be wholly unprepared for the worft that can happen, however unexpected it may be; and any where elfe you can be ready for no trial, however light it may feem, or however much you was aware of its coming. This is that chamber of fafety, which is recommended by the Spirit of God himfelf in fuch a time as this. "Come, my people, "enter thou into thy chambers; fhut the doors about "thee; hide thyfelf, as it were for a little moment, "until the indignation be overpaft. For behold the "LORD cometh out of his place, to punifh the inha- "bitants of the earth for their iniquity; the earth "alfo fhall difclofe her blood, and fhall no more cover "her flain*."

(2.) Maintain a conftant impreffion of your own demerit, and of the many juft caufes of the Lord's contending againft you. The man who is not fenfible of any caufe, why God fhould plead a controverfy with him, cannot be fuppofed to lay his account with the pleading of it. If it is pleaded, it will be matter

* Ifa. xxvi. 20, 21.

matter of furprife to him; and he will be in danger of charging God both with folly and injuftice. But he whofe fin is ever before him, and who knows the exceeding finfulnefs of it, will ever be fenfible that God may juftly contend againft him on account of it. If he does contend, the man is in cafe to afcribe righteoufnefs to him, while he takes fhame and confufion of face to himfelf. And, inftead of finding fault with God's procedure, as too fevere, he is ready to acknowledge that he is punifhed lefs than his iniquities deferve; and to fay, with the church, " It is of the " Lord's mercies, that we are not confumed, and be- " caufe his compaffions fail not *."

(3.) Live always denied to the world, and all that it contains. The greateft part of the afflictions of this life arifes from our being deprived of fome fuppofed good, that we either enjoyed or hoped for. When we lofe our health, our reputation, our worldly fubftance, or our earthly relations; thefe are among the fevereft trials that we meet with. And never will you be properly ready to bear any fuch trial, till you be convinced that all fublunary enjoyments are but vanity, and give over looking for folid or lafting happinefs in them. As the child, while it continues to fuck, will not be pleafed without the breaft, whatever elfe you give it, but after it is weaned, can be as happy without it, as it was with it before; fo you, while you continue unduly attached to any earthly good, will find it impoffible either to be happy or content without it. Indeed, you can neither enjoy it, nor part with it in a becoming manner, till your foul be, with regard to it, " even as a weaned child." You
are

* Lam. iii. 22.

are incapable of behaving as you ought, either when you have it or when you come to want it, unless you are ready and willing either to have it or to want it, as God sees best for you.

(4.) Pretend not to be a Christian without first counting the cost; nor think of following Christ, and becoming his disciple, without *taking up* your *cross*. Our Lord does not mean to entice any to his service by false and delusive hopes, that he never intends to gratify. He, therefore, assures us, in the entry, that through " much tribulation we must enter into the " kingdom." He that would be his disciple must " take up his cross, and follow *him;*" that is, he must lay his account with trials, not only in the way of following Christ, but even on that account. Not only must he suffer reproaches, cruel mockings, and some lesser evils; he must look for the severest persecutions, if God be pleased so to permit; even to the ignominious death of the cross. And he must be resolved, that, if ever it is put to his choice, he will take his cross on his shoulder, as malefactors used to do, and carry it forth to the place of execution, in order to be immediately nailed to it; rather than escape that barbarous death, by turning his back upon Christ, in whole or in part. If a man looks only for sunshine and fair weather in the way of godliness, he must needs be surprised, and disconcerted, and discouraged, when he sees the clouds to gather, and feels the storms to blow. But the man who expected no better, " thinks it not strange concerning the " fiery trial; *because he knows* that the same afflic-
" tions are accomplished in *his* brethren that are in
" the world." He considers what he suffers as an
accomplishment

accomplifhment of the word of God : and inftead of being thereby difcouraged, he confiders it as a pledge, that " not one good word *fhall* fail, of all that the " Lord hath fpoken."

(5.) Beware of ever giving yourfelf up to fecurity, or putting the evil day far away. If you have long enjoyed profperity, dream not that you fhall enjoy it always. The longer it has continued with you, the nearer it is to a period; and you fhould be fo much the more ready for the approach of adverfity. If you have been long under trouble, and now have obtained a little revival; that muft not be confidered as an evidence that you will enjoy any long exemption. On the contrary, for ought you know, God may have vifited you with leffer trials heretofore, with a view to prepare you for heavier trials that may be yet a-coming. If ever you imagine that your " mountain ftands ftrong; " and *you* fhall not be moved," even though you impute it to the love of God; you may be fure that it is but a little, if indeed you are an object of God's love, when your *profperous ftate* will be *turned into mifery*. And the lefs the change was looked for, the more difficult will you find it to behave properly under it. Job found it no eafy matter to be rightly exercifed under his affliction, though he met with nothing but what he had *greatly feared*. How much more would it have been fo, if he had been *in fecurity*, or *in reft*, or *in quiet*, when *trouble came* *?

(6.) Be ever denied to your own will, and let it be funk in the will of God. Chrift himfelf is our beft pattern in this, as well as in every other branch of the

* Job iii, 25, 26

Chriſtian practice. Though he prayed moſt fervently, and repeated his prayer thrice in the ſame words, about a matter that was of the greateſt importance to him, yet he concludes the whole with this memorable expreſſion, " Nevertheleſs, not my will, but thy " will be done." A ſimilar prayer he taught his diſciples; and every genuine diſciple will be concerned to uſe it in ſincerity. If ſuch a prayer became his lips, whoſe will could never be contrary to his Father's; how much more does it become us, whoſe wills are ſo perverted, that we are incapable of chuſing or following, of ourſelves, either what tends to the glory of God, or what tends to our own advantage? Our will muſt needs be croſſed, ſo far as it is contrary to the will of God; for his " counſel ſhall " ſtand, and *he* will do all *his* pleaſure." The man who has not learned to ſubmit his will to God's, muſt needs rage, when his ſchemes are diſconcerted, " like " a wild bull in a net." But he who has learned to bring his own will into ſubjection to the will of God, will be in a condition to hear the heavieſt tidings without undue emotion; and without any other reply, than that which old Eli made to Samuel's meſſage, " It is the Lord, let him do what ſeemeth him " good."

(7.) Keep it ever in mind, that you are not your own, but bought with an immenſe price; and, by your own voluntary deed, given away and devoted unto God. While a man conſiders himſelf as his own maſter, he doubtleſs will think that he has a right to diſpoſe of himſelf at his own pleaſure. And no wonder that he take it amiſs, when he finds his lot otherwiſe diſpoſed than he wiſhed it to be. But it is impoſſible

possible for any person to be a Christian, without having dedicated himself to God as one of his people; because such a dedication is necessarily included in his acceptance of the covenant of grace. And after having devoted himself to God, he cannot reasonably find fault, because God disposes of him as his own; even though it should be in a manner not very agreeable to his inclinations. If you would always maintain a due impression of this, you would have a ready answer to all temptations to repining under trials, as well as to all other temptations to sin of any kind, in the words of Jephtha the Gileadite; " I have opened " my mouth to the Lord; and I cannot go back[*]."

(8.) Learn always to consider your own interest as subordinate to the glory of God. This is the ultimate end of your being. It is the ultimate end of all God's dealings with you. And, so far as you are exercised like your profession, it will be your ultimate aim in all your actions. Satan could never fall upon a more effectual method, to baffle the whole design of divine revelation, than to persuade men, that self-love, interest, or pleasure is, or ought to be, the principal motive of religious actions. Nor did he ever fall upon a scheme better calculated to establish his own kingdom, upon the ruins of the kingdom of Christ, in this world, than the selfish mode of religion which he is now endeavouring to introduce. So far as that prevails, the consequence must be, that whenever the methods that God takes with us, or the duties that he requires of us, are inconsistent with our mistaken and contracted views of interest; the latter must preponderate with us, to the neglect of our duty, and to the

condemning

[*] Judg. xi. 39.

condemning of God's difpenfations. It will never be an eafy matter to perfuade carnal fenfe, or bewildered reafon, that trials and afflictions are not contrary to the perfon's intereft. And unlefs he has learned to acquiefce in them, from a perfuafion that they are for God's glory, and from a fuperior regard to that, as the end of his being; he will never find it eafy to be reconciled to them.

(9.) Study always to live by faith, and to view every difpenfation of Providence in the light of the word of God. It is not in human nature; perhaps it is not confiftent with any nature; for a perfon to acquiefce, with fatisfaction, in what he really believes to be againft him. Though our own intereft ought never to be our ultimate end, it will ever be a fubordinate end, in the view of every perfon that is influenced by a principle of felf-prefervation. Refignation, therefore, to the will of God, under afflicting providences, is an abfolute impoffibility, while you look upon God as your enemy, and confider his difpenfations as intended for your hurt. But if you look into the word of God, you fhall find reafon, from his own gracious grant and promife, to confider God as your kind and loving Father; to confider all his chaftifements as intended for your profit, both in this world and in the world to come; and to fee them all working, together with every other difpenfation, for your good, as well as for his glory. And then, inftead of repining againft them, you fhall find good reafon to fubmit to them all, as juft and neceffary; to acquiefce in them all, as good; and even to be thankful for the worft that you fuffer. Thus, faith in God's word

word of grace and promise is the best preparative for an afflicted lot.

Finally, Be concerned daily to imitate the example of Paul and his primitive brethren, by " looking, not " at the things which are seen, *and* are temporal; but " at the things which are not seen, *and* are eternal*." If you compare the verse to which we refer, with the preceding part of that chapter; you will find that this was the happy mean by which they were prevented from fainting under their adversities; so that they could be " troubled on every side, *without be-* " *ing* distressed; perplexed, *and yet* not in despair; " persecuted, and not forsaken; cast down, and not " destroyed." By this means they came to be satisfied, that their " light affliction, which *was* but for a " moment, *wrought* for *them* a far more exceeding " and eternal weight of glory." And hence they were not only resigned to tribulation, but even gloried in it. And the same exercise will have the same influence upon you. If your attention is fixed upon the unseen objects of an eternal world, you will find so little proportion between them and the transient vanities of a present life, that you will not count these worthy of a look, in comparison of the other. The good things of a present world you will consider as being so empty, and so transitory, that you will be ashamed, either to rejoice in the possession or to grieve for the loss of them. And the evil things of this seen world you will also consider as so light and momentary, that you will count it unworthy of a person that was made for eternity, to make himself uneasy on account of them. In a word, The blessed hope of an eternal

* 2 Cor. iv. 18.

eternal and uninterrupted enjoyment of those unseen things, upon which you now look by faith, will be found the most powerful cordial, to support you under all the troubles of this passing world. By this means you will be enabled, under the heaviest of them, to "rejoice with joy unspeakable and full of "glory."

If these things be in you and abound, they will make you ready for all that you can be called to; and for all that you can be visited with in the present world. You will never be unprepared, either for work or warfare, for prosperity or adversity, for life or death. And all these are included in the shoes that our heavenly Father has provided for the feet of his returning prodigals. It will now be a native question, among all those who are truly attentive to their own interest, How these shoes are to be attained? Or in what manner it is that they are put on?

II. And this was the *second* thing of which we proposed to speak. All that we intend on this head, you may take in the following observations.

1. God himself, and he only, can effectually put these shoes on our feet. It will readily have occurred to every exercised Christian, that the several pieces of preparation which have been mentioned, are so many fruits of the Spirit of God, and can only be attained by his saving and efficacious operation. This might be particularly evinced concerning each of them. It shall suffice to give one general proof, comprehending them all. The inspired Preacher assures us, that " the preparations of the heart in man, as
" well

" well as the answer of the tongue, are from the " Lord *." All our endeavours to attain such preparations would be vain, if we had not reason to expect success from God's concurring operation; and they will be vain, unless he concur with them indeed. We could have no reason to hope for such concurrence, if he had not graciously promised it; nor will any persons enjoy it, unless their endeavours are accompanied with a believing dependence upon him, for the accomplishment of his promise. But if we continue in the use of appointed means, depending upon him for success, and wrestling with him, by humble supplications to that effect; we may be assured that our " labour shall not be in vain in the Lord. Lord, " thou hast heard the desire of the humble: thou wilt " prepare their heart, and thou wilt cause thine ear " to hear †."

2. The gospel of the grace of God is the principal mean of furnishing those shoes, and putting them on. They are the " preparation of the gospel of peace." They who have never heard the gospel, nor enjoyed divine revelation, can be prepared for nothing. No work that they do is capable of being viewed as an acceptable service to God. Instead of accomplishing a warfare against their spiritual enemies, they are all combined with the enemy for their own destruction, as well as for breaking God's bands, and rejecting the government of his anointed. Their corruptions are fed by every prosperous, and irritated by every adverse dispensation. Every change that passes over them finds them unprepared; and therefore every thing leaves them worse than it found them. The same

* Prov. xvi. 1.   † Psal. x. 17.

fame is indeed the cafe with all thofe who hear the gofpel, and never yet felt its powerful efficacy for changing the heart. But every one, whofe heart the Lord has opened to attend to the things that are fpoken in the gofpel, knows in his happy experience, that all the branches of preparation which have been mentioned, and every other which has not been mentioned, are to be attained through its inftrumentality.

The gofpel reveals and exhibits Chrift, as the only hiding-place for perifhing fouls, in which, as you heard, every perfon may be habitually ready for every thing; and out of which none can be ready, either habitually or actually, for any thing. The gofpel is the vehicle which the Spirit of God makes ufe of for conveying into the heart, that almighty power by which alone the finner can be determined to come to Chrift, and to embrace the favour of God, as exhibited through him. The gofpel fets before us, as in a glafs, thofe unfeen and eternal things, which may attract our attention, and draw us off from all undue attachment to the vanities of a prefent life. The gofpel is the mean by which the Holy Ghoft works in fubduing corruption; in implanting every grace, and drawing it forth into exercife; and in working in us " all " the good pleafure of his goodnefs." It animates us to prefs after every piece of neceffary preparation, by affuring us of fuccefs, not by might nor by power, but by the Holy Spirit of God. And it fets before us all thofe great and precious promifes, upon which our faith may reft in every cafe; fo that we may neither be furprifed, nor difconcerted, nor difmayed; whatever

ever should happen to ourselves in particular, or take place in the world around us.

3. The servants of God, particularly they who labour in word and doctrine, are the happy instruments of bringing forth those shoes, and putting them upon the feet of returning prodigals. Hence the command in the text is addressed, by the prodigal's father, to the servants of the family. Indeed, every Christian may be useful to his brethren in this respect; and he ought to make it his study to be so. We are all bound to strengthen one another's hands, in the work and way of God. We are to " strengthen the weak hands, " *to* confirm the feeble knees;" to stir up and awaken the secure, and to give warning to every one of every danger that we see approaching; that our brethren, as well as we, may be ready to meet our God. But this is the province, in a peculiar manner, of the ministers of the gospel. As the publication of the gospel is their main work, whatever the gospel is a mean of accomplishing, they have the honour of being instruments in it; though the effect is neither owing to any intrinsic efficacy in the mean, nor any kind of activity in the instrument; but solely to him, who has chosen, " by the foolishness of preaching, to save " them that believe."

4. In this whole matter, returning prodigals themselves must be " workers together with God." Though we can do nothing of ourselves, and though it is God that does all our works in us, yet he does all, in a way of stirring us up to be active and diligent, in a humble dependence upon his gracious assistance. Indeed, there are some things that God does, both in us and for us, in which we are not capable of any activity.

vity. Thus, in regeneration we are as little active as Adam was in his own creation, or as the dead will be at the laſt day in their own reſurrection. But, in all that belongs to the progreſs of ſanctification in us, we neceſſarily muſt be active. And in this way it is that our ſhoes muſt be put on. While Chriſtians continue inactive, the work of God makes ever ſlow progreſs in their ſouls; and in that ſtate they are not duly prepared for any thing. But when their loins are girded, their lamps burning, their garments on, and themſelves watching, and occupying their Maſter's talents; then the Spirit of God is alſo buſy, carrying on his work in them, and making them ready, not only for all that can befal them in time, but alſo for an approaching eternity, and for their Lord's coming. Indeed, their activity is the neceſſary effect; and therefore the beſt evidence of his being preſently at his work.

Much is incumbent upon you, Chriſtian, in this reſpect. You muſt wait diligently upon thoſe means of grace, in the uſe of which you are warranted to expect the " preparations of the heart." You muſt wreſtle with God, fervently and conſtantly, that he may prepare your " heart, and cauſe *his* ear to hear." You muſt daily improve the *goſpel of peace*, as the only mean of furniſhing, or repairing your ſpiritual ſhoes; receiving the teſtimony that it brings you of God and his will; truſting in its promiſes, and in the faithfulneſs of him that hath promiſed, for every branch of preparation, and for all that you need; and relying upon the righteouſneſs which it exhibits, as the only ground of your title both to the promiſe itſelf, and to the accompliſhment of it. You muſt watch

the preparation of the Gospel of Peace. 427

watch continually against all the attempts of the enemy, whether to deprive you of that preparation which you have attained, or to prevent your attaining more. All this, and much more than this, you must do, in a way of maintaining a fixed persuasion that you can do nothing; and that all that you do, in agreeableness to the will of God, as well as all that is done for you, in agreeableness to his promise, must be the work of God himself; and under a fixed resolution to give him all the glory, counting yourself no more than an *unprofitable servant*.

III. We shall now conclude with some improvement of the subject. And,

1. It affords us information, in various particulars; such as,

(1.) It shews that a man in a natural estate is ready for nothing; every sinner is a prodigal, wanting shoes, as well as other necessaries. He is therefore unprepared for all that is required of him, and for all that he meets with in the course of providence. If God calls him to any piece of work, he is otherwise engaged; he neither attends to the call, nor is at leisure to comply with it. If spiritual enemies assail him, he is so far from being prepared to repel their assaults, that he fondly mistakes them for friends, and takes part with them in promoting his own ruin. If he enjoys prosperity, it destroys him. Like a ship without ballast which is ready to be overset by a wind that would otherwise be most favourable, he is unable to bear the gale of prosperity. His " table *proves* a " snare, and his welfare *is* a trap to take him." When adversity befals him, he is suddenly overwhelmed.

He enjoys nothing to balance it, therefore his heart fails; and he vents his impotent rage against God, in such murmurings as tend more to make him miserable than all the rest that he suffers. And so far is he from being ready for death or eternity, that he really knows nothing about what preparation is necessary for either.

(2.) They who are brought back to the family of God, and put, by divine grace, among his children, are never wholly unready for any thing; no event can overtake them wholly unprepared. It is among the first things that their heavenly Father does for them, to order shoes for their feet. The truth is, there is a twofold readiness necessary, in view of whatever may take place in this world, as well as of death and another world. A *habitual readiness*, consisting in our being secured against any real injury, by any thing that may happen; and an *actual readiness*, consisting in our present fitness to be active in fulfilling whatever is the will of God concerning us. The first of these every Christian enjoys; for it is the immediate result of his union to Christ, and of his interest in the favour of God. And the other he likewise enjoys in some degree, though he finds it always necessary to press after more.

(3.) Even they who are brought back to the house and family of God have need to beware of apprehending that they are come to their rest; or considering themselves as at home while, they continue in this world. Among the Jews, and other nations in that climate, it was unusual to wear shoes, unless when they were abroad, and had a journey of some kind to accomplish. Our being provided with shoes

when

when we return to our Father's houfe, is a fure evidence that our journey is not finifhed; but we are ftill in the condition of travellers here. Think not, Chriftian, that becaufe you are returned from that far country in which you was in your natural eftate, you are ftill to enjoy reft and tranquillity for the time to come. Nay, you are ftill in a *foreign land.* Your inheritance, and the houfe where you are to dwell for ever, are in " the land that is *yet* afar off." Still you have a long journey before you; and you muft lay your account with toil, and hardfhips, and dangers, and difficulties of various kinds. Yea, your road lies through an enemy's country. You muft fight every inch of your way. Your fhoes are neceffary, as a piece of armour to defend your feet from the enemy's weapons, as well as to preferve them from the injuries of the way. And, if you duly attend to your fituation, you will find reafon to be thankful to your heavenly Father, who has provided fhoes for your feet.

2. This fubject likewife affords matter of trial. You have all need to examine your feet, and confider whether you have on the fhoes mentioned in the text or not. For your affiftance, we fhall fuggeft a few queftions, that you may afk every one at his own confcience. Are you fenfible that you meet with nothing for which you do not need much preparation, beyond all that you have? Are you convinced, that you can never prepare yourfelf for any thing; and defirous always to look to God for the " preparations " of the heart ?" Are you careful, through divine grace, to obferve what is a-coming in the courfe of providence, and to be prepared for all that you forefee?

fee? Are you fenfible of your fhort-fightednefs, convinced that it is impoffible for you to be apprized beforehand of every thing, or almoft of any thing that you meet with; and therefore concerned to be alfo ready for what you cannot forefee? Is it your main concern to be ready for the fecond coming of Chrift, and for your folemn appearance before him to judgement; and that you may be fo, is it your daily ftudy to improve every talent, and fpend every part of your time, as you would wifh to be found doing when he comes: In one word, any meafure of preparation that you think you have attained, has it been wrought in you by means of the *gofpel of peace?* Have you felt the power of the Holy Ghoft, coming along with his word of grace, transforming you gradually into his image, and fo preparing you for every branch of his will? If you can anfwer thefe queftions affirmatively, and upon good grounds; then you have your feet fhod after the manner of God's children; and this you have as a comfortable evidence that you belong to that happy family. But if you have never had experience of any of thefe things, you may be affured that you continue in the far country ftill.

3. In this fubject we might find ample matter for exhortation. We fhall content ourfelves with fuggefting to you the following advices. (1.) Be concerned, whoever you are, to get on thefe fpiritual fhoes. You are all on a journey to an eternal world. You are fure it is a long journey, and you neither know, nor can we tell you how rough and difficult you may find it. Neither is it poffible to forefee what methods enemies may take to render it ftill more uneafy. And how can you undertake fuch a

journey,

journey without shoes on your feet? Unless you are prepared in the manner you have been hearing, your way will afford no pleasure to you, but every step of it will be more painful than another. Neither will God have pleasure either in it or in you. But if your feet are covered with these shoes, they will appear beautiful in Chrift's eyes; for thus he speaks to his bride and spouse: " How beautiful are thy feet with " shoes, O prince's daughter*?" God will delight greatly in the way wherein you walk. And, to yourself, the ways of wisdom will be found " pleasantness, " and all her paths *will be* peace."

(2.) Be careful always to keep them on. Indeed, if once your *feet* be truly *shod with the preparation of the gospel of peace*, you can never totally or finally lose that preparation. Your habitual preparation will always continue; because your union to Chrift can never be dissolved. But your actual preparation may in a great measure be lost; so that you may be much more in readiness either for doing or suffering to-day than you will be to-morrow, or for a long time afterwards. Yea, even your union to Chrift must continue, in the way of being maintained by the exercise of faith on your part, as well as by the inhabitation of the Spirit on his part. Hence is his exhortation to his disciples, " Abide in me, and I in you; " as the branch cannot bear fruit of itself, except it " abide in the vine; no more can ye, except ye abide " in me." Having taken hold of Chrift, therefore, by faith, be careful to abide in him, by a continued exercise of the same faith. And whatever you attain, serving to prepare you for any part of what is the will

of

---

* Song vii. 1.

of God concerning you, be careful never to lose it, nor suffer yourself to be deprived of it by any means. For instance, if you are concerned about preparation, in the view of a solemn sacramental occasion; and, by the good hand of your God upon you, attain some degree of it; beware of thinking it useless for the time to come, and suffering it to slip. The same thing that serves to prepare you for an approach to God at his table, will also serve as a branch of preparation for every thing else that may be before you, and even for death and eternity. You should, therefore, not only continue in the same state, but you should also strive to maintain the same frame, in every part of your after life. Satisfy not yourself with retaining the habits of grace; but, as far as possible, continue in the exercise of it. Consider always who he is that has said, "Behold, I come quickly; hold that fast "which thou hast, that no man take thy crown *."

(3.) Use every method of divine appointment to have your shoes more and more fortified. It is the excellency of the shoes mentioned in the text, that, like those of the Israelites in the wilderness, they "wax not old upon *one's* feet;" they can never be worn out; but, under proper management, will every day wax stronger and stronger. Every Christian should grow in grace, and in the knowledge of our Lord Jesus Christ. Growing in grace, you will grow in readiness for every thing that you may have to meet with. And this should be one argument, by which you should be stirred up to aim daily at such a growth. How this is to be attained, we cannot now stay to inform you at large. But, in a few words, you will find

it

* Rev. iii. 11.

it of ufe to wait diligently upon all the appointed means of grace; to think much about the reafonablenefs of fubjection to the will of God; to be much employed in the mortification of pride, and the other corruptions of your nature; and to be much in prayer to God, from whom alone you can receive *the preparations of the heart.*

(4.) In one word, Study to be daily ready, not only for all that you have to meet with in time; but likewife for your appearance before the tribunal of Chrift at his coming; and for that eternal eftate, upon which you muft enter as foon as you leave the prefent world. We fpake not at large concerning the preparation that is neceffary in the view of judgment and eternity; becaufe we apprehend that the fhoes in the text fignify properly that preparation which is neceffary during the continuance of our journey, to fecure us againft injury by the hardfhips of the way. But it is obvious, that it is as neceffary to be prepared for thefe, as for any thing that can happen in this life; and more fo, in proportion as eternity is of more importance than time. If you have all the branches of preparation already mentioned, you will be, in a great meafure, ready for thefe alfo. And if you are ready for thefe, you will not be unready for any thing that can occur here. That you may be fo, be careful to improve every talent that the Mafter has beftowed upon you, in the view of that account which you muft give of them all when he comes. See that you have the work which he has affigned you in fuch forwardnefs, as that, when he comes, he may find it finifhed. And let every part of your time be fpent, as you would wifh to fpend the laft hour of it. Ne-

ver suffer yourself to be employed in a manner in which you would be ashamed to be employed, when you shall be summoned to the judgment-seat of Christ. Let your heart be always in heaven, and your conversation heavenly; so shall you be fit for a personal residence in heaven in a little. And be much employed in learning that new song, which you wish and hope to sing eternally in your Father's house. In one word, Be much in the exercise of faith. Learn more and more to depend upon God for these spiritual shoes, as well as for every thing else that you need. These, as well as all the rest, are secured to you by the promise; for what Moses said to Asher, may be considered as the word of God to every one of you:
" Thy shoes shall be iron and brass; and as thy days
" are, so shall thy strength be*."

* Deut. xxxiii. 25.

SERMON XIV.

The returning Prodigal's Entertainment; or, *The Penitent Sinner abundantly satisfied with the Fatness of God's House.*

LUKE xv. 23.

—AND BRING HITHER THE FATTED CALF, AND KILL IT; AND LET US EAT AND BE MERRY.

THESE words contain the fourth and last branch of the orders, that the prodigal's father is represented as giving to the servants of the family in relation to his son, who was just now restored from the far country, whither he had wandered, and from that abandoned course of life which he had there pursued. He enjoins them to prepare a magnificent feast for the entertainment of the whole family, and of all the friends of the family, as well as of the returning prodigal; that he might testify his joy, for the reclaiming of his lost son; and give them all an opportunity to partake with him in that joy. More parti-

particularly, the words contain the three things following.

1. The provision with which the returning prodigal was to be entertained, *the fatted calf*. As, among all the robes that might be suppofed to be in fuch a man's houfe, the very beft was ordered for his fon; fo, among all the calves which were in his ftall, one was fuperior to all the reft; and was known in the family, and among the fervants, by the defignation of *the fatted calf;* and this was it that was to be now ufed. In how much efteem this kind of food was among the Hebrews, appears from various inftances. Abraham had nothing better, wherewith to entertain a company of angels*. And the forcerefs at Endor thought it not too mean to be fet before a king †. Among the Greeks, too, we are told it was confidered as one of the moft fumptuous and magnificent repafts.

2. What was given in charge to the fervants, concerning this fatted calf, in two particulars. (1.) They were to *bring* it *forth*, from the place where it then was, to the very place where the mafter of the family met with his fon: *bring* hither *the fatted calf*. (2.) It was to be killed in that place. The word properly fignifies *to kill in facrifice;* and fo it is rendered by various interpreters. We know it was ufual when a facrifice was offered, to invite friends to feaft upon the flefh of it; and, when a magnificent feaft was intended, nothing was more common than firft to offer the beaft in facrifice whofe flefh was to be eaten. This father was not fo lifted up with the reftoration of his loft fon, as to forget that he owed that happy event to the Providence of God. And therefore

fore he appointed that the fatted calf should first be offered to God as a sacrifice, in the place where he and his son met; and afterwards be fed upon by the whole family in the house.

3. The design of this preparation, intimated in the last words of the verse; *and let us eat and be merry*. The word signifies, to indulge one's self in all manner of joy; and in all those actions and gestures whereby the highest degree of joy and gladness is evidenced, which are usual at a great feast. Had he only intended to refresh the prodigal himself, and relieve him from that hunger with which he was ready to perish, such preparation had not only been needless; it had even been hurtful, by occasioning too much delay. But it was his intention that himself, his friends, his other children, and even his servants, should all *eat and be merry*.

It is agreed among all expositors, so far as I know, that this circumstance in the parable is emblematical of that *feast of fat things*, which God makes *unto all people* in a gospel-dispensation; wherein penitent sinners, together with the whole family of their heavenly Father, are entertained and feasted upon the flesh and blood of the Son of God. In the keeping of this feast, the whole company, both in heaven and on earth, are allowed and required freely to indulge themselves in holy joy and festivity. The sense of the words may accordingly be expressed in the following proposition.

The most delicious and exquisite provision being ready in the house of God, for the entertainment of returning Prodigals; the whole family of grace are warranted and invited to eat and be merry.

We shall not detain you by searching for mysteries, where we apprehend none were intended by the great speaker of the parable. Neither shall we strain the similitude, and disgust the sober part of the audience, by pursuing the resemblance between the emblem and the thing represented by it, as far as a wanton imagination might carry us. We shall not, therefore, trouble you with any enquiry about who are the servants to whom those orders are given. The main thing intended seems to be, that God has taken effectual care, that such provision should be made, for the entertainment of returning sinners, as might fitly be represented by the fatted calf. And, as such provision is not usually made, in the house of any great man, without the intervention of servants; it was necessary, to make the parts of the parable hang together, that the servants of the family should be represented as receiving injunctions concerning it; though no created servant of God could have any considerable hand, in providing for that spiritual feast which is represented by the parable.

All that is proposed, therefore, is only to mention a few things, which I take to be imported in the words; and then to conclude with a brief improvement.

The words, I conceive, import, among others, the following things.

1. That every returning sinner finds abundance of provision in the house of God. This prodigal, when he came to himself, said, " How many hired servants, " in my father's house, have bread enough, and to " spare?" And, now when he returns, he not only finds plenty of bread, to satisfy those cravings of nature

ture that could not be allayed in the famifhed country from which he came; he even finds a fatted calf on his table; and is much better entertained than ever he was during his riotous courfe of life. In like manner, when finners come fo far to themfelves, as to be convinced that happinefs is not to be found among the perifhing objects of fenfe; they are taught, by the gofpel of the grace of God, to expect that fatisfaction in God himfelf, which they fought for in vain among the creatures. In that hope they return to him, being affifted by his holy Spirit; and they find all that they hoped for, and incomparably more. Like the queen of Sheba, in relation to the wifdom of Solomon, they find that the one half was not told them. They met with nothing but difappointment upon difappointment, while they fought their provifion in the far country; but here they find all that is requifite to gratify their moft extenfive defires. A difappointment, indeed, they meet with, upon their returning to God; but of a very different nature from what they formerly experienced. Now their hopes are exceeded as far as they were baulked before. They meet with fuch a happy difappointment as he does, who expects but the bread of a hired fervant; and is feafted, among the children of the family, upon *the fatted calf.*

2. That, befides the ordinary provifion of God's family, there is fomewhat prepared for the reception of penitent finners that is of peculiar excellence in itfelf, and peculiarly adapted to their condition. This prodigal was not only permitted to fhare in the daily provifion of the family; but the fatted calf was killed for him, and a feaft was made for his reception. All the

the family of God have abundance of provifion; and would have enjoyed abundance, though no prodigal of our finful tribe had ever returned to his houfe. But that which fupplied the reft of the family, was not judged fufficient for the entertainment of returning prodigals. Something more noble was provided.

To fpeak without allegory, every rational creature, continuing in obedience to God, enjoys a fulnefs of happinefs in him, fuited to its nature and capacity. Adam, in his innocent eftate, was completely happy in God. So are the angels that never finned. But neither what was enjoyed by innocent Adam, nor what is ftill enjoyed by unfinning angels, was fufficient to make them happy who had once played the prodigal, and been alienated from the family. Our heavenly Father does not mean to make us only as happy as our firft parents were in Paradife. A happinefs is intended for thofe who are faved by Chrift, in many refpects fuperior to what Adam enjoyed, and even to what is enjoyed by elect angels. Some new provifion was therefore to be made, that the houfe of God had never afforded, if there had been no prodigals to entertain. For this purpofe the covenant of grace was made from all eternity; the Son of God was incarnate in the fulnefs of time; and, in our nature, fulfilled all that he undertook to the Father. Thus a foundation was laid for bringing us to happinefs in a new way; and likewife for affording us a happinefs containing various new ingredients, that had never otherwife been enjoyed by creatures, nor known among them. You fhall not only be reftored, Chriftian, to the fame condition from which Adam fell; your eternal eftate fhall be incomparably fuperior to what Adam, or any of his pofterity would ever have enjoyed, if he had never fallen. Not only fhall you eat angels food, in your Father's houfe; you fhall feed, through eternity, upon food that angels fhall not tafte; upon food that angels had never feen, if you had not been reftored to the family. Yea, even in this world, you have provifion fet before you, both in word and facrament; that God's houfe would never have afforded, if it had not been prepared for fuch as you. The flefh and blood of the Son of God would never have been any part of the food of the family, unlefs he had firft given it for the life of a loft world. God's *fatted calf* had never been *killed*, if there had been no returning prodigals to entertain.

3. That this noble provifion is made, for the entertainment of mankind finners, by the exprefs warrant and command of God, the great Mafter of the houfe and family. The fervants did not go of their own accord to kill the fatted calf and prepare it; but their mafter gave them pofitive orders for that purpofe. When we call you to a participation of the gofpel-feaft, we do not, like the ftrange woman, invite you to *ftolen waters*, or to *bread* that muft be *eaten in fecret;* without the knowledge of him who bears the expence. The feaft of fat things, which we prefent unto you, is a feaft of God's own making; and he has provided it for the entertainment of prodigals, fo that nothing in your paft life can give you reafon to doubt of his making you welcome to it.

4. That the provifion which God has made, for the entertainment of returning finners, is the flefh of a flain facrifice. The fatted calf, you have heard, was to be facrificed, before it was ferved up. And, in the cafe

case supposed, there was much propriety in that circumstance. The prodigal had *sinned against heaven,* as well as in his Father's sight. It was proper that his sin should be expiated, when he returned to his father's house; and it could not be expiated without a sacrifice. The calf was accordingly to be sacrificed, to make atonement for his sin, before it could be used as his feast. In all this, the figure corresponds exactly with the thing signified. The course of life in which all mankind are naturally engaged, is so egregiously sinful, *against heaven and in* God's *sight;* that it was impossible for any of us to be admitted back into his family, unless upon the footing of a sacrifice. The inexorable justice of God had passed a sentence of condemnation against us all. And the honour of that, and other divine perfections, was pledged, that the sentence should be fully executed. Had it been executed upon us, we could never have been restored to the family of God; but must have continued eternally under that punishment, which we could never have borne to the full. The infinite wisdom and goodness of God provided a remedy for this seemingly desperate case. The eternal Son of God condescended to substitute himself in our room and place; and to suffer the full execution of our dreadful sentence upon himself. Thus he became a sacrifice of atonement for our sin; and, in consequence hereof, his flesh and blood are served up, for our entertainment, in our Father's house. It is only by the killing of this sacrifice, that guests are furnished for the table of God, and that the table is furnished for the guests.

5. That

5. That God's fatted calf behoved to be flain in the place where he meets with returning finners. In other words, Chrift behoved to offer himfelf a facrifice, in the fame place and in the fame condition, in which the grace of God finds us, when he is about to bring us back to his houfe and family. The fervants, we hear, were to bring the fatted calf and kill it in the place where their mafter now ftood, and where he had met with his fon. And, if we compare ver. 20. we fhall fee that it was at fome diftance from the houfe. In order to his being a proper facrifice for us, it was neceffary that Chrift fhould come into our world, and take upon him our nature; that he fhould fubject himfelf to the law that we had broken, and to the fame curfe under which we lay ; that, in one word, he fhould become like one of us, and be in the fame ftate in which we were, fin only excepted. All this he really fubmitted to. Though " he was in the form " of God, and thought it not robbery to be equal with " God ; *yet* he took on him the form of a fervant, and " humbled himfelf *to* become obedient unto death, " even the death of the crofs. *Though* he did no e- " vil, neither was guile found in his mouth;" yet he condefcended to be accounted a malefactor, and dealt with as fuch, both by God and men. He who was the original author of the law, was fubjected to the law which he made. And he who was " God over " all, bleffed for ever, *was* made a curfe for us. In " all things, *he was* made like unto his brethren ;" not only like what they are after they become his brethren ; but like what they were in their natural eftate ; fave only that he was not ftained with the pollution, nor fubject to the power of fin. This was

utterly

utterly incompatible with the divinity of his person; and, had it been possible, would have rendered him altogether unfit to be a sacrifice for sin. And now, in consequence of being sacrificed for us, Christ himself is become the happy meeting-place between God and us; for " God is in Christ, reconciling the world " to himself; not imputing their trespasses unto " them *."

6. That the provision which God has made is the most exquisite; possessed of all that can recommend it to every sinner, and to every saint. Two things here intimate the excellency of it; its being compared to a *fatted calf*, and to a calf that had been offered in sacrifice.

First, Its being compared to a fatted calf, intimates to us the following things.

(1.) That it is most delicious and palatable, suited to every taste. Some persons have a liking for one sort of provision, and some for another. Some have an aversion to one kind of food, and some to another. But nothing is more universally agreeable than the flesh of a *fatted calf*. It pleases almost every palate. So is the case with this spiritual provision. The desires of every soul are boundless, and can never be satisfied with any finite good. But the desires of particular persons are extremely various, and diversified one from another. So long as we look for the gratification of them among the creatures, we must be disappointed; because no created good can be infinite. But in Christ they may all be gratified to the utmost. That desire of riches, which, when fixed on the things of the present world, is termed covetousness,

ness, and justly deemed idolatry; if turned towards Christ is laudable, and shall be fully gratified in the event; for "riches and honour are with *him*; yea, "durable riches and righteousness." That desire of honour, which is a vain and sinful ambition, when terminating upon those shadows that men have to bestow, if taught to centre in Christ, would be commendable, and shall be gratified with a crown of immortal glory. That desire of pleasure, which, in carnal men, degenerates into luxury, resting in the vain objects of sense, and proving the man to be dead while he liveth, if sanctified and fixed upon Christ, is abundantly consistent with spiritual life; and shall be completely gratified, by the possession of that "ful-
" ness of joy *that is* before God's face; *and those* ri-
" vers of pleasures *that are at his* right hand for ever-
" more." The Spirit of God, by his saving operations, destroys not any of those faculties or appetites, that himself, as the God of nature, has implanted in any soul. His business is to destroy that corrupt bias which sin has given them; and bring them back to himself, in whom alone they possibly can be gratified. And whatever is suited to gratify them all, is to be found on the gospel-table.

(2.) That it is substantial, and full of nourishment. Some kinds of provisions, though they are bulky enough, and serve to fill the belly; yet have little substance in them, and therefore afford little nourishment. But the flesh of a *fatted calf* is one of the most substantial, and nutritive kinds of food. So the flesh and blood of Christ, which are the provision here signified, afford the most copious nourishment to the souls of men. By the use of this provision, you may not only have your hunger and thirst allayed, and your desires satisfied for the present; you may likewise be nourished up to the day of complete redemption, so as to grow, every day, in grace, and in the knowledge of our Lord Jesus Christ, till you arrive at the stature of a perfect man in him. Yea, such is the virtue and efficacy of this food, that he who eats it shall never decay, nor wax old; but, through eternity shall flourish, in the vigour of youth, and in all the bloom of spiritual health, without any fear, either of diseases or death.

(3.) It is the most harmless and wholesome provision. Some kinds of food, though sufficiently agreeable to the taste, are prejudicial to the health, and ruinous to the constitution. And some things that agree well enough with one constitution, may be very hurtful to another. But a *fatted calf* is a kind of meat that seldom disagrees with any constitution, more than with any taste. It is wholesome, as well as nourishing. So this spiritual meat, that God has provided for the entertainment of his prodigals, is the most wholesome that can be imagined. It agrees with every constitution, and is adapted, in the best manner, to persons of every age, sex, and quality. The weakest babe finds it not too hard of digestion, and the strongest man has no reason to undervalue it as too light. No man ever contracted any disease from the use of it; nor was any person's appetite or constitution impared by using it freely. So far is it from being hurtful, that it is in the highest degree medicinal. It is an universal remedy for all the diseases of the soul. Yea, it is a sovereign antidote against death itself; for " he that eateth *of it* shall ne-
" ver

" ver die." Not only does it maintain life where it is, and effectually prevent the perfon from dying; it even cures death, where it has already prevailed, and reftores the dead man to life and health. The fmalleft morfel of this provifion put into the mouth of one that is dead in trefpaffes and fins, will immediately caufe him to rife out of his grave, and join in that holy joy and feftivity, which obtains among returning prodigals, in the houfe of God *.

(4.) It is the moft fumptuous and magnificent provifion. You have heard, that of old, before thofe refinements of luxury were invented that difgrace the prefent age, a *fatted calf* was counted an entertainment fit for the tables of the greateft princes. And furely it is proper that the provifion upon God's table fhould excel in magnificence. When the Perfian monarch made a feaft to his nobles and great men, it was *according to the ftate of fo great a king*. And, doubtlefs, the feaft that is made by the King of heaven, muft be incomparably beyond any thing of which there ever was an example among men. Every perfon who has ever tafted of this provifion, or knows any thing of the qualities of it, the expenfive rate at which it was purchafed, or the diftant country from which it comes, will be fatisfied, that the richeft provifion that ever ftood on the table of an earthly potentate, bears no comparifon with this.

Secondly, Its being compared to a calf previoufly facrificed, imports two things:

(1.) That it contains a fecurity to all who partake in it, againft the wrath of God, and againft all the punifhments of fin, both in this world and in the world

---

* See John vi. 33, 50, 57, 58.

to come. You have heard, that Chrift, when he became a facrifice for us, fubjected himfelf to all the punifhment that was juftly due to us for our fin. And now, every perfon who eats his flefh and drinks his blood, being thereby interefted in his facrifice, is fecured in eternal exemption from punifhment in his own perfon. As God could not be juft, in fuffering the fanction of his own law to fall to the ground without any execution; fo neither could he be juft in exacting punifhment twice for the fame crime. Having received a full fatisfaction to all the demands of his law, from the hand of your Surety, believer; God may as foon deny himfelf, and violate his juftice and holinefs, as well as his mercy and goodnefs, as he may fuffer the fmalleft degree of legal punifhment to fall upon you, either in time or through eternity. Nay, his juftice is as ftrictly engaged to preferve you from punifhment, in confequence of your intereft in Chrift, as it is to inflict punifhment upon all who are ftrangers to him. You may, nay you fhall be fubject to chaftifements; and perhaps you may find them both fore and of long continuance. But no part of what you fuffer fhall be the effect of the curfe. In all, God fhall be influenced, not by vindictive wrath, but by fatherly love. Inftead of being a punifhment, every chaftifement fhall prove a bleffing, though it comes in difguife. And it is but a little when you fhall have a comfortable outgate from them all. You have eaten of the flefh of that facrifice, by which fin was expiated. This is a fure evidence that God has accepted it, as an atonement for *your* fin. And herein you have the fulleft affurance, that God, having *forgiven* your *iniquity*, will *remember* your *fin no more*. As this

this is really secured to you, by your participation of God's provision; it is visibly sealed to you, as often as you partake in it symbolically, in the *sacrament* of the *supper*.

(2.) That it affords a like security for the actual communication of all the benefits of God's covenant to the person, in grace here, and in glory hereafter. Even under the law, every sacrifice that was offered, according to divine appointment, contained a seal and confirmation of that covenant by which God stood related to the church. And if this was the case with those typical sacrifices, that could never make any real expiation of sin; how much more must it be so with this all-sufficient sacrifice, which is the sole antitype of the others? In offering this sacrifice, upon which you are called to feed, our Lord Jesus Christ perfected his fulfilment of the condition of the covenant of grace. By that means, he laid a sure foundation for the accomplishment of all its promises. Yea, in consequence of it, God became indispensibly bound to fulfil every promise of the covenant, to all who should have an interest in this sacrifice. By eating the flesh of the sacrifice, you become a partaker of all the virtue of it; and therefore have security, not only for deliverance from punishment, but also for the final enjoyment of all the blessings that were purchased by the shedding of Christ's blood; and promised in that covenant which was confirmed by it. Thus, every time that you eat of God's provision, you have all the promises of his covenant sealed over to you; and a renewed security is afforded you, for the gradual accomplishment of them all; till you be " filled, *at last*, with all the fulness of God." You may not, indeed, look for the full accomplifhment of them here. In this world you are but heirs in minority; and it is enough if you have your neceffary charges borne. Even this you fhall not always have in the fame manner, nor yet in the fame meafure that you may think beft. While you are children, you muft think and act like children; and fo may be oft in danger of finding fault with the manner in which your heavenly Father difpenfes to you the bleffings of his covenant. But when once you come to the years of fpiritual difcretion, you fhall be put in full and perfonal poffeffion of your inheritance; and yourfelves fhall be witneffes, that " not one good word " hath failed of all that the Lord hath fpoken." Then alfo, your judgment being fo far ripened, as to be able, in fome degree, to underftand the defign and tendency of his paft dealings with you; you fhall be difpofed, readily to acknowledge, to the praife of his grace, that, even in the years of your minority, " he " did all things well."

7. The words of the text import, that God's defign, in making fuch provifion for prodigal finners, is, that they may eat it, and feed upon it. The moft delicious food, fet upon the table before a man, will never be of any ufe to him, unlefs he put forth his hand, and take it into his mouth and eat it. The end for which the fatted calf was to be brought and killed, was that the family might eat it and be merry. All the provifion that God has made for finners of mankind would continue ufelefs, if none were to eat of it; and never will *you* have any fhare of its ufefulnefs, unlefs you take it, and eat it. By eating it, we do not mean your attending outwardly upon the difpenfation

fation of the gofpel. By fuch an attendance, indeed, you fit down at the table of God; but this you may do without ever tafting of his fupper. Neither do we barely mean an external participation of the facrament of the *Lord's Supper*. You may eat the facramental bread, and drink the facramental cup, without feeding upon the body and blood of Chrift, as therein exhibited. Far lefs do we mean any corporeal eating of Chrift's flefh, either in word or facrament. His glorious body is now in heaven; and would to God it were as much beyond the power of antichrift and his followers, to wound, perfecute, and opprefs his myftical members, as it is to tear his human body with their teeth. Nay, the provifion of which we fpeak is fpiritual, it was intended for the nourifhment of fouls; and it muft be fed upon by the foul in a fpiritual manner. The eating here required, includes the following things.

(1.) A believing appropriation of Chrift, and all the bleffings of his purchafe, to the perfon in particular. While the meat ftands on the table, every gueft has an equal accefs to it. But none of them has it in actual poffeffion, nor can any of them really feed upon it, till he put forth his hand, take it up from the table, and put it in his mouth. In like manner, as Chrift is offered in the gofpel, every finner has an equal accefs to him, and an equal right to receive him. But, notwithftanding of this, we can have no real intereft in him, nor any real advantage by him, unlefs we receive and appropriate him to ourfelves by faith. That faith which does not include a perfonal appropriation, as it differs not, in the nature of it, from the faith of devils; fo it can produce no better effects upon us than theirs does upon them. They who fatisfy themselves with such a faith, may *believe and tremble*. And I have no doubt but they will do so through eternity, if they live and die pleasing themselves with such a fancy. But it is utterly impossible that, in the sense of this text, they should " eat and be " merry."

(2.) An uniting with Christ, who is our provision, so as to be in him, and to have him in us. You all know, that those things which feed and nourish the body must first be taken into it, and become one with it. Yea, they must be so digested and transformed, as really to become a part of the body itself; otherwise they speedily pass into the draught, and the body receives no advantage by them. So, if you really feed upon Christ, you must so receive him as to become one with him. You must abide in him by a lively faith, and he must abide in you by his Holy Spirit; and unless this is the case, you do not feed upon him either in word or sacrament; nor have you any more advantage by him, than a man has by that food which he tastes not. " Abide in me, (says " Christ,) and I in you; for without me ye can do " nothing *."

(3.) A believing improvement of Christ, and of all the benefits of his purchase, for all those ends and purposes for which they are useful to us; and particularly, for our spiritual nourishment and growth in grace. The bodies of men, you know, must be nourished, till they arrive at their full stature, by new accessions, both of strength and substance, to their several parts and members. And even after they are at their full growth, they stand in need of daily supplies,

to

---

* John xv. 4, 5.

to counter-balance the waste of nature, and prevent a too early, or too rapid decay. These accessions and supplies they receive from the food that they eat; which, as you heard, is changed, for that purpose, into a part of themselves. The people of God, in this world, are all children, in a spiritual sense. And unless they *grow in grace, in the knowledge of Christ*, and in conformity to his image; they can never arrive *at the stature of perfect men in him*. This growth can only be promoted, and a spiritual decay prevented, by a constant improvement of Christ and his benefits, in the daily exercise of faith. But the man who feeds upon this noble provision, draws supplies from thence to strengthen him for all the work that God has called him unto, to make up the defects of which he is daily sensible, and to enable him to make daily progress in faith, in holiness and comfort, till he arrive at the state of perfection.

(4.) It includes a believing acquiescence in Christ, as being, to the soul, instead of all those vanities which it formerly pursued; and as yielding a happiness that was sought for in vain among the objects of sense. Men eat for the allaying of hunger, as well as for the nourishment of the body. And we feel a pleasure, both in eating and after eating, proportioned to the pain that we endured by the gratings of hunger before. This prodigal is represented as having been ready to perish with hunger, before he returned to his father, and longing to " fill his belly with the " husks that the swine did eat." And, doubtless, such a person would feel an exquisite pleasure, in feeding upon *the fatted calf.* His pinching hunger would be allayed, and he would no longer have any desire after those empty husks which he coveted before. In like manner, if you really eat of this wonderful provision, that God is setting before you, it will more than supply the place of those empty and transient vanities, in which you fondly expected happiness before. You will find a satisfaction in using it, that all these could never afford you. Your hunger after them will be allayed, and you will consider the bread of your Father's house, as superseding all necessity for your seeking the food of your souls any where else.

8. The words of the text import, That, in making use of this noble provision, every returning prodigal has communion with God himself, and with his whole family. *Let* us *eat*, says the father of the prodigal, *and be merry;* plainly including himself, his other children, the friends of the family; and even the servants to whom he spake, as well as the young man lately returned to him. So the feast that God has provided, in consequence of the sacrifice of Christ, is intended for the entertainment of his whole family. They all sit at the same table, partake of the same provision, join in the same spiritual mirth; and, in every respect, hold such communion with one another, as fellow guests do in the celebration of a feast. Yes, Christian, whether you feed upon this provision in the gospel, or at the sacramental table, you therein have communion with the whole family of God; and with all the friends of the family, whether in heaven or on earth. God himself sits at the head of his own table; and though he cannot eat of the provision in the same sense as you do; yet there is nothing else upon which he feeds with equal satisfaction. Even typical sacrifices

fices are sometimes called " the bread of God*; with how much more propriety may this all-sufficient sacrifice be so denominated? No creature is capable of taking such pleasure in the most delicious food, as may bear a comparison with that infinite satisfaction which God has in the sacrifice of Christ, and in entertaining his people with the flesh and blood of a crucified Redeemer. In feeding upon this sacrifice, therefore, you are honoured to have communion with God himself. You have communion with all the children of God on earth; for this is the only food, by which they are all nourished up to the day of complete redemption. You have communion also with the saints in glory; for there is nothing else served up, nor, indeed, would any other provision have any relish at the table in the upper house. You have communion even with the elect angels. Though they have no need of this provision, to prevent their longing for husks as you once did, nor yet to cure those spiritual diseases of which they have contracted none; yet there is no other provision upon which they feed with more satisfaction. To speak more plainly, though angels have no need of the sacrifice of Christ, as an atonement for sin, and though they can make no appropriation of him as their Redeemer; yet there is no subject which they contemplate with more pleasure, or in consideration of which they are more filled with heavenly joy, admiration, and praise, than the giving of Christ to be a sacrifice for sin, or the redemption of sinners to God by his blood; these " things " the angels desire to look into †."

9. They import, that, in making use of this provision,

---

* See Lev. xxi. 6, 8. † 1 Pet. i. 12.

sion, all the family of God, and especially prodigals lately returned to it, should concur in the exercise of spiritual mirth and gladness. Every *feast is made for gladness;* and it is very unseemly for a person to be dull, sullen, or melancholy on such an occasion. There never was, nor will be, any other feast, affording such cause of joy as this does. All who truly eat of it will do it with gladness; and all who are invited to it, are called both to *eat and be merry.* God himself rejoices in his Son, and over his people, at the feast. To Christ, the feast-day being " the day of his espousals, " *is also* the day of the gladness of his heart. *There* " *is* joy in heaven, *and* before the angels of God," when prodigals return and feed upon this provision. And why should prodigals themselves be sad or melancholy? The feast was made for their reception. All the other guests rejoice at their happiness; and why should they, to whom all the advantage redounds, be the only persons to spoil the melody, or mar the joy of the feast? It is a shame for any of you to sit even at the gospel-table, without having your hearts filled with holy joy, and your mouths with a song of praise, on account of the glad tidings which the gospel brings, and of the rich provision with which it supplies you. Still more unseemly will it be, if any of you shall be seen at the *communion-table,* with sadness in your countenance, and nothing but complaints in your mouth. Has your heavenly Father slain the *fatted calf* for your entertainment? Has he given commandment to " bring forth the best robe and put it on *you;* " *to* put a ring on *your* hand, and shoes on *your* feet?" Has he brought you, an outcast prodigal, into his house; set you down at his own table, and even *put*

you

you *among the children?* Does your Father himself, and the whole family, in heaven and in earth, rejoice at your restoration? Is the feast appointed, to give every one occasion to manifest his joy at the happy event? And shall you, who reap all the advantage, be the only person to disgrace the solemnity, by your unseasonable fears and complaints? Nay, Christian, " Eat thy bread with gladness, and drink thy wine " with a merry heart;" it is the voice of thy heavenly Father, that saith, " Let us eat and be merry."

Finally, The words of the text import, That in this heavenly festivity there can be no excess. It was hinted in the entry, that the word here rendered to *be merry*, signifies to indulge one's self without restraint, in all those gratifications, and in all those signs of gladness, that are common at a magnificent feast. It is usually taken in a bad sense, to express those revellings and debaucheries that are practised by epicures and sensualists at their feasts. And it is remarkable, that words of such import are frequently used in Scripture, with relation to this spiritual feast. One instance of this we had occasion formerly to take notice of, in these words, " Drink, yea drink abundantly, " O beloved *." The word, as you then heard, signifies literally, *drink and be drunken*. Of a similar meaning is the word used in this text. And the design of using such a word is, to intimate, that neither in making use of this provision, nor in the spiritual mirth here recommended, is it possible to exceed. Though you should indulge yourself in it, to the same degree as the grossest sensualists do in carnal gratifications, it will be so far from offending, or degenerating

---

* Song v. 1. See page 3·3, of this volume.

ting into vice, that it will be no more than what is expresly warranted, and required of you, by the command of God. You may eat as much as you pleafe at this feaft; you can neither furfeit yourfelf nor exhauft the provifion. Though you drink ever fo plentifully, your fenfes cannot be difordered, nor yourfelf intoxicated. Neither can your joy rife to excefs at this feaft. The joy of the world foon becomes exceffive, and degenerates into madnefs; becaufe the caufe of it is but trivial, and the degree of it is beyond the value of the object. But it is impoffible for your joy ever to rife fo high, as to bear any proportion to the caufe, or to the object of it. In a word, You cannot ftay too long in the banqueting-houfe, nor indulge your feftivity till it become unfeafonable. Not only while time remains, but even through the lafting ages of eternity, fhall this feaft continue to be celebrated. And no perfon, that has once tafted of the wonderful provifion, fhall ever rife from the table. Nay, Chriftian, you fhall always continue to feed upon this bread of heaven, while you remain in the wildernefs, whether you be fenfible of it or not. And when you leave this world, you fhall feed upon it ftill in the houfe above, where you fhall be completely *fatisfied* with the *fatnefs of* your Father's *houfe;* and fhall drink eternally of *the rivers of* his *pleafures.*

We are now to conclude with the following inferences from what has been faid.

1. We here fee what a happy change there is in the condition of every perfon, who, by divine grace, is enabled to return from fin unto God. The prodigal, clothed with the beft robe, adorned with the family

mily ring, fortified with shoes on his weary feet, introduced into his father's house, restored to his father's favour, and feasted at his father's table upon the *fatted calf*, was a very different man from what he was a little ago; when his clothes were worn to mere tatters, his jewels forfeited to glut his appetite, his shoes worn quite off his feet, his whole stock spent up, himself enslaved to a cruel master, employed in the meanest drudgery; so much pinched for sustenance, that he longed to feed with the swine; and even that denied him, so that he felt himself ready to perish by hunger. Yet this is no more than a faint shadow of the happy change that is made, by divine grace, about every one who is brought back to the house and family of God. As far as the soul is more valuable than the body, and eternity of more importance than time; so far is the misery of our natural estate, beyond what any earthly similitude can represent: and so far is the happiness to which we are restored, beyond any thing that is set before us by this, or can be set before us by any other sensible image. On the one hand, *the power of* God's *wrath* cannot be known by any finite capacity; and that is it to which we are all exposed in our natural estate. And, on the other hand, no " eye hath seen, nor ear heard, neither " have entered into the heart of man the good things " which God has laid up for them that love him." And yet, in all these good things every person obtains an indefeasible interest, the moment that he returns to God as his Father.

2. We here see what is the real business about which we are assembled to-day. It is not barely to join together in the outward celebration of divine ordinances. It is not that ministers may speak, and

people

people hear, a few things about God and about eternal concerns. Nor is it that we may difpenfe, and you receive, the vifible fymbols of the broken body and fhed blood of Chrift. All this we may do, and yet do nothing to the purpofe. Our proper bufinefs is, to join together, with fpiritual mirth and gladnefs, in keeping a folemn feaft upon God's *fatted calf* that has been *facrificed for us;* or, in other words, to feed upon the flefh and blood of a crucified Redeemer, by an applying faith. This is not only the bufinefs of thofe who intend to partake at the facramental table: it is the proper work of every one who hears the gofpel. If this is not the errand upon which you came to this place, your external appearance belies you; you mock God to his face, and juftly may he judge and condemn you out of your own mouth. The food that is to be ferved up on the facramental table, is the fame that ftands before every one in this company on God's table in the gofpel. The fame feaft is materially prefented to you on both tables. All the difference lies either in the manner of exhibition, or in the perfons who are welcome to each. In the gofpel, the flefh and blood of Chrift are exhibited immediately, to the faith of thofe that hear it; in the facrament, they are exhibited to the bodily fenfes of communicants in a figure. They are exhibited to the eye, to the tafte, and to the touch, under the fymbols of bread and wine; as they have juft now been to the ear, under the emblem of a fatted calf. In the gofpel, this feaft is made *unto all people.* God's provifion is fet before all indifcriminately; and every one is invited to eat of it, without waiting for any previous qualifications. But in the facrament, it is prefented sented only to the children of God's family; and no person is warranted to intermeddle with it, till he first return from his prodigal courses, be reconciled to God as his Father, be clothed with the robe of imputed righteousness, and brought into the house of God, so as to be secured against going any more out. Yet still it is the indispensible duty of all present, to feed upon the same provision. Since the fatted calf is killed, the marriage supper of the King's Son on the table, and an invitation tendered to every one of us; why should we not all *eat and be merry?*

3. We see how noble and excellent this provision is, which God has ordered for our entertainment. You have heard of various excellencies which may serve to recommend it. But one half has not been told you. You heard that it is delicious and palatable, wholesome and even medicinal, substantial and nutritive, sumptuous and magnificent. You have been told that it affords security against the wrath of God, and ensures the accomplishment of all the promises of God's covenant, to every person that feeds upon it. You might likewise have been informed, that it is expensive and costly provision. All the gold and precious stones that lie hid in the bowels of the earth could not purchase a crumb of it. The whole creation of God amounts not to half its price. Even the treasures of eternity could not go higher. Though it is represented by the homely similitude of a fatted calf, it was actually purchased with the blood of the Son of God. It is mysterious and wonderful provision. Every thing about it is full of mystery, and will afford matter of eternal admiration. It is the flesh of a slain sacrifice, and yet it is *living bread*. It is bread to which all

that

that hear the gospel are invited, and yet bread that none but the children of God shall ever taste. Like the *paschal Lamb*, one of its most lively types, it must be wholly eaten up the day we begin to feed upon it, and yet it shall last through all eternity. It must be wholly eaten by every guest at God's table; and yet it is sufficient for them all. It effectually quenches thirst, and allays hunger; so that he who feeds upon it shall never hunger nor thirst any more; and yet no person is capable either to hunger or thirst, till he eat of it. But why should I spend time in pretending to tell you what it is? All the redeemed from among men will eternally be employed in recounting its excellencies; and yet they will never be able to describe it so clearly, as to give a distant idea of it to any person who has not himself tasted it. If, therefore, you wish to know what it is, much better than I, or any such worm, or even an angel from heaven, can tell you; come, taste, " O taste and see that God " is good."

4. We may here find much assistance in the duty of self-examination, that is so necessary as a preparative for the great work of the day. None can be welcome to eat at the sacramental table, but they who have been enabled to return to God as their Father, and have previously fed upon the *fatted calf* in his house. Let every one who intends to communicate examine himself, and every one who intends not to communicate. It cannot be a loss to any of you, to know whether you live in God's family, or continue a slave to the devil; whether you are fed in the house of God, among his children, or starved in the open fields, among the devil's swine. It will be an unspeakable

speakable advantage. That you may know it we would ask you,

(1.) Have you ever been sensible of the famine that prevails in the *far country?* Have you felt yourself longing to fill your belly with those empty husks which the devil's swine do eat, and been made sensible that such a thing was impossible? The prodigal, till he *came to himself,* still hoped to earn his bread in the stranger's service, and expected to cram his belly with the swine's provision. And every man that continues in a natural estate, though he may feel himself miserable for the present, still dreams of happiness among the creatures; and therefore continues his mad pursuit. But the man who has returned to God, has first been convinced that all earthly things are but empty husks; he despairs of finding happiness among them; he resolves to pursue it no longer, where he finds that it is not; and looks for it only in the house of his heavenly Father.

(2.) What appetite have you for the provision that stands upon God's table? All who ever tasted of it hunger vehemently, and thirst after righteousness; after the flesh and blood of Christ, as " the bread " which cometh down from heaven, that a man may " eat thereof and not die." Their earnest petition is, " Lord, evermore give us this bread." Nothing can satisfy them without Christ. They long for an interest in his sacrifice, as that which alone is sufficient to take away their sin. They look for satisfaction to their immortal souls, only in the enjoyment of that fulness which God has lodged in his hand. And from thence they draw all their supplies, for spiritual nourishment, and growth in grace.

(3.) What

(3.) What think you of the company at God's table? You have heard, that in feeding upon Chriſt you have communion with God, with angels, and with ſaints; and is this the company that you chooſe, or with whom you deſire to aſſociate? He who loves to aſſociate with the wicked, is himſelf a wicked man, let his pretenſions be what they will. He only is returned to God's family, who, like Chriſt, looks upon " the ſaints *as* the excellent ones of the earth, with " whom is all *his* delight." He loves them for their conformity to the image of God; and, on this account, has pleaſure in communion with them; becauſe he loves God above all things, and conſiders communion with him as the only happineſs that is commenſurate to the boundleſs deſires of an immortal ſoul.

(4.) What do you know about that ſpiritual mirth that ſhould ever accompany this feaſt. In the dwellings of the righteous is heard the melody of joy and ſalvation. All God's children have learned, in ſome degree, to rejoice in Chriſt Jeſus, though they have no confidence in the fleſh. They rejoice in God, even when deprived of all earthly comforts, and ſubject to the heavieſt earthly miſeries. They know ſomething of a joy which may be, and is exerciſed even when they mourn and are in heavineſs; either for ſin itſelf, or for any of the conſequences of it which they either feel or fear. And every new taſte of this proviſion ſerves to increaſe their joy; the more they eat, the more are they diſpoſed to be merry.

(5.) In a word, Are you willing to be God's ſervant, at the ſame time that you hope to be acknowledged

ledged by him as a son? When the prodigal first thought of returning, he resolved to apply for the place of a hired servant. And though this part of his resolution was not put in practice, nor ought to be imitated by us in every respect; it surely intimates to us this much, that every penitent sinner is weary of his former course of life, and abhors himself on account of it; *i. e.* To make provision for the flesh no longer; that he is pleased with the laws of God's house, is willing to subject himself to God's authority, and to be employed in his work; that though he looks for the privileges of a son, he resolves to employ himself as a servant, in a course of regular obedience to all God's holy commandments.

5. From this subject we may see in what frame of spirit communicants should go forward to the Lord's table. Consider, my dear brethren, the nature, the plenty, and the excellence of the provision; and see that you come forward with an appetite. *Blessed are they* who come to this feast, *hungering and thirsting after righteousness;* we dare promise, nay, the Lord himself has promised, that *they shall be filled.* Consider the solemnity of the feast; and come forward in the exercise of that reverence which is due to him who sits at the head of the table; and of that self-diffidence which must arise from a sense of your liableness to miscarry. By all means see that you come forward arrayed in the best robe. Consider the occasion of the feast; and come forward, mourning deeply for that riotous course of life in which you was once engaged, resolving never more to return to it; influenced by the deepest gratitude, and the most fervent love to your heavenly Father, who gives you such a

kindly reception; and remembering with faith, love, admiration, and thankfulnefs, your glorious elder Brother, who made himfelf your facrifice, and gives himfelf for your provifion. Confider the happy relation in which you ftand to the Mafter of the feaft; and ufe all holy boldnefs and confidence, in taking and eating your Father's provifion; nothing difcouraged even by the confideration of your former prodigality. In a word, Confider the exprefs command of your Father; and in obedience to it, come forward in the exercife of that heavenly joy and gladnefs which become fuch an occafion. Away with all your unbelieving fears, complaints, and down-caftings; and " let " us eat and be merry."

6. To conclude, We here fee what ample encouragement prodigals of all forts have to return to God as their Father; and to expect the moft kindly reception, and the moft plentiful entertainment in his houfe. Whatever be the riotous courfe that you have purfued, however far you have departed from God, however deeply you have been engaged in the devil's fervice, however long you have fought to fill your belly with hufks, forgetting, and even defpifing all the bread of your Father's houfe; ftill, ftill you are welcome to return. God will not only meet you while you are yet afar off; he even comes to the far country to feek you back. He is ready to accept your acknowledgement, and to forgive and forget all that is paft. You fhall find every thing ready for you that you can ftand in need of. The beft robe is brought forth to be put upon you. There is a ring for your hand, and fhoes for your feet. The fatted calf is facrificed;

crificed; and behold it ſtands upon the table! Come then, without any further delay, and eat to the ſatisfying of your ſoul. Come, and eat ſo as to hunger no more. Come, and eat, without money and without price. Let *the poor, the halt, and the maimed come;* the robber that infeſts the *high-ways*, and the thief that lurks among the *hedges;* we have authority to *compel them* all *to come in*. Let every ſinner, of every denomination, in this numerous aſſembly come; and *let us* all *eat and be merry*.

END OF THE SECOND VOLUME.

www.ingramcontent.com/pod-product-compliance
Lightning Source LLC
Chambersburg PA
CBHW022100300426
44117CB00007B/535